Crossings:

Mexican Immigration
in Interdisciplinary Perspectives

Crossings:
Mexican Immigration in Interdisciplinary Perspectives

Edited by
Marcelo M. Suárez-Orozco

Published by
Harvard University
David Rockefeller Center for Latin American Studies

DISTRIBUTED BY
HARVARD UNIVERSITY PRESS
CAMBRIDGE, MASSACHUSETTS
LONDON, ENGLAND

Library of Congress Cataloging-in-Publication Data

Crossings: Mexican immigration in interdisciplinary perspectives /
   edited by Marcelo M. Suárez-Orozco.
      p.   cm.
   Includes bibliographical references and index.
   ISBN 0-674-17766-5 (hardcover). —ISBN 0-674-17767-3 (pbk.)
   1. Mexican Americans—Social conditions.   2. Immigrants—United States—Social conditions.   3. Mexico—Emigration and immigration.   4. United States—Emigration and
immigration.   I. Suárez-Orozco, Marcelo M.,   1956-   II. David Rockefeller Center for
Latin American Studies.
E184.M5C76   1998
305.868'72073—dc21   98-18176
                                                                            CIP

Contents

Acknowledgments

This book is the product of a two-day international conference entitled Immigration and the Socio-Cultural Remaking of the North American Space held at Harvard University in April 1997. The conference and this book were made possible by generous support from the Antonio Madero Endowment for the Study of Mexican and Latin American Politics and Economics and the David Rockefeller Center for Latin American Studies at Harvard.

I would like to thank John Coatsworth, Monroe Gutman Professor of Latin American Affairs and Director of the David Rockefeller Center for Latin American Studies, for his unwavering commitment to this project. Since much of Latin America no longer sits still south of the border, new visions of area studies and new institutional structures will be required of universities in the decades ahead. The Center's support for this and a number of other initiatives in the area of immigration and Latino cultures in the United States represents a fresh new approach to area studies.

I am indebted to Professor Wayne Cornelius for giving me much needed guidance, particularly during the gestation of this project. Dr. Carola Suárez-Orozco, Co-Director of the Harvard Immigration Projects, provided invaluable advice during various phases of this book. Also a big thanks to Debra-Lee Vasques, the conference coordinator at the David Rockefeller Center for Latin American Studies, for her meticulous work in preparation for the conference. Hilary Burger, Ph.D. candidate in Latin American history at Harvard and research associate for the immigration initiative, did a brilliant job preparing this manuscript for publication. ¡Gracias!

PART I

Overview

Photo by Anna LeVine

Marcelo M. Suárez-Orozco Growing up in a multiethnic neighborhood in Buenos Aires, I first learned about immigration in my hometown's plaza where the children and grandchildren of Italian, Spanish, German, Armenian, Syrian, Japanese, Irish, and Anglo-Argentine parents gathered together to kick around soccer balls on lazy summer afternoons. In a five-mile radius of the house where I was born, and spent the first 17 years of my life, there was an Italian-language school, a Hebrew-language school, a German-language school, and several English-language schools. Although Spanish was the lingua franca, ethnic loyalties remained high. The nicknames we gave each other in those dusty soccer fields—"El Tano" (the Italian), "El Vasco" (the Basque), "El Arabe" (the Arab)—told of the history of the "other" great country of immigration in the Americas.

A few years later, while graduate students in anthropology at Berkeley, Jonathan Habarad and I organized a study group involving a number of graduate students working on issues related to immigration. In the early 1980s, there was no graduate-level course taught at Berkeley on immigration. Soon it became clear to us that a large number of graduate students—in anthropology and beyond—were doing basic research on issues relating to refugees and immigrants. With the support of George De Vos and Elizabeth Colson we organized what became one of the most popular courses at Berkeley: the Anthropology of Immigration. Graduate students from all the social sciences and the professional schools took the course. After years of neglect, immigration was once again emerging as a topic of scholarly concern.

Since leaving Berkeley, the bulk of my empirical work has been focused on the psychosocial experiences of Central American and Mexican immigrants in California. I have also considered recent developments in European immigration. My new basic research, in collaboration with Carola Suárez-Orozco, Co-Director of the Harvard Immigration Projects, is interdisciplinary, comparative, and longitudinal. We freely borrow tools from various social science disciplines, especially research psychology and research anthropology, to explore the adaptations of immigrants (of Asian, Caribbean, and Latino origin) in American schools.

Currently, I am Professor of Human Development and Psychology and Learning and Teaching, and Co-Director of the Harvard Immigration Projects at the Harvard Graduate School of Education. My most recent book, co-authored with Carola Suárez-Orozco, *Transformations: Immigration, Family Life, and Achievement Motivation among Latino Adolescents* (Stanford University Press), won the 1996 Social Policy Book Award from the Society for Research on Adolescents.

1

Crossings: Mexican Immigration in Interdisciplinary Perspectives

Marcelo M. Suárez-Orozco
Harvard University

Immigration is the driving force behind a significant transformation of American society taking place at the end of the millennium. Few other social phenomena are likely to affect the future character of American culture and society as much as the ongoing wave of "new immigration."[1] The nature of this change is indeed momentous (Figure 1.1). In 1945, just fifty years ago, the U.S. population was 87 percent white, 10 percent black, 2.5 percent Hispanic, and 0.5 percent Asian. Fifty years from now, in the year 2050, demographic projections suggest a strikingly different population profile: 52.8 percent of the population will be white, 13.6 percent of the population will be black, 24.5 percent of the population will be Hispanic, and 8.2 percent of the population will be of Asian ancestry (Bureau of the Census 1996; National Research Council 1997).[2] These census projections are quite problematic (see Waters, this volume). In a sense, these projections are another version of the Rorschach test—the original projective test: Nobody quite knows what that ink-blot means but everyone has the urge to interpret it. These census projections assume that ethnic and racial categories are enduring and more or less static formations. Given ethnic socioeconomic mobility and the high rates on interethnic marriage in the U.S. along with changing cultural models and practices around ethnicity, there is reason to suspect that these categories, fluid and in constant formation and transformation, may be quite irrelevant in three generations. It is, however, quite likely that by then the United States will be the only postindustrial world power with ethnic minorities approaching nearly half of the total population.

FIGURE 1.1

U.S. Demographics

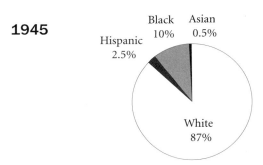

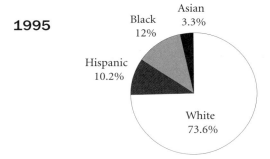

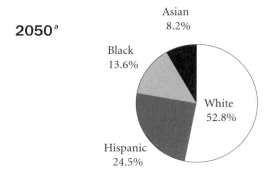

[a] Projected from Census Bureau, 1996.

In the United States immigration is at once history and destiny. It is a dominant theme in the foundational narrative that accounts for how the country came into existence.[3] It was foreordained, therefore, that all subsequent immigration—including what we call in this volume "the new immigration"—would be framed by this quasi-sacred narrative.[4] This, then, suggests the broad question that will guide much of the labor of the next generation of immigration researchers: Just how is the current wave of immigration both like and unlike the large-scale immigration of a century ago? Are today's Mexicans, Haitians, and Koreans simply replicating the grammar of a narrative already told—albeit with different accents— by Irish, Italian, and Polish immigrants a century ago? Or are the experiences of today's immigrants an entirely different phenomenon, requiring new categories of understanding and new policy responses?[5]

This book brings together a number of original essays by leading scholars of the most significant feature of the new immigration: Mexican immigration to the United States. By the year 1990, there were more legal immigrants from Mexico than from all of Europe combined. Today, there are some 7 million Mexican immigrants residing in the United States, constituting roughly a third of the total foreign-born population of the country (González Baker et al., this volume). More than one-quarter of all Mexican immigrants to the United States arrived in the last five years (Binational Study on Migration 1997, ii). Mexican immigrants now constitute 40 percent of the total Mexican-origin population of the United States.

Talk of "the new immigration" refers largely to immigration from Latin America, the Caribbean, and Asia. Mexican immigration has come to dominate the new immigration to the United States. In the rapidly growing area of immigration studies, Mexican immigration is where some of the most important basic research and theory is now taking shape.

Three features distinguish this volume. First, the authors focus on aspects of the recent immigration experience that are new and that differentiate this wave of immigration from earlier experiences in this century. Second, this book represents an ambitious interdisciplinary exercise. Immigration has become such a complex—and charged—phenomenon that it cries out for perspectives that go beyond the sometimes confining boundaries of traditional social science disciplines. Third, the book brings together the contributions of a binational group of scholars. Mexican and U.S. scholars of immigration bring different perspectives to an issue that links the two nations more than ever before (Bean et al. 1997).

The volume includes an array of diverse empirical and theoretical perspectives on Mexican immigration to the United States. The authors rely on various methodologies, from sophisticated statistical analyses of large data sets to complex psychoanalytic interpretations of intrapsychic processes. All of the authors present new, heretofore unpublished findings. Although the chapters rely on quite distinct methodologies and theoretical baggage, a set of recurring themes gives the volume an intellectual core.

First, the research suggests that the deep economic and sociocultural changes taking place on both sides of the border virtually ensure that Mexican immigration to the United States will be a long-term phenomenon. While it is likely that the extremely high flows of Mexican immigration to the United States during the 1980s and 1990s will eventually decrease (see Binational Study on Migration 1997), we must assume that Mexican immigration will continue to dominate immigration to the United States over the next decades. Second, new data suggest that the Mexican immigration momentum is structured by powerful economic and sociocultural forces not easily contained by unilateral policy initiatives, such as the various border control efforts now taking place. Third, the data suggest that Mexican immigrants are here to stay. Indeed, Mexican immigrants today are more likely to permanently settle in the United States than return to Mexico. Given these three fundamental features of the new immigration, two basic areas of inquiry will become increasingly relevant in the study of the Mexican experience in the United States.

First, we need to know more about how this unprecedented pattern of Mexican immigration is changing the U.S. side of "the line." In many parts of the country it is now obvious that the demographic momentum generated by Mexican immigration is visibly transforming the texture of the American fabric. Soon the United States will have the second-largest number of Spanish-speakers in the world.[6] As in the "new" *New York Times,* ethnic life in the United States will no longer be dominated by "black" and "white" headlines. Mexican immigration is palpably changing our public space (see Ainslie, this volume; Gutiérrez, this volume) and our social institutions, including schools (Trueba, this volume; Orfield, this volume), jobs (Waldinger 1997), and businesses (Cornelius, this volume).[7]

Second, we need to know more about how the immigrants themselves change over time. The permanence of Mexican immigrant life on the U.S. side of the border will require that we develop more sophisticated models for understanding the long-term adaptations of immigrants and especially their children. We need a robust research agenda on the schooling experiences of the children of immigrants, their health, and their transition to the world of work to help us map out the long-term patterns of immigrant insertion into American life. Longitudinal research will be very important to the next generation of scholars of the new Mexican immigration.

In the rest of this chapter, I present a broad outline of new developments in Mexican immigration to the United States, with specific reference to larger features of the new immigration. Then I introduce the substance of each of the chapters in the volume.

EVERYTHING YOU EVER WANTED TO KNOW
ABOUT THE NEW IMMIGRATION BUT WERE AFRAID TO ASK

What is "new" about the new immigration? In the scholarly literature, *new immigrants* generally refers to post-1965 immigrants (Espin 1987; Portes and Rumbaut 1996; Hing 1993). The new immigrants (about 80 percent of them) tend to be nonwhite, non-English-speaking, non-Europeans emigrating from developing countries in Latin America, the Caribbean, and Asia (Edmonston and Passel 1994, 41). They are more socioculturally diverse than ever before. Today, public schools in the two largest U.S. cities (New York and Los Angeles) enroll children who speak well over 100 different languages; just thirty years ago, and indeed for most of this century, a smaller number of European languages dominated immigrant schools.

In terms of educational background and skills, immigrants today are a much more complex group than ever before. They are at once among the most educated and skilled and the least educated and skilled people in the United States. Immigrants tend to be overrepresented in the category of people with doctorates—or, indeed, winners of the Nobel Prize—just as they are overrepresented in the category of people without a high school diploma. Mexican immigrants are an extremely heterogeneous group. While most are low-skilled workers—entering a highly segmented American labor market—many are professionals: over one-seventh of them (Binational Study on Migration 1997, iv). In technical language, immigrants today tend to be much more "bimodal" in their socioeconomic profile than ever before.[8]

In recent years, anthropologists and sociologists have claimed that what is novel about the new immigrants is that they are actors on a new transnational stage (Levitt 1997; Mahler 1997; Basch et al. 1995). The ease of mass transportation and new communication technologies seem to conspire to structure the journeys of the new immigrants into American society in ways incommensurable to the patterns characteristic of the old immigrants from Europe.

Today, there is a more massive back-and-forth movement of people, goods, information, and symbols than ever before.[9] Compared with Mexican or Dominican immigrants today, the Irish immigrants of last century simply could not maintain the level and intensity of contact with the "old country" that is now possible (see Ainslie, this volume). Furthermore, the ongoing nature of Mexican immigration to the United States constantly replenishes social practices and cultural models that would otherwise tend to ossify (see Gutiérrez, this volume). Indeed, in certain areas of the Southwest, Mexican immigration is generating a powerful infrastructure dominated by a growing Spanish-speaking mass media (radio, TV, and print), new market dynamics (Steinhauer 1997),[10] and new cultural identities.

Another relevant feature of the new transnational framework is that even as they enmesh themselves in the social, economic, and political life in their new lands (see Cornelius, this volume; Durand, this volume), immigrants remain powerful protagonists in the economic, political, and cultural spheres back home. Immigrant remittances and investments have become vital to the economies of varied countries of emigration, such as El Salvador—where in 1996 remittances were the largest source of foreign exchange, at over $1 billion—Haiti, and Mexico. The Binational Study on Migration (1997, vii) estimates that remittances to Mexico were the "equivalent to 57 percent of the foreign exchange available through direct investment in 1995, and 5 percent of the total income supplied by exports."[11]

Politically, likewise, immigrants are emerging as increasingly relevant actors with influence in political processes in both their new and old lands. Some observers have noted that the outcome of the most recent Dominican presidential election was largely determined in New York City, where Dominicans are the largest group of new immigrants (Pessar 1995). Likewise, Mexican politicians—especially those in opposition parties—have recently discovered the political value of the seven million Mexican immigrants living in the United States. The new Mexican dual nationality initiative, whereby Mexican immigrants who become nationalized U.S. citizens would retain a host of political and other rights in Mexico, is also the product of this emerging transnational framework.

Culturally, immigrants not only significantly reshape the ethos of their new communities (see the chapters by Ainslie and Gutiérrez, this volume) but are also responsible for significant social transformations "back home" (see Durand, this volume). Peggy Levitt (1997) has argued that in many settings immigrant "social remittances" affect the values, cultural models, and social practices of those left behind. Because of both a new ease of travel and new communication technologies, it seems that immigration is no longer structured around the sharp break with the country of origin that once characterized the transoceanic experience (see Ainslie, this volume). Immigrants today are more likely to be at once "here" and "there," bridging increasingly unbounded national spaces (Basch et al. 1995) and in the process transforming both home and host countries.

Another feature of the new immigration to the United States is that immigrants today are entering a country that is economically, socially, and culturally unlike the country that absorbed—however ambivalently—previous waves of immigrants. Economically, the previous large wave of immigrants arrived on the eve of the great industrial expansion, in which immigrant workers and consumers played a key role (Higham 1955).

Immigrants now are actors in a thoroughly globalized and rapidly changing economy that is increasingly taking an hourglass shape. High-skilled immigrants are moving into well-remunerated knowledge-intensive industries at a heretofore unprecedented rate (Waldinger and Bozorgmehr 1996). On the other end of the hourglass, low-skilled immigrants may be locking themselves into the low-wage sector in large numbers. Some scholars have argued that unlike the low-skilled industry jobs of yesterday, the kinds of jobs typically available to low-skilled new immigrants today do not offer prospects for upward mobility (Portes 1996).

Another current feature of immigration is the increasingly segregated concentration of large numbers of immigrants in a handful of states (see González Baker et al., this volume; Gutiérrez, this volume) in large urban areas polarized by racial tensions. Some 85 percent of all Mexican immigrants in the United States reside in three states (California, Texas, and Illinois). A number of distinguished sociologists have argued that as a result of an increasing segmentation of the economy and society, many low-skilled new immigrants "have become more, not less, likely to live and work in environments that have grown increasingly segregated from whites" (Waldinger and Bozorgmehr 1996, 20).[12]

Yet another way the new immigrant experience seems incommensurable with earlier patterns relates to the cultural ethos today's immigrants encounter. New immigrants are entering American society at a time when what we might term a "culture of multiculturalism" permeates the public space. Certainly a century ago there were no cultural models or social practices celebrating—however superficially—"diversity," "multiculturalism," and "ethnic pride" (Glazer 1997).

It is, however, far from clear how the new culture of multiculturalism will affect, if at all, the long-term adaptations of immigrants and, especially, their children. If we take the heated issue of immigration and language, the data suggest that the new multiculturalism is indeed superficial. Today employers in Miami, the American city with the highest concentration of foreign language speakers, have trouble finding competent office workers with the ability to function in professional Spanish (Mears 1997, 1). Immigrant children are likely to learn English rapidly *while* they lose their mother tongue (Portes and Hao 1997; Snow 1997).

NEW DEVELOPMENTS IN U.S.-MEXICAN IMMIGRATION

Immigration has become too important an issue to leave it to generalists. This volume includes a dozen original essays by a number of distinguished social scientists representing the fields of anthropology, demography, economics, education, government, health science, history, political science, psychoanalysis, and sociology. Each chapter is followed by substantial commentary by an established scholar in the field.

The authors, while grounded in their own scholarly techniques and cultures, were encouraged to think beyond disciplinary boundaries in addressing broad empirical and analytical questions related to new patterns of Mexican immigration to the United States. The purpose of the volume is to initiate a dialogue that will locate immigration research in a robust interdisciplinary and transnational context.

The intellectual parameters of the book are structured along broad thematic clusters. The authors explore the causes and consequences of international migration as a regional formation involving the flow of people, resources, and symbols across an increasingly problematic international boundary.

Immigration is best framed in the context of powerful—and little understood—globalizing trends.[13] In this volume we examine a number of economic and sociocultural processes implicated in these new immigration dynamics. Economic factors include increasingly "borderless" economies predicated on new patterns of capital flows, newly opened markets, and immigrant-dependent economic niches. Sociocultural factors include transnational networks, such as family reunification networks, communication networks, and transportation networks.[14]

BACKGROUND:
ANTECEDENTS AND NEW DEMOGRAPHIC FORMATIONS

Economic arguments, for better or worse, have dominated the debate over the antecedents and consequences of immigration.[15] Earlier research on economic antecedents explored, among other things, the "push" and "pull" economic vectors relevant to an understanding of why and when individuals and groups choose—or are forced—to migrate. Economic factors in host countries—such as the need for workers to do jobs natives can't or won't do—are said to "pull" immigrants into a new setting, while economic factors in the home country— such as unemployment and low wages—are said to "push" them out.[16]

More recently the vast changes brought about by various restructuring strategies in a variety of settings have come under the gaze of economists interested in new immigration dynamics. Enrique Dussel Peters, an associate professor at the Graduate School of Economics, Universidad Nacional Autónoma de México, presents us with an overview of recent changes in the Mexican economy. The broad changes outlined in Dussel's chapter are of relevance to an understanding of recent, as well as likely future, Mexican migratory dynamics and potentials.

Dussel's data suggest that through 1994 the Mexican economic restructuring plan was relatively successful in terms of its stated objectives: Between 1987 and 1994, inflation was reduced, the fiscal deficit was brought under control, and capital flows in the form of foreign investment soared—from $2.8 billion in 1987 to $32.7 billion in 1993. While the massive flow of foreign capital was a particular success, there was also a surge in exports.

Dussel examines the effect of the new Mexican strategy on two economic factors closely related to emigration: wages and employment. In terms of real wages, Dussel's data reveal that since 1980 the average Mexican worker has been losing ground. In 1997, real wages were 60 percent of what they were in 1980, although in some sectors of the economy (such as the automobile industry) real wages have increased.[17]

Dussel's data on recent patterns of employment suggest that presently there are some 15 million working-age individuals in Mexico who are not formally employed. During the 1980–1996 period, manufacturing, thought to be a key element in the liberalization strategy, actually expelled labor.[18] Dussel estimates that the Mexican gross domestic product (GDP) would have to grow by 12 percent, and manufacturing by 9 percent, to keep up with population growth.

The data on wages and employment, combined with the data on the enduring demand for Mexican immigrant labor in the United States (see González Baker et al., this volume; Cornelius, this volume), suggest that in the short and medium term there remains an enormous potential for Mexican emigration to the United States.

Dussel's study suggests that the restructuring or liberalization of the Mexican economy has generated a process of deep polarization in economic, regional, and social terms. While there have been some important gains, there have also been impressive losses. Of particular relevance to immigration to the United States is the negative association between liberalization policies, the generation of employment, and real wages.[19]

Susan González Baker and her colleagues present us with a thorough analysis of the most recent demographic data on new patterns of Mexican immigration to the United States. Their materials highlight a basic theme in this volume: Mexican immigration is generating a new demographic trend whose effects are rapidly spreading over large sectors of U.S. territory.

Their data indicate that flows of legal immigrants, refugees and asylees, undocumented immigrants, and nonimmigrant entrants have all increased since the 1950s. There is a marked transition in country of origin from European stock to Asian, Caribbean, and Latin American background.

Susan González Baker et al. document how Mexicans have come to dominate the new immigration. Their numbers have increased in all categories of immigrants, except refugees and asylees. Some two-thirds of all immigrants from Latin America are Mexicans, and three-fourths of those who legalized their status under the 1986 Immigration Reform and Control Act (IRCA) were Mexicans. Mexican immigrants today constitute 40 percent of the Mexican-origin population in the United States—an impressive figure considering that the U.S.-born Mexican population has higher than average fertility rates.[20]

González Baker et al. claim that new Mexican immigration is becoming decoupled from the traditional socioeconomic variables that characterized previous patterns of immigration to the United States. Mexican immigration to the United States is no longer primarily a short-term economic strategy exemplified by the sojourner pattern, that is, men in search of cash migrating temporarily to the United States with the intention of returning to Mexico (see also Cornelius, this volume; Durand, this volume). Immigration is now becoming common for large numbers of Mexican women and children (Hondagneu-Sotelo 1994).[21] We are also witnessing burgeoning naturalization rates among Mexican immigrants in the United States (see Gutiérrez, this volume). These and other findings suggest that Mexican immigrants today are much more likely to develop strong roots on the U.S. side of the border than ever before.[22]

ECONOMIC THEMES

Few topics today are more heated than the economic consequences of immigration.[23] Do the new immigrants help or hurt the U.S. economy? Do immigrants carry their own weight or do they represent a burden to citizens and other established residents? Do complex postindustrial economies need low-skilled immigrant workers or have they become redundant? The most recent debate over immigration and the economy has tended to focus on a handful of concerns. These have included the fiscal implications of immigration, the issue of immigrant competition with native workers, and the related issue of immigration and wages. Another important theme has been the economic integration and progress of immigrants over time (Espenshade 1997; National Research Council 1997).

The research findings on the economic consequences of immigration are far from conclusive. Indeed, they are often contradictory, with some economists claiming that the new immigrants are a burden to taxpayers and an overall negative influence on the U.S. economy (Huddle 1993) and others suggesting that they continue to be an important asset (Simon 1995).

The most authoritative and recent study on the economic, demographic, and fiscal effects of immigration by the National Research Council (NRC) concludes that "immigration produces net economic gains for domestic residents" (NRC 1997, 3). Not only do immigrants "increase the supply of labor and help produce new goods and services" but their presence also "allows domestic workers to be used more productively, specializing in producing goods at which they are relatively more efficient. Specialization in consumption also yields a gain" (NRC 1997, 3–4). The NRC estimates that the immigration-related "domestic gain may run on the order of $1 billion to $10 billion a year" (NRC 1997, 5). On the other hand, in fiscal terms the NRC data suggest that "immigrants receive more in services than they pay in taxes" (NRC 1997, 7). Although there are important differences by state—California, for example, is more negatively affected than other states—the panel calculates that "if the net fiscal impact of all U.S. immigrant-headed households were averaged across all native households the burden would be . . . on the order of $166 to $226 per native household."[24]

The NRC study further suggests that while immigration is a plus in overall economic terms, low-skilled new immigrants have contributed to a modest drop in the minimum wage of low-skilled workers: A five percent drop in wages since 1980 among high school dropouts can be attributed to the new immigrants. There is, however, no evidence to suggest that new immigration has hurt the economic condition of African Americans (NRC 1997, 5).

Two chapters in this volume are devoted to the sensitive topic of Mexican immigration and the U.S. economy. Wayne Cornelius, the Theodore Gildred Professor of Political Science and International Relations at the University of California, San Diego, engages the theoretical debate over the role of immigrant workers in a global, postindustrial economy. In the context of the increasingly advanced knowledge-intensive economies of the *fin de siècle,* are low-skilled immigrant workers simply anachronistic leftovers from other eras of production? Just why do businesses continue to hire immigrant workers?

Cornelius' data are derived from a comparative study of the use of immigrant labor in two paradigmatic postindustrial economic settings: San Diego County, California, and Hamamatzu, Japan. The results of this study suggest a remarkable convergence in patterns of growing reliance on immigrant labor, in spite of rather marked differences in national context.

In the San Diego study, Cornelius interviewed a sample of 112 employers together with a sample of 501 immigrant workers.[25] The firms involved in the study represent a broad range of sectors including high-tech manufacturing, construction, hotels, restaurants, agriculture, services, and food processing. Over 50 percent of the workers were undocumented; 79 percent were Mexican, along with 12 other nationalities.[26]

Wayne Cornelius' data reveal a pattern of enduring, indeed voracious, U.S. demand for Mexican immigrant labor: 92 percent of the workers in agriculture and food processing were immigrants, as were 72 percent of the workers in service, 67 percent of the workers in hotels, and 50 percent of the workers in manufacturing.[27] Overall, two-thirds of the workers in the sample were foreign-born.[28] Nearly 50 percent of the employers in the San Diego study reported that there "were no tasks in their business that they could not assign to immigrant workers." Cornelius argues that the use of immigrant labor in California has become largely independent of the business cycle: "As immigrants become a preferred labor force, employers do more to retain them, even in a recessionary economy" (Cornelius, this volume).

Cornelius claims that Mexican immigrants are desirable to a wide variety of employers for three basic reasons: (1) immigrants are willing to do low-pay work that is boring, dirty, or dangerous,[29] with no prospects for upward mobility, and that even in firms involving highly advanced technologies such work is critical; (2) they are perceived favorably by employers as being reliable, flexible, punctual, and willing to work overtime and therefore are often preferred over native-born workers; and (3) immigrant transnational labor recruiting networks are a powerful method for "delivering eager new recruits to the employer's doorstep with little or no effort on his part" (see also Waldinger 1997).

Cornelius' study suggests that the San Diego labor market has become increasingly segmented into immigrant-dominated and native worker–dominated sectors. In certain sectors of the California economy immigrants have all but replaced native workers. Cornelius reports that nearly half of all the employers in his sample said that U.S.-born workers simply never apply for the types of jobs held by immigrants. In such contexts, it is meaningless to suggest that native-born workers and immigrant workers "compete" in the labor market.[30]

Cornelius suggests that the general trend since the 1970s has been for Mexican immigrants to stay for longer periods and to wish to settle in California rather than return to Mexico. Cornelius concludes with a cautionary note with important policy implications: Immigrant-dominated labor markets are not easily subject to manipulation by policy initiatives such as border controls and employer sanctions. Powerful socioeconomic forces continue to subvert policy attempts to control immigration.[31]

Is the San Diego pattern singular or does it apply to other areas as well? After all, San Diego is a unique city just half an hour from the Mexican border. Given that San Diego, because of history and geography, is such a visible center of Mexican immigration, is it not quite predictable to find firms heavily dependent on immigrant labor?[32] In his commentary, Robert Smith, an assistant professor of sociology at Barnard College, suggests that isomorphic processes may now be taking place in other regions of the country—even in areas that have until recently not been traditional destinations for Mexican immigrants. He notes, for example, the significant growth of Mexican immigration to New York.[33]

Dowell Myers, an associate professor at the School of Urban Planning and Development, University of Southern California, tracks, over time and across generations, various dimensions of the economic adaptations of Mexican-origin men in the Southern California region. His chapter explores three sequential outcomes: educational attainment, occupational mobility, and earnings. In some fundamental ways, the recent Mexican male experience in Southern California seems to replicate earlier patterns of immigrant adaptation. Yet in other ways, Myers' findings suggest new, and disturbing, patterns.

Myers' data reveal that on arrival Mexican immigrant men tend to be poorly educated, work in low-skilled occupations, and earn low incomes. Over time Mexican immigrant men make modest improvements in their economic condition. However, he also suggests that important changes occur across younger cohorts within the first generation. These changes, according to Myers, are strongly related to the much higher educational attainment of immigrant children. In other words, Myers finds an old story with a new set of characters: Poorly educated immigrant men make modest gains over time, but their children are able to attain more education in the new country.

Still, Myers' data reveal a disturbing new pattern: Among the children of immigrants, higher education "does not appear to fully convert into higher occupational status or earnings, and higher occupational status translates even less well into higher earnings. These under-returns are most pronounced for the more recent arrivals and for young cohorts, including native-born, both of whom newly entered the labor market in the 1970s and 1980s." Myers concludes that "young Latinos who stay in high school, graduate, and advance into skilled occupations have adapted reasonably well. Their low earnings despite this effort could be seen more as a failure of the reward system in a restructured economy than as a sign of personal failure or declining quality. The social implications are regrettable, because this declining reward system may discourage other" immigrant children from investing in schooling as the route for status mobility.[34]

SOCIAL THEMES

Jorge Durand's contribution captures another facet of the increasing embeddedness of Mexican immigrants in the United States. While Myers and Cornelius examine various economic aspects of the Mexican immigrant experience, Durand explores another basic social indicator: marriage patterns. Durand, professor of social anthropology and cultural geography at the University of Guadalajara, introduces new data derived from an ethnographic study of Ameca, a town of 56,000 inhabitants some 50 miles west of the city of Guadalajara.

Durand notes that historically U.S. immigration policies and market forces did not encourage the long-term integration of Mexican immigrants into American society. Rather, the emphasis was on their eventual return to Mexico. Hence a sojourner pattern came to dominate Mexican immigration to the United States. The 1986 Immigration Reform and Control Act (IRCA) profoundly altered the nature of the Mexican immigrant experience in the United States. IRCA provided for the legalization of some two million undocumented Mexican immigrants. Durand explores how IRCA contributed to the trend toward permanent Mexican immigrant settlement in the United States.[35]

Durand's research suggests that an important and novel feature of the Mexican experience in the United States is the increase in intermarriages between immigrants and U.S. citizens.[36] Intermarriage is an important mark of social integration. Durand's arguments are based on a study of Ameca, a locus of Mexican emigration to the United States (55 percent of its households include a member who has worked in the United States). The first intermarriage of an Amequense with a U.S. citizen took place in 1965; since then mixed marriages have steadily increased.[37] As intermarriages among Amequenses residing in the United States increase, Durand detects significant changes in the cultural expectations and social practices of those left behind.

Durand argues that the experiences of Amequense immigrants in the United States suggest that a fundamentally new chapter in the long history of Mexican immigration to the United States is now being written. The new Mexican immigration is characterized by a significant increase in intermarriages and a tendency to remain on the U.S. side of the border. Durand speculates that new patterns of intermarriage among Mexican immigrants are related to the emergence of new ethnic identities, such as the recent appearance of the variegated "Latino" construct.

Durand's chapter is a good example of why we need more interdisciplinary research combining methodologies and data sets.[38] While his data suggest that

Amequenses have in recent years become more fully integrated in American life, large-scale data sets suggest that Mexican immigrants today are growing increasingly segregated from other groups. A number of studies suggest that Mexican immigrants tend to be highly segregated in the workplace (Waldinger 1997), in schools (see Orfield, this volume), and in neighborhoods (Waldinger and Bozorgmehr 1996).

While immigration is affecting nearly all aspects of American society, public debate has tended to concentrate narrowly on a handful of controversies. Likewise, in the scholarly literature certain aspects of the immigrant experience have been theorized about more systematically than others. In recent years, for example, economic and demographic processes have been major topics of empirical work. Although such work is certainly necessary, it tends to address only the tip of what is proving to be a gigantic iceberg.

Arguably no other aspect of the new immigration is more important than the adaptation of the children of immigrants. The number of immigrants in the total U.S. child population is rapidly growing. The children of today's immigrants will become key players in the remaking of American economy, society, and culture. Their long-term adaptations to the institutions of the host society are of paramount importance. The essays by Richard Brown and colleagues and Enrique Trueba examine two basic aspects of the experience of Mexican immigrant children that will have profound relevance for the future: health and education.

Richard Brown and his colleagues at the UCLA Center for Health Policy Research present new data on health and immigration, including access to health insurance and health care among Mexican immigrant children. These data are very important to consider in light of the policy changes that terminate Medicaid eligibility for most new immigrants (see Hagan, this volume).

The broader aim of the work by Brown et al. is to explore how local, state, and federal policies affect the access of disadvantaged populations—including new immigrants—to health care. The authors note that access to health insurance and services is related to children's current and future well-being:

> Access to health services is particularly important for children to ensure that acute and chronic conditions are diagnosed and treated in a timely manner, that health and development are adequately monitored, and that preventive services are provided as recommended. . . . These issues are particularly salient for Mexican immigrants in the United States, who have poorer socioeconomic status than many other immigrant groups.

Are immigrant families and their children disadvantaged in their access to health care? The UCLA team introduces data based on two separate surveys, the 1996 March Current Population Survey and the National Health Survey.[39]

Brown and his colleagues found that over half (55 percent) of Mexican immigrant children in their study lack health insurance. Even more worrisome is the fact that noncitizen children are at greater risk of being without health insurance regardless of their length of stay in the United States. The authors note that when it comes to lack of insurance, Latino children in general are the most disadvantaged group—even if they are citizens or have U.S.-born parents. In addition to ethnicity and immigration status, two other factors are powerfully correlated with insurance rates: poverty and education. Children in families near or below the poverty line have four times the odds of being uninsured. Low levels of parental education also was related to children being more likely to be uninsured.

The effects of insurance on access to health care are quite strong. Access is typically measured by the use of physician services. The authors report that over one-third (35 percent) of all Mexican immigrant children do not have a regular source of care, and fully 42 percent of all Mexican immigrant children reported no physician visits within the past year. In short, the UCLA study suggests that many Mexican immigrant children are at risk of lacking insurance and, therefore, of lacking access to vital health services.[40]

The disturbing picture outlined in the UCLA study is made even more alarming by the fact that recent federal legislation will dramatically reduce access to care for immigrant children. The provision of publicly funded services to immigrants—including schooling and health services—has become a highly charged political issue in states such as California that have been heavily affected by immigration. While many—both politicians and others—are angry about the costs of providing health care and schooling to large numbers of immigrant children, few have paused to calculate the long-term costs of not providing such services, considering that access to such services is so deeply implicated in current as well as future emotional, economic, and social well-being.[41]

Enrique Trueba's contribution examines another critical aspect of Mexican immigration to the United States: the educational adaptations of immigrant children. For immigrant children, schools are the primary entry point into the host society. How immigrant children fare in schools can forecast their contributions to society as citizens. Immigrant adaptation to schooling is an extremely complex process. While all immigrant groups undergo certain similar processes (e.g., the upheaval of resettling in a foreign land, culture shock, linguistic and cultural discontinuities), Enrique Trueba discusses the unique historical, sociocultural, and economic contexts that have shaped the schooling experiences of Mexican immigrant children living, in Trueba's words, "in a binational world."

Trueba's work can be read as a contribution to a series of ongoing theoretical debates in the fields of cultural psychology and the anthropology of education. Two broad questions are pertinent in the context of this volume: Why is it that some immigrant children thrive in schools while others give up on schools as the route to a better tomorrow? And how do the adaptations and experiences of immigrant children in schools change over time? These questions have important implications for the future well-being of Mexican immigrant children in the United States.

Like previous generations of immigrants, many Mexican immigrant children do brilliantly in American schools (see Myers, this volume). In general, studies examining patterns that lead to school success tend to emphasize "the ideologies of opportunity" and "cultures of optimism" that motivate immigrant parents to migrate (Gibson 1988; Rumbaut and Cornelius 1995; Kao and Tienda 1995; Suárez-Orozco 1989; Suárez-Orozco and Suárez-Orozco 1995; Tuan 1995). Some scholars have argued that successful adaptations among immigrants may relate to the patterns of cultural, economic, and social "capital" that immigrants bring to the new land. Other scholars more specifically single out immigrant "cultural values" said to promote educational success (Sue and Okazaki 1990). Yet others suggest that some immigrant families succeed by inoculating their children—via culturally specific strategies—against the hostilities and negative attitudes they encounter in the new culture (De Vos and Suárez-Orozco 1992). Other studies emphasize that successful immigrant parents are able to maintain social cohesion by orienting the children away from various negative interpersonal and cultural aspects of the host culture (Zhou 1996).

A number of studies have concentrated on school failure among the children of immigrants. As Gary Orfield notes in his commentary, for many Mexican-origin youth poor achievement in school is a serious problem (see also Gandara 1995; Claude et al. 1992; Goldenberg and Gallimore 1995; Orfield 1995; Reese, Gallimore et al. 1991; Reese, Goldenberg et al. 1995; Romo and Falbo 1996; Suárez-Orozco 1989; Suárez-Orozco and Suárez-Orozco 1995; Trueba 1996).

Enrique Trueba and others (Trueba 1989a, 1989b; Delgado-Gaitan and Trueba 1991; Trueba 1993) have carefully examined the processes by which failure occurs within school settings (see also Hymes 1974; Mehan 1978; Gumperz 1981, 1982, 1983). In a series of detailed ethnographic studies, Trueba and others have documented the structural inequalities as well as language and other cultural discontinuities separating Mexican immigrant students from the English-speaking middle-class school system (see, for example, Carter and Segura 1979; Cazden 1988; Mehan 1978; Trueba et al. 1989; Trueba 1993).[42]

According to this line of research, face-to-face interactions in small-scale settings such as schools often capture and recreate certain class and ethnic inequalities permeating the larger sociocultural environment. In brief, these scholars tend to see the classroom as a microcosm of the larger socioeconomic power structure, recreating or reproducing social inequality through interethnic and interclass miscommunication between immigrant students and teachers from the dominant culture.[43]

Another issue of relevance to the work of Trueba relates to recent cross-sectional data suggesting another unsettling pattern: Among a number of immigrant groups today, length of residence in the United States seems to be associated with *declining* school achievement and aspirations (Kaminsky 1993; Kao and Tienda 1995; Suárez-Orozco and Suárez-Orozco 1995; Steinberg 1996; Vernez et al. 1996; Portes and Hao 1997; Rumbaut 1997). A central paradox in need of careful theoretical treatment relates to the fact that according to a number of studies, *new arrivals* from Central America (Suárez-Orozco 1989), Mexico (Trueba, this volume; Suárez-Orozco and Suárez-Orozco 1995), the Caribbean (Waters 1996), and Asia (Gibson 1988; Helweg and Helweg 1990; Sue and Okazaki 1990; Rumbaut and Cornelius 1995; Tuan 1995; Maira 1996; Zhou 1996) display highly adaptive attitudes and behaviors for succeeding in school. Yet the longer many immigrant youth are in the United States, the more negative they become in terms of school attitudes and adaptations (Suárez-Orozco and Suárez-Orozco 1995; Waters 1997).

Ruben Rumbaut, for example, surveyed over 15,000 seniors, juniors, and sophomores. He writes, "An important finding supporting our earlier reported research, is the *negative* association of length of residence in the United States with both GPA and aspirations. Time in the United States is, as expected, strongly predictive of improved English reading skills; but despite that seeming advantage, longer residence in the United States and second-generation status (that is, being born in the United States) are connected to declining academic achievement and aspirations, net of other factors" (Rumbaut and Cornelius 1995, 46–47, emphasis in the original).[44]

These and other data suggest that the new-immigrant experience may subvert the predictions of "assimilation" models that argue that in the United States each new generation tends to do substantially better in schools than the previous one, eventually reaching parity with the mainstream population (Chavez 1991) [for a critique of Chavez see Chapa 1996 and also Alba and Nee

1997; Rumbaut 1997]. Among many immigrants, exposure to certain aspects of American socioeconomic structure and culture today appears to be negatively associated with school orientation.[45]

As Gary Orfield notes (this volume), in 25 years there will no longer be a white majority in schools. Students in California and Texas will soon be predominantly Latino—the large majority of them of Mexican origin. The dropout rate among Mexican-origin students is a serious social problem because the U.S. economy today generates virtually no jobs for high school dropouts. Also worrisome is the fact that while the overall percentage of college-aged Americans is rising, Mexican-origin college attendance remains flat. Indeed, the low college graduation rate for Mexican-origin students forecasts problems for a community that is rapidly becoming the largest minority group in the United States (Orfield, this volume).

The problematic school performance of Mexican-origin children needs to be seen in the context of broader urban dynamics. In addition to widespread segregation, Mexican immigrant children are enrolling in growing numbers in school districts that are collapsing.[46] Orfield notes that these central-city school systems are attempting to deal with the incredible cultural changes brought about by immigration, without the necessary funds and without a coherent policy. We cannot avoid the conclusion that these schools are perpetuating inequality—a departure from the idea that schools provide (especially) immigrants the means to mobility in American society (Orfield, this volume).

PSYCHOCULTURAL THEMES

The process of immigration sets in motion multiple changes. Immigrants are changed by the experience of immigration. The process of uprooting and resettlement renders immigrants comparativists who come to experience significant aspects of their lives in terms of a double consciousness spanning the "here and now" of their new home with the "there and then" of their old world (Suárez-Orozco 1989; Suárez-Orozco and Suárez-Orozco 1995). As such, immigrants have become the muse of theorists of the human experience interested in issues of hybridity in the making and remaking of identities (Chambers 1994).

Second, immigrants change their host societies in multiple and profound ways. Our schools, places of work (Waldinger 1997), places of worship (Eck 1996), and media have all been transformed because of immigration. The contributions by Ricardo Ainslie, David Gutiérrez, and Thomas Espenshade and Maryann Belanger examine various responses to the changes brought about by recent Mexican immigration to the United States.

Ricardo Ainslie, associate professor of psychology at the University of Texas, Austin, presents us with a perspective on immigration with implications for our understanding of the changes immigrants undergo in settling in a new land *and* the anxieties generated by immigration among nonimmigrant citizens. Nearly all postindustrial democracies today find themselves experiencing very similar concerns in managing their distinct immigration problems: The French have their Algerians, the Germans their Turks, just as the United States has its "new immigrants." The anxieties generated by the changes brought about by immigration today cannot be divorced from the more general cultural dystopia now afflicting various postindustrial settings, including most of Western Europe and the United States (Suárez-Orozco, Roos, and Suárez-Orozco 1997).

This malaise is rooted in factors both internal and external to the various countries of immigration. Internally, taking the United States as an example, some scholars have argued that there is a crisis of authority and corrosion of trust in the ability of structures of the state to address, let alone resolve, elemental problems such as justice, education, and poverty. The research by Nye Jr., Zelikow, and King (1997) suggests that over the last three decades there has been a major decline in public confidence in the American government.[47]

This decline in public trust is generating a range of responses. At one end of the spectrum there is considerable citizen detachment and cynicism, while at the other there are the increasingly angry antigovernment militant groups such as the militias. In addition to these internal dynamics—which are also structured by increasing socioeconomic inequality and ethnic strife—there are new, little understood, external transnational impulses powerfully reshaping the economic, social, and cultural order in various countries of immigration. These factors conspire to generate an unsettling feeling that on seemingly all fronts we are "losing control"—of our borders, of the economy, of our culture.[48]

It is in the context of this general malaise that, borrowing from Sartre (who was borrowing from Nietzsche), we might say that if we did not have immigrants we would have to invent them because they simply make a natural target on which to focus and vent anxiety. In many countries today immigrants are the "usual suspects" to account for all kinds of chagrins, from economic downturns to youth crime and the cultural transformation of the public space.

Theoretically, Ainslie's work presents us with an interdisciplinary project involving certain psychoanalytic and social science tools to explore the issue of mourning, an important psychological problem in the immigrant experience. Psychodynamically speaking, there are two sides to every immigration story.

Immigration is at once about losses and about gains. While a great deal of social science research has examined how immigrants gain—materially and otherwise—in the process of resettling in a new land, there is much less basic research on immigrant losses—and how immigrants psychologically defend against such losses.

To the list of what is "new" about the new immigration, Ainslie adds the subtleties of a form of what we might call "low-intensity mourning." Ainslie suggests that "the immigrant experience represents a special case of mourning in which mourning revolves around the loss of people and of places loved, occasioned by geographic dislocation."[49] Among old-world immigrants a pattern of what we might call "high-intensity mourning" was engendered by a more definitive break with the country of origin—with old places and loved ones left behind. The Irish simply could not afford to return, en masse, to their villages in western Ireland every Christmas the way the Tehuixtlateño immigrants described in Ainslie's chapter return to their town in the mountains of Puebla. Ainslie argues that "immigrants" from Tehuixtla "retain a vibrant and intense connection to the town from which they migrated." He relates how immigrants in various U.S. destinations, including New York, California, and Texas, coordinate their activities to raise funds to rebuild the church, the cemetery, and to solve the town's water problems.

Ainslie notes that many of them are building houses "back home" because of a shared understanding that "they are only temporarily living in the United States, and that it is only a matter of time before they return to take up their lives more or less where they left off. Psychologically speaking, for these immigrants Tehuixtla remains part of their psychic present, not a lost past." What is important here is not whether in the end they will or will not go back to settle in their beloved town—if the general pattern described by Cornelius and Durand applies to Tehuixtla, it is very likely that many of them will *not* return—but rather the emotional power of these "return fantasies." Ainslie writes,

[T]he earnestness of these return fantasies, as well as their intensity, is impressive. The proximity of Mexico fuels these hopes. In the lives of these immigrants, Tehuixtla remains a powerful emotional beacon, orienting them toward their homeland. They remain, relative to the experience of many other immigrants, more tightly connected and identified with that community because Tehuixtla is so close and readily accessible. This emotional proximity has implications for the character of their cultural mourning. Their loss is not so complete. Indeed, many believe it to be only transient.

But to be sure, even low-intensity mourners do not live on hold until their powerful fantasies of the mythical return are, if ever, realized. As Ainslie observes, "In the character of their mourning, in the manner in which immigrants' mourning plays itself out in their individual and collective ties, powerful motivational forces are at work that shape how immigrants alter the worlds into which they come to live."

Immigrants come to reshape the cultural ethos of their new communities—substantially in broad areas of the Southwest and more subtly in nearly all other areas of the country. It could not be otherwise. Culture, in the Geertzian sense of human "webs of meaning" (Geertz 1973), is implicated in generating a psychological "background of safety" (Gumpel 1996). Culture, defined as a symbolic field of shared meanings and shared understandings and their embodiment in facts and artifacts, provides the safety net that humans need to balance the difficult walk between what is "me" and "not me." Immigrants entering a new cultural space manage their anxieties concerning the need to survive without their cultural safety net by fabricating new cultural spaces, by generating new meanings, and by establishing new shared understandings.

This is the psychocultural work of the immigrant. These new safety nets are woven not simply from the transplanted relics of the "old culture," nor are they created by a psychoculturally barren mechanical appropriation of the new culture. Immigrants today, to borrow from Woody Allen's film, are the anti-Zelig: They refuse to quietly disappear into the new cultural space. Rather, they weave, with threads borrowed from each of their two worlds, a new tapestry: a hybrid blending of the two systems of meaning that they struggle to integrate. The new cultural spaces that immigrants construct cannot be reduced or entirely contained by either of the cultural traditions in the immigrant's life. Psychoculturally speaking, "La Pulga"—the flea market vividly portrayed by Ainslie—is no more "Mexico" than it is "Austin." Rather, it is, in Ainslie's technical expression, a "restorative" space saturated with new hybrid signs and symbols, facts, and artifacts that mimic the immigrants' internal efforts to integrate, psychically and culturally, the new and the old.

And here is a paradox of immigration. As immigrants struggle to generate a new background of safety, they change the cultural space of the host society. In Ainslie's words, "These immigrants have seized the flea market and made it their own. In so doing they have simultaneously reconstructed a lost world *and* created a vehicle for effective engagement in the new one. This is precisely what immigrants have always done, thereby shaping the receiving culture, altering its configurations, and all too often provoking deep anxieties among those being changed." Sometimes the immigrant's new background of safety becomes the native's background of the uncanny, a term I borrow from the Israeli psychoanalyst Yolanda Gumpel (1996).

Among many established citizens, large-scale immigration generates a destabilizing sense that their cultural background of safety is changing in unsettling ways. Barbara Coe, a leader of the anti-immigration Proposition 187 in California (the initiative that would deny access to a host of publicly funded programs to undocumented immigrants) became involved in the anti-immigration cause after a visit to an Orange County social service agency when she

> became frightened by the changes immigration had brought into her community. "I walked into this monstrous room full of people, babies, little children all over the place, and I realized nobody was speaking English," . . . "I was overwhelmed with this feeling: Where am I? What's happened here?" [Barbara] Coe was trying to help an elderly friend secure some public health benefits but was turned down. "When the counselor told me that lots of those people waiting were illegal aliens and they were getting benefits instead of citizens like my friend, I walked out of there so outraged I decided I had to do something" (Suro 1994).

Psychological theorists from disparate perspectives, including Freudians (Freud 1930), neo-Freudians (Fromm 1973), post-Freudians (Kohut 1972; Mitchell 1993), and non-Freudians (Dollard et al. 1939), have claimed that frustration, injury, endangerment, and upheaval offer a powerful matrix for hatred and aggression. But heuristic models are only relevant when they can elucidate God in the details. Why, we must ask, is this anxiety over immigration emerging as an epidemic now? Beyond psychocultural insight we are in urgent need of a theory of new social formations. New information technologies, new idioms of communication, new patterns of capital flows, and a new ease of mass travel are making meaningless many of the boundaries that delineated much of the twentieth century.

These new social forces are engendering unprecedented opportunities but also remarkable contradictions, paradoxes, and anxieties. The meaning- and safety-making systems that structure identities and give us a sense of rootedness and continuity with our social space are undergoing a profound transformation. The anxieties about immigration must be placed at the center of these global changes. When immigration is framed as endangering cultural forms (language, shared understandings, values, etc.) or the economy (i.e., generating unemployment, depressing wages, fiscally burdening the native born, etc.), the result is anger and anxiety.

David Gutiérrez, associate professor of history at the University of California, San Diego, examines various historical and political themes specifically relating to Mexican immigration to Los Angeles. Los Angeles is the region most affected by Mexican immigration to the United States: The total Mexican-origin population in Los Angeles today is over 3.7 million, up from 1.1 million in 1970. He concentrates on issues of ethnicity and culture in the remaking of public culture and institutional life. He examines both continuities and changes in the character of the new Mexican immigration to Los Angeles.[50]

Immigrants from Mexico—and indeed from other Latin American countries—have steadily transformed the Los Angeles region over the last few decades. Gutiérrez describes processes of cultural rejuvenation taking place in neighborhoods nourished by continuous Mexican immigration, a paradigm of a wave of "Latinization" taking place in large areas of the Southwest and elsewhere.

Gutiérrez argues that the recent immigrant experience differs from previous immigration in fundamental ways: "[T]he magnitude of the most recent influx of immigration has contributed to the expansion of a Latino ethnic infrastructure and social world that dwarfs that which emerged in the first third of this century." An ubiquitous new formation is the stunning expansion of the Latino print media, television, and radio market. There has also been massive growth in the Latino consumer market, generating new business practices, consumer trends, and market tastes (Steinhauer 1997).

It has been argued that because of historical, cultural, and class reasons there is an enduring divide in the United States between new immigrants and more established Mexican Americans. Gutiérrez speculates that this too may be changing. Parts of Los Angeles have become a complex mosaic of Mexican-origin families: "The presence in the same neighborhoods (and indeed, often in the same households) of virtually any combination of U.S.-born Mexican Americans, permanent immigrants (both officially sanctioned and undocumented), long-term and short-term sojourners, and the U.S.-born and foreign-born children of all these groups has greatly complicated the sociocultural matrices in the United States in which individual and collective identities are evolving among ethnic Mexicans in the border region." There are, he claims, new possibilities of emerging political alliances where Mexican immigrants and more established Latino citizens meet.

Gutiérrez also examines the development of a significant Mexican-origin political mass. Latino immigrants are taking up U.S. citizenship—and registering to vote—in unprecedented numbers. The political implications of this trend over the long term are far from clear. Gutiérrez's contribution raises a number of significant questions. With population growth, will there be a commensurable growth of Latino participation in electoral politics? What will the political process be like in regions of the country where Mexican-origin U.S. citizens will soon be majorities? Will the growth of the Latino population necessarily be equated with increased political power? How will the culturally conservative Mexican-origin voters behave in the context of bipartisan American politics?[51] Will there be new forms of transnational alliances involving recent immigrants, more established Mexican Americans, and Mexicans in Mexico? Will the Mexican dual nationality initiative affect, if at all, the long-term political behavior of naturalized Mexican immigrants in the United States? With increasing transnationalism has the political appeal of citizenship and nationhood diminished? Is the growth of citizenship applications among Mexican-origin immigrants the result of instrumental need in light of new punitive legislation limiting immigrant access to certain publicly funded services? What, then, of the emotional or expressive appeal of citizenship? Such questions will surely preoccupy the next generation of observers of the Latino political experience in the United States.[52]

Thomas Espenshade and Maryann Belanger of Princeton University examine new data on American public opinion about immigration. Their research is based on an analysis of national surveys by 20 different organizations over a 30-year period. In their chapter they focus on the most recent (post-1990) data. They specifically examine public opinion on immigration and the economy and on legal versus illegal immigration, and attempt to evaluate the relative importance of immigration in the context of other national issues.

Espenshade and Belanger suggest that in recent years there has been "growing anxiety over the presence of immigrants in the United States." Indeed, their data reveal that by the year 1990 over 60 percent of the American public wanted immigration decreased. They found that Mexicans, along with other Latin Americans and Caribbeans, rank among the least favored immigrants in U.S. public opinion. They are perceived by many as less likely to work hard and more likely to use welfare than other immigrants such as Asians or Europeans. While most Americans (by a 2 to 1 ratio) say that the U.S. government should do more to control immigration, the Princeton researchers note that African Americans, Asian Americans, and Hispanic Americans tend to have more pro-immigrant views than whites.

The Princeton study suggests that the public is very concerned about illegal immigration. However, while the American public thinks immigration is a serious issue and wants the government to take action, especially against illegal immigration, they rank immigration way below more urgent concerns such as crime, jobs, and the economy.

The Princeton team suggests that historically there is a powerful correlation between anti-immigrant sentiment and unemployment. They conclude that macroeconomic conditions are clearly implicated in the making of public opinion. Other important findings include the following. Public opinion about immigration is ambivalent; responses depend on the specific wording and the symbolism implicit in phrasing each question (e.g., when the word "children" is included, attitudes seem to soften. On the other hand, when the word "welfare" is included, attitudes seem to harden). Attitudes toward immigration seem to lack intensity (e.g., in public opinion "immigration ranks below 'don't know' among the most important problems facing the United States today").

Public anxieties over immigration—especially illegal immigration—have inspired a great deal of new legislative and policy initiatives. These include the new welfare law that bars new immigrants from a host of publicly funded services, the 1997 immigration legislation that requires a person sponsoring a family member from abroad to demonstrate earnings of 125 percent of the poverty level ($19,500 a year for a family of four), and a number of border control initiatives designed to deter illegal immigration.[53]

Peter Andreas discusses the nature and efficacy of the massive new law enforcement efforts at the southern border of the United States. The border region is one of the fastest growing areas of North America. The California-Baja 130-mile-wide border area is home to over 11 million residents—6.1 million on the U.S. side and 5.1 million on the Mexican side. The region generates an estimated $150 billion in annual output (Migration News 1997). Two features characterize recent developments at the southern border: increasing liberalization of commercial flows and increasing criminalization of human flows.

In 1996, President Clinton announced "the end of the era of big government." That same year the Immigration and Naturalization Service (INS) experienced explosive growth. On September 30, 1996, President Clinton signed the Illegal Immigration and Reform and Immigration Responsibility Act. The act, among other things, will double the current size of the Border Patrol over the next five years—from some 5,000 agents to 10,000 agents in 2001.[54]

As part of the administration's overall strategy of "prevention through deterrence," Attorney General Janet Reno appointed a border czar to oversee the various border initiatives in the Southwest. Doris Meissner, the U.S. Commissioner of Immigration, promising to "reinvent" what had been a "dysfunctional" INS, announced that her office, too, will give top priority to securing the southern border. Likewise, Andreas documents the growing role of U.S.

military personnel at the southern border, who assist the INS in various initiatives including surveillance, maintenance, and operation of highly sophisticated military equipment.

The first intensive "prevention through deterrence" field operation was conducted in El Paso, Texas, and quickly adopted in other sectors of the southern border, including San Diego, Nogales, and Brownsville. The effort was designed to concentrate massive amounts of resources, including personnel and equipment, in the areas most trafficked by unauthorized immigrants. The idea was to apprehend as many illegal immigrants as possible in the border region, which would, in turn, reduce unauthorized immigration flows.

What has been the result of this unprecedented deployment of force? Has the INS been able to significantly reduce the flow of illegal immigration to the United States? Andreas' findings are quite alarming: "Noticeably missing from INS progress reports is any claim that illegal migration is actually down. The total increase in the number of Southwest border apprehensions may actually reflect more border crossings. Illegal entry is certainly more difficult and dangerous, but there is little evidence to suggest that migrants are giving up and heading home."

It seems that although the INS remains highly self-congratulatory, claiming that the southern border is harder to cross than ever before, the new efforts may simply be redirecting unauthorized immigration flows to more remote—and more dangerous—regions of the border.

Another new development is the criminalization of the border region. Unauthorized crossings went from being mostly acts of self-smuggling to a process structured by widening circles of illegality. Andreas argues that unauthorized immigrants must increasingly rely on the work of professional alien smugglers and document forgers—a high-profit growth industry on both sides of the border. Because immigrants now try to cross the border at more difficult points of entry, the price of being smuggled has also gone up: The price of being smuggled from Tijuana to Los Angeles doubled from 1994 to 1996.

Researchers at the Center for Immigration Research, University of Houston report an increase in the number of immigrant deaths in New Mexico, West Texas, and Arizona due to dehydration, exposure, and hypothermia as unauthorized immigrants attempt to cross the border in more remote and more dangerous areas. Likewise, the human rights of unauthorized immigrants have been seriously corroded as a result of the various new efforts at the southern border (Eschbach et al. 1997).

In short, Andreas claims that these new efforts, while making for dramatic symbolic politics, have largely failed to actually reduce illegal immigration flows through the southern sector of the international border. The initiatives generate a seductive imagery of state control and reinforce the myth that the answer to the problem of illegal immigration is to be found on the border.[55]

Because Mexican immigration to the United States—including undocumented immigration—is structured by powerful economic, social, and cultural processes, the problem of undocumented immigration will require more intelligent, long-term, binational responses than we have seen to date.

ACKNOWLEDGMENTS

I would like to thank Hilary Burger for her invaluable assistance in preparing this manuscript for publication. This research was made possible by the generous support of the David Rockefeller Center for Latin American Studies, the W. T. Grant Foundation, and the National Science Foundation.

NOTES

1. Scholars of immigration generally refer to post-1965 immigration as the "new immigration." Prior to 1965, the vast majority of new immigrants to the United States were of European (and Canadian) origin. After 1965, Afro-Caribbeans, Asians, and Latin Americans became the largest groups of immigrants.

2. The Native American population will be less than 1 percent.

3. Arguably all of the defining themes in the American experience, including the landing at Plymouth Rock, the involuntary transport of enslaved Africans, and the great industrial expansion of the twentieth century, are framed against the background of immigration.

4. The elemental structures of this narrative might include the following "mythemes" (Lévi-Strauss 1963, 206–231): (1) poor but (2) hard-working European peasants (3) pulling themselves up by their bootstraps, (4) willingly giving up their counterproductive old-world views, values, and languages—if not their accents!—to (5) become prosperous, proud, and loyal Americans. These mythemes frame the various hot-button issues in today's immigration debate, such as whether immigrants should be allowed access to welfare and social services and whether immigrant children should be given bilingual education.

5. In addition to attending to diachronic matters, a good case can be made that scholars of the new immigration have a great deal to learn from the recent experience of immigration in other postindustrial democracies such as France, Germany, and Japan. This, then, suggests a synchronic or comparative program for research: Just

how is the new immigration to the United States both like and unlike immigration in other postindustrial democracies? Again, because of the mythico-historical place of immigration in the national imagination, research on the new immigration continues to be filtered through the powerful lenses of "American exceptionalism."

6. Because Mexican immigrants display a pattern of "linguistic loyalty," retaining their home language after settling in the United States more than other new immigrants such as those from Asia (Estrada 1997; Portes and Hao 1997), and because there is now a massive Spanish-speaking media and business infrastructure in many large American cities, we can predict that the Spanish language—as well as new hybrid versions of "Spanglish"—will continue to thrive in the United States in the next century. George Sanchez suggests in his commentary that throughout the Southwest, where there is a critical mass of Mexican immigrants, new questions will need to be articulated: How are established citizens changing as a result of the massive immigration of the last two decades? Will *they* learn Spanish in significant numbers?

7. There is evidence to suggest that these changes, when combined with economic stagnation—especially unemployment—generate unsettling psychocultural anxieties and anti-immigrant sentiment among more established citizens. For example, public opinion data suggest that the U.S. public today seems most anxious about immigration from Latin America—of which Mexico is the principal source (see Espenshade and Belanger, this volume). Because Mexican immigration will continue to dominate patterns of immigration to the United States in the near future, it is important to develop a better understanding of, and help contain, this anxiety.

8. Some scholars, such as George Borjas (1994), have suggested that what is new about immigration is that large numbers of immigrants today tend to be less educated and less skilled relative to nonimmigrant citizens. This argument, unfortunately known as the "declining quality argument," in essence claims that what is new is that since 1965 the United States has been "importing poverty" (for a critique of the declining quality argument, see Myers, this volume).

This new immigration pattern, some observers have claimed, has over the years placed overwhelming demands on the structures of the welfare state—particularly on the education, health, and criminal justice systems (Huddle 1993). Other scholars of immigration have rejected those claims (Simon 1995). The declining quality argument provided much of the intellectual framework for the rather punitive new immigration legislation. For example, the immigration law enacted in April 1997 requires that a person sponsoring a family member from abroad must demonstrate earnings of 125 percent of the poverty level ($19,500 a year for a family of four). The message is clear: no more importing poverty. (For an overview of various new immigration-related legislative initiatives, see Hagan, this volume).

9. Borrowing the delicious words of Luis Rafael Sánchez, many new immigrants today live neither here nor there but rather in "la guagua aérea"—the air bus (Sánchez 1997).

10. Since 1990, while the Hispanic population in the United States grew by more than 30 percent, its buying power has grown by more than 65 percent, to about $350 billion in 1997. This is changing the way business is conducted in many parts of the country (see Steinhauer 1997, 3).

11. Cornelius (this volume), however, argues that over time Mexican immigrants in the United States are less likely to invest in capital improvements in their sending communities. In fact, he argues that a new feature of the Mexican experience in the United States is that as Mexican immigrants become increasingly rooted in the U.S. side of "the line," they mainly go back to their sending communities for rest and relaxation.

12. Indeed, new data suggest that children of Mexican immigrants today are enrolling in large numbers in poor and racially segregated schools (see Orfield, this volume).

13. New patterns of capital flows and communication, new information technologies, and the ease of mass transportation generate dynamics that transverse, and indeed, at times seem to overwhelm, the traditional boundaries of the nation-state.

14. Scholars of immigration have long maintained that cultural and social practices can generate and sustain substantial migratory flows. People tend to migrate because others—especially kith and kin—migrated before them. Roger Waldinger (1997) has explored the social dynamics of one such practice: immigrant labor recruiting networks. Immigrants, voilà, find their kith and kin jobs. Waldinger suggests that immigrant networks provide employers with a nearly unlimited supply of people with little or no outlay. Networks provide connections to people able to fill jobs, at times even before the jobs are vacant. The social networks function optimally when they efficiently and economically generate quality information about jobs, applicants, and bosses.

   Over time, social networks seem to generate such a momentum that companies simply prefer not to hire off the street, relying instead on their own established immigrant sources. Waldinger suggests that eventually network recruitment tends to create forms of "social closure," detaching employers from the open labor market. By their very nature, networks tend to provide a homogeneous group of workers: Immigrant workers recruit their fellow immigrant kith and kin (Waldinger 1997).

15. Clearly, economics do matter but not uniformly and not universally. It is worth noting that war and other social factors were basic to an understanding of earlier patterns of Mexican immigration to the United States, as well as the large-scale migration patterns from Central America during the 1980s (Domínguez 1997; Suárez-Orozco 1989).

16. Wayne Cornelius (this volume) and González Baker et al. (this volume) argue that the demand for Mexican labor on the U.S. side of the border has been a powerful and enduring pull or magnet factor regulating immigration flows. While push and pull factors generate an important context for immigration, immigrants are not automatons exclusively driven by economic forces: Human agency, social relations, and cultural practices are powerfully implicated in the migration process.

17. Another factor that will remain a critical issue in the Mexican economic landscape is the foreign debt. The foreign debt service now represents 8 percent of gross domestic product (GDP), a fact that, along with negative growth, puts an intense strain on the Mexican economy.

18. Mexican employment generated since 1988 has been in construction and state-related services, not in high technology and knowledge-intensive fields. Another important feature of the recent Mexican experience has been the increasing exclusion of small and medium-sized firms from the new economic arena.

19. In his commentary on Dussel's paper at the Harvard conference (where it was first presented), John Coatsworth, Monroe Gutman Professor of Latin American Affairs at Harvard, observed that the economic crisis afflicting Mexico over the last 15 years is the longest in this century. Coatsworth argued that Mexico may not recover its 1980 level of GDP per capita before well into the next century. Furthermore, he pointed out that there is always the possibility that a U.S. recession in the not-too-distant future would affect the Mexican economy dramatically, given that the two economies are linked more than ever since the signing of the North American Free Trade Agreement (NAFTA). What is remarkable about this period, Coatsworth claimed, is not just the polarization detected in Dussel's data, but the prolongation and depth of stagnation taking place. While such polarization also occurred during the *porfiriato*, the turn of the century was a period of growth. Polarization while incomes are stagnating is a new and troubling phenomenon in the Mexican economy.

20. The authors suggest that in addition to economic factors—including the enduring demand for Mexican labor in the context of the restructuring of the U.S. economy, with its boon in the service sector and the downturn of unionization—policies to recruit temporary workers, such as the *bracero* program, seem to have generated a powerful migratory momentum. The post-1965 family reunification policy, they argue, has also favored the Mexicanization of U.S. immigration.

21. Better data are needed to examine issues of gender and Mexican immigration to the United States. For example, what are the implications of the new pattern of immigration among women and children, in light of recent policy measures limiting immigrant access to a host of publicly funded services? Mexican families are more likely to be both intact and poor (40 percent of all Latino children today live

below the poverty level). We need better models for understanding how marriage, kinship, and poverty interplay to shape the opportunities available to immigrant men and women today.

22. There is an interesting contradiction in much current research on the new immigration. On the one hand, robust data suggest that immigrants are increasingly rooted in the U.S. economy and society. Large numbers of immigrants are pursuing citizenship and, as Wayne Cornelius claims, more Mexican immigrants now express an unequivocal intention to remain in the United States than ever before. Cornelius notes that in the past ten years, many more Mexicans have arrived to try to establish a viable economic base on the U.S. side of the border, discarding any plans to return to Mexico. Cornelius' research suggests that there is a sharply higher number of immigrants coming with plans to settle and pursue citizenship, including even the "street corner laborers" he has interviewed. Naturalization is now seen by many immigrants as essential to securing a viable economic base in the United States. Other research suggests that "the rate of back-and-forth labor movement seems to be slowing" (Binational Study on Migration 1997, iii).

How are we to reconcile this tendency with the pattern of transnationalism that has been described among immigrant groups, including Mexicans? At the Twentieth Latin American Studies Association (LASA) International Congress in Guadalajara, a substantial number of presentations on Mexican immigration to the United States privileged the "transnationalism" said to characterize the new Mexican experience. The question in urgent need of theoretical elaboration is, What does it mean to talk about transnationalism when the data suggest a robust momentum toward increasing immigrant embeddedness in the U.S. setting?

23. It is important to highlight that the portion of the U.S. economy that is affected by immigration is rather minor. The total size of the U.S. economy is $7 trillion; immigrant-related economic activities are a small portion of that total (a domestic gain in the order of $1 to $10 billion a year, according to the National Research Council [1997, 5]). It is obvious that immigrants will neither make nor break the U.S. economy. What is curious, therefore, is the degree of public and media concern over immigration and the economy. My hypothesis is that some other anxieties, such as those relating to the cultural and demographic changes brought about by immigration, are finding an outlet in the current concern over immigration and the economy.

24. The NRC study suggests that there are "three main reasons why immigrants receive more in services than they pay in taxes in these annual calculations: (1) immigrant-headed households include more school-aged children than native households on average, and therefore currently consume more educational services; (2) immigrant-headed households are poorer than native households on average, and

therefore receive more state and locally funded income transfers; and (3) immigrant-headed households have lower incomes and own less property than native households on average, and thus pay lower state and local taxes" (NRC 1997, 8). Of relevance to this volume is the panel's findings regarding differences across various immigrant populations: "Across the immigrant population, the size of the net fiscal burden imposed on native residents varies significantly. It is by far heaviest for households of immigrants originating in Latin America. . . . These differences arise because households of Latin American immigrants tend to have lower incomes and to include more school-age children than do other immigrant households" (NRC 1997, 8). In terms of long-term fiscal implications of immigration, it is clear that an important issue will be the educational adaptation of the children of today's immigrants: More education today means less fiscal burden down the road.

25. In addition, Cornelius' research team interviewed 116 irregularly employed "street corner workers," who typically find work in construction and landscaping.

26. Cornelius' data suggest that immigrant workers in San Diego county are key players in small and medium-sized establishments employing a median number of 46 people. These firms do not appear to be in financial danger. Nor were they paying substandard or minimum wages. Fully one-third of businesses in Cornelius' sample were immigrant owned. He notes that the workforce of Mexican-owned firms is largely Mexican or Latin American. Roger Waldinger (1997) has suggested that in immigrant-dominated firms in neighboring Los Angeles there exists a cultural and linguistic climate that tends to exclude nonimmigrant workers: In some cases non-Spanish-speaking workers simply feel "out of place."

27. Whereas in the past Mexican immigrant workers were concentrated in a more limited range of economic sectors (Gamio 1971), immigrant labor is now found in much broader sectors of the economy, such as highly advanced technologies, service, food processing, construction, restaurant-hotels, manufacturing, and, of course, agriculture.

28. The mean entry-level wage was $5.62 (1996); agricultural and restaurant work paid closer to the minimum wage. Cornelius found that the difference between the wages of legal and illegal workers was small (a 45 cent difference per hour, which he attributes to length of stay in the United States and ability to do jobs requiring English-language skills).

29. Note that immigrant workers in Japan are sometimes called the "3-K" workers for the Japanese words for "dirty, demanding and dangerous" jobs (Tsuda 1996).

30. What is the impact of policy changes on the use and supply of immigrant labor? Following Operation Gatekeeper—the effort at the San Diego sector of the international border to curtail illegal immigration (see Andreas, this volume)—only 8 percent of employers interviewed perceived a change in the labor supply. Some

employers actually reported an *increase* in labor supply since the implementation of Operation Gatekeeper! Cornelius argues that the explosive growth in the Southern California retail and service sectors has created such a powerful demand for immigrant workers that the presence of both legal and illegal immigrants will not be easily contained via border control initiatives (see also Andreas, this volume).

31. The studies by González Baker et al. and Cornelius reveal a contradiction between the attitudes and practices of businesses—who seem to thrive from having access to a large pool of Mexican immigrant labor—and public sentiment, which is increasingly "anti-immigrant" (see Espenshade and Belanger, this volume). Whereas immigrant-dependent firms are enjoying the fruits of immigrant labor, they do not have to proportionally absorb the costs associated with the presence of large numbers of immigrant families and children who are in need of basic services such as schooling and health care. These costs are the responsibility of taxpayers who are increasingly angry about such costs. The potential political implications of this contradiction are explosive. Recently there has been a wave of political and legal activity around the costs associated with providing services to large numbers of immigrants. For example, California's Proposition 187, the anti-immigrant initiative that would deny illegal immigrants access to publicly funded services, as well as the state of California suing the federal government for reimbursement for the costs of providing services such as education, health, and the justice system to immigrants relate to the basic tension around who "gains" and who "pays" for immigration (Suárez-Orozco 1996). In addition to the immigrants themselves and immigrant-dependent firms, the federal government may be the other big winner. The federal government keeps the largest share of the immigrant-generated tax base. On the other hand, states must pay the bill for some of the more expensive services immigrants need. Therefore, some observers have claimed that the federal government should reimburse the immigrant-impacted states a proportional share of the immigrant-generated tax dollars it collects.

32. It is perhaps not surprising that in immigrant-saturated areas, firms become immigrant dependent. The interesting question is, of course, the nature of the causality implied in the equation. Do immigrant-dependent firms become so because they are in immigrant-saturated areas? Or do immigrant-dependent firms saturate an area with immigrants because they hire immigrant workers? The data suggest that immigrants, too, "follow the money" (Sassen 1994). Of course, cultural and social practices are also powerful factors in migratory flows.

33. In his commentary, Robert Smith concurs with others in this volume in suggesting that as Mexican immigrants become firmly established in various U.S. settings, we will need to pay more attention to the long-term process of incorporation, particularly for second-generation immigrants. He suggests that there are signs for con-

cern. For example, whereas in 1980 Mexicans in New York City were quite close economically to Cuban Americans, today they appear to be struggling—along with Dominican immigrants—at the bottom of the economic ladder. They have lower rates of employment and educational standing, an ominous condition given the shrinking options for mobility for those at the lower end of the opportunity structure (see also Orfield, this volume).

34. In his commentary, Nathan Glazer, Professor Emeritus of Education and Sociology at Harvard, raises an urgent question: Is the pattern of declining returns from education among the children of immigrants a temporary dynamic, or is this likely to be an enduring trend? There is reason to suspect that graduating from high school is no longer enough to achieve meaningful mobility in the posteducational opportunity structure. Myers' findings are even more alarming when we consider that only about half of all Mexican-origin students who start high school graduate. These two social phenomena—declining returns from education and continued high dropout rates among Mexican-origin students—have broad sociological implications given that the U.S. economy is no longer generating the jobs that traditionally provided mobility for those who do not complete higher education.

Glazer suggests that the pattern of decline in educational returns may also be related to the declining quality of education. Myers' paper suggests many other questions, all of which require further empirical treatment and theoretical framing: Are the diminishing returns from education due to large-scale immigration or a consequence of global economic trends? Does the pattern of declining returns affect the children of Mexican immigrants in the same way that it affects the native-born white population? Or is there an additional penalty that Mexican immigrants and their children pay? Are there any important gender differences between the earnings of male versus female immigrants based on education?

35. Durand argues that IRCA had the following effects: (1) large numbers of Mexican immigrants were legalized; (2) there was an increase in the immigration of women and children, who could now more easily join their relatives in the United States; (3) there was a significant increase in urban-origin emigration from Mexico; and (4) IRCA put an end to the dominant pattern of seasonal or return migration to Mexico.

36. He notes that in Ameca the high levels of intermarriage now taking place were unheard of in the past. Durand speculates that in the past intermarriages would have caused jealousy and social disruption but are now tolerated and even celebrated with pride.

37. In most cases (74 percent), the marriages took place while Amequense immigrants were in the United States without proper documentation—the majority of the marriages were, in fact, to "regularize" the situation of an undocumented

immigrant. These marriages, however, have proven quite stable over time. The vast majority of intermarried couples have chosen to reside in the United States (82 percent). Intermarriage patterns included the following combinations: 44 percent married Chicanos, 42 percent married white Americans, 3 percent married African Americans, and 11 percent married people of other national origin. Mexican immigrant women, Durand observes, have broadened the marriage panorama more than men.

38. Merilee Grindle, Edward S. Mason Professor of International Development at the Kennedy School of Government, Harvard University, addresses her commentary to the kinds of problems that typically surface while dealing with the various data sets needed to generate an adequate picture of immigration and integration. Large data sets cannot capture the subtle dynamics of immigration that underlie long-term trends. They simply do not allow for detailed analyses of complex microscopic processes such as those described in Durand's work. On the other hand, detailed microscopic ethnographies do not always yield generalizable findings.

Professor Grindle also highlights the implicit causality in Durand's paper. Durand's position is that government policies regulating residence and citizenship rights frame the social practices that come to shape immigrant life. Policy changes—such as the IRCA—generate new realities by stimulating changes in the social and economic opportunities opened to immigrants. After legalization Amequense immigrants were free to enter new sectors of the economy and society, where, Durand suggests, there was more contact between the sexes and between Amequenses and other groups. These new social relations generated new social practices, including intermarriage patterns.

39. The National Health Survey does not provide information on citizenship status.

40. In his commentary, Felton Earls, professor of human behavior and development, Department of Maternal and Child Health at Harvard School of Public Health and professor of child psychiatry at Harvard Medical School, points out that immigrants today are entering a society where there are 42 million uninsured and 40 million poorly insured Americans. Earls refers to the three competing theories on uninsurance and health care utilization patterns among immigrants: (1) *Assimilation theory,* which holds that the longer an immigrant is in the United States, the more assimilated she should become, and the more access she will have to health care; (2) *human capital theory,* which holds that as immigrants gain education, their access to health care should also increase; and (3) *structural theory,* which holds that despite education and time spent in the United States, there are structural barriers to immigrants' access to health care.

According to Earls, the data generated by the UCLA study, as well as a number of other recent studies, suggest that structural theory best accounts for recent patterns of immigrant access to health care. Immigrants today are not achieving equality in access to health services despite long periods of residence or educational attainment. In fact, Earls suggests that the estimates in the UCLA study may be quite conservative. In the Current Population Survey, for example, the definition of coverage is whether one had insurance coverage at any time in the last twelve months. This is particularly unrevealing in a volatile health care market.

41. Dr. Earls claims that in addition to violating the International Convention on the Rights of the Child, current U.S. policy is surely generating excess suffering, with attendant long-term financial, physical, and social costs.

42. Another intellectual current has influenced Trueba's approach to the issues facing Mexican immigrant children in schools: L. S. Vygotsky's theoretical work on child development. One of the most important contributions of Vygotsky to our understanding of children's cognitive development, especially those undergoing situations of rapid sociocultural change, such as immigrant children, was his theory of the relationship between cognitive and social phenomena (Vygotsky 1978, 1981; Wertsch 1981; Cole 1985; Moll 1986; Tharp and Gallimore 1988; Moll 1990; Wertsch 1991).

Vygotsky and his followers argue that the development of uniquely human higher mental functions find their origin in day-to-day social interactions. At the foundation of Vygotsky's theory is the proposition that in order to translate socially constructed experiences into cognitive categories, children move from the interpersonal plane to the intrapsychological plane. The process of internalization that permits the translation of interpsychological experience to intrapsychological cognitive categories presupposes culturally and linguistically meaningful interaction. Because of the intimate relationship between language and thought, it follows that lack of intellectual performance and school achievement in immigrant children may well have to do with their experience of abrupt transitions and discontinuities from familiar to unfamiliar sociocultural environments, which are particularly detrimental to children when they lack both linguistic and cultural knowledge to interact meaningfully with adults and peers.

43. In addition to sociolinguists, social reproduction theorists have also argued that schools tend to replicate social inequities by such practices as offering the least challenging curriculum to working-class, ethnic, and immigrant students and by systematically devaluing their cultural capital, such as linguistic patterns, modes of dress, and other cultural orientations (Bowles and Gintis 1976; Bourdieu and Paseron 1977; Willis 1977; Giroux 1983; Macedo 1994). Enrique Trueba's work has explored structural barriers to advancement as well as sociocultural and linguistic factors involved in the schooling of children in poor inner-city schools—the schools many newly arrived immigrants, especially those from Mexico, tend to

attend (see Orfield, this volume). Other scholars have argued that "tracking" has had particularly devastating influences in the immigrant school experience, particularly among Mexican-origin youth (Romo and Falbo 1996).

44. Likewise, in his study based on a national survey of over 20,000 teenagers from nine high schools, Steinberg reports a very alarming trend:

> The longer a student's family has lived in this country, the worse the youngster's school performance and mental health. . . . Foreign-born students—who, incidentally, report significantly more discrimination than American-born youngsters and significantly more difficulty with the English language—nevertheless earn higher grades in school than their American-born counterparts.
>
> . . . The more Americanized students—those whose families have been living here longer—are less committed to doing well in school than their immigrant counterparts. Immigrants spend more time on homework, are more attentive in class, are more oriented to doing well in school, and are more likely to have friends who think academic achievement is important.
>
> Differences between immigrants and nonimmigrants are also apparent when we look at various manifestations of mental health. Immigrant adolescents report less drug use, less delinquency, less misconduct in school, fewer psychosocial problems, and less psychological distress than do American-born youngsters.
>
> The adverse effects of Americanization are seen among Asian and Latino youngsters alike (that is, within each of the two largest populations of immigrant youth in this country), with achievement decreasing, and problems increasing, with each successive generation. Instead of finding what one might reasonably expect—that the longer a family has been in this country, the better the child will be faring in our schools—we find exactly the reverse. Our findings, as well as those from several other studies, suggest that becoming Americanized is detrimental to youngsters' achievement, and terrible for their overall mental health (Steinberg 1996, 97–98).

45. Gary Orfield highlights some of the broader issues involved in the schooling of Mexican immigrant youth today. He notes that because immigration is mainly affecting the Southwest and the West, and cities like Chicago and New York, the rest of the country has not yet realized the magnitude of the change now taking place. Mexican immigrants are an intensely metropolitan population. The Los Angeles Unified School District today enrolls 20 percent of all U.S. Latinos. The

chances that a Mexican-origin youth will go to college are very small. Mexican-origin families are becoming increasingly segregated from whites and from the middle class. Today if a child is enrolled in an all-Latino or all-black school, she is much more likely to be impoverished.

46. On July 1997, parents of children attending schools in Compton, California, "filed a lawsuit asserting that the classrooms in the state-run district are so dilapidated and school management so inept that the students are being deprived of a basic education and are at an increased risk of injury" (*New York Times* 1997). The parents "complain of classroom floors covered with buckets to catch leaking rainwater, boarded-up windows, graffiti, exposed electrical wiring, playgrounds littered with broken glass, meager libraries, and bathrooms that are perpetually flooded with human waste and lacking toilet paper. They also say that teachers are unqualified, that playground equipment is either nonexistent or broken, and security is so lax that parent meetings cannot be held on school grounds" (*New York Times* 1997, 12). The population of the Compton schools is mostly of African American and Mexican origin.

47. In 1964, three-quarters of all Americans said they trusted the federal government "to do the right thing." Today merely a quarter do (Nye et al. 1997).

48. In the words of Michael Sandel, the sense of losing control defines "the anxiety of the age" (Sandel 1996).

49. An issue of importance here, not examined in Ainslie's chapter, is the problem of pathological mourning. The pathological mourning of losses is often implicated in the creation of psychologically powerful cultural narratives structured around what Vamik Volkan has called "chosen traumas" (Volkan 1996). Psychologically speaking, much of American history is the history of the work of mourning, both healthy and pathological among various immigrant groups involved in the creation of the American ethos: the early WASPS, the Germans, the Irish, the Eastern Europeans, the Southern Europeans, and now, the "new immigrants." By one interpretation, before entering the Golden Door immigrants had to make a Faustian bargain: They could dream of achieving the dream but first they had to check out some baggage at the door—particularly cultural baggage.

If Ainslie's general model is correct, then how these earlier groups managed—and did not manage—to mourn the losses of immigration, and the type of psychic baggage they transmitted to the next generation, would have important implications for their attitudes toward new immigrants. More work in this area would be quite fruitful.

50. Gutiérrez notes that the Los Angeles Unified School District is 68 percent Latino. In some downtown areas the percentage is much higher, along with a high percentage of limited-English-proficiency students (over 50 percent).

51. Will the more "pro-immigrant" Democrats get the lion's share of their votes? Or will the culturally conservative—but more hostile to immigration—Republicans reap the benefits?

52. It can be argued that in some ways, the expressive appeal of citizenship has been decoupled from its instrumental aspects. In other words, people are taking on citizenship today almost entirely for instrumental purposes. Is it then the case that the current immigration-related legislation will cheapen the concept of citizenship? (See Jones-Correa, this volume.)

53. In her commentary, Jacqueline Hagan claims that the new immigration legislation will have a negative effect on large sectors of society. She suggests that the internal security provision of the new act may usher in a nationwide effort at fingerprinting, wiretapping, INS linkages with local and state law enforcement, and other measures to combat links between immigration, the drug trade, and terrorism. The act has obvious implications for the civil rights of immigrants and citizen alike.

     The new law changes in significant ways the process by which citizens and permanent residents can bring family members to permanently reside in the United States. Hagan claims that this feature of the law will decidedly undermine the principle of family reunification—a cornerstone of U.S. immigration policy since 1965. The law, for example, requires that a person sponsoring a family member from abroad must demonstrate earnings of 125 percent of the poverty level. This will limit the ability of poorer citizens and permanent residents to sponsor family members, disproportionately affecting the Mexican-origin population in the United States, who tend to be poorer than other groups. The new law will also adversely affect asylum seekers. It is quite likely that this new act will further encourage illegal immigration to the United States.

54. The new legislation also requires building a 14-mile triple fence in the San Diego area, in the most heavily trafficked sector of the international border.

55. Andreas claims that while there has been a massive buildup of resources in the border region, workplace enforcement and employer sanctions for knowingly hiring an illegal immigrant are minimal.

REFERENCES

Alba, R., and V. Nee. 1997. Rethinking assimilation theory for a new era of immigration. Paper presented at the Second Generation Conference at the Jerome Levy Economics Institute of Bard College, Annandale-on-the Hudson, New York.

Basch, L., N. G. Schiller, et al. 1995. *Nations Unbound: Transnational Projects, Postcolonial Predicaments and Deterritorialized Nation-States.* Basel, Switzerland: Gordon and Breach Science Publishers.

Bean, F., R. de la Garza, et al., eds. 1997. *At the Crossroads: Mexico and U.S. Immigration Policy.* Lanham, Md.: Rowman & Littlefield Publishers, Inc.

Binational Study on Migration. 1997. Binational Study: Migration Between Mexico and the United States. Washington, D.C.: Prepublication Copy.

Borjas, G. 1994. Tired, poor, on welfare. In *Arguing Immigration,* ed. N. Mills. New York: Simon and Schuster.

Bourdieu, P., and J. Paseron. 1977. *Reproduction in Education, Society and Culture.* Beverly Hills, Calif.: Sage Publications.

Bowles, S., and H. Gintis. 1976. *Schooling in Capitalist America.* New York: Basic Books.

Bureau of the Census. 1996. *Population Projections of the United States by Age, Sex, Race, and Hispanic Origin: 1995 to 2050.* Washington, D.C.: Government Printing Office.

Carter, T. P., and R. D. Segura. 1979. *Mexican Americans in School: A Decade of Change.* New York: College Entrance Examination.

Cazden, C. 1988. *Classroom Discourse: The Language of Teaching and Learning.* Portsmouth, N.H.: Heinemann.

Chambers, I. 1994. *Migrancy, Culture, Identity.* London and New York: Routledge.

Chapa, J. 1996. *Mexican American Education: First, Second, and Third Generation Adaptations.* Current Issues in Educational Research Workshop, Harvard University Graduate School of Education.

Chavez, L. 1991. *Out of the Barrio: Toward a New Politics of Hispanic Assimilation.* New York: Basic Books.

Claude, G., L. Reese, et al. 1992. "Effects of Literacy Materials from School on Latino Children's Home Experiences and Early Reading Achievement." *The American Journal of Education* 100(4): 497–536.

Cole, M. 1985. The zone of proximal development: Where culture and cognition create each other. In *Culture, Communication and Cognition: Vygotskian Perspectives,* ed. J. B. Wertsch. New York: Cambridge University Press.

Delgado-Gaitan, C., and H. T. Trueba. 1991. *Crossing Cultural Borders: Education for Immigrant Families in America.* London: The Falmer Press.

De Vos, G. A. 1992. *Social Cohesion and Alienation: Minorities in the United States and Japan.* Boulder, Colo.: Westview Press.

Dollard, J. L., W. Doob, N. E. Miller, O. H. Mower, and R. R. Sears. 1939. *Frustration and Aggression.* New Haven, Conn.: Yale University Press.

Domínguez, J. 1997. Immigration and foreign policy. Paper presented at the Harvard Graduate School of Education, Cambridge, Massachusetts.

Eck, D. L. 1996. "Neighboring Faiths." *Harvard Magazine* 99.

Edmonston, B., and J. Passel, eds. 1994. *Immigration and Ethnicity: The Integration of America's Newest Arrivals.* Washington, D.C.: The Urban Institute.

Eschbach, K., J. Hagan, et al. 1997. *Death at the Border.* Houston: University of Houston, Center for Immigration Research.

Espenshade, T., ed. 1997. *Keys to Successful Immigration: Implications of the New Jersey Experience.* Washington, D.C.: The Urban Institute Press.

Espin, O. M. 1987. "Psychological Impact of Migration on Latinas: Implications for Psychotherapeutic Practice." *Psychology of Women Quarterly* 11(4): 489–503.

Estrada, L. 1997. Demographics and the new immigration. Paper presented at the Spencer Foundation Conference on Immigration and Education, 8 October, UCLA, Los Angeles, California.

Freud, S. 1930. *Civilization and Its Discontents.* New York: W W Norton and Company.

Fromm, E. 1973. *The Anatomy of Human Destructiveness.* New York: Henry Holt.

Gamio, M. 1971. *Mexican Immigration to the United States.* New York: Dover Publications, Inc.

Gandara, P. 1995. *Over the Ivy Walls: The Educational Mobility of Low Income Chicanos.* Albany, N.Y.: SUNY Press.

Geertz, C. 1973. *The Interpretation of Cultures.* New York: Basic Books.

Gibson, M. A. 1988. *Accommodation without Assimilation: Sikh Immigrants in an American High School.* Ithaca and London: Cornell University Press.

Giroux, H. 1983. "Theories of Reproduction and Resistance in the New Sociology of Education: A Critical Analysis." *Harvard Educational Review* 53(3): 257–293.

Glazer, N. 1997. *We Are All Multiculturalists Now.* Cambridge, Mass.: Harvard University Press.

Goldenberg, C., and R. Gallimore. 1995. "Immigrant Latino Parents' Values and Beliefs about Their Children's Education: Continuities and Discontinuities across Cultures and Generations." *Advances in Motivation and Achievement* 9: 183–228.

Gumpel, Y. 1996. Reflections on the prevalence of the uncanny in social violence. Paper presented at the Conference on Cultures Under Siege, Rockefeller Foundation Conference Center, Bellagio, Italy.

Gumperz, J. 1981. Conversational inferences and classroom learning. In *Ethnography and Language in Educational Settings,* ed. J. L. Green and C. Wallat. Norwood, N.J.: Ablex.

Gumperz, J. 1982. *Language and Social Identity.* Stanford: Stanford University Press.

Gumperz, J. 1983. The communicative basis of social inequality. In *Minorities: Communities and Identity,* ed. J. L. Green and C. Wallat. New York: Garland.

Helweg, A., and U. Helweg. 1990. *An Immigrant Success Story: East Indians in America.* Philadelphia: University of Pennsylvania Press.

Higham, J. 1955. *Strangers in the Land: Patterns of American Nativism.* New Brunswick and London: Rutgers University Press.

Hing, B. O. 1993. *Making and Remaking Asian America through Immigration Policy.* Stanford: Stanford University Press.

Hondagneu-Sotelo, P. 1994. *Gendered Transitions: Mexican Experiences of Immigration.* Berkeley and London: University of California Press.

Huddle, D. 1993. *The Costs of Immigration.* Washington, D.C.: Carrying Capacity Network.

Hymes, D. 1974. *Foundations in Sociolinguistics.* Philadelphia: University of Pennsylvania Press.

Kaminsky, M. 1993. "On the Site of Loss: A Response to Antokeletz's Paper on Cross-cultural Transformation." *The American Journal of Psychoanalysis* 52(3): 103–108S.

Kao, G., and M. Tienda. 1995. "Optimism and Achievement: The Educational Performance of Immigrant Youth." *Social Science Quarterly* 76(1): 1–19.

Kohut, H. 1972. "Thoughts on Narcissism and Narcissistic Rage." *Psychoanalytic Study of the Child* 27: 360–400.

Levi-Strauss, C. 1963. *Structural Anthropology.* New York: Basic Books, Inc.

Levitt, P. 1997. Future allegiances: The social and political implications of transnationalism. Paper presented at the David Rockefeller Center for Latin American Studies, Harvard University, Cambridge, Massachusetts.

Macedo, D. 1994. *Literacies of Power: What Americans Are Not Allowed to Know.* Boulder, Colo.: Westview Press.

Mahler, S. 1997. Immigration and gender in transnational perspective. Paper presented at the Harvard Graduate School of Education, Cambridge, Massachusetts.

Maira, S. 1996. Ethnic identity development of second-generation Indian American adolescents. Unpublished manuscript, Harvard Graduate School of Education, Cambridge, Massachusetts.

Mears, T. 1997. Miami Hispanics losing their Spanish. *Boston Globe,* 5 October.

Mehan, H. 1978. "Structuring School Structure." *Harvard Educational Review* 45(1): 31–338.

Migration News. 1997. The border region economy grows. 1 July.

Mitchell, S. A. 1993. "Aggression and the Endangered Self." *Psychoanalytic Quarterly* LXII: 351–382.

Moll, L. 1986. "Writing as Communication: Creating Strategic Learning Environments for Students." *Theory to Practice* 26(2): 102–108.

Moll, L. 1990. Introduction. In *Vygotsky and Education: Instructional Implications and Applications of Sociohistorical Psychology,* ed. L. Moll. Cambridge: Cambridge University Press.

National Research Council. 1997. *The New Americans: Economic, Demographic, and Fiscal Effects of Immigration.* Washington, D.C.: National Academy Press.

New York Times. 1997. California parents sue state over schools in their city. 14 July.

Nye, J. S. Jr., P. Zelikow, and D. C. King, eds. 1997. *Why People Don't Trust Government.* Cambridge, Mass.: Harvard University Press.

Orfield, G. 1995. Latinos in Education: Recent Trends. Paper presented at the Harvard Graduate School of Education, Cambridge, Massachusetts.

Pessar, P. R. 1995. *A Visa for a Dream.* Boston: Allyn and Bacon.

Portes, A. 1996. Children of immigrants: segmented assimilation and its determinants. In *The Economic Sociology of Immigration: Essays on Networks, Ethnicity, and Entrepreneurship.* New York: Russell Sage Foundation.

Portes, A., and L. Hao. 1997. English first or English only? Paper presented at the Second Generation Conference at the Jerome Levy Economics Institute of Bard College, Annandale-on-the Hudson, New York.

Portes, A., and R. Rumbaut. 1996. *Immigrant America.* Berkeley and Los Angeles: University of California Press.

Reese, L., R. Gallimore, et al. 1991. *The Concept of Educación: Latino Family Values and American Schooling.* Annual Meetings of the American Anthropological Association.

Reese, L., C. Goldenberg, et al. 1995. Ecocultural context, cultural activity and emergent literacy: Sources of variation in home literacy experiences of Spanish-speaking children. In *Class, Culture, and Race in American Schools: A Handbook,* ed. S. W. Rothstein. Westport, Conn.:, Greenwood Press.

Romo, H., and T. Falbo. 1996. *Latino High School Graduation: Defying the Odds.* Austin: The University of Texas Press.

Rumbaut, R. 1997. Achievement and ambition among children of immigrants in Southern California. Paper presented at the Jerome Levy Economics Institute of Bard College, Annandale-on-the Hudson, New York.

Rumbaut, R., and W. Cornelius. 1995. *California's Immigrant Children: Theory, Research, and Implications for Policy.* La Jolla, Calif.: Center for U.S.-Mexican Studies.

Sánchez, L. R. 1997. Mainland Puerto Ricans. Paper presented at the Harvard Graduate School of Education, Cambridge, Massachusetts.

Sandel, M. 1996. *Democracy's Discontent.* Cambridge, Mass.: Harvard University Press.

Sassen, S. 1994. *The Mobility of Labor and Capital.* New York: Cambridge University Press.

Simon, J. 1995. *Immigration: The Demographic and Economic Facts.* Washington, D.C.: The Cato Institute and the National Immigration Forum.

Snow, C. 1997. The myths about being bilingual. *Boston Globe,* 13 July.

INTRODUCTION

Steinberg, L. 1996. *Beyond the Classroom: Why School Reform Has Failed and What Parents Need to Do.* New York: Simon and Schuster.

Steinhauer, J. 1997. A minority market with major sales. *The New York Times,* 2 July.

Suárez-Orozco, C., and M. M. Suárez-Orozco. 1995. *Transformations: Immigration, Family Life, and Achievement Motivation among Latino Adolescents.* Stanford: Stanford University Press.

Suárez-Orozco, M. 1989. *Central American Refugees and U.S. High Schools:* A *Psychosocial Study of Motivation and Achievement.* Stanford: Stanford University Press.

Suárez-Orozco, M. 1996. "California Dreaming: Proposition 187 and the Cultural Psychology of Racial and Ethnic Exclusion." *Anthropology & Education Quarterly* 27(2): 151–167.

Suárez-Orozco, M., P. Roos, and C. E. Suárez-Orozco. 1997. Cultural, educational and legal perspectives on immigration: Implications for school reform. In *New Perspectives on School Reform,* ed. J. Heubert. New Haven, Conn.: Yale University Press.

Sue, S., and S. Okazaki. 1990. "Asian-American Educational Achievements: A Phenomenon in Search of an Explanation." *American Psychologist* 45(8): 913–920.

Suro, R. 1994. California's SOS on immigration. *The Washington Post,* 29 September.

Tharp, R., and R. Gallimore. 1988. *Rousing Minds to Life: Teaching, Learning, and Schooling in Social Context.* New York: Cambridge University Press.

Trueba, H. T. 1989a. *Raising Silent Voices: Educating the Linguistic Minorities for the 21st Century.* Cambridge, Mass.: Newbury House.

Trueba, H. T. 1989b. Rethinking dropouts: Culture and literacy for minority empowerment. In *What Do Anthropologists Have to Say about Dropouts?,* ed. H. T. Trueba, G. Spindler, and L. Spindler. New York: The Falmer Press.

Trueba, H. T. 1993. "Race and Ethnicity: The Role of Universities in Healing Multicultural America." *Educational Theory* 43(1): 51–54.

Trueba, H. T. 1996. Latinos in the United States: The Emerging Majority in Our Schools and Society. Unpublished manuscript, Harvard Graduate School of Education, Cambridge, Massachusetts.

Trueba, H. T., G. Spindler, et al., eds. 1989. *What Do Anthropologists Have to Say about Dropouts?* New York: The Falmer Press.

Tsuda, T. 1996. *Strangers in the Ethnic Homeland: The Migration, Ethnic Identity, and Psychosocial Adaptation of Japan's New Immigrant Minority.* Ph.D. dissertation, University of California at Berkeley, California.

Tuan, M. 1995. Korean and Russian students in a Los Angeles high school: Exploring the alternative strategies of two high-achieving groups. In *California's Immigrant Children: Theory, Research, and Implications for Educational Policy,* ed. R. Rumbaut and W. Cornelius. La Jolla, Calif.: Center for U.S.-Mexican Relations, University of California, San Diego.

Vernez, G., A. Abrahamse, et al. 1996. *How Immigrants Fare in U.S. Education.* Santa Monica, Calif.: Rand Corporation.

Volkan, V. 1996. Modern Greek and Turkish identities and the psychodynamics of Greek Turkish relations. Paper presented at the Conference on Cultures Under Siege, Rockefeller Foundation Conference Center, Bellagio, Italy.

Vygotsky, L. S. 1978. Interaction between learning and development. In *Mind in Society: The Development of Higher Psychological Processes,* ed. B. J.-T. M. Cole, S. Scribner, and E. Souberman. Cambridge, Mass.: Harvard University Press.

Vygotsky, L. S. 1981. The genesis of higher mental functions. In *The Concept of Activity in Soviet Psychology,* J. V. Wertsch. Armonk, N.Y.: M E Sharpe.

Waldinger, R. 1997. Social capital or social closure? Immigrant networks in the labor market. Paper presented at the Conference on Immigration and the Socio-Cultural Remaking of the North American Space, David Rockefeller Center for Latin American Studies, Harvard University, Cambridge, Massachusetts.

Waldinger, R., and M. Bozorgmehr. 1996. *Ethnic Los Angeles.* New York: Russell Sage Foundation.

Waters, M. C. 1996. West Indian family resources and adolescent outcomes: Trajectories of the second generation. Paper presented at the Annual Meeting of the American Association for the Advancement of Science, Baltimore, Maryland.

Waters, M. C. 1997. The Impact of Racial Segregation on the Education and Work Outcomes of Second Generation West Indians in New York City. Unpublished manuscript, Harvard University, Cambridge, Massachusetts.

Wertsch, J. 1981. *The Concept of Activity in Soviet Psychology.* New York: M E Sharpe.

Wertsch, J. 1991. Beyond Vygotsky: Bakhtin's contribution. In *Voices of the Mind: A Sociocultural Approach to Mediated Action,* ed. J. Wertsch. Cambridge Mass.: Harvard University Press.

Willis, P. 1977. *Learning to Labour: How Working Class Kids Get Working Class Jobs.* Farnborough, England: Saxon House.

Zhou, M. 1996. *Growing Up American: The Adaptation of Vietnamese Children.* The Current Issues in Educational Research Workshop, Harvard University Graduate School of Education, Cambridge, Massachusetts.

PART II

Antecedents and New Demographic Formations

Photo by Anna LeVine

Enrique Dussel Peters   I was born in Paris, where I lived for a few months, then I lived in Germany for one year, where my sister was born, and my family moved finally to Argentina in 1967. My father, being an Argentine academician, was persecuted after Peron's death in Argentina by the right-wing "Triple A" and we were forced to leave the country in 1975. We moved to Mexico City that year.

As in any such experience, there are several perspectives. Thousands of Argentines were killed in these years; some had to flee from Argentina in different ways. Being a nine-year-old boy, I remember when the bomb exploded in our house, destroying a significant part of it. However, probably due to my age and the beauty and spirit of the country and the Mexican people, my immigration experience was not traumatic. I remember my first years in Mexico for having missed my family (grandparents, uncles, cousins), as well as street friends with whom I played soccer in the streets, chess, and other games. The change from living in a provincial city and moving to a chaotic megacity was also difficult in these first years. However, I believe that due to my age, I was able to integrate rather quickly into Mexican society, and in a few weeks I was able to speak "Mexican" Spanish. After several years, I felt like a Mexican, even though I am not originally of Mexican nationality.

In contrast to some of my Argentine and Chilean friends, my studies and work were not significantly influenced by these past experiences. On several occasions while studying in the United States (in South Bend, Indiana, and San Diego, California), I have made friends with Mexican immigrants, both documented and undocumented. Nevertheless, I strongly believe that there are many different immigration stories and experiences. Mexican immigration to the United States, for example, has been significantly different from Argentine and Chilean immigration to Mexico in the 1970s: The relative openness of Mexico's institutions and society, the relatively higher levels of education and income among South American immigrants, the differences in distances and the impossibility, in some cases, of returning "home" radically change the immigration experience. I returned to Mendoza, where I had lived in Argentina, after 20 years in 1995. Before, I could not return with my family because of the rule of the military junta. I felt, after 20 years, besides the joy of meeting part of my family and new family members, like a stranger and a foreigner.

Associate Professor at the Graduate School of Economics, Universidad Nacional Autónoma de México (UNAM), 1993 to present. B.A. and M.A. at the Free University of Berlin, and Ph.D., University of Notre Dame. Publications include *La Economía de la polarización. Teoría y evolución del cambio estructural manufacturero mexicano (1988–1996)* (México: Editorial JUS/UNAM, 1997); and, with Michael Piore and Clemente Ruiz Durán, *Pensar globalmente y actuar regionalmente. Hacia un nuevo paradigma industrial para el siglo XXI* (México: Editorial JUS/UNAM/Fundación F. Ebert, 1997).

2

Recent Structural Changes in Mexico's Economy: A Preliminary Analysis of Some Sources of Mexican Migration to the United States

Enrique Dussel Peters
Facultad de Economía, UNAM

Mexico's economy has gone through deep structural changes recently. At the beginning of 1997, just two years after the most profound crisis since the 1930s, Mexico was able to repay $12.5 billion of the emergency loan from the United States. Moreover, since mid-1996 there have been significant signs of an economic recovery. In spite of these recent tendencies, it is important to point out some of the difficulties and contradictions that Mexico is currently facing and will continue to confront into the beginning of the next century. This realization is not a matter of pessimism or frustration, as some high-ranking officials have said, but rather a matter of discussing and trying to prevent or mitigate some of these problems through appropriate policy measures.

To understand the recent dynamics of the domestic economy and Mexico's potential for growth, this chapter will focus on Mexico's macroeconomic conditions and the most significant challenges that have resulted from the liberalization strategy. Several of Mexico's political and economic challenges are strongly related to Mexican migration to the United States.

The chapter will be divided into four sections. The first section will briefly introduce the discussion in the literature regarding the relationship between economic activity in Mexico and its impact on Mexican migration to the United States. The second section will analyze Mexico's macroeconomic development during the 1990s and will highlight some of the most significant challenges and difficulties. The third section will examine the topics of employment and real wages in Mexico in greater depth, as two significant causes of Mexican migration to the United States. The fourth and final section will present the conclusions reached.

ISSUES IN THE DISCUSSION OF MEXICO'S ECONOMY AND MIGRATION TO THE U.S.

There are multiple causes of migration. The World Bank (World Bank 1995), for example, refers to a variety of economic and political causes of migration that depend strongly on the particular regions of origin and destination. Similarly, the causes of Mexican migration to the United States have been discussed in depth; however, there is no final and conclusive evidence on the topic. There is also a consensus regarding the insufficiency of data and information concerning these processes. In this ongoing discussion, at least the following issues have been highlighted:

1. There is no single issue or variable that determines migration to the United States. Moreover, both the source of labor power for the United States and its demand are critical to understanding the issue, that is, it is not sufficient to study independently the labor market conditions in Mexico or those in the United States. Cultural, regional, familial, economic, legal, and, more recently, military issues in Mexico and the United States, as well as the interaction of some or all of these processes, play a role in the final decision to migrate to the United States (Cornelius 1978; Massey, Goldring, and Durand 1994; Verduzco Igartúa 1995).

2. Mexican migration to the United States has been going on for a long time and is usually parallel to the growth and development of infrastructure, agriculture, and critical economic sectors in the United States (Espinoza Valle 1990; Verduzco Igartúa 1995).

3. As in other cases, Mexican migration has a variety of causes. Nevertheless, and contrary to migration from other nations to the United States, Mexicans' motivations for migration are mainly economic.[1] Chávez, Flores, and López Garza (1989), for example, not only show that economic motives are the most significant for Mexican immigration but also that there are a variety of economic motives, particularly, for both women and men, low wages in Mexico and high wages in the United States. A recent study on this issue (COLEF, CONAPO, and STPS 1994) observes that 27.5 percent of Mexican immigrants did not

have a job before going to the United States and concludes that the lack of a stable and well-paid job, as well as the recurrent immigration to the United States, is significant for understanding this phenomenon. The gap between gross domestic product (GDP) per capita in Mexico and the United States seems to be particularly important and has not yet received sufficient analysis. As reflected in Figure 2.1, the "lost decade" of the 1980s, which resulted mainly from a fall in the generation of employment, as well as declining GDP per capita and real wages, seems to have affected migration to the United States. The increasing gap since the Mexican crisis of December of 1994 might increase potential Mexican migration to the United States.

5. Mexico's northern border region (*zona fronteriza*) provides a significant demand for employment in maquiladoras and is an important buffer zone for Mexican migration to the United States. Ciudad Juárez, Nuevo Laredo, and particularly Tijuana are border cities where since the beginning of this century demographic growth has depended on migration from other regions of Mexico as well as migration to the United

FIGURE 2.1

GDP per Capita in Mexico and the United States, 1820–1996 (1980=100)

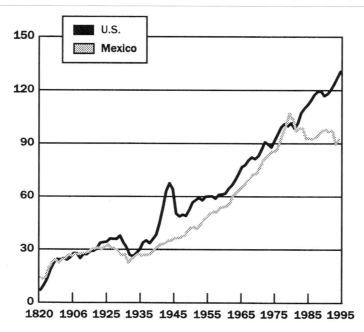

Source: Data obtained from Maddison (1995); GDP per capita values for 1995 and 1996 were estimated.

States (Browning and Zenteno 1993; Carillo 1993; COLEF, CONAPO, and STPS 1994; Piñeiro 1992).

6. It is most important to understand that migration may be either permanent or temporary. Historically, and particularly in recent decades, Mexican migration to the United States has been characterized by being seasonal, temporary, and seen as a complement to family income, wages, and employment (COLEF, CONAPO, and STPS 1994; Verduzco Igartúa 1996).

RECENT MACROECONOMIC EVOLUTION AND CHALLENGES FOR MEXICO'S ECONOMY

Since the beginning of the 1980s, and particularly since 1988, Mexico embarked on a radically new policy of economic development. It abandoned its commitment to import substitution industrialization (ISI) accompanied by various forms of active government intervention in the economy. Since then, economic policy moved toward an increasing reliance on market mechanisms and macroeconomic policies to direct the evolution of the microeconomic structure and thus achieve an export orientation for Mexico's manufacturing sector. As part of this liberalization strategy, it liberalized imports, controlled inflation and the fiscal balance, and generated incentives to attract massive foreign investment.

The liberalization strategy has not been modified significantly during the Zedillo administration, in spite of some changes imposed by the crisis of December of 1994. It is important to establish a clear understanding of the various components of this strategy.

Pillars of the Present Macroeconomic Policy: The Liberalization Strategy (1988–1994)

Mexico's liberalization strategy was consolidated through a series of *Pactos Económicos*, originating in December of 1987. The respective *Pactos*—which included wage ceilings and allowed for an ex post facto indexation of wages—were negotiated among official unions, the government, and the private sector, and became the centerpiece of the new strategy. The major reforms and guidelines of the liberalization strategy are described below (Aspe Armella 1993; Córdoba 1991; Dussel Peters 1997).

1. Since 1988 the government has viewed controlling inflation rates and the fiscal deficit, as well as import liberalization and the attraction of foreign investments, as the principal mechanisms of the liberalization strategy. These macroeconomic changes were designed to induce microeconomic incentives for economic restructuring. From this per-

spective, the liberalization strategy attempted to create new patterns of specialization and comparative advantages so that the export-oriented private sector would be at the center of the new growth model.

2. Reprivatization of the banks, since the mid-1980s, and the overall reduction of state intervention in the allocation of credit and in the financial sector in general have been critical mechanisms of the liberalization strategy (Garrido and Peñaloza 1996).

3. The Banco de México has pursued orthodox and restrictive monetary and credit policies to achieve the main objectives of the strategy (Banco de México 1996) and was granted an autonomous constitutional status in order to pursue such policies. Moreover, the nominal exchange rate was used as an anchor to control inflation, which resulted in an appreciation of the real exchange rate.

4. The process of import liberalization began at the end of 1985, when most official import prices and import licenses were replaced by tariffs. Since then, tariffs fell continuously until 1994. The implementation of the North American Free Trade Agreement (NAFTA) on January 1, 1994, overshadowed previous agreements and negotiations and marks the final stage of Mexico's import liberalization and overall trade policies.

5. Privatization or disincorporation of state-owned companies was one of the main structural changed at the macroeconomic level and was intended to produce microeconomic structural change in the private sector. Furthermore, it became an important source of revenue for the government (Rogozinski 1993).

6. Different mechanisms were implemented to enhance foreign investments, particularly high interest rates and more open laws and regulations. Moreover, NAFTA changed investment-related issues significantly, since each nation has to treat other investors and their investments no less favorably than national investors.

It is important to mention that these institutional and macroeconomic changes generated an overwhelmingly positive attitude toward Mexico internationally, particularly during the Salinas administration, and thus fueled private capital flows to Mexico.

Results of the Liberalization Strategy, and Challenges for Mexico's Economy at the End of the 1990s

Since the imposition of the liberalization strategy, several important economic issues arose. In the tradition of prior development strategies, the liberalization strategy is still highly dependent on political events. On one hand, the end of one administration (or *sexenio*) and the beginning of another have almost always been accompanied by an economic crisis. On the other hand, the evolution of Mexico's economy has been associated with the evolution of the main political party, the Partido Revolucionario Institucional (PRI). Since the end of the 1980s this party has had to adjust to a more democratic and participatory society and political system, and therefore is in the midst of either a transition process or crisis (Ibarra 1996). The economic situation in Mexico in the late 1990s will thus critically depend on the PRI's transition away from being a state institution and its potential for becoming an authentic political party, as well as the response of the main opposition parties. Moreover, economic developments in Mexico will also depend on the behavior of other social and political actors in the country and their relationship with the government. The resulting political interaction will be crucial for national and foreign investors in Mexico. Finally, the solution offered for a different way of dealing with social uprisings as well as guerrilla movements will also be critical for Mexico's future economic development.

On the positive side of the liberalization strategy, it is important to stress that inflation and the fiscal deficit were under control until 1994, and that the country was able to attract massive foreign investment. Most important, exports have become one of the main pillars of economic growth and have increased continuously during 1980 to 1996, particularly during periods of crises, such as in 1982 and 1994 to 1995 (Table 2.1). However, inflation levels began to surge again during 1995 to 1996.

On the negative side, growth of GDP and GDP per capita have been far below historical levels (see Figure 2.1), employment has not yet achieved the dynamism necessary in order to incorporate the growing economically active population into the formal labor force, and real wages are significantly below the levels prevailing at the beginning of the 1980s. Similarly, the savings ratio has declined steadily since 1980, as well as the gross fixed investment/GDP coefficient. Moreover, the issue of foreign indebtedness, which triggered the crisis of 1982, is still a very critical issue for the economic evolution of Mexico and remains a latent problem as well as an immense burden on Mexican society. Finally, Mexico's economy, particularly private manufacturing, has not yet been able to create a link between the export sector and the rest of the economy, as evidenced in the high trade deficit until 1994, particularly in the export-oriented manufacturing sector. These processes have produced increasing economic, social, and regional polarization.

From this perspective, Mexico's economy faces many economic structural challenges for the late 1990s. So far, the liberalization strategy has not been able to generate growth rates similar to those attained between 1940 and 1980. After the "lost decade" of the 1980s, the crisis of 1994 to 1995 produced the strongest fall in the rate of GDP of Mexico since the 1930s. For the period from 1988 to 1995, for example, GDP grew at an average rate of 1.7 percent, which was slightly below the level of population growth.

One of the most significant structural changes in Mexico's economy has been the increasing incapacity to integrate its growing population into formal employment. On the contrary, and as analyzed more in depth in what follows, the Mexican economy not only failed to integrate the growing economically active population but also massively expelled labor power from several economic activities. Moreover, employment growth during the liberalization strategy has been far below the levels achieved before 1982. This exclusion process is critical for understanding the dimension and potential of the informal labor market and migration to the United States.

The liberalization strategy has also resulted in an increasing polarization of Mexico's economy. A few branches—mainly automobiles and auto parts, basic petrochemicals, glass, and electronic products—have been able to substantially increase their share of GDP, employment, and exports, as well as improving labor and capital productivity. These branches feature the highest capital intensity of Mexico's economy. This tendency has sharpened export concentration since NAFTA and the crisis of December of 1994. The increasing capital intensity of these dynamic branches underlines some of the contradictions and difficulties for job creation in the future.

As stressed earlier, the export-oriented manufacturing sector was at the center of the liberalization strategy. However, until today, Mexico's economy has not been able to overcome one of its most striking structural conditions: its high dependency on imports, particularly in the most dynamic sectors and branches during periods of growth. This "import-oriented industrialization" (Dussel Peters 1997) is also reflected in the worsening of the trade balance/GDP coefficient of manufacturing, that is, the relationship between net exports and value added, which accounted for −44 percent in 1994. This evolution is most significant since it reflects the high and increasing import dependency of the sector, particularly of the most dynamic branches, the difficulties the most dynamic branches and manufacturing in general have in generating linkages with the rest of the national economy, and the incapacity of manufacturing to substantially integrate itself into the world market.

The prior analysis leads to the conclusion that the private manufacturing sector was at the root of the crisis of December of 1994 given the rapid liberalization strategy and this sector's incapacity for integration into the world

TABLE 2.1

Main Macroeconomic Variables (1980–1996)

	1980	1981	1982	1983	1984	1985	1986	1987
GDP	8.2	8.8	-0.6	-4.2	3.6	2.6	-3.8	1.7
GDP per capita	5.4	6.1	-3.0	-6.5	1.2	0.5	-5.5	0.0
Employment	14.7	6.2	-0.3	-2.3	2.3	2.2	-1.4	1.1
Real wages (1980=100)	100.0	105.2	97.4	85.2	84.2	84.1	83.5	79.9
Real wages (1980=100), minimum wage	100.0	101.3	104.7	84.8	71.8	70.9	63.2	60.3
Open unemployment	4.7	2.5	7.0	6.6	5.7	4.4	4.3	3.9
Gross fixed investment/GDP	24.8	26.4	23.0	17.5	17.9	19.1	19.5	18.4
Private	14.1	14.3	12.3	11.0	11.3	12.5	12.9	13.2
Public	10.7	12.1	10.2	6.6	6.6	6.6	6.5	5.2
Inflation	29.8	28.7	98.8	80.8	59.2	63.7	105.7	159.2
Financial deficit/GDP	7.5	14.1	16.9	8.6	8.5	9.6	16.0	16.1
Exports of goods and services	25.7	11.4	22.6	14.2	5.7	-4.5	4.5	9.5
Imports of goods and services	35.2	17.7	-37.9	-33.8	17.8	11.0	-7.6	5.1
Trade balance[b]	-4.7	-5.7	8.7	12.6	11.9	7.7	3.3	5.9
Current account[b]	-10.7	-16.1	-6.2	5.4	4.2	1.2	-1.7	4.0
Capital account[b]	11.4	26.4	9.8	-1.4	1.3	-1.5	2.7	-1.2
International reserves[b]	4.2	5.0	1.8	4.7	8.0	5.7	6.7	13.7
Foreign investment[b]	2.1	3.5	2.6	-0.2	-0.4	-0.5	0.7	2.8
Foreign direct investment[b]	2.2	2.5	1.7	0.5	0.4	0.5	1.5	3.2
Foreign portfolio investment[b]	-0.1	1.0	0.9	-0.6	-0.8	-1.0	-0.8	-0.4
Total foreign debt[b]	57.5	78.3	86.1	93.1	94.9	96.9	100.9	109.5
Public[b]	34.0	43.1	51.6	66.9	69.8	72.7	75.8	84.3
Private[b]	7.3	10.2	8.1	14.8	16.3	15.7	15.1	14.1
Total external debt service[b]	9.4	10.6	12.3	13.0	15.9	15.3	12.9	12.1
Interest payments[b]	4.6	6.1	7.8	8.2	10.3	10.2	8.4	8.3
Principal repayments[b]	4.8	4.5	4.5	4.8	5.7	5.1	4.6	3.8
Total external debt/GDP	26.9	32.2	79.9	93.4	93.0	91.8	116.1	117.1
Total external debt/exports of goods and services	216.1	259.3	334.8	345.1	222.1	356.8	459.5	370.9
Total external debt service/ exports of goods and services	38.3	22.9	75.3	37.5	59.1	49.3	53.5	49.6
Real exchange rate (1978=100)[d]	85.2	78.6	116.3	131.5	115.8	116.2	150.7	151.9

Notes: All data refer to growth rates, unless otherwise specified. Maquiladora activities are not included.

[a] Data for some of the variables are preliminary.

[b] Billion $U.S.

[c] Estimations.

[d] The real exchange rate is calculated as the nominal exchange rate deflated by the consumer price index for Mexico and the U.S. (1978=100).

Source: Own estimations based on data from INEGI, CEPAL, Banco de México, and Oxford Economic Forecasting.

TABLE 2.1 (CONTINUED)

Main Macroeconomic Variables (1980–1996)

	1988	1989	1990	1991	1992	1993	1994	1995[a]	1996[c]
GDP	1.2	3.5	4.4	3.6	2.9	0.9	4.6	-7.0	5.1
GDP per capita	-0.2	1.7	2.5	1.7	0.9	-0.9	1.7	-8.7	3.3
Employment	0.9	1.3	0.9	2.6	0.4	0.2	1.2	-7.5	3.4
Real wages (1980=100)	76.4	73.9	71.5	73.6	77.5	79.2	81.6	69.7	60.0
Real wages (1980=100), minimum wage	53.6	49.4	43.1	40.7	39.3	38.9	38.8	34.0	27.0
Open unemployment	3.6	3.0	2.8	2.6	2.8	3.4	3.7	6.3	5.5
Gross fixed investment/GDP	19.3	18.2	18.6	19.5	21.9	21.1	22.1	16.9	15.7
Private	14.2	12.7	13.7	14.9	16.6	16.6	17.3	11.9	11.4
Public	5.0	4.7	4.9	4.6	4.2	3.3	3.6	3.5	3.6
Inflation	51.7	19.7	29.9	18.8	11.9	8.0	6.9	54.5	27.7
Financial deficit/GDP	12.5	5.6	3.9	-1.5	1.6	0.7	-0.1	0.1	1.0
Exports of goods and services	5.8	2.3	3.6	4.6	1.7	3.7	17.3	32.0	20.7
Imports of goods and services	36.7	21.3	19.7	16.8	20.9	-1.2	16.7	-25.6	23.5
Trade balance[b]	-0.9	-4.1	-6.3	-13.4	-23.0	-21.4	-27.3	-3.8	0.8
Current account[b]	-2.4	-5.8	-7.5	-14.9	-24.8	-23.4	-29.7	-1.6	-1.8
Capital account[b]	-1.2	3.2	8.3	24.5	26.3	32.5	14.6	-15.7	3.6
International reserves[b]	6.6	6.9	10.3	18.1	19.3	24.3	6.1	15.7	18.0
Foreign investment[b]	5.6	3.5	6.0	16.9	23.6	32.7	15.6	-3.1	21.5
Foreign direct investment[b]	2.9	3.2	2.6	4.8	4.4	4.4	8.0	7.0	6.4
Foreign portfolio investment[b]	2.7	0.3	3.4	12.1	19.2	28.4	7.6	-10.1	15.1
Total foreign debt[b]	99.2	93.8	100.8	103.8	112.9	127.6	136.5	161.1	172.3
Public [b]	80.6	76.1	77.8	80.0	75.8	78.7	85.4	100.9	94.5
Private [b]	5.9	13.9	16.5	17.0	37.1	48.9	51.1	60.2	77.8
Total external debt service[b]	8.1	14.5	11.2	16.1	25.7	24.7	32.9	31.6	33.6
Interest payments[b]	6.4	6.9	5.5	5.8	5.3	4.8	5.4	6.3	15.6
Principal repayments[b]	1.7	7.6	5.7	10.3	20.4	19.9	27.5	25.3	18.0
Total external debt/GDP	58.9	49.5	43.7	40.8	34.8	35.1	36.2	64.0	62.0
Total external debt/exports of goods and services	273.8	225.2	209.4	223.2	205.8	208.0	191.8	179.6	150.0
Total external debt service/ exports of goods and services	56.8	41.2	27.9	37.7	55.6	47.6	54.0	34.3	33.0
Real exchange rate (1978=100)[d]	122.4	115.8	110.3	100.5	91.9	86.8	90.2	130.7	105.0

market; so far this has not been acknowledged by the government or reflected in its policies.

External debt, which triggered the crisis of 1982, has apparently disappeared as one of the main problems for the successive administrations (Gurría Treviño 1993). However, Table 2.1 shows that the amount of external debt has continued to increase since 1988 and reached an estimated $170 billion in 1996; in 1996 alone Mexico's total external debt service was estimated at $33.6 billion, or around 13 percent of its GDP (SHCP 1996). Thus, the issue might be one of the most important variables for generating overall uncertainty due to debt payment difficulties or as a result of political or economic events that affect foreign investments flows.

Other issues, such as the crisis in the financial and banking sectors and the critical conditions of individuals and firms that are highly indebted, are not examined here. Nevertheless, they are still highly significant in the country's present economic context and will result in high economic costs for the Mexican government: Government intervention in buying bad loans from financial institutions was estimated at around 10 percent of GDP in 1996.

Increasing economic concentration and heterogeneity, the dynamism of a few branches representing the highest intraindustry trade, and access to foreign markets and international financial markets have contributed to economic, social, and regional polarization, a process that began with the liberalization strategy and that has intensified since the crisis of December 1994. Domestic demand is below the levels for the 1980s; the polarization between domestic-oriented firms and export-oriented firms has grown rapidly since 1994, which also affects their respective real wages and the overall structure of income distribution.[2]

RECENT PATTERNS IN DEMOGRAPHY, EMPLOYMENT, AND REAL WAGES

In the first section we observed that low levels of employment and real wages are two of the important causes for Mexican migration to the United States, although they are only part of the explanation of this process. In this section we will analyze some basic demographic tendencies in Mexico and their impact on employment, the evolution of employment, and, finally, the performance of real wages. For this analysis we will use data from 1980 on and some projections up to the year 2000.[3]

Mexico's population has been growing rapidly since 1980. Total population growth has been on average 2.2 percent from 1980 to 1990 and has declined only slowly to 1.8 percent since 1994. Similarly, the economically active population (EAP)[4] showed an average annual growth rate (AAGR) of 3.6 percent during 1980 to 1990, with levels between 3.6 percent and 3.8 percent during the 1990s (Table 2.2).

From this perspective, one of the most critical aspects for employment is the annual growth of the EAP with respect to total existing employment. The required employment coefficient reflects the growth of employment required in order to capture total labor supply, including the growth of the EAP, and depends, thus, on the growth of the EAP and on total employment. The gap—either positive or negative—between required employment growth and employment growth is important, since it highlights the basic conditions of the labor market (Figure 2.2).

In Mexico's case, required employment should have grown at around 5.2 percent[5] during the 1990s, when in fact employment's AAGR was −0.2 percent during 1990 to 1996. That is, throughout this period the EAP increased by more than 7.6 million, while the economy expelled almost 260,000 workers from their jobs (Figure 2.3). This tremendous gap of more than 7.8 million jobs for the 1990 to 1996 period reflects, on the one hand, the incapacity of

TABLE 2.2

Total Population and Economically Active Population

	1980	1985	1990	1991	1992	1993	1994	1995	1996	2000	1980–96	1996–2000
Thousands												
Total population	67,003	74,036	81,290	82,884	84,502	86,092	87,687	89,267	90,848	99,199	—	—
Economically inactive population	45,007	48,183	49,851	50,244	50,672	51,022	51,337	51,597	51,798	54,199	—	—
Economically active population	21,996	25,853	31,439	32,640	33,830	35,070	36,350	37,670	39,050	45,000	—	—
Structure[a]												
Total population	100.00	100.00	100.00	100.00	100.00	100.00	100.00	100.00	100.00	100.00	100.00	100.00
Economically inactive population	67.17	65.08	61.32	60.62	59.97	59.26	58.55	57.80	57.02	54.64	60.48	55.77
Economically active population	32.83	34.92	38.68	39.38	40.03	40.74	41.45	42.20	42.98	45.36	39.52	44.23
Growth Rates[b]												
Total population	—	2.0	2.0	2.0	2.0	1.9	1.9	1.8	1.8	—	1.9	2.2
Economically inactive population	—	1.4	1.0	0.8	0.9	0.7	0.6	0.5	0.4	—	0.9	1.1
Economically active population	—	3.3	3.6	3.8	3.6	3.7	3.6	3.6	3.7	—	3.7	3.6

[a] As a percentage of total population.
[b] Data for 1985 and 1990 refer to the annual average growth rate for 1980–1985 and 1985–1990, respectively.

Source: Own estimations based on INEGI and Oxford Economic Forecasting.

FIGURE 2.2

Required Employment Growth and Employment Growth

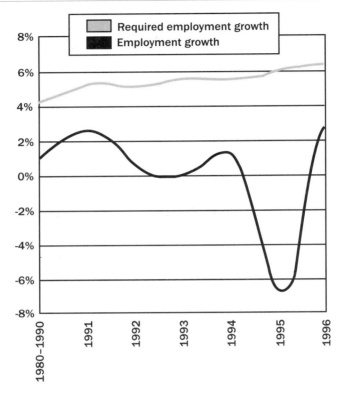

Mexico's economy to provide employment for the growing EAP, contrary to prior periods under ISI (Dussel Peters 1996). On the other hand, it also explains the massive growth of the informal labor market and of potential migration to the United States as well.

Considering these tendencies as the basis for understanding Mexico's labor market, during 1980 to 1996 employment in Mexico has been characterized by an increase in the EAP of 17.05 million with an increment of less than 2 million formal jobs; that is, 15.05 million individuals had to search for a job either in the informal sector or in the United States. In this context, Figure 2.4 shows, on the one hand, that manufacturing has been the only subsector that has expelled workers for the whole period, and, on the other hand, that both communal services[6] and construction have been the most important subsectors of Mexico's economy in terms of generating employment.

The following tendencies have been exacerbated by the performance of Mexico's economy during the liberalization strategy:

FIGURE 2.3

EAP and Employment (1,000s)

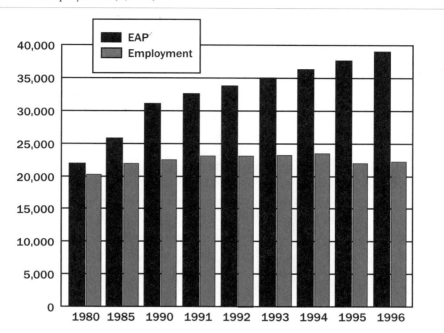

1. A slow but continuous decline in the share of the labor force absorbed by agriculture and manufacturing and an increase in service sector employment. It is important to stress that this tendency was accentuated after the December 1994 crisis, but has been consistent since 1980. This apparent tertiarization of Mexico's economy does not necessarily reflect a dynamic development of services, but rather the incapacity of agriculture and manufacturing to generate employment.

2. Manufacturing's share of total employment fell from 12.04 percent in 1980 to 9.42 percent in 1996 and presents an AAGR of −2.35 percent for 1988 to 1995. With the exception of other manufacturing industries, all subsectors show an expulsion of labor, which is particularly pronounced for more traditional subsectors such as textiles, apparel and leather, wood and its products, and structural metal products. However, even metal products, machinery and equipment, which includes automobiles and auto parts, showed a decline in its share on total employment from 2.70 percent in 1980 to 1.79 percent in 1995.

3. After communal services, construction has been the most important subsector for generating employment since the 1980s, and particularly

FIGURE 2.4

Employment Creation by Sectors (1,000s)

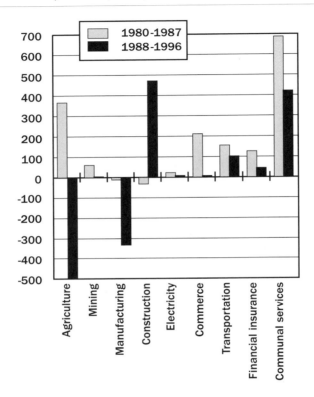

for the period from 1988 to 1996, with an AAGR of 2.80 percent. This tendency reveals a lot about the quality of employment generation, since construction has the lowest level of real wage per worker (Dussel Peters 1996).

4. It is important to stress that within services, communal services (social and personal) has remained the most important economic activity in terms of employment since the 1980s, representing around 30 percent of total employment. Moreover, transportation, storage, and communications, as well as financial insurance and real estate, have significantly increased their share in total employment, particularly since the end of the 1980s.

5. Maquiladora activities have been the most dynamic in terms of employment generation since the beginning of the 1980s. They presented an AAGR for 1980 to 1996 and 1988 to 1996 of 12.5 percent and 9.76 percent, respectively. In other words, this has been the only sector

in the economy that has generated employment at a level superior to that required by Mexico's growing population and EAP. Even in absolute terms the evolution of the maquiladoras has been significant: from less then 125,000 workers in 1980 to around 800,000 in 1996. Even during periods of crisis for Mexico's economy, such as in 1982 and from 1994 to 1995, employment growth was positive for maquiladoras. Similarly, maquiladora employment as a share of manufacturing employment has increased substantially, from 5 percent in 1980 to almost 40 percent in 1996. On the other hand, and in spite of this impressive dynamism, the maquiladoras should not be overestimated: In 1996 they employed just above 50 percent of the required increase in annual employment (Mendiola 1997).

6. The employment issue also has a strong regional component, as was suggested by the performance of the maquiladora sector, which is heavily concentrated along Mexico's northern border. As already stressed, the crisis of December of 1994 produced a decline in employment of more than 7 percent. The relative recovery of the employment level since then is most important and reflects a regional polarization within the country. From July 1995—the worst month after the crisis in terms of employment—to October of 1996—the last month for which it was possible to obtain regional and sectorial employment data[7]—employment increased by 854,470 jobs; the northern border states[8] accounted for 240,000 jobs, or 28 percent of total employment growth. According to the same data source and period, maquiladoras generated more than 20 percent of total employment, in spite of its small share of total employment.

This is the situation of employment and the challenge posed by unemployment in Mexico. Official statistics attempting to measure unemployment, particularly what is defined as the open unemployment rate, are useless in the Mexican context. By definition, the open unemployment rate refers to the share of the EAP who have not worked for even one hour a week, even though they have searched for a job. Given the Mexican labor market conditions— particularly the inexistence of institutions that support the unemployed population—the open unemployment rate in Mexico is inappropriate; it is even surprising that there is any openly unemployed population at all. Moreover, it does not capture the massive increase of employment in the informal sector and of Mexican migration to the United States, as already discussed.

Real wages as well as real minimum wages[9] have declined substantially throughout 1980 to 1996. Real wages showed an AAGR of –0.5 percent during

1980 to 1996 and in real terms represent in 1996 only 60 percent of their 1980 value, while the real minimum wage in 1996 represents only 27 percent of its 1980 value (Table 2.1). This dramatic decline of income can be observed in all economic subsectors. As highlighted in Figure 2.5, none of the subsectors has real wage levels above the ones achieved at the beginning of the 1980s. This decline, which has had a significant impact on effective demand and has also polarized the economic and social structure in Mexico, was accentuated by the crisis of December 1994.

These tendencies show that Mexico's economy has not been able to incorporate most of its EAP into formal employment; on the contrary, the expulsion of labor from various subsectors and the incapacity to significantly increase formal employment throughout 1980 to 1996 mean that most of the growing EAP has to search for employment in the informal sector or through migration to the United States. The apparent tertiarization of Mexico's economy is a result of the declining participation in total employment by agriculture and manufacturing, as well as generation of employment in construction and communal services. The shift in the employment structure during 1980 to 1996 reflects a decline in the quality of available employment.

FIGURE 2.5

Real Wages by Sectors (1980=100)

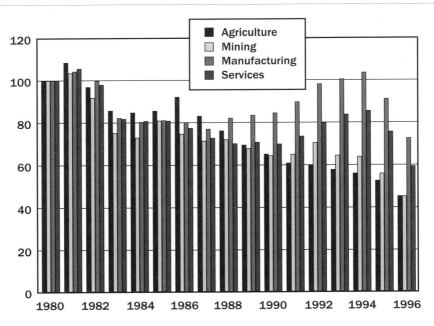

CONCLUSIONS

This chapter concludes that the liberalization strategy, as implemented since 1988, has had an extremely heterogeneous impact on Mexico's economy and was characterized by a general process of exclusion even before the crisis of December of 1994. The emphasis of the liberalization strategy on macroeconomic and market-oriented mechanisms has also resulted in an increasing social, economic, and regional polarization since only a few branches and export-oriented sectors have been able to benefit from these policies.

This strategy has achieved important effects on productivity and exports, and controlled inflation and the fiscal deficit, at least until 1994. However, most successful branches have increased capital intensity and productivity by expelling labor; this has been particularly evident in the case of manufacturing since 1988. Moreover, it is important to stress that the economic recovery achieved since 1996, both in terms of GDP and export growth, has not reversed the tendencies analyzed before. On the contrary, export growth has been highly concentrated in the same dynamic branches since 1988 and, as a result of GDP growth, imports are again growing much faster than exports, which reflects the unsustainability of this growth model.

Just as it is for other nations, generating employment is a crucial task for Mexico and there does not seem to be a solution in the near future given the massive dimensions of the challenge. According to some estimates, total GDP would have to increase by more than 10 percent annually in order to absorb the increasing EAP in the years ahead (Dussel Peters 1996), a rather difficult goal given Mexico's current economic conditions. Moreover, real wages have declined substantially since 1980 and again throughout the 1990s, which increases the pressure on the labor market.

From this perspective, and considering that neither employment nor real wages in Mexico are the only causes of immigration to the United States, it is at least possible to say that there is a vast potential of labor power in Mexico that is willing to work and desperate enough to join the informal labor market and/or to cross the border to the United States. The increasing gap in GDP between Mexico and the United States since the 1980s seems to sharpen this tendency. Regional issues within Mexico have also become important from this perspective, since in the north maquiladoras have been able to function as a buffer zone for Mexican migration to the United States whereas other regions in Mexico, particularly south of Mexico City, have suffered most under the liberalization strategy.

ACKNOWLEDGMENTS

I am very thankful to the conference participants for their comments, particularly to John H. Coatsworth and Marcelo M. Suárez-Orozco.

NOTES

1. The study by Chávez, Flores, and López Garza (1989), for example, is very clear in pointing out that Central Americans have migrated to the United States only recently; their main reason for migrating has been the political and economic instability in their respective countries.

2. One of the most dramatic cases that reflects this process relates to the automobile sector, probably the branch that benefited most under the liberalization strategy. Exports' share of total production was 3.9, 33.9, and 83.4 percent in 1980, 1990 and 1995, respectively. This shift in the production structure, due to the drastic fall in domestic sales, was also a result of intraindustry trade and the linkages of these transnational corporations to other firms and nations, particularly the United States. However, only a few Mexican firms were able to move in that direction. Small and medium firms in particular saw their production drastically diminished and yet had no opportunity to integrate to export networks (Ruiz Durán, Dussel Peters, and Taniura 1997).

3. Data on employment for 1995 and 1996 at the branch level were estimated by Oxford Economic Forecasting.

4. The EAP is defined as the group of persons, male or female, that are ready to contribute with work for producing goods and economic services. In Mexico, this includes all individuals 12 years old or older who are looking for a job (CELADE 1996; Instituto Nacional de *Estadística Geografía e Informática* [INEGI]).

5. The coefficient of required employment is calculated as the growth of the EAP in relation to total existing formal employment.

6. According to INEGI, communal services (social and personal) include activities such as professional services, educational services, and medical services, among others.

7. These data were obtained from IMSS and refers only to employed persons with social security. The data are not compatible with data provided by INEGI.

8. Coahuila, Chihuahua, Durango, Nuevo León, San Luis Potosí, Tampico and Zacatecas.

9. In 1995, 50 percent of the EAP obtained two minimum wages or less.

References

Aspe Armella, Pedro. 1993. *El Camino Mexicano de la Transformación Económica.* México, D.F.: Fondo de Cultura Económica.

Banco de México. 1996. *The Mexican Economy 1996.* México: Banco de México.

Browning, Harley, and René M. Zenteno. 1993. "The Diverse Nature of the Mexican Northern Border: The Case of Urban Employment." *Frontera Norte* 5(9), pp. 11–31.

Carrillo, Jorge V. 1993. *Condiciones de Empleo y Capacitación en las Maquiladoras de Exportación en México.* México: Secretaría del Trabajo y Previsión Social y El Colegio de la Frontera Norte.

CELADE (Centro Latinoamericano de Demografía). 1996. *Boletín Demográfico* XXIX, no. 57, Santiago de Chile.

Chávez, Leo R., Estévan T. Flores, and Marta López Garza. 1989. "Migrants and Settlers: A Comparison of Undocumented Mexicans and Central Americans in the United States." *Frontera Norte* 1(1): 49–75.

COLEF (El Colegio de la Frontera Norte), CONAPO (Consejo Nacional de Población), and STPS (Secretaría del Trabajo y Previsión Social). 1994. *Encuesta sobre Migración en la Frontera Norte.* Tijuana: El Colegio de la Frontera Norte.

Córdoba, José. 1991. "Diez Lecciones de la Reforma Económica en México." *Nexos* 158: 31–49.

Cornelius, Wayne. 1978. *Mexican Migration to the United States: Causes, Consequences and U.S. Responses.* Cambridge, Mass.: Massachusetts Institute of Technology, Center for International Studies.

Dussel Peters, Enrique. 1996. "Recent Developments in Mexican Employment and the Impact of NAFTA." *International Labor Studies* 5: 45–69.

Dussel Peters, Enrique. 1997. *La Economía de la Polarización. Teoría y Evidencia del Cambio Estructural en el Sector Manufacturero Mexicano (1988–1996).* México: Editorial JUS/UNAM.

Espinoza Valle, Víctor Alejandro. 1990. *Don Crispín. Una Crónica Fronteriza.* Tijuana: El Colegio de la Frontera Norte.

Garrido, Elso, and Tomás Peñaloza. 1996. *Ahorro y Sistema Financiero Mexicano. Diagnóstico de la Problemática Actual.* México, D.F.: Grijalbo/UAM.

Gurría Treviño, Angel. 1993. *La Política de la Deuda Externa.* México, D.F.: Fondo de Cultura Económica.

Heath Constable, Jonathan. 1996. "La Problemática del Empleo y Desempleo en México." *Ejecutivos de Finanzas* (December): 35–76.

Ibarra, David. 1996. *Transición o Crisis? Las Contradicciones de la Política Económica y el Bienestar Social.* México: Nuevo Siglo Aguilar.

Maddison, Angus. 1995. *Monitoring the World Economy.* Paris: OECD.

Massey, Douglas S., Luin Goldring, and Jorge Durand. 1994. "Continuities in Transnational Migration: An Analysis of Nineteen Mexican Communities." *American Journal of Sociology* 99(6): 1492–1533.

Mendiola, Gerardo. 1997. Las empresas maquiladoras de exportación 1980–1995. In *Pensar Globalmente y Actuar Regionalmente,* ed. E. Dussel Peters, M. Piore, and C. Ruiz Durán, 185–228. México: Editorial JUS/UNAM.

PEF (Poder Ejecutivo Federal). 1996a. *Plan Nacional de Desarrollo. Informe de Ejecución 1995.* México: Poder Ejecutivo Federal.

PEF. 1996b. *Segundo Informe de Gobierno.* México: Poder Ejecutivo Federal.

Piñeiro, Rodolfo Cruz. 1992. "La Fuerza de Trabajo en los Mercados Urbanos de la Frontera Norte." *Cuadernos* 5: 1–75. Tijuana: El Colegio de la Frontera Norte.

Rogozinski, Jacques. 1993. *La Privatización de Empresas Paraestatales.* México, D.F.: Fondo de Cultura Económica.

Ruiz Durán, Clemente, Enrique Dussel Peters, and Taeko Taniura. 1997. *Changes in Industrial Organization of the Mexican Automobile Industry by Economic Liberalization.* Joint Research Program Series no. 120. Japan: Institute of Developing Economies.

SHCP (Secretaría de Hacienda y Crédito Público). 1996. *Informes sobre la Situación Económica, las Finanazas Públicas y la Deuda Pública.* México: Secretaría de Hacienda y Crédito Público. Tercer trimestre de 1996.

STPV (Secretaría del Trabajo y Previsión Social). 1996. *Informe de Labores 1994–1995.* México: Secretaría del Trabajo y Previsión Social.

Verduzco Igartúa, Gustavo. 1995. "La Migración Mexicana a Estados Unidos: Recuento de un Proceso Histórico." *Estudios Sociológicos* XIII, 39: 573–594. México: El Colegio de México.

World Bank. 1995. *World Development Report.* Washington, D.C.: World Bank.

Zapata, Francisco. 1997. *International Baseline Study. Mexico.* Warwick, U.K.: Institute for Employment Research. Draft.

Commentary

John H. Coatsworth, Harvard University

Enrique Dussel Peters' chapter provides a thoughtful review of economic trends, policies, and problems in Mexico since the country's leaders opted to open its market and shrink its government a decade ago. He is surely correct to remind us that higher wages constitute an important (if not the only) attraction that beckons Mexican immigrants, both legal and undocumented, to the United States. Correcting for differences in purchasing power, Mexicans probably earn about a fifth to a quarter of the wages earned by inhabitants of the United States.[1]

This gap has fluctuated over the years, but stands today roughly where it was 100 years ago.[2] For much of the twentieth century, in fact, real wages in Mexico and the United States have tended to rise and fall together. For example, real hourly wages in most sectors of the U.S. economy have stagnated for the past 15 years or so, while Mexican wages have declined somewhat. Thus, even though the Mexican economy has stagnated while that of the United States has grown since 1980, the wage gap has not increased apace.

If the wage gap between Mexico and the United States has not changed in a hundred years, why are so many more Mexicans coming to the United States now than a century ago? Part of the answer to this question is demographic. Mexico's population has grown at high rates since the 1930s, so the population available to be enticed northward is now much larger than it was a century ago. Since the Revolution of 1910, the Mexican population has increased from barely 15 million to over 90 million. So, with a constant wage gap, one would expect annual Mexican immigration to the United States to increase fivefold over this period, even if nothing else had changed.

Though precise data are lacking, most experts appear to believe that the proportion of Mexicans who think seriously about coming to the United States and the proportion that actually do move north have increased over the past century and may still be rising.[3] That is, a constant wage gap (over the long run) appears to be associated with a rising immigration rate. Much has changed over the past century to raise the rate of immigration, but two key factors stand out: (1) the long-term rise in the income levels of most Mexicans (and thus of the pool of potential immigrants) and (2) the long-term decline in the costs associated with immigrating (with or without documents) to the United States.

Mexicans who decide to come to the United States know that they must save up enough cash to cover all the expenses of the journey and still have something left over to carry them until their first payday. Over the course of the twentieth century, the proportion of the Mexican population earning enough to cover these expenses has increased substantially.[4] Should Mexican wages begin to rise again in the coming years, rates of undocumented immigration to the United States will probably increase, ceteris paribus, as more people manage to save what they need to immigrate.

The costs of immigrating to the United States have been reduced by social networks that help new immigrants to get settled and find work. U.S. border control efforts focus on keeping the costs up by forcing undocumented immigrants to finance repeated attempts to breach the border, longer travel times via more circuitous routes, and higher prices to "coyotes" and producers of forged documents. Enforcement within the United States concentrates on increasing the risk of apprehension and reducing job opportunities through employer fines, factory raids, and the like.

Border control and enforcement measures, to be truly effective against undocumented immigration, must raise the net costs of immigration as a proportion of the income of the immigrant pool in Mexico. If social networks continue to lower costs and Mexican incomes begin to rise again, the United States will have to spend even more on these efforts just to prevent the numbers from increasing. No one knows how much would be required.

It may be true (as many politicians but few scholars have it), that the rate of immigration from Mexico would decline if the wage gap could be reduced, not just for a few years (as in the late 1970s when oil exports ran up the peso), but permanently and irreversibly. If the Mexican economy had grown as fast as any one of the Asian tigers over the past quarter century or so and wages had more or less kept pace, Mexican wages would be in the range of two-thirds the U.S. level by now.[5] Would Mexican immigration to the United States be less today as a result? Will Mexicans cease moving to the United States in large numbers when they can improve their incomes by only 50 percent instead of 300 or 400 percent as is the case now?

For the foreseeable future, as Dussel Peters suggests, we are not likely to be given an opportunity to answer this question. The wage gap is more likely to rise than to fall over the next decade or so. As the U.S. economy reaches the end of the Clinton boom, U.S. wages have begun to rise, albeit slowly, as many local and regional labor markets become tighter. On the other side of the border, massive underemployment of labor in Mexico is likely to keep real wages stagnant for many years to come. While the rate of increase of new entrants to the labor market will decline in the coming decade because population growth has slowed, free trade in grain under NAFTA will force many, perhaps millions, of Mexican farmers off the land during the first decade of the next century. And the next recession is likely to treat Mexico and Mexican wages more harshly than it does the United States.

For the foreseeable long-term future, as Dussel Peters concludes, Mexican citizens will continue to view immigration to jobs in the underground economy of the United States as a reasonable alternative to unemployment or underemployment in lower-paying jobs in Mexico. The subterranean integration of the labor markets of the two countries is likely to proceed unabated even if the United States continues to spend unprecedented billions of tax dollars trying to stop it. Surely the time has come to consider more orderly, economically sensible, and humane alternatives.

NOTES

1. Mexican per capita gross national product (GNP), adjusted for purchasing power parity (PPP), declined from 27.8 to 23.7 percent of the U.S. level between 1987 and 1995 (World Bank 1997, 215). Trends in real wages in Mexico from the 1940s to the 1970s are the subject of much controversy. The gap in wages tends to track the gap in GNP per capita over the long run.

2. According to Angus Maddison, PPP-adjusted rates of economic growth for Mexico and the United States from 1900 to 1987 were roughly 1.6 and 1.8 percent per annum, respectively (Maddison 1989, 15). The difference between the two rates is partly accounted for by the Mexican decline between 1981 and 1987.

3. See the excellent review by Susan González Baker, Frank D. Bean, Augustin Escobar Latapi, and Sidney Weintraub in this volume.

4. PPP-adjusted per capita gross domestic product (GDP) in Mexico has more than tripled over the twentieth century (Maddison 1994, 22–23, Table 2-1).

5. The growth of PPP-adjusted GDP per capita of Hong Kong, South Korea, Singapore, and Taiwan averaged 6.7 percent per annum between 1965 and 1990, to cite the most dramatic cases (Asian Development Bank 1997, 2). The Mexican

economy did not even keep pace with the much slower pace of U.S. economic growth in this period.

REFERENCES

Asian Development Bank. 1997. *Emerging Asia.* Manila: Asian Development Bank.

Maddison, Angus. 1989. *The World Economy in the Twentieth Century.* Paris: OECD.

Maddison, Angus. 1994. Explaining the economic performance of nations. In *Convergence of Productivity: Cross-National Studies and Historical Evidence,* ed. W. Baumol, R. Nelson, and E. Wolff. Oxford: Oxford University Press.

World Bank. 1997. *World Development Report, 1997.* New York: World Bank.

Photo by Anna LeVine

Susan González Baker   My interest in Mexican immigration to the United States is rooted in my own family history. I have always seen the González family as a microcosm of the issues that I discovered in college—the key problematics in sociology—issues like migration, settlement, incorporation, and social mobility. At the personal level, these issues were just stories: stories of my grandfather's transition from a *vaquero* and traildrive cook in northern Mexico to a beer-joint proprietor in southwest Texas, to a foreman on a small ranch, to a small rancher himself; stories of my grandmother's determination to see her eldest daughter be the first in the family to go to college, and to help her start over by taking us all in when youthful marriage, motherhood, and divorce derailed those early efforts. So profound were these stories in shaping my intellectual interests and my career ambitions, that to this day, I preface most of my public presentations on Mexican-origin people in the United States with a quiet moment alone in front of a mirror, usually in some well-appointed hotel room the likes of which Teodoro and Susie González have never visited, and a whispered reminder to remember where I came from. It is this remembering, as much as my training in the discipline of sociology, that affords me some confidence that my research will ask the important questions and recognize the right answers.

Assistant Professor, Department of Sociology, University of Texas, Austin. Faculty Affiliate, University of Texas Population Research Center. Member, Section Council of the Latino/a Section, American Sociological Association.

3

U.S. Immigration Policies and Trends: The Growing Importance of Migration from Mexico

Susan González Baker
University of Texas at Austin
Frank D. Bean
University of Texas at Austin
Augustin Escobar Latapi
CIESAS, Guadalajara, Mexico
Sidney Weintraub
CSIS, Washington, D.C.

Immigration issues have risen markedly on the U.S. public policy agenda over the past decade. Scholarship and commentary on U.S. immigration policy is abundant (e.g., Brimelow 1995; Teitelbaum and Weiner 1995; Beck 1996; Waldinger and Bozorgmehr 1996), and policy reforms have been frequent, from the 1986 Immigration Reform and Control Act (IRCA) targeting illegal immigration (Bean, Vernez, and Keely 1989), to the 1990 Immigration Act (IMMACT), which increased employment-based visa allotments while limiting overall immigration, to current efforts aimed at further border control and restrictions on public benefits. In 1990, the creation of the U.S. Commission on Immigration Reform further ensured that the issue would maintain a high profile (Bean and Fix, 1992). The 1996 federal passage of antiterrorist and welfare bills with substantial implications for U.S. immigrants, and, at the state level, California's passage of Proposition 187, limiting immigrant access to public services, demonstrate the continuing salience of immigration as a major public issue.

The profound importance of immigration derives in part from the nature of post–World War II migration flows, which include (1) rising numbers of legal immigrants, (2) increasing numbers of unauthorized immigrants, (3) increasing numbers of refugees and asylees, and (4) enormous jumps in the temporary admission of persons on so-called nonimmigrant visas. Furthermore, the share of persons from non-European countries has grown and now constitutes a majority in each of these flows. Within the first two categories, Latin American and Caribbean countries constitute the single largest proportion, sending nearly 38 percent of legal entrants in 1994 (INS 1995) and over 80 percent of unauthorized entrants (INS 1997). Within that broad regional category, Mexico predominates.

This chapter examines the nature of and basis for Mexican migration to the United States. The rationale for a Mexican focus derives not only from the fact that Mexican flows are large but also from the fact that U.S.-Mexico relations are as significant for both nations as they have ever been. The mounting importance of Mexico to the United States is reflected in the recent U.S. publication of numerous books concerning that country (e.g., Oppenheimer 1995; Castañeda 1995; Fuentes 1996). It is also illustrated by the bipartisan emphasis on Mexico-relevant policy, such as the Democratic Clinton administration's stewardship in 1993 of the North American Free Trade Agreement (NAFTA), which had also been a high priority of the previous Republican administration. Further evidence of Mexico's importance can be seen in the U.S. loan-guarantee package assembled to assist the Mexican government through the economic difficulties created by the peso devaluation of December 1994. Given these relations, Mexican migration to the United States is a phenomenon particularly worthy of thorough, systematic investigation.

We begin by documenting the post-war changes in general immigration flows to the United States and the ways in which they illustrate the importance of Mexico. We then examine the broad contours of Latino migration, the specifics of Mexican migration, and their significance for U.S. population patterns. We then analyze labor market and demographic changes that shape the demand factors attracting Mexican flows to the United States, changes in policy that affect migration flows, and the implications of NAFTA and changing trade relationships for Mexican migration. Finally, we explore the settlement and citizenship patterns likely to characterize the Mexican-origin population in the United States in the twenty-first century.

Migrant Flows

Legal Immigrants

After a lull between 1925 and 1945, legal U.S. immigration grew steadily for nearly 50 years, reaching levels in the late 1980s and early 1990s that approached the all-time highs set early in the twentieth century (Bean, Vernez, and Keely 1989). With legalizations through the 1986 IRCA programs included, the 1990/1991 levels exceed all previous annual highs (INS 1995).

The national origins of immigrants have also been changing. Before 1960, the vast majority came from European countries or Canada (often over 90 percent over a decade). Even as late as the 1950s, 67.7 percent of all arrivals came from these countries. However, in the 1960s family reunification criteria replaced national-origin quotas as the basis for entry (Bean, Vernez, and Keely 1989; Reimers 1983). By the 1980s, only 12.5 percent of legal immigrants came from Europe or Canada, while 47.7 percent were Latin American or Caribbean, and 39 percent were from Asian countries (INS 1995). Of those Latin American/Caribbean entrants, 68.7 percent were from Mexico between 1990 and 1994 (INS 1995).

Unauthorized Migrants

Persons who enter the United States illegally or who enter legally and then violate the terms of their visas, constitute another major flow. The Immigration and Naturalization Service (INS) refers to the former as EWIs, those who enter without inspection, while the latter are called visa overstayers. Almost all EWIs enter at the U.S.-Mexico border, with the vast majority being Mexican nationals, supplemented recently by Central American migrants (Bean et al. 1990). Visa overstayers come from a wide variety of countries. As a group, they represent nearly half the illegally resident U.S. population (Warren 1990; INS 1997). Together, the numbers of these unauthorized immigrants started growing in the 1960s and increased rapidly in the 1970s. Today, the U.S. Bureau of the Census includes an annual net gain of 200,000 illegal immigrants in its annual population estimates (Campbell 1994). Other sources estimate the sector at about 300,000 persons per year (Warren 1992). Of all unauthorized immigrants who legalized their status under the 1986 IRCA provisions, 69.9 percent were of Mexican origin, and 92.4 percent were either Latin American or Asian (Department of Justice 1992).

Refugees and Asylees

Like most other Western democracies, the United States began focusing on refugee acceptance after World War II, when it recognized victims of political persecution as "a distinct category of international migrants to whom [it] owed special obligations" (Zolberg 1992, 55). Crafted and implemented largely ad hoc, U.S. refugee policy introduced another immigrant flow. Since the end of World War II, nearly 3 million refugees and asylees have been granted lawful permanent resident status (INS 1995). The number averaged 50,000 a year in the 1940s and 1950s, declining to 20,000 annually in the 1960s, and rising to over 50,000 annually in the 1970s. Well over 100,000 refugees and asylees were admitted each year by the 1990s. As with legal immigrants, the vast majority (49.2 percent since 1945 and 82.2 percent during the 1980s) come from Asia, Latin America, and the Caribbean.

Nonimmigrant Entrants

During fiscal year 1993, 21.4 million nonimmigrant admissions to the United States were recorded, an increase of 650,000 (3.1 percent) over the previous year (INS 1995). The dramatic increases reflect the mounting demand for both tourism- and business/employment-related entry resulting from increased economic globalization. Nonimmigrant flows produce visa overstayers. To the extent that visa overstayers eventually become legal residents, a growing nonimmigrant volume pressures the legal immigration system even if the rate of visa overstaying remains constant. Unlike the other flows described, nonimmigrant entrants hail from a wide range of countries. Still, the percentage from Asia, Latin America, and the Caribbean increased from 41 to 54 percent in 1993, and Mexico finds itself high on the list of top sending countries each year for student, business, and tourist nonimmigrant visas.

IMMIGRATION AND THE U.S. MEXICAN-ORIGIN POPULATION

The cumulative effects of Mexican dominance in legal and undocumented flows is readily apparent in Table 3.1, which presents data on the stock of Mexican foreign-born persons relative to other Latin American groups and the total foreign-born population over the past 15 years. Mexican-born persons were 15.0 percent of the total foreign-born population in 1980. The figure rose to 20.7 percent by 1990 and to 28.4 percent by the mid-1990s. Mexican immigrants have come to constitute the largest single foreign-born group in the United States.

This growth has contributed greatly to the overall growth in the U.S. Mexican-origin population, which includes several distinct subgroups. Mexican-origin people include those born in the United States who trace their ancestry to Mexico, as well as those born in Mexico who have migrated to the United States, be they naturalized citizens, legal immigrants, or undocumented immigrants.

TABLE 3.1

Number and Percentage of Foreign-Born Persons, 1980–1994/95

Place of Birth	1980 Number	1980 %	1990 Number	1990 %	1994/95 Number	1994/95 %
Central/ South America	**4,021**	**28.6**	**7,407**	**37.5**	**10,299**	**46.2**
Mexico	2,108	15.0	4,098	20.7	6,322	28.4
Cuba	588	4.2	698	3.5	768	3.4
Other	1,325	9.4	2,611	13.2	3,209	14.4
Dominican Republic	160	1.1	321	1.6	478	2.1
Central America[a]	252	1.8	941	4.8	1,312	5.9
Colombia	136	1.0	249	1.3	170	0.8
Other	777	5.5	1,100	5.6	1,249	5.6
Asia/Pacific Island	**2,540**	**18.0**	**4,979**	**25.2**	**5,855[b]**	**26.3**
Other	**7,519**	**53.4**	**7,381**	**37.3**	**6,116**	**27.5**
Total Foreign Born	**14,080**	**100.0**	**19,767**	**100.0**	**22,270**	**100.0**

[a] El Salvador, Guatemala, Honduras, Nicaragua, and Panama.
[b] Asian/Pacific Islanders data tabulated from 1996 March CPS.

Source: 1980 and 1990, Public Use Microdata Samples (PUMS); 1994 and 1995, March Current Population Survey (CPS).

Assessing the size and growth of the Mexican-origin population requires an understanding of each component—a challenging task given the changes in the ways Mexican-origin people have been identified over time by official U.S. efforts.

We focus first on changes in the U.S. census definitions of Mexican-origin persons, then discuss patterns of growth over the past century. Bean and Tienda note (1987, 38) that "Ethnicity denotes a social identity deriving from group membership based on common race, religion, language, national origin, or some combination of these factors." Given those many dimensions, definitions have changed over the years (see Table 3.2). Before 1970, Mexican ethnicity was measured through various objective markers, including place of birth, parents' place of birth, language, and Spanish surname. These markers identified the foreign born and their children fairly well, but overlooked third- or higher-generation persons, particularly those who spoke no Spanish or carried a non-Spanish surname. In response to concerns, a new ethnicity measure entered the 1970 census, whereby Mexican ethnicity could be identified through use of a subjective term: "Hispanic origin." This allowed respondents of any generation to self-affiliate as possessing Mexican or other Latino ethnic status.

Even considering these changes, the Mexican-origin population has grown steadily (Table 3.3). Some growth can be attributed to natural increase by the

TABLE 3.2

Identifiers Available in the United States Census for the Hispanic Population,
1950–1990

Year	Birthplace	Foreign Parentage	Mother Tongue	Other Language at Home	Spanish Surname[a]	Spanish Origin or Descent	Ancestry
1994/96	yes	no	no	no	no	yes	yes
1990	yes	no	no	yes	no	yes	yes
1980	yes	no	no	yes	yes	yes	yes
1970	yes	yes	yes	no	yes	yes	no
1960	yes	yes	yes[b]	no	yes	no	no
1950	yes	yes	no	no	yes	no	no

[a] Data available for only five southwestern states.
[b] Data available for 25 percent of the foreign-born population.

Source: 1950–1980 data from Bean and Tienda (1987); 1990 census information and 1994/96 CPS information constructed by authors.

U.S. born, since Mexican American fertility rates are roughly 35 to 40 percent higher than those of non-Mexican whites (Bean and Tienda 1987). Even absent migration, then, the size of the Mexican-origin population would have increased relative to its non-Mexican counterpart throughout this century.

However, the present size of the Mexican-origin population is mostly attributable to migration processes. Edmonston and Passel (1994) estimate that the Mexican-origin population in 1990 would be only 14 percent its current size had there been no immigration from Mexico after 1900. Table 3.4 presents the size of the Mexican-born population in the United States by decade. The immigrant flow fluctuated considerably throughout this period, but it is clear that it has become an increasing share of the total.

Mexican population growth in the United States has varied with economic and political conditions on both sides of the border (Dussel, this volume; Freeman and Bean 1997; Szekeley and de la Garza 1997). The border attained its modern definition in 1848, but records on Mexico-U.S. crossings were not kept until 1908, and were themselves dubious, as the border was largely unsupervised. Two border states (Arizona and New Mexico) were only territories until 1912. The first large-scale, officially measured migration from Mexico into U.S. territory occurred between 1910 and 1919. Increased labor demand spurred by Chinese worker exclusion in 1882, Japanese worker exclusion in 1907, and a shortage of European immigrants during World War I encouraged Mexican migration. Mexican migration rates continued to increase as the U.S. government exempted the Western Hemisphere from the national-origin quota laws of the 1920s and 1930s in the name of Pan Americanism, which was also

TABLE 3.3

Total Mexican-Born Population in the United States, 1900–1995

Year	Mexican-Born Population (1,000s)	Percentage of Total Foreign-Born Population	Percentage of Total Mexican-Origin Population[a]
1996	6,895	25.8	38.2
1995	6,060	27.2	35.6
1990	4,298	21.7	32.1
1980	2,199	15.6	25.2
1970	759	7.9	16.7
1960	576[a]	5.9	33.2
1950	454	4.4	33.7
1940	377	3.2	35.0
1930	617	4.3	43.4
1920	486	3.5	65.7
1910	222	1.6	57.7

[a] Mexican-origin population is the sum of the Mexican-born population and U.S. natives of Mexican parentage.

Source: Immigration and Naturalization Service and *Historical Statistics of the United States, Part 1* (1975).

encouraged by Southwesterners looking to Mexico for cheap labor (Reimers 1992). When labor demand waned during the Great Depression, the United States repatriated many Mexican-origin persons, including U.S.-born children.

Immigration from Mexico increased again with the Bracero program (1943–1964). When non-Mexican farm workers in California sought higher-paying jobs in World War II defense industries, labor supply for growers tightened. This prompted growers to pressure Congress for temporary workers from Mexico—the braceros. During its peak in 1956, the program recruited 445,197 workers (Reimers 1992). Although the braceros were expected to remain temporarily, many stayed, along with their family members. Although growers fought to retain their cheap labor supply, Congress refused to extend the program past 1964.

Since that time, both legal and undocumented migration from Mexico has grown steadily. The legal population, in particular, grew dramatically in the late 1980s and early 1990s. The 1986 IRCA legalization provisions conferred legal status on nearly 3 million undocumented immigrants, overwhelmingly of Mexican origin, who had been working in agriculture or living illegally in the United States before 1982. When the legalized population is removed from official estimates, the size of the Mexican immigrant population from 1981 to 1994 drops substantially.

TABLE 3.4

Immigration from Mexico to the United States, 1900–1994

Years	Number Arriving from Mexico in the Decade	Percentage of All Immigrants Arriving in the Decade
A. Published Totals		
1991–1994	1,400,108	31.0
1981–1990	1,655,843	22.6
1971–1980	640,294	14.2
1961–1970	453,937	13.7
1951–1960	299,811	11.9
1941–1950	60,589	5.9
1931–1940	22,319	4.2
1921–1930	459,287	11.2
1911–1920	219,004	3.8
1901–1910	49,642	0.6
B. Revised Numbers: Mexican Arrivals, Excluding IRCA Legalized[a]		
1991–1994	353,702	11.1
1981–1990	693,213	11.6

[a] Numbers of those legalized through IRCA were obtained from INS *Statistical Yearbooks* for 1989 to 1994.

Source: Immigration and Naturalization Service, 1996. 1994 *Statistical Yearbook of the Immigration and Naturalization Service.* Washington, D.C.: Government Printing Office.

TABLE 3.5

Number of Naturalized Citizens of Mexican Origin in the United States, 1950–1996

Year	Number of Naturalized Citizens of Mexican Origin	Percentage of Total Mexican Foreign-Born Population in the United States
1996	851,803	12.4
1990	969,704	22.6
1980	518,218	23.6
1970	306,403	40.3
1960[a]	—	—
1950	318,594	70.1

[a] Number of naturalized citizens of Mexican origin not available for 1960.

Source: U.S. Bureau of the Census, 1950–1990; March 1996 Current Population Survey.

TABLE 3.6

Estimated Size of the Enumerated Undocumented Mexican Migrant Population, 1980–1995

Year	Estimated Undocumented Mexicans (1,000s)	Percentage of Foreign-Born Pop. in the U.S.	Percentage of Mexican-Born Pop. in the U.S.	Percentage of Mexican-Origin Population	Percentage of Total U.S. Population
1995	2,150	9.7	35.5	12.6	0.8
1990	1,321	6.7	30.7	9.9	0.5
1980	1,131	8.0	51.4	12.9	0.5

Source: Estimates of enumerated undocumented Mexican migrant population from Warren and Passel 1987 (for 1980), Warren 1992 (for 1990), and author tabulations (for 1995).

Table 3.5 presents data on Mexican-born naturalized U.S. citizens. Compared with other immigrant groups, Mexicans have been slow to naturalize (Grebler 1966; Bean and Tienda 1987). English-language ability is frequently cited as the largest barrier to citizenship for Mexicans (Reimers 1992). The proportion of Mexican immigrants who naturalize has decreased over time, largely due to the large number of recent arrivals. However, in 1996, Mexican naturalization increased substantially, as those IRCA-legalized immigrants became eligible and as other Mexican immigrants more generally sought to maintain eligibility for public benefits in the wake of new restrictive legislation (INS 1997).

The final component of Mexican population in the United States is the undocumented population. Table 3.6 presents estimates of the Mexican undocumented population from 1980 to 1995. Mexican undocumented immigrants counted in the 1980 U.S. census constituted about 8 percent of the U.S. foreign-born population, 51 percent of the total Mexican-born population, and about 13 percent of the total Mexican-origin population. By 1995, the estimated undocumented population was about the same relative size (just under 10 percent of the total foreign-born population) but had dropped to only 36 percent of the total Mexican foreign-born population (Bean et al. 1997a), a function of the expanded opportunity structure for acquiring legal status in the post-IRCA period.

FACTORS AFFECTING THE DEMAND FOR MEXICAN MIGRATION

What drives Mexican migration to the United States? Numerous theories have been put forth, and empirical support has been found for some of the predictions of each (Massey and Espinoza 1997). While the U.S. demand for Mexican labor does not drive the process to the exclusion of all other influences, it is a clear and profound force. Hence, analyses of labor demand changes are particularly useful for understanding Mexican migration. It is also useful to ask how recent changes in U.S. immigration policy have affected the demand for Mexican labor. Finally, we must ask how NAFTA, which was intended to change trade conditions between the two nations, has affected Mexico-U.S. migration.

U.S. Economic Restructuring and the Demand for Mexican Labor

Both U.S. income and occupational statistics attest to the process of economic restructuring occurring in recent decades. In 1979, 32 percent of all male U.S. workers earned between $20,000 and $30,000 annually (in 1988 dollars) (Levy and Murnane 1992). Despite six years of slow growth starting in 1973, this general income profile was stable until 1979, when income polarization began to emerge. Thereafter, the poor became poorer while the rich became richer. Jobs providing middle-range incomes dropped from 32 to 26 percent of total jobs by 1987. Some speculate that the polarization emerged from deindustrialization, with many new jobs emerging in a tertiary sector marked by a distinct mix of low- and high-paying jobs. However, Levy and Murnane (1992) suggest that this is not the case. While the service sector grew, so did the manufacturing sector. The issue became one of manufacturing jobs increasingly resembling those of the service sector, with lower skill demands and wage offers over time. Most of this job expansion took place in the Southwest (particularly in California), where the 1980s boom opened many low-paid assembly and personal service jobs.

The Sunbelt boom and its expanded low-end manufacturing and service job base were significant factors in the demand for Mexican labor. By 1990, 37 percent of young Mexican immigrant men and 50 percent of young Mexican immigrant women were employed in manufacturing, overwhelmingly in direct production tasks (Vernez and Ronfeldt 1991). Other studies show that these workers were employed not only by labor-intensive traditional industries (e.g., shoe and garment manufacture, construction) but also by high-technology firms with seemingly safe market positions (Cornelius 1989; Fernandez-Kelly 1983).

In this context, Mexicans in the United States shifted from agricultural and seasonal jobs to urban jobs with less demand variation. This shift had precedent. During World War II, Mexicans had performed many urban manufacturing jobs. The transition took place again in the 1970s and 1980s, prompted by the increased availability of Mexican workers (an outcome of the Mexican crisis and adjustment) and by the rise in world market competition. The Southwest boom was prompted by localized growth and firm relocation. The same factors that led to the fivefold growth of employment in maquiladoras through the 1980s spurred growth in Mexican employment in manufacturing and services in California.

Mexican labor became attractive to U.S. employers for other reasons as well. With the closure of old, unionized plants and the transition to nonunionized shops came changing employer hiring practices. As Martin (1986) explains, Mexican-immigrant supervisors contributed significantly to the concentration of Mexican workers in large and small firms (see also Waldinger 1997). Once hiring and firing power rested with Mexican-immigrant supervisors, those powers led to increasing portions of the firm's workforce including Mexican kin and countrymen. Employers initiated and supported such practices not only because they lowered search costs but also because many of these homogeneous work groups became self-managing. Eventually, the development of language and cultural barriers between U.S.- and foreign-born work groups led to high levels of shop floor segregation and, in some cases, the exclusion of the U.S.-born working poor from the low-paying positions that provide entry into work hierarchies.

Still, analyses of metropolitan labor markets in Texas and California suggest that Mexican immigration tends to push native minorities up the occupational scale, not down, although there are some segments of that population that do become unemployed (Newby 1996). Nevertheless, the displacement thesis suggested by Waldinger, Martin, and others has an important implication: Since foreign-born workers in U.S. firms are less likely than U.S.-born workers to climb to positions demanding education, English proficiency, and legal status, a new tier of low-paid workers consolidates in the lower echelons. Thus the fluidity of the U.S. job structure is diminished in two ways. First, with less access to low-skilled jobs, the U.S. poor remain marginal to employment. Second, many foreign-born workers never ascend within firms, but must become independent or wait for their offspring to acquire the schooling and language abilities necessary for better jobs—a process documented for Latino men in southern California by Myers in this volume.

U.S. Immigration Policies and Labor Demand

U.S. responses to the perceived costs of Mexican migration constitute another set of influences on Mexican emigration dynamics. The major post–World War II initiative to curtail illegal immigration was the 1986 Immigration Reform and Control Act (Bean, Vernez, and Keely 1989). IRCA attempted to reduce the flow and stock of Mexican undocumented immigrants through the legalization of many undocumented U.S. residents, employer sanctions against hiring undocumented labor, and increased border enforcement resources. One criterion by which IRCA's effectiveness can be judged is the extent to which undocumented flow and stock actually diminished, beyond the reduction attributable to legalization.

Some answers can be derived from INS apprehensions data. Apprehension statistics come from monthly tallies of the number of times persons crossing into the United States are apprehended by the U.S. Border Patrol or other INS personnel. The data include various migrant types (Bean et al. 1994), persons apprehended multiple times, and persons who return to Mexico within the year. Thus, the peak of 1,767,400 apprehensions in fiscal year 1986 substantially overstates the size of the undocumented population. Conversely, the statistics can also lead to underestimates if many entrants go undetected.

Even given these cautions, apprehensions data are of great value for tracking flow and gauging changes over time. Since almost all apprehensions (92 percent in fiscal year 1987, for example) involve Mexicans, they are the only data from which to gauge Mexican flows. Border Patrol apprehensions declined after IRCA's passage, from 1.7 million in fiscal year (FY) 1986 to 1.2 million in FY 1987, to 1 million in FY 1988, and to 954,253 in FY 1989. However, this trend reflects, in part, the vigor of INS enforcement. The number of hours dedicated to actual border patrol has fluctuated over time. Thus, it is useful to examine apprehensions per hours of effort expended and per "line-watch" hour (the hours spent in direct border patrol). Data on line-watch apprehensions, line-watch hours, and line-watch apprehensions per hour from fiscal years 1977 to 1995 are presented in Table 3.7. Five distinct periods emerge. From 1977 to 1982, a period of relative boom in the Mexican economy, line-watch apprehensions were relatively stable. From 1983 to 1986, after the slowdown in the Mexican economy and before IRCA's passage, line-watch apprehensions jumped sharply. After a lag, line-watch hours also increased. Most important, apprehensions per line-watch hour climbed substantially.

The next period covers 1987 to 1989, immediately after IRCA's passage. During this period, apprehensions declined, as did apprehensions per line-watch hour. However, apprehensions did not fall to their 1977–1982 levels. While IRCA stemmed some of the increase in illegal flows resulting from the 1982 recession, it did not reduce illegal crossings to earlier levels.

NAFTA Trade Relations and the Peso Devaluation

Increasing liberalization of trade policies, evidenced by the General Agreement on Trade and Tariffs (GATT), the North American Free Trade Agreement (NAFTA), and rapidly shifting international investment and monetary

TABLE 3.7

Yearly Line-Watch Apprehensions and Hours, Fiscal Year 1977–1995

Fiscal Year	Line-Watch Apprehensions	Line-Watch Hours	LWAs per Hour
1977	441,265	1,740,446	0.254
1978	481,612	1,762,616	0.273
1979	488,941	1,935,926	0.253
1980	428,966	1,815,797	0.236
1981	452,821	1,929,448	0.235
1982	443,437	1,871,173	0.237
1983	646,311	1,976,126	0.327
1984	623,944	1,843,179	0.339
1985	666,402	1,912,895	0.348
1986	846,341	2,401,575	0.394
1987	750,954	2,546,397	0.295
1988	614,653	2,069,498	0.297
1989	521,899	2,436,788	0.214
1990	668,282	2,549,137	0.262
1991	711,808	2,390,500	0.298
1992	814,290	2,386,888	0.341
1993	840,326	2,713,024	0.310
1994	687,163	3,074,060	0.224
1995[a]	480,580	1,891,413	0.254
Fiscal Year	Mean	Mean	LWA/Hour
1977–1982	456,174	1,842,568	0.248
1983–1986	720,750	2,033,444	0.354
1987–1989	629,169	2,350,894	0.268
1990–1993	758,677	2,509,887	0.302
1994–1995[a]	699,247	2,973,337	0.235

[a] FY 1995 includes only September 1994 to April 1995.

Source: INS *Statistical Yearbooks* and special INS tabulations provided to authors.

exchange patterns (such as those contributing to the recent peso devaluation) also have migration implications. Mexico's development model went through profound transformation during the 1980s. Dussel outlines this process in Chapter 2 of this volume. Briefly, the policy of the postwar period was one of almost unmitigated import substitution industrialization (ISI). Mexico, under ISI, required prior licenses and levied high duties on imports, imposed domestic-content requirements on foreign investors, and, as a rule, limited foreign direct investment to a minority share. The policy was referred to as "development from within." Little regard was given to promoting exports.

In overall growth terms, the policy succeeded. Gross domestic product increased five to six percent a year from the 1950s through the 1970s. Benefits were not equally distributed, however, with income distribution highly skewed in favor of upper-income families. Emigration to the United States was substantial throughout this period owing to persistent poverty, particularly in rural areas. The migration networks that had been established during the bracero period consolidated during the ISI period.

In 1982, Mexico abandoned its traditional model and began to build an export structure model. In 1986, during the de la Madrid administration (1982–1986), Mexico acceded to the GATT, a step explicitly rejected during the previous López Portillo administration (1976–1982). The adjustment was painful. The Mexican economy grew modestly over the next five years, and hardly at all in per capita terms (Lustig 1992). The minimum wage fell by some 40 percent. As noted above, apprehensions of Mexican undocumented immigrants rose steadily over this period, from 970,000 in 1982 to 1.7 million in 1986.

Mexico entered 1994 with great hopes. NAFTA formally entered implementation on January 1. Inflation was dropping. Foreign reserves exceeded $25 billion. Gross domestic product (GDP) growth was projected at 4 percent. However, the balance of payments deficit was growing dangerously high, reaching 8 percent of GDP in 1994. Still, capital flows to finance the deficit and augment reserves were flowing into Mexico. Although there was no lessening of income inequality, the overall sentiment was one of optimism.

As it turned out, 1994 was a year of setbacks. A group in the state of Chiapas calling itself the Zapatista National Liberation Army chose January 1 to stage an uprising. In March, Luis Donaldo Colosio, the presidential candidate of the ruling Partido Revolucionario Institucional (PRI), was assassinated. The August presidential and congressional elections generated conflict over voter fraud allegations. Later in the year, José Francisco Ruis Massieu, the number two official in the PRI, was murdered. These internal shocks were aggravated by rising U.S. interest rates as the Federal Reserve raised the federal funds rate six times. U.S. treasury notes became increasingly attractive to investors in light of the disquieting events in Mexico.

The combination of horrors in Mexico and the attraction of U.S. fixed-income investments led to episodic capital flight from Mexico. By December 20, when Mexico had largely depleted its reserves, the peso was devalued by 15 percent, widening the upper limit of the band within which the peso was traded.

Within a day or two, the market grasped that the amount of outstanding Mexican dollar-indexed, short-term treasury obligations—*tesobonos*—was several times greater than Mexico's foreign reserves. Although denominated in pesos, the dollar indexing made these bonds equivalent to dollar instruments purchased by investors precisely as a hedge against devaluation.

Panic ensued. Mexican authorities dedicated most of their activities in 1995 to dealing with the financial and economic catastrophe. GDP fell in 1995 by 6.9 percent. Real wages declined by 15 percent and urban unemployment rose by 2 million persons. By early 1996, the financial situation seemed to have stabilized. The peso was steady; the stock market was high. Mexico was able to borrow on world money markets.

All these actions—policy changes, adjustments to them, and the economic declines of 1982 and 1995—had significant migration impacts. They helped spur much internal migration, and much emigration to the United States as economic prospects shifted. Because the peso devaluation raised Mexican unemployment and increased the peso value of dollar remittances from the United States, it selected for labor migration. Although current research is still inconclusive, it appears that Mexican migration flows, as measured by border apprehensions, did increase as a result of the peso devaluation, along with other factors such as lower overall U.S. unemployment rates, appreciably higher aggregate U.S. unemployment from the beginning of 1994 to early 1995, and more hours devoted to border enforcement. Research by Bean and Cushing (1995) suggests these factors could account for as much as two-thirds of the increase in apprehensions during early 1995. Thus, U.S. conditions, including labor demand and policy implementation, appear to have affected migration as much as conditions in Mexico.

CITIZENSHIP AND SETTLEMENT

Given the continuing importance of Mexican migration, and given that such migration is at least in part the product of labor demand in the United States, the question of Mexican migrant incorporation into U.S. society becomes particularly significant. Mexican immigrants are more than workers. Over time, they become neighbors, community members, and, potentially, U.S. citizens. Especially important is the issue of citizenship. Naturalization rates vary widely among U.S. immigrants, from highs in excess of 75 percent among European immigrants to lows in the 10 to 15 percent range among Mexicans. Most social science scholarship suggests that individual and social factors interact to produce differential naturalization rates across country-of-origin groups and immigration status categories. The tendency to adjust to U.S. citizenship seems to be associated with three primary factors: relatively high levels of human capital (i.e., education, English fluency, occupational skill), distance from the country of origin, and having entered the U.S. in refugee/asylee status (as opposed to family- or employment-based migration).

Given these factors, immigrants from most Latin American countries would not be expected to naturalize in great numbers. Such has been the case. Nearly 40 percent of the Latino population in the United States is foreign born, and less than 20 percent of those have naturalized. With the exception of Cubans, who meet the criteria listed above and whose naturalization rates exceed 50 percent, Latinos tend to remain legal permanent residents throughout their lives.

The political potential implied by Latino naturalization is substantial. If all noncitizen Latinos of voting age were to naturalize, the upper bound of new Latino voters would exceed 7 million (Baker 1996). Furthermore, given the geographical concentration of Latino immigrants, the state and local impact of such a change in voter composition would be even more dramatic. Texas and California alone, for instance, account for over half the Latino foreign-born population in the United States.

In 1995, naturalization application rates doubled nationwide from 1994 levels, and increased by a factor of five in California, where over 40 percent of all foreign-born Latinos in the United States are found. From August 1995 to September 1996, roughly 1.3 million legal permanent residents applied for U.S. citizenship. Scholars and policymakers alike seem to agree that the surge in naturalization applications, while composed of increases from many groups, is disproportionately attributable to Latino immigrants, both those who have become eligible recently and those who have been long-term residents (Baker 1997).

Does the Latino immigrant trend toward U.S. citizenship signify any subjective change in the orientation toward home or host country? As Latino immigrants become U.S. citizens, potential outcomes may include an increase in U.S. political participation, increased investment in U.S.-based capital (e.g., property, English-language instruction, U.S.-centered social networks), and corresponding decreases in the social and economic investments made in the sending country (e.g., remittances, extended periods of residence abroad, and the endurance of home-country kinship networks). On the other hand, it may be that the surge in Latino citizenship is driven largely by the exogenous shock of policy reforms that have heightened the instrumental value of acquiring formal status, with little or no change in the way Latino immigrants see themselves or live their lives. Ainslie's research, for example, presented in Chapter 9, documents the powerful connection to home country maintained by Latino immigrants well after their settlement in the United States appears secure. Indeed the whole discourse in immigration research on "transnationalism" suggests a new form of settlement through which immigrants capitalize on the technologies of transportation and communication to create lives imbued with elements of both home and host culture. To the extent that citizenship acquisition is largely instrumental, it may be less likely that it will have profound effects for immigrants over their own life course, even if it facilitates the settlement and incorporation of their children and subsequent generations on the U.S. side of the border.

Some preliminary evidence suggests that the shift toward naturalization among Latinos is indeed being fueled by instrumental concerns and fear regarding access to U.S. social services. Surveys with INS officials, immigrant-assistance organizations, and public service providers suggest that this fear factor operates in two ways. Not only is the fear of losing benefits eligibility (whether or not those benefits are actually being accessed) motivating immigrants to seek naturalization, but the "door slamming shut" metaphor is also being employed aggressively by the advocacy community in its outreach and appeals extended toward immigrants. In other words, the fear exists on its own terms and is being used through collective action as a mobilization lever by the advocacy community (Baker 1997; Freeman et al. 1996).

Three additional factors enter into the naturalization equation: (1) changes in Mexican policy that allow for dual-nationality maintenance and retention of Mexican property rights while living abroad; (2) changes in U.S. immigration policy that now require a renewal process for the green card, giving immigrants an opportunity to come into contact with the INS and discover that a modest increment in their investment could lead to citizenship; and (3) sheer timing for a large cohort of eligibles, as the mid-1990s usher in 13 to 15 years of residence for those 1.7 million immigrants who legalized through IRCA's main legalization program. The combined result of these Mexican and U.S. policy changes has been a burgeoning naturalization rate. Ironically, the instrumental bases for the rising rate have also given rise to new criticism from immigration restrictionists, who decry the fact that naturalization motivations, when expressed by Latino applicants in particular, are defensive, exploitative, and cynical, rather than representing the embrace of U.S. identity assumed to have motivated earlier cohorts and those from other parts of the world (Baker 1997).

And yet, even with such instrumental rationales, Latino naturalized citizens do harbor the potential for bringing about sociopolitical change. For example, although California's controversial Proposition 187 limiting immigrant access to social services passed by a healthy margin, nearly four out of five Latino voters rejected it—a fact made more significant by the changing composition of the California electorate. Latino voting rates in California rose from a 1988 level of 7 percent of total votes to 11 percent of the 1996 vote, all the more informative when compared with the drop in African American voting share from 8 to 6 percent during the same time period. While much of the increase is attributable to registration drives and turnout dynamics among U.S.-born Latinos, it would be naive to regard the surge in Latino political mobilization as wholly independent of the increasing Latino naturalization trend, particularly when field research on naturalization documents the active role of advocacy groups like the National Association of Latino Elected Officials in distributing voter registration materials at citizenship swearing-in ceremonies (Freeman et al. 1996). In sum, as some policy walls rise for the foreign born in the United States, and as others drop on the home side for the emigrants from key countries like Mexico, one underemphasized consequence has been an increased claim to full access to U.S. institutions through the acquisition of U.S. citizenship when possible.

Citizenship and settlement, however, are two different phenomena. U.S. citizens live in Mexico, just as Mexican citizens live in the United States. Questions about settlement, therefore, cannot be answered by relying on the assumption that one's immigration status determines where one lives. If for no other reason than the explosion in transportion and communication technologies, options for physical settlement in geographical space will be more varied in the twenty-first century than they have ever been. Just as distance from the sending country has been a powerful predictor of U.S. citizenship acquisition, so has proximity to the sending country been associated with the persistence of a lifestyle in which immigrants adjust their residential patterns throughout the year and throughout the life course to include periods in the United States and periods in the country of origin. In the U.S. case, Mexicans are the archetype, but similar patterns are observed for Central American immigrants (Hondagneu-Sotelo 1994; Hagan 1994).

Mexican immigrants have always tended to initiate their U.S. residence during the prime years of labor force activity. Tracking the modal settlement pattern at this point in the life course across cohorts of Mexican immigrants, a transition emerges from the agricultural pattern of splitting the year between the harvest in the United States and the rest of the year in Mexico to a more prolonged U.S. stay in an urban environment, interspersed with shorter, predictable visits to Mexico, often centered on holiday seasons. The transition is a classic one—from sojourner to settler. An increasing rate of U.S. citizenship may amplify this tendency and result in an increasingly settled Mexican population in the United States. In the long term, as the work of Cornelius and Gutiérrez documents in this volume (see also Waldinger 1997), there is every reason to expect such an outcome, in which the Mexican presence in the United States transforms sociocultural and economic space, and in which U.S. institutions like the workplace, schools, and the health care system are called on to adapt to the changing composition of the population.

Indeed, it appears that the chances of primary settlement in the United States are being heightened substantially by the increasing tendency for Mexican migration to include women, be they wives, daughters, other relatives, or solo migrants. In contrast to the "mourning process" for Mexican men that Ainslie identifies in Chapter 9, women's settlement aspirations seem to consistently favor remaining in the United States, particularly when U.S.-born children are part of the household. Although separation from the home country takes a clear toll on male and female immigrants alike, it remains the case that women express far more enthusiasm for settlement than do men, whose "myth of return" provides psychic solace, given their advantaged status in the home country relative to their female counterparts (Hondagneu-Sotelo 1994). This gendered preference for settlement in the United States hinges on the opportunity structures available to Mexican women in the labor market and on the social services available to them and to their children. Thus, it comes as no surprise that the tendency of Mexican migration to include more and more women and families has spurred new backlash campaigns to cut off access to precisely those institutions of which women and families avail themselves. While the restrictionist line against male target-earners has always been one of wage depression and higher unemployment for native workers, the corollary concern with pressure on the public purse has been mobilized rather effectively in light of the gendered demographic changes in the Mexican immigrant population seeking to settle in the United States and acquire full access to the benefits of that settlement.

Still, in the short term, what can be seen as U.S.-centered transitions, from undocumented to legal status, from alien to citizen, have had the counterintuitive effect of increasing flow back and forth across the international border and placing settlement predictions in flux. It is in this climate that the construct of transnationalism has ascended in migration theory and research. At present, residential choices seem to be transcending formal immigration status categories. For instance, the 1986 U.S. legalization program conferred travel rights to a large cohort of previously undocumented immigrants who had been at high risk for apprehension every time they tried to cross between the two countries. Those travel rights unleashed a short-term boom in border travel, as the newly legalized returned to Mexico, and, in the process, reinvigorated social and economic ties to home (Hagan and Baker 1993). The result, ten years later, has been a continuing fluidity in which a second wave of migration (typically family based) to the United States is being sponsored by those legalized immigrants, even as steady, periodic returns to Mexico are becoming an institutionalized part of the family's life course (Baker 1997).

The U.S.-Mexico border itself is also emerging as a unique region in which the formalities of legal status have less explanatory power for people's settlement choices than is true in the interior. For instance, since the 1970s, estimates of Mexican illegal immigrant settlement along the border are lower than many observers would suspect, particularly in Texas (Bean et al. 1997a; Bean et al. 1994). The border population is much more residentially fluid than the interior population on either side. As the border population grows, a transnational lifestyle may well become an increasing share of the total set of residential options evident for Mexican immigrants, up to and including Mexican-born U.S. citizens taking up primary residence on the Mexican side of the border even as their schooling, commerce, and certain health care services take place on the U.S. side. In other words, nation-state borders and technical immigration status definitions are becoming somewhat decoupled from the actual residential practices of Mexicans and U.S. citizens of Mexican birth. While both the Mexican and U.S. states continue to exert their authority over the immigration process through policy reforms, the social process of migration continues, adapting rapidly to those reform efforts. In this way, the Mexican migration of today may well be considered as a new form. Past waves of migration were profoundly affected by both the business cycle and by policy reforms. Explicit exclusion of Asian immigrants, for example, effectively cut off the flow for decades. Boom economies encouraged migration, while depressions slowed the flow to a trickle. In contrast, today's migration from Mexico continues at a steady clip, policy restrictions and economic restructuring notwithstanding.

It is this constant replenishment of the first generation, moving in alongside more established cohorts, that may make immigrant incorporation more difficult to achieve, and more difficult to see even when achieved, than was the case in the past. On balance, the work in this volume suggests that such incorporation is taking place. However, it comes with a distinct character. Neither assimilation into a non-Latino mainstream nor the strict reproduction of Latino culture and institutions on a U.S. landscape, Mexican incorporation into the United States is instead producing a complex web of social, economic, cultural, and policy relations.

The sheer size and complexity of the Latino population in the United States invites much speculation about these changes. With fully 40 percent of the Latino population in the United States today having been born abroad, and with nearly one out of ten U.S. residents being of Latino origin, even a total moratorium on immigration could not forestall a national debate on the implications of the Latino presence. For instance, the debate on the "declining quality" of immigrants, now over a decade old, continues to fuel concern that the next generation of Latino children will fall farther behind their parents, and behind their non-Latino counterparts, than has been the case in recent U.S. immigration history (Borjas 1996). Likewise, dedicated research comparing children of immigrants with U.S.-born children suggests that the risk of downward assimilation is as significant as the opportunities for upward assimilation, depending on the complexities of race, national origin, and population concentration (Portes 1996). Thus, the twenty-first century research agenda on immigration must incorporate time directly into predictive models of immigrant outcomes, through longitudinal data collection efforts and more sophisticated efforts to harness time trends from repeated cross-sectional data (Myers and Lee 1996).

U.S. immigration from Mexico, in particular, defies most attempts at simplified research sound bites or simplistic policy control. Neither an unqualified boon to the United States nor the root of all social ills, it gives little quarter to those seeking easy answers or foolproof predictions. But its complexity is no excuse for abandoning it as a central concern of social science and public policy. No policy, however restrictive, whether implemented domestically, abroad, or as part of an international compact, can stop the sheer demographic momentum by which the United States and Mexico are already transforming the North American social and demographic landscape. Under these circumstances, the scholarly and policy tasks of the next century will be to meet the complexity of this transformation head-on, in the hope that more complete answers might guide more enlightened policymaking and minimize the risks of surprise, overstatement, and overreaction so prevalent in the immigration history of the region.

ACKNOWLEDGMENTS

The support of the Center for the Study of Western Hemispheric Trade, the Ford Foundation, the Hewlett Foundation, and the Mellon Foundation is gratefully acknowledged. Thanks are expressed to Jennifer Glick, Maureen Meko, and Jennifer Van Hook for their assistance in this project.

REFERENCES

Baker, Susan González. 1996. Demographic trends in the Chicana/o population: Policy implications for the twenty-first century. In *Chicanas/Chicanos at the Crossroads: Social, Economic and Political Change*, ed. I. Ortiz and D. Maciel, 5–24. Tucson: University of Arizona Press.

Baker, Susan González. 1997. "The Amnesty Aftermath: Current Policy Issues Stemming from the Legalization Programs of the 1986 Immigration Reform and Control Act." *International Migration Review* 31(1): 5–27.

Bean, Frank D., and Robert G. Cushing. 1995. "The Relationship between the Mexican Economic Crisis and Illegal Migration to the United States." *Trade Insights* 5 (August): 1–4.

Bean, Frank D., and Michael Fix. 1992. The significance of recent immigration policy reforms in the United States. In *Nations of Immigrants: Australia and the United States in a Changing World*, ed. G. P. Freeman and J. Jupp, 41–55. New York and Sydney: Oxford University Press.

Bean, Frank D., and Marta Tienda. 1987. *The Hispanic Population of the United States*. New York: Russell Sage Foundation.

Bean, Frank D., et al. 1990. Post-IRCA changes in the volume and composition of undocumented migration to the United States: An assessment based on apprehensions data. In *Undocumented Migration to the United States: IRCA and the Experience of the 1980s*, ed. J. S. Passel, F. D. Bean, and B. Edmonston, 111–158. Washington: The Urban Institute Press.

Bean, Frank D., Roland Chanove, Robert G. Cushing, Rodolfo O. de la Garza, Gary Freeman, Charles Haynes, and David Spener. 1994. *Illegal Mexican Migration and the United States/Mexico Border: The Effects of Operation Hold-the-Line on El Paso and Juarez*. Washington: U.S. Commission on Immigration Reform.

Bean, Frank D., Rodolfo Corona, Rodolfo Tuiran, and Karen Woodrow-Lafield. 1997a. *Mexico/U.S. Migration Patterns: The Magnitude of Stocks and Flows*. Washington: U.S. Commission on Immigration Reform.

Bean, Frank D., Rodolfo O. de la Garza, Bryan R. Roberts, and Sidney Weintraub, eds. 1997b. *At the Crossroads: Mexico and U.S. Immigration Policy*. Lanham, Md.: Rowman and Littlefield.

Bean, Frank D., George Vernez, and Charles B. Keely. 1989. *Opening and Closing the Doors: Evaluating Immigration Reform and Control*. Washington: The Urban Institute Press.

Beck, Roy Howard. 1996. *The Case Against Immigration: The Moral, Economic, Social, and Environmental Reasons for Reducing U.S. Immigration Back to Traditional Levels*. New York: W. W. Norton Press.

Borjas, George. 1996. "The New Economics of Immigration." *Atlantic Monthly*, 278 (November): 73–80.

Brimelow, Peter. 1995. *Alien Nation: Common Sense About America's Immigration Disaster*. New York: Random House.

Campbell, Paul R. 1994. *Population Projections for States, by Age, Sex, Race, and Hispanic Origin: 1993–2020*. Washington: U.S. Bureau of the Census, 25–1111.

Castañeda, Jorge G. 1995. *The Mexican Shock: Its Meaning for the United States*. New York: The New Press.

Cornelius, Wayne A. 1989. The U.S. demand for Mexican labor. In *Mexican Migration to the United States: Origins, Consequences, and Policy Options*, ed. W. A. Cornelius and J. A. Bustamante, 25–48. La Jolla, Calif.: University of California-San Diego, Bilateral Commission on the Future of United States-Mexican Relations, Center for U.S.-Mexican Studies.

Edmonston, Barry, and Jeffrey Passel, eds. 1994. *Immigration and Ethnicity: The Integration of America's Newest Arrivals*. Washington: The Urban Institute Press.

Fernandez Kelly, Patricia. 1983. *For We Are Sold, I and My People: Women and Industry on Mexico's Frontier*. New York: State University of New York.

Freeman, Gary P., and Frank D. Bean. 1997. Mexico and U.S. worldwide immigration policy. In *At the Crossroads: Mexico and U.S. Immigration Policy*, ed. F. D. Bean, R. O. de la Garza, B. R. Roberts, and S. Weintraub. Lanham, Md.: Rowman and Littlefield.

Freeman, Gary P., Rodolfo O. de la Garza, Luis F. B. Plascencia, Susan González Baker, and Manuel Orozco. 1996. "The Texas Citizenship Initiative Program: A Preliminary Discussion." Report to the Office of Immigration and Refugee Affairs. 12 December.

Fuentes, Carlos. 1996. *A New Time for Mexico*. New York: Farrar, Straus and Giroux.

Grebler, Leo. 1966. Mexican immigration to the United States: The record and its implications. Mexican American Study Project, University of California, Los Angeles.

Hagan, Jacqueline. 1994. *Deciding to be Legal*. Philadelphia: Temple University Press.

Hagan, J. M., and S. G. Baker. 1993. "Implementing the U.S. Legalization Program: The Influence of Immigrant Communities and Local Agencies on Immigration Policy Reform." *International Migration Review* 27(3): 513–536.

Hondagneu-Sotelo, Pierrette. 1994. *Gendered Transitions: Mexican Experiences of Immigration*. Berkeley: University of California Press.

Levy, F., and R. J. Murnane. 1992. "U.S. Earnings Levels and Earnings Inequality: A Review of Recent Trends and Proposed Explanations." *Journal of Economic Literature* (September): 1333–1381.

Lustig, Nora. 1992. *Mexico: The Remaking of an Economy*. Washington: The Brookings Institution.

Martin, Philip L. 1986. Illegal immigration and the colonization of the American labor market. CIS Paper No. 1. Washington, D.C.: Center for Immigration Studies.

Massey, Douglas S., and Kristin Espinoza. 1997. "What's Driving Mexico-U.S. Migration? A Theoretical, Empirical, and Policy Analysis." *American Journal of Sociology* 102(4): 939–999.

Myers, Dowell, and Seong Woo Lee. 1996. "Immigration Cohorts and Residential Overcrowding in Southern California." *Demography* 33 (February): 51–65.

Newby, Alison. 1996. "A Shift-Share Analysis of U.S. Metropolitan Areas Containing Substantial Mexican-Origin Populations." *Texas Population Papers*. Austin: The University of Texas at Austin, Population Research Center.

Oppenheimer, Andres. 1995. *Bordering on Chaos: Guerillas, Stockbrokers, Politicians, and Mexico's Road to Prosperity*. Boston: Little, Brown and Company.

Portes, Alejandro, and Robert L. Bach. 1985. *Latin Journey: Cuban and Mexican Immigrants to the United States*. Berkeley: University of California Press.

Portes, Alejandro, ed. 1996. *The New Second Generation*. New York: Russell Sage Foundation.

Reimers, David M. 1983. "An Unintended Reform: The 1965 Immigration Act and Third World Migration to the United States." *Journal of American Ethnic History* (Fall): 9–28.

Reimers, David M. 1992. *Still the Golden Door: The Third World Comes to America*, 2nd ed. New York: Columbia University Press.

Szekely, Gabriel, and Rodolfo O. de la Garza. 1997. Policy, politics and emigration: Reexamining the Mexican experience. In *At the Crossroads: Mexico and U.S. Immigration Policy*, ed. F. D. Bean, R. O. de la Garza, B. R. Roberts, and S. Weintraub. Lanham, Md.: Rowman and Littlefield.

Teitelbaum, Michael, and Myron Weiner, eds. 1995. *World Migration and U.S. Policy*. New York: Norton Press.

U.S. Department of Justice. 1992. *Immigration Reform and Control Act: Report on the Legalized Population*. Washington: Government Printing Office.

U.S. Immigration and Naturalization Service (INS). 1995. *Statistical Yearbook of the U.S. Immigration and Naturalization Service, 1994*. Washington: Government Printing Office.

U.S. Immigration and Naturalization Service (INS). 1997. *Statistical Yearbook of the U.S. Immigration and Naturalization Service, 1996*. Washington: Government Printing Office.

Vernez, George, and David Ronfeldt. 1991. "The Current Situation of Mexican Immigration." *Science* 251 (March): 1189–1193.

Waldinger, Roger, and Mehdi Bozorgmehr. 1996. *Ethnic Los Angeles*. New York: Russell Sage Foundation.

Waldinger, Roger. 1997. "Black/Immigrant Competition Re-assessed: New Evidence from Los Angeles." *Sociology Perspectives* (40)3: 365–386.

Warren, Robert, and Jeffrey S. Passel. 1987. "A Count of the Uncountable: Estimates of Undocumented Aliens Counted in the 1980 United States Census." *Demography* 24: 375–394.

Warren, Robert. 1990. "Annual estimates of nonimmigrant overstays in the United States 1985–1988." In *Undocumented Migration to the United States: IRCA and the Experience of the 1980s*, ed. F. Bean, B. Edmonston, and J. Passel, 77–101. Washington: Urban Institute Press.

Warren, Robert. 1992. *Estimates of the Unauthorized Immigrant Population Residing in the United States, by Country of Origin and State of Residence, October 1992.* Washington: Immigration and Naturalization Service, Statistics Division.

Zolberg, Aristide. 1992. "Response to Crisis: Refugee Policy in the United States and Canada." In *Immigration, Language, and Ethnicity: Canada and the United States*, ed. B. R. Chiswick, 55–109. Washington, D.C.: AEI Press.

Commentary

Mary C. Waters, Harvard University

The chapter by Susan González Baker and colleagues raises a number of important questions. How are Mexicans different from other immigrants, both in their numbers and in the existence of a shared border? What are the factors determining immigration from Mexico to the United States? What are the long-term consequences of current immigration laws and policies? Are we witnessing a new pattern of settlement, or a new kind of transborder, transnational relationship? The chapter takes a demographic and historical perspective on Mexican immigration that illuminates several important, unique characteristics of Mexican immigration.

These authors stress a number of important themes about Mexican immigrants. First, they document the increasing numbers of Mexican immigrants and their descendants in the United States, and the growing share that Mexicans constitute of all immigrants in the United States. While Mexicans represented 15 percent of the foreign-born population in 1980, they represented 28.4 percent in the mid-1990s. The authors also pay attention to the wide variety of groups of Mexicans in the United States. Mexicans are a very heterogeneous group in terms of birthplace, generation, legal status, and citizenship status.

All too often migration from Mexico to the United States is understood in terms of changes in U.S. laws, the U.S. economy, and American society. This chapter provides a needed corrective to that perspective, stressing the role of economic, political, and social developments in Mexico in determining flows of immigration. The authors also stress the ongoing nature of Mexican immigration. In the early twentieth century it was possible to speak of waves of immigration coming from Mexico, but as we approach the end of the twentieth century, immigration has been very constant.

Finally, the authors examine the patterns of naturalization among the Mexican-origin population. They argue that the shift toward naturalization is leading to a border population that is more transnational in its orientation and behaviors. Citizenship frees people to actually live more of their lives in Mexico because as citizens they can easily move back and forth across the border. The question of settlement patterns and the development of a transnational space at the border is identified by the authors as an important topic for further research.

This rich chapter suggests two important themes for students of immigration and for policymakers to think about: the unintended consequences of laws pertaining to immigrants, and the challenges of understanding immigration to the United States that is characterized by constant replenishment of immigrants rather than distinct waves of high and low periods of immigration. Each of these will be examined in turn.

Immigration laws have often produced consequences that are the opposite of those the lawmakers intended. The most glaring historical example is the 1965 immigration act, which lawmakers at the time thought would increase European immigration. Most could not foresee the ways in which the provisions of the law favored Asian and Latin American immigrants. U.S. policy on immigration now increasingly includes laws other than immigration laws. As González Baker and colleagues point out, U.S. policy on immigration now includes schools, hospitals, the welfare office, and the voting booth. The recent welfare reform bill was passed under the mistaken idea that immigrants come to the United States for welfare benefits. However, when one controls for refugee status, legal immigrants to the United States are actually less likely to use welfare than natives with the same characteristics. Conservative policymakers who restrict benefits for legal immigrants in an effort to reduce immigration create incentives for immigrants to naturalize, which has the unintended consequence of allowing them to move with greater ease back and forth to Mexico, perhaps even slowing assimilation and incorporation into American life. Radical proposals to deny citizenship and schooling to the children of illegal immigrants could also have unintended negative effects on the target population, creating for the first time a population of second-class noncitizens who continue to live in the United States but have no reason to feel any civic loyalty and few skills with which to participate in a productive way in the economy.

The distinction the authors make between effects on settlement patterns of citizenship and long-term patterns of incorporation highlights the issue of understanding the long-term patterns of Mexican assimilation in conditions of constant immigration. Are the heightened patterns of transnationalism at the border short-term responses to the freedom to move back and forth that citizenship brings or a long-term phenomena that might also characterize the second generation? In comparing patterns of incorporation of earlier waves of immigrants to the United States and the post-1965 immigrants, long-term demographic trends make a key difference. The hiatus in immigration to the United States between the immigration restriction laws and the depression in the 1920s and 1930s and the economic growth and social mobility that characterized the American economy between World War II and the 1970s led to sustained economic assimilation for the vast majority of European immigrants and their children. The demographic hiatus in immigration laid bare assimilation, as each generation was less ethnic and more socially mobile. Without new European immigrants arriving, the ethnic groups themselves aged, losing language fluency and residential and occupational concentration.

Mexican immigrants, on the other hand, are an example of an immigrant group with constant replenishment. As a result the assimilation of Mexican immigrants and their descendants that has occurred has not been as visible as the European case. Assimilation is masked by new arrivals who replenish the culture and distinctiveness of Mexicans as a group in American society. This has enormous implications for public opinion and policymakers and how they think about issues of immigration.

Take language as an example. Many Americans are worried that Spanish-speaking immigrants are refusing to learn English. The English Only movement has succeeded in passing laws in many states declaring English as the official language of the state. Yet very few second- or third-generation Americans have trouble speaking English fluently. Indeed, the vast majority cannot speak Spanish. Descendants of recent immigrants, including Spanish-speaking people, are speaking English. Yet with the constant supply of new immigrants it appears to many Americans as if there were a problem with language assimilation.

Population projections of the Latino population also fail to take into account assimilation that is occurring behind the scenes. When the Census Bureau project that one in ten Americans will be Latino by a certain date, what does that mean? Census Bureau projections currently do not take into account intermarriage. Yet Latinos, especially in later generations, have high intermarriage rates with non-Latino whites as well as other ethnic groups. Many descendants of Mexican immigrants who intermarried with other groups may no longer identify themselves solely or even partly as Mexican. Yet future projections assume that all people who are currently identified as Mexican will have descendants who will forever identify that way. If population projections had been done in the early twentieth century of the various European-origin groups who were so troubling to the nativist anti-immigrant groups of the time, they would have missed the great deal of intermarriage and identity changes that have occurred in this population.

A demographic concentration of Mexicans in the United States can indeed have long-term effects—keeping alive a vibrant ethnic community, sustaining Spanish language use, providing ethnic marriage partners. Yet a demographic preponderance of this group can also mask real social change. Later generations who speak English, intermarry with non-Mexicans, and live in nonresidentially concentrated communities are also part of the story of Mexican immigration to the United States. Data presented here by González Baker et al. (see also Myers, this volume) suggest that there is a great deal of change taking place, but that it may be behind the scenes. Recognition of the existence of this behind the scenes assimilation would go a long way toward calming the fears of those concerned with the impact of immigration on American society and culture.

Overall, the Mexican experience is critical in representing change over the long-term among immigrants. Yet the Census Bureau has not asked a question about the birthplace of parents since 1970, making it very difficult to contrast the experiences of the first, second, and later generations. The longitudinal data that are very important in looking at long-term incorporation of immigrants and their children are scarce but increasingly very important. Immigration to the United States from a wide variety of countries shows no sign of an abrupt cutoff anytime soon. Thus all immigration to the United States will reflect conditions of constant replenishment. A clear understanding of the Mexican experience, such as González Baker et al. provide here, is crucial to understanding wider issues of immigration to the United States in general.

PART III

Economic Themes

Photo by Anna LeVine

Wayne A. Cornelius was born and raised in a small town in western Pennsylvania. His work on international migration began with an interest in internal migration, specifically, the political consequences of rural-to-urban migration in Mexico and other Latin American countries. Having studied the political attitudes and behavior of low-income migrants in Mexico City for his dissertation, he chose as his first postdoctoral research project a study of the determinants of emigration from nine rural communities in Los Altos de Jalisco, which according to census data had one of the highest rates of out-migration among Mexican regions during the 1960s.

Once he began his fieldwork, Cornelius found that more than half of the emigrants from his research typically went to the United States rather than cities within Mexico. This entirely serendipitous discovery led him to focus on the international component of migration from rural Mexico. For more than 22 years, he has been tracking shifts in U.S.-bound migration and return migration patterns in one community in Jalisco, and since 1990 he has also done fieldwork on international migration to Japan and Spain as well as the United States. His most recent books on the subject are *Controlling Immigration: A Global Perspective* (Stanford University Press, 1995), edited with Philip Martin and James Hollifield, and *The Transformation of Rural Mexico* (Center for U.S.-Mexican Studies, UCSD, 1998), edited with David Myhre.

Wayne Cornelius is the Gildred Professor of Political Science and U.S.-Mexican Relations at the University of California-San Diego, and founding Director of UCSD's Center for U.S.-Mexican Studies. He was formerly on the faculty of the Massachusetts Institute of Technology. His Ph.D. in political science is from Stanford University.

4

The Structural Embeddedness of Demand for Mexican Immigrant Labor: New Evidence from California

Wayne A. Cornelius
University of California, San Diego

A central paradox posed by the most recent wave of Mexican migration to the United States is that poorly educated, low-skilled Mexican immigrants are being incorporated readily into a high-tech, knowledge-intensive, postindustrial economy that ostensibly has no real need for this type of labor. The orthodox, neo-classical labor economics paradigm commonly used to rationalize more restrictive immigration policies stresses that the economic benefits resulting from an ample supply of predominantly unskilled Mexican and other foreign workers are minimal and constantly diminishing (see, for example, Borjas 1994, 1996; Briggs 1996). It follows that purging these superfluous workers from U.S. labor markets would involve, at most, disruptions that are very short term and entirely manageable through rationalization of production, greater investment in labor-saving technologies, more aggressive recruitment of native-born workers, and other means. It is further assumed that native workers—ethnic and racial minorities, women, the elderly, the disabled—can be substituted almost infinitely for low-skilled immigrants now in the labor force, if both employers and native-born residents can be suitably "incentivized" by government. In sum, unwanted immigrants—particularly the undocumented—can be dislodged from the workplace, and penetration of industries and job categories in which immigrants are not yet dominant can be reversed or prevented. Failure to do so is simply a reflection of employer greed and lack of political will.

This line of argument rests on a series of largely untested assumptions about the character and determinants of the demand for immigrant labor in the United States. Why do employers use this labor source? (We cannot simply assume, "Because it's cheaper.") How did they come to rely on it—through what processes or mechanisms? Why do many employers actually prefer to hire immigrants even if native-born workers are theoretically available to be recruited? What alternatives to the use of foreign labor do employers perceive, and if they have pursued any of these options, how well have they worked?

If the demand for immigrant labor has become a structural feature of the receiving economy, what are the empirical indicators of such structural embeddedness? Does demand expand or contract significantly with the business cycle, or does it remain constant or continue to grow at a steady pace, regardless of macroeconomic fluctuations? Do major changes in the regulatory environment—in public policies, laws, and law enforcement strategies—affect the propensity of employers to rely on immigrant workers?

Finally, how do changes in law and public policy affect the supply of immigrant labor that is available to employers? For example, has the supply of undocumented immigrant workers in California been affected in any way by the passage of restrictive measures like the state's Proposition 187 (which seeks to deny public education, health care, and other basic human services to undocumented immigrants and their children) or by tighter border controls? Or is the employment of immigrant labor so highly institutionalized that it is no longer sensitive to changes in the legal and public policy environment that are intended to deter new immigration or discourage permanent settlement by immigrants already here?

RESEARCH DESIGN AND METHODOLOGY

This paper is based primarily on data from a comparative study of how immigrant labor is being utilized in the economies of San Diego County, California, and the city of Hamamatsu, Japan. Fieldwork in both research sites was conducted simultaneously during the first half of 1996. In San Diego, a randomly selected sample of 112 employers were interviewed, together with 501 immigrant workers who were employees of the same firms in which employers were interviewed and 116 irregularly employed "street-corner workers"—migrant workers who seek day labor in construction and landscaping by standing along public thoroughfares in various parts of San Diego County.

The universe for our survey of San Diego employers consists of firms that were known, through telephone screening interviews, to be employing immigrant workers. All sectors of the regional economy in which immigrants constitute a significant portion of the labor force (except private household service) are represented in the study. Interviews with employers and immigrant workers were distributed evenly across ten sectors: agriculture and horticulture, high-tech manufacturing, low-tech manufacturing (except clothing), apparel, food processing, construction, hotels and motels, restaurants, landscape and building maintenance, and miscellaneous services (dry cleaners, car washes, laundries, and convalescent homes). These industries account for 34.4 percent of nongovernmental employment in San Diego County. Four out of five of the sample firms were chosen at random from complete lists of businesses in the ten sectors covered by the study, compiled by a market research firm. The remainder consisted of firms that had been studied in two previous surveys of immigrant-using businesses in California, conducted by the author in 1983–1984 and 1987–1988 (see Cornelius 1989). The sample firms were distributed geographically throughout San Diego County, including rural areas.

All interviews were conducted in person, using standardized questionnaires developed for each of the three groups of interviewees (employers, their immigrant employees, and street-corner workers). In each firm, the person having primary responsibility for hiring decisions was interviewed (in most cases, this proved to be the firm owner). Five or six randomly chosen immigrant employees per firm were interviewed. Interviews with employers averaged about one hour in duration; interviews with immigrant workers lasted about 45 minutes. Over half of the workers interviewed were undocumented (77 percent among the street-corner workers). More than 90 percent of the workers whom we classified as undocumented admitted to our interviewers that they had entered the United States on their most recent trip without papers or with fraudulent documents; the remainder reported that they entered on short-term tourist or student visas or local border crossing cards, none of which authorize employment in the United States. Seventy-nine percent of the workers were Mexican nationals, although a dozen other nationalities are also represented in the sample.

In most respects, San Diego County, with a population of about 2.9 million, is representative of the large metropolitan areas that now absorb the bulk of both legal and illegal Mexican migrants to the United States. Its economy differs from that of other major immigrant-receiving cities like Los Angeles, Chicago, Houston, and New York in only one key way: the San Diego region has a major, still-expanding agricultural and horticultural industry, which in 1996 produced $1.1 billion in crops and flowers. Agriculture and horticulture in San Diego are highly labor intensive, and this sector is among the heaviest users of Mexican migrant labor (mostly originating in the impoverished southeastern state of Oaxaca). Like the other major destinations for long-distance Mexican migrants to the United States, San Diego has lost much of its traditional manufacturing base since the 1980s, but growth in the service, retail, and construction sectors has more than offset the loss of manufacturing employment, and high-tech manufacturing is robust.

Until the early 1980s San Diego served primarily as a corridor for Mexican migrants headed to Los Angeles and other cities to the north and east; during the last 15 years, however, San Diego County has become an important destination for Mexicans seeking U.S. employment. Much tighter border enforcement by the U.S. Immigration and Naturalization Service in the San Diego sector since October 1994 has further reduced San Diego's role as a mere way station for Mexican migrants in transit (see the discussion of public policy changes, below). San Diego's immigrant population is dominated to a greater extent than in other major immigrant-receiving cities by a single nationality: Mexican. As a consequence, Mexican immigrants in San Diego usually do not find themselves in competition for the same kinds of jobs with immigrants from the Caribbean (as, for example, Mexicans versus Dominicans in New York City), or from Central America and the Asia-Pacific region (as in Los Angeles).

We found high levels of reliance on immigrant labor throughout the San Diego economy. While the percentage of immigrant workers varies considerably by sector, from 50 percent in manufacturing to 92 percent in agriculture and food processing (see Figure 4.1), on average, two-thirds (66.7 percent) of the production workers in our sample firms were foreign born, according to the employers interviewed. One out of five firms in the sample reported that more than 90 percent of its local workforce consists of immigrants, and one out of ten admitted that they have a 100 percent foreign-born labor force, that is, they "never" hire U.S.-born people, at least as production workers. This stratum of firms is not just immigrant dependent; it is totally reliant on this labor source.

CHARACTERISTICS OF IMMIGRANT-DEPENDENT FIRMS

What types of firms use immigrant labor? In San Diego, the vast majority of them are small businesses: The median total number of employees in our sample of firms is 46. But many of these firms do not fit the stereotype of the small, financially precarious, high-turnover enterprise that hyperexploits immigrant workers.

The vast majority of our sample firms do not seem financially endangered. In fact, 74 percent of them described their current operations as somewhat or very profitable. Looking ahead, 92 percent of the firms were somewhat or very optimistic about their profitability and sales during the next three years.

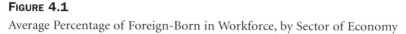

FIGURE 4.1

Average Percentage of Foreign-Born in Workforce, by Sector of Economy

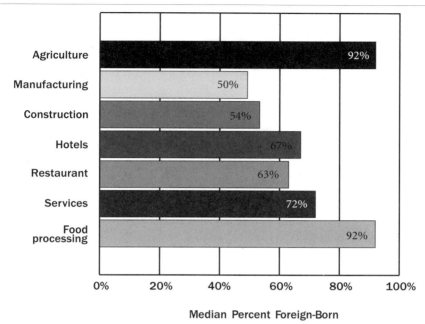

Median Percent Foreign-Born

Source: Sample survey of 112 San Diego County firms that use immigrant labor, conducted by the Center for U.S.-
Mexican Studies, University of California-San Diego, 1996.

Another indicator of financial viability is the fact that nearly half (48 percent) of these firms are involved to some extent in exporting, and more than one out of ten has at least one production site in a foreign country (usually Mexico).

The firms in our sample are not rock-bottom, sub-minimum-wage employers. The mean hourly wage paid to entry-level production workers in 1996 was $5.62. Only agricultural enterprises and restaurants were paying their entry-level workers close to the legal minimum wage (see Figure 4.2). Average wages were not being kept down by employer-induced turnover aimed at preventing workers from accumulating seniority and demanding higher pay: Average annual turnover among production workers in the sample firms was only 10 percent, and most employers claimed that they wanted as stable a workforce as possible.

Nor were these firms discriminating significantly on the basis of immigration status: The difference in average hourly wages between legal and illegal immigrant workers in our employee sample was small ($6.50 per hour for legals; $6.05 for the undocumented), and overall monthly earnings including overtime pay were also similar (averaging $1,167 for legals; $1,066 for illegals).

FIGURE 4.2

Average Hourly Wages Paid to Entry-Level Production Workers, by Sector of Economy

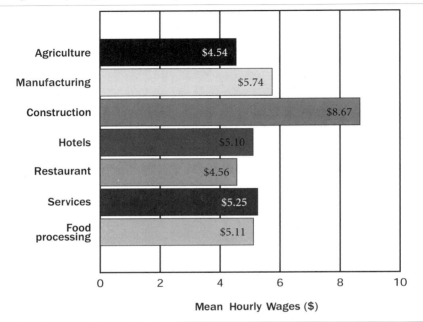

Mean Hourly Wages ($)

Source: Sample survey of 112 San Diego County firms that use immigrant labor, conducted by the Center for U.S.-Mexican Studies, University of California-San Diego, 1996.

Nearly all of the wage gap can be attributed to the legal immigrants' greater job seniority, longer residence in the United States, and ability to do jobs requiring English—not to legal status per se.

   The job skill requirements of the immigrant-using firms in our sample are of particular interest. While many of these firms use highly advanced technologies, they nevertheless require substantial numbers of low-skilled workers. On average, our San Diego employers classified 83 percent of their production workforce as unskilled or low skilled. This is a key finding, in view of the conventional wisdom that the new information-based technologies require numerous highly skilled, college-trained workers but very few of the less skilled. The reality is exemplified by one of our sample firms that grows gourmet-quality mushrooms, using the latest hydroponic techniques developed in Japan. The company nevertheless relies on Mexican immigrants as production workers, to harvest and package the product. This high-tech agricultural employer is just as dependent on immigrant labor as the average tomato grower in San Diego County, who typically uses the most traditional methods of production.

The employers in our sample reported that newly hired, entry-level production workers in their firms typically need only about eight days of training to do their jobs, which was corroborated by the immigrant employees whom we interviewed. And nearly half (46 percent) of the employers told us that there were no tasks in their business that they could not assign to immigrant workers. Among those who said that there were some tasks that they could not give to immigrants, 90 percent characterized these as jobs that required English speaking or comprehension ability, or tasks requiring direct contact with English-speaking customers (so-called front-of-the-house jobs).

All this suggests that there are many types of businesses that continue to serve as easy points of entry into the U.S. labor market for newly arriving immigrants, irrespective of skill level: not just farms and restaurants, but even high-tech manufacturing operations. In every sector of the economy, San Diego firms that hire immigrant workers use them in nearly every type of production job, and often in supervisory jobs as well. The proportion of low-skilled jobs in immigrant-using firms has actually risen during the past 13 years. In 1983, when we first surveyed such firms in San Diego, 58 percent of them reported that more than three-quarters of their workforce was unskilled; in our 1996 survey of the same firms, 68 percent said that more than three-quarters of their workers were unskilled.

The Highly Immigrant-Dependent Firm: An Empirical Profile

To identify the principal defining characteristics of immigrant-dependent businesses, we divided our 1996 sample of immigrant-using firms in San Diego into two groups: those that scored above and below the median on a summative index of immigrant dependence, constructed from 18 items in our employer survey. These included questions about the proportion of foreign-born persons in the workforce, the nationality of persons who apply for production jobs in the firm, English language requirements, employer perceptions of foreign-born as compared with native-born workers, whether immigrant employees are called on to work night shifts and overtime, the anticipated role of immigrants in meeting future labor requirements, and the perceived effectiveness of alternatives to employing immigrant workers. Based on their ranking on this overall index of immigrant dependence, the most immigrant-dependent firms in our sample differ from the less dependent firms in the following respects:[1]

- They are more likely to be very small businesses (the median number of total employees is 30, versus 50 in less immigrant-dependent firms;

median gross sales in 1996 were only half as large as those of less immigrant-dependent firms).

- They are more likely to be owned by immigrants (especially Mexican nationals) and by Mexican Americans.
- They are somewhat less profitable businesses (but only 36 percent are just breaking even or losing money).
- They rely more heavily on illegal immigrant workers (65 percent of their employees are undocumented, versus 50 percent in the less immigrant-dependent firms).
- Their immigrant workers are more likely to be purely "economic migrants" (motivated to come to the United States by job availability, higher wages, or economic crisis in their home country), as contrasted with migrants who came to the United States because of the presence of relatives or for other noneconomic reasons.
- Their immigrant workers are more likely to have worked in agriculture immediately before coming to the United States.
- Their immigrant workers are more likely to be first-timers or persons with a limited history of U.S.-bound migration and shorter total residence time in the United States.
- Their immigrant workers have lower levels of educational attainment (average of 8.0 years of schooling, versus 9.6 years among workers in less immigrant-dependent firms).
- They are more likely to have no specific training requirements for entry-level production jobs, and less likely to provide job training to the workers they hire.
- They are more likely to recruit workers through social networks, that is, referrals by current immigrant employees or supervisors (80 percent of their production workforce in 1996 had been hired in this way, versus 64 percent in the less immigrant-dependent firms).
- They are much less likely to require workers to have English language proficiency (27 percent, versus 64 percent in less immigrant-dependent firms).
- They are more likely to have a sharp division of labor between native-born and foreign-born employees (i.e., U.S.-born workers, if present, rarely do the kinds of jobs performed by immigrants in these firms).
- They pay lower wages (averaging $5.04 per hour for entry-level production workers, versus $6.02 per hour in less immigrant-dependent firms).
- They believe it would be necessary to raise entry-level wages by an average of $3.10 per hour (a 62 percent increase over the current level) in order to attract U.S.-born job applicants; less immigrant-dependent firms believe

they would need to raise hourly wages by $2.08 (a 35 percent increase).

- They are much less likely to provide employer-paid health insurance and pension plans to production workers (but there is no difference in legally mandated employee benefits, paid vacations, and sick leave).
- During the 1990s recession, they were more likely to reduce wages, overtime, and employee benefits to adjust for lost business, but not to reduce their workforce through layoffs.
- They have lower turnover among production workers (13 percent annually) than less immigrant-dependent firms (17 percent).
- U.S.-born workers are much less well represented in their job applicant pools (in 71 percent of highly immigrant-dependent firms, native-born workers never apply for the kinds of jobs held by immigrants, versus 35 percent of less immigrant-dependent firms).
- They expect to have an even more immigrant-dominated workforce in the future, with foreign-born workers accounting for 80 percent of new hires (versus 50 percent in less immigrant-dependent firms).

To assess the relative importance of these factors in explaining dependence on immigrant labor, we constructed a multivariate model that regresses ten firm characteristics on the percentage of foreign-born persons in the firm's production workforce (the dependent variable) while controlling for sector of the economy. As summarized in Table 4.1, this model explains nearly 73 percent of the variance in immigrant dependence among our San Diego sample firms. The strongest predictors of immigrant dependence are firm age (established more recently), entry-level wages (lower), whether U.S.-born persons sometimes apply for the kinds of jobs now held by immigrants in the firm (no), whether the company owner is an immigrant or U.S.-born Latino (yes), and whether the firm reduced its labor force during the 1990s recession (no). The very large and highly significant negative coefficient for the variable concerning native-born applicants for the types of jobs done by immigrants is of particular interest. As discussed below, native-born workers are virtually absent from the applicant pools of most of our sample firms, at least for entry-level production jobs. This is strong evidence supporting the hypothesis that the demand for immigrant labor has become structurally embedded in the San Diego economy. The wage variable is also highly significant but has a rather small coefficient, indicating that cheapness is not the primary reason for hiring foreign workers, or at least that the wage differential is small.

These findings suggest that the stratum of most-immigrant-dependent businesses consists of those that are "immigrant enclave" or "Mexican co-ethnic"[2]

TABLE 4.1

Regression of Firm Characteristics on Percentage of Foreign-Born Persons in Workforce

Independent Variable	Coefficient	Standard error	Significance
Years company has been operating	-.375	0.119	0.003[a]
Wages for entry-level workers	-1.581	0.726	0.033[a]
Average age of workers (years)	0.288	0.394	0.467
Provides health insurance for production workers	-3.290	3.857	0.397
Skilled workers = more than 25% of labor force	-7.250	4.463	0.110
Company owner is immigrant or U.S.-born Latino	8.508	3.979	0.037[a]
Native-born persons sometimes apply for same jobs held by immigrants	-23.401	3.966	0.000[a]
Has some difficulty recruiting U.S.-born workers with or without recession	4.350	3.603	0.232
Immigrants are more hard-working than native-born (dummy)	3.866	3.470	0.270
Reduced overall labor force during last recession	-8.317	3.346	0.016[a]
Agricultural-horticultural sector (dummy)	22.488	7.750	0.005[a]
Construction sector (dummy)	16.168	8.032	0.049
Hotel sector (dummy)	39.874	10.968	0.001[a]
Food sector (dummy)	21.732	7.776	0.007[a]
Service sector (dummy)	14.811	7.078	0.041[a]
Manufacturing sector (dummy)	5.992	6.618	0.369
Constant	67.874	14.618	0.000[a]

Note: Coefficients are unstandardized, ordinary least-square regression coefficients. The intercept in the model represents the restaurant sector, which is the sector with the proportion of foreign-born workers that is closest to the sample mean.

[a] $p<.05$ in a two-tailed significance test.

R square: .852

Adjusted R square: .726

Standard error of estimate: 13.678

Source: Sample survey of 112 San Diego County firms that use immigrant labor, conducted by the Center for U.S.-Mexican Studies, University of California-San Diego, 1996.

firms that recruit almost exclusively through social networks, tapping the lowest stratum of the Mexican immigrant population (impoverished, recently arrived, undocumented, economically motivated migrants with limited education and English proficiency). Despite offering less attractive wages and fringe benefits, they have more stable workforces (some possible explanations are offered below). They offer employment opportunities to the least skilled, least educated, least English-proficient members of the Mexican immigrant population. During recessionary periods, these firms may find it necessary to cut wages, overtime, and benefits, but they are unlikely to shed immigrant labor because they depend so heavily on this labor source and have no realistic alternatives to it. Thus, the most immigrant-dependent firms are the least responsive to the business cycle in terms of immigrant worker hiring and layoffs. They do not attract U.S.-born job applicants for production jobs, and they are pessimistic about their future ability to compete for native-born workers, given the numerous disincentives (unattractive wages, benefits, working conditions, etc.), which they can do little to change.

These results underline the crucial role played by immigrant labor in the creation, survival, and growth of a significant stratum of businesses in San Diego. These firms are, in many ways, the most extreme manifestation of a demand for immigrant labor that is structurally embedded.

CREATING STRUCTURAL EMBEDDEDNESS

The continuing need of even knowledge-intensive businesses for substantial numbers of relatively low-skilled production and maintenance workers helps to explain the pervasive demand for immigrant workers in large metropolitan areas like San Diego. But other factors are clearly at work, most important being (1) the nature of the jobs typically offered to entry-level workers in immigrant-using firms (not just low-paying, but involving boring, often dirty and even hazardous tasks, with no career ladder), (2) the proliferation of social networks that keep delivering eager new immigrant job-seekers to the employer's doorstep with little or no effort on his or her part, and (3) the way in which employers perceive and evaluate immigrant workers in comparison with potential native-born substitutes. Data from our surveys of San Diego employers and immigrant workers demonstrate the importance of all of these factors in creating a structurally embedded demand for foreign labor.

Making new hires through immigrants' kinship and friendship networks has become the most common labor recruitment mechanism for immigrant-using firms in the San Diego area. Seventy percent of the employers whom we interviewed reported that their most important way of recruiting production workers was through referrals from current employees. This coincides exactly with what the immigrant workers in our employee sample told us: Seventy percent had found their current job through a relative or friend employed at the same firm where they now work (only 16 percent had applied for their job directly, without benefit of social network contacts). The proportion of immigrant workers hired through network referrals ranged from 55 percent in the hotel and motel industry to 80 percent in restaurants, landscape and building maintenance, and low-tech manufacturing firms.

From the employer's perspective, immigrants' social networks provide an ideal mechanism for labor recruitment. No costly advertising is required; no employment agency fees need be paid. Job vacancies can be filled almost immediately; in most cases, immigrants already working in the firm know that a vacancy is about to occur even before the employer does. High-quality workers are virtually guaranteed, even without screening of job applicants, since the immigrant's social network vouches for his or her reliability, productivity, and good character. As Waldinger has also observed in Los Angeles and New York City, the existence of such a convenient, no-cost, highly reliable labor recruitment mechanism in itself serves to perpetuate and, over time, expand the immigrant presence in many firms, while reducing the representation of native-born residents in their applicant pools (Waldinger 1996c).

However, it is also clear from our interviews that many employers who use immigrant labor do so not just as a matter of convenience; employers develop a distinct preference for it—a preference that strongly influences the level of effort that they make to recruit outside of immigrant networks. Employers like the fact that immigrants are highly reliable and punctual. They appreciate the immigrants' flexibility—their willingness to work overtime, weekends, or night shifts if needed (the illegals in our immigrant worker sample were especially more likely than legal immigrants to be working the night shift). Employers also value the immigrants' strong work ethic: 54 percent of our San Diego employers told us that, in general, immigrants were more hard-working than native-born employees, which is up from 28 percent who expressed this belief in our 1983 survey of San Diego employers.

Immigrants and native-born workers tend to be channeled (or channel themselves) into quite distinct segments of the California labor market. Native-born workers seldom compete directly with immigrants for low-skilled production jobs in firms and industries that have come to be dominated by immigrant workers. If there is job competition, it occurs between recently arrived and long-settled immigrant residents. As shown in Figure 4.3, immigrants have all but replaced U.S.-born workers in nine of the most common types of low-paying jobs in California, statewide. The representation of immigrants in all of these job categories has increased dramatically during the last 16 years.

This phenomenon is very evident in San Diego, where nearly half (49 percent) of the employers whom we interviewed reported that U.S.-born persons never apply for the same types of jobs held in their firm by immigrants, or apply only rarely for these jobs. In just one-third of our sample firms do the immigrant and native-born job applicant pools overlap substantially. The segmentation of San Diego's labor markets into immigrant-dominated and native-worker-dominated sectors is partly a product of network-mediated labor recruitment, which effectively removes jobs filled through referrals by other immigrants from the open labor market. However, such segmentation also reflects the prevailing attitudes of native-born workers—especially the young—toward certain types of jobs and industries. Employers who get few, if any, native-born applicants may not be trying very hard to recruit them, but it is also true that native-born workers typically avoid jobs that have become stereotyped

FIGURE 4.3

Immigrant-Dominated Job Categories in California (Percentage of Jobs in Each Category Held by Foreign-Born Workers, Statewide)

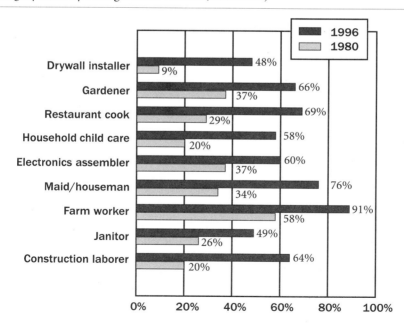

Source: U.S. Census Bureau.

as "immigrant jobs," particularly in firms where immigrants already comprise a high percentage of the total workforce. In those firms, the culture of the workplace, including the predominant use of Spanish among production workers and between workers and their immediate supervisors, constitutes an additional disincentive for native-born workers to seek jobs there (Waldinger 1997b).

A final factor that contributes to the demand for immigrant labor in San Diego and other major cities where Mexican migrants have clustered since the 1970s is the growth of immigrant entrepreneurship. Increasingly, Mexican immigrants—like other immigrant groups—are not just employees but owners of the businesses where they work. Among the firms in our 1996 San Diego sample, more than one-third were immigrant owned, with Mexico-born entrepreneurs being the most numerous.

A recent survey of 102 Mexican-owned businesses in Los Angeles (Guarnizo 1996) found that 81 percent of their employees were Mexican immigrants and another 17 percent were Latino immigrants of other nationalities; only 2 percent of the workers were non-Latino immigrants and U.S. natives. This closely resembles the ethnic composition of the workforce in the Mexican-owned businesses represented in our 1996 San Diego sample. These firms are more dependent on foreign-born labor (especially undocumented Mexicans) than Anglo-owned businesses in San Diego, they recruit almost exclusively through referrals from their immigrant employees, and they pay lower wages than U.S.-born employers (but not subminimum wages). Surprisingly, labor turnover rates in immigrant-owned businesses are lower than in U.S. native-owned firms in San Diego, which suggests the importance of a workplace culture in which ethnic solidarity, ease of communication (in Spanish), and family ties provide incentives for stability.

THE IMPACT OF BUSINESS CYCLES

As immigrants become a preferred labor source, employers do more to retain them, even in a recessionary economy. In San Diego we found that most employers who had been using immigrant labor before the recession of the 1990s tried to keep as many of those workers as possible. During the recession, 63 percent of our San Diego sample firms did not lay off a single foreign-born worker; in fact, 36 percent of the employers had put new immigrant workers on their payrolls during this period. Seventy-two percent of our sample firms reported that there had been no net change in the proportion of immigrants in their workforce since 1990, despite the severity and duration of the recession in California.

Moreover, the recession apparently did little to expand the supply of native-born labor for the firms we studied in San Diego. Only one out of five of our sample firms reported that it had been easier to find U.S.-born workers to fill low-level jobs in their company during the recession. These findings are consistent with the hypothesis that the use of immigrant labor in California's economy has become largely independent of the business cycle.

Nor is it accurate to portray immigrant labor simply as a countercyclical cushion that employers can expand or contract almost at will to buffer their firms against recessions or seasonal fluctuations in product demand. The impressive stability of the immigrant workforce in the San Diego firms that we surveyed both in 1983 (immediately following the 1981–1982 recession) and in 1996 (following the recession of the early 1990s) belies this notion. The typical employer of immigrants in San Diego clearly does not treat them as highly disposable workers relative to native-born employees. Employers certainly can and do use immigrants as a flexible labor source, but in San Diego this normally takes the form of using immigrant workers on night shifts and for overtime work to respond to peaks in demand. Layoffs of nontemporary, full-time immigrant employees during slack periods are no more prevalent than among native-born workers.

IMPACTS OF PUBLIC POLICY CHANGES

What impacts have changes in the legal and public policy environment had on the use of foreign labor? In the case of San Diego, the most important change in the two years preceding our 1996 survey of employers and immigrant workers had been the implementation of Operation Gatekeeper, a $300 million effort by the Border Patrol to fortify the San Diego County segment of the U.S.-Mexico border through manpower, hardware, and technology enhancements. More than 2,000 Border Patrol agents have been stationed in the San Diego sector to carry out Gatekeeper. By sharply increasing the probability of apprehension for illegal border crossers along the most fortified, westernmost segment of the U.S.-Mexico border (where 45 percent of illegal immigrant apprehensions all along the border occurred in the 1993 fiscal year), Gatekeeper has sought to force crossings into the much less hospitable, mountainous terrain in the eastern portion of San Diego County and into the desert of neighboring Imperial County. In theory, as the risk of apprehension increased, professional people-smugglers (coyotes) raised their fees, and their clients were exposed to life-threatening physical hazards (including death from dehydration or hypothermia), prospective illegal migrants would be deterred from leaving their places of origin or, upon reaching the border and failing repeatedly to gain entry, would become discouraged and return home.

We were interested in how this intensified border enforcement effort had affected the actual supply of immigrant labor available to San Diego employers. We found that only 8 percent of the employers whom we interviewed had noticed any decrease in the number of immigrant workers seeking jobs at their company during the 15 months preceding our interviews—a period that coincided with the implementation of Operation Gatekeeper. More than two-thirds (69 percent) of the employers had seen no change in the supply of immigrant labor, and 23 percent had noticed an increase in immigrant job applicants since Gatekeeper began.

Our observations and interviewing in street-corner labor markets where recently arrived undocumented migrants from Mexico often congregate, conducted from January 1996 through July 1997, revealed no shortage of job seekers. Indeed, the most common complaint voiced by migrants seeking work as day laborers is the persistent oversupply of Mexican labor, that is, too much competition from other migrants, who continue to make their way to San Diego's labor markets despite the formidable new obstacles at the border.

While Gatekeeper has certainly raised the probability of apprehension at certain points along the border, illegal migrants are still crossing successfully in other areas. Among our sample of illegal migrant workers, those who entered the San Diego labor market before January 1995 made an average of 1.42 crossing attempts before gaining entry; those who entered between January and December 1995 made 1.18 attempts; and those who came to San Diego from January through June of 1996 made 1.63 attempts (mean statistics). Seventy-eight percent of the undocumented workers entering the San Diego labor market before January 1995 made it into the United States on their first try, 87 percent of those coming in 1995 (the first full year of Gatekeeper operations) made a single crossing attempt, and 81 percent of those entering in the first half of 1996 attempted entry only once. These findings, together with Border Patrol apprehension statistics, clearly indicate that as enforcement has been stepped up along the westernmost portion of San Diego County's border with Mexico, prospective illegal migrants have learned quickly to avoid the most heavily fortified segments of the border altogether and cross elsewhere (see Cornelius 1997, 385–395; Gross 1997).

We hypothesized that the highly publicized implementation of Gatekeeper could have a chilling effect on some employers and make the search for a job more difficult for undocumented workers entering the San Diego labor market, but our survey data do not support this expectation. In fact, job-seeking time in San Diego among undocumented migrants remained constant or declined during Gatekeeper's implementation period. The median number of job-search days for undocumented migrants, excluding street-corner day laborers, remained constant at 7; the mean job search declined from 35.1 days for those arriving before 1995 to 26.8 days during 1995 and to 23.7 days in the first half of 1996. These figures refer to the amount of time needed to secure a steady job; they do not include street-corner labor market participants. Clearly, whatever chilling effect Gatekeeper may have had on the hiring of undocumented workers during its first 21 months of activity, it was more than offset by the increase in demand for labor as California's recovery from the early 1990s recession gathered momentum.

Gatekeeper has made would-be illegal entrants more dependent on *coyotes*, while bidding up the fees such smugglers can charge. Among illegal immigrants in San Diego whom we interviewed, the proportion using the services of coyotes rose steadily as Gatekeeper was implemented. Forty-two percent of those who entered the United States most recently before January 1995 used coyotes, 44 percent of those who entered during 1995 did so, and 52 percent of illegals entering during the first six months of 1996 found it necessary to use coyotes. Fees paid to coyotes for assistance in evading the Border Patrol and transportation to a safe house or worksite rose sharply, from a mean of $143 in the pre-Gatekeeper period to $490 in 1995.

Concentrated border enforcement operations like Gatekeeper (San Diego, October 1994 to the present), Operation Hold-the-Line (El Paso, Texas, September 1993 to the present), and Operation Rio Grande (McAllen, Texas, September 1997 to the present) appear to be failing as deterrents to illegal immigration, in the sense of persuading would-be migrants to stay home, causing those who fail repeatedly to gain entry clandestinely to give up, and keeping those who succeed from getting jobs in the United States. However, such operations may have the unintended consequence of prolonging the stays of undocumented Mexican migrants and raising the probability that they will settle permanently in the United States (see Andreas, this volume).

Every major U.S. government effort to tighten border enforcement or restrict access to the labor market for undocumented immigrants in the past 15 years has aroused the "psychology of the closing door" and at least temporarily increased the costs and risks of illegal entry. The effect of such measures is clearly reflected in the behavior of undocumented Mexican migrants to the United States following enactment of the 1986 Immigration Control and Reform Act (IRCA), which included penalties against employers who "knowingly" hired unauthorized migrants. Among undocumented migrants from three Mexican sending communities studied by the author in 1988–1989, those who had gone to the United States most recently in the pre-IRCA period spent 16.7 months there, on average; unauthorized migrants who had gone to the United States since IRCA's enactment were spending 20.6 months there before returning to their home community (Cornelius 1990, 241). Among the undocumented Mexican workers whom we interviewed in San Diego during the first half of 1996, 77 percent of those who had entered the San Diego labor market during the January to December 1995 period (Gatekeeper's first full year of operation) had already stayed in the United States longer than they had expected on arrival.[3]

Another key change in the public policy environment in the period leading up to our 1996 surveys in San Diego was the movement to deny basic social services to undocumented immigrants. California voters approved Proposition 187 some 14 months before our field interviewing began in San Diego County. While implementation of most of its provisions was blocked almost immediately by federal court rulings, the passage of the state ballot initiative by a 59 to 41 percent majority sent a strong signal to immigrants—legal and illegal alike—that the tolerance of the aging Anglo residents who constitute the bulk of the participating California electorate for the current wave of predominantly Latino immigration was ending, and punitive measures were likely to be taken against them. Nevertheless, as its advocates readily acknowledged, Proposition 187 contained virtually nothing that would make undocumented immigrants less employable in California; the initiative was aimed at denying them social services. Hence, in our fieldwork we expected to find no significant labor market impacts of Proposition 187.

The results of our survey of immigrant workers in San Diego County were largely consistent with this expectation. Only one out of five regularly employed workers had experienced any type of problem that they could attribute to Proposition 187; a considerably higher proportion (41 percent) of the street-corner workers whom we interviewed reported problems resulting from "la 187." Except among the street-corner workers, the Proposition 187–related problem experienced most frequently by our immigrant worker interviewees was increased discrimination and hostility of a generalized character (i.e., not limited to hiring discrimination).

Only 1.5 percent of the regularly employed immigrants reported that they had found it more difficult to get work because of Proposition 187, but 16 percent of the street-corner migrant laborers had found it harder. If the street-corner workers' perceptions are accurate, it is reasonable to hypothesize that some casual employers of undocumented workers (typically individual homeowners and small subcontractors in construction, painting, and landscaping) were frightened off—at least temporarily—by the media hype surrounding

Proposition 187 and, more important, by their own misunderstanding of the measure. Nevertheless, for the vast majority of undocumented immigrants—even street-corner workers—it has been business as usual in San Diego's labor markets.

THE FUTURE DEMAND FOR MEXICAN IMMIGRANT LABOR

The U.S. economy and society are being transformed in ways that inevitably increase the demand for immigrant labor. Growth in low-level service and retail employment has been particularly explosive in recent decades: hotels and motels, restaurants and fast-food outlets, car washing, dry cleaning, convalescent care, and domestic service. Some of these industries (like fast food) are slowly becoming more automated, but many others have already reached a more or less permanent plateau of technological modernization and are unable to further reduce their labor requirements in this way. A simple example: Virtually all restaurants have installed automatic dishwashers, but those machines must still be loaded, unloaded, and maintained by someone—almost invariably an immigrant, in San Diego and other California cities.

In some sectors of the economy, the utilization of Mexican and Central American labor has been driven partly—or at least facilitated—by the rapidly expanding supply of immigrant workers. In California, this phenomenon of supply-driven employment of immigrants can be observed most easily in the domestic service and agricultural sectors. Since the 1970s there has been an exponential increase in the demand for private household service workers who provide house cleaning, gardening, child care, and elder care services. In a society where both parents now typically work outside the home, such workers are considered a necessity, not a luxury, even by middle-class families—which is why this common source of employment for immigrants is virtually recession-proof. Census data show that twice as many gardeners and private household servants were employed in the Los Angeles region in 1990 than in 1980 (Waldinger 1997a, 457), a trend that has been documented in other major metropolitan areas (see Repak 1995).

The same rapid growth in employment has been observed in California's agricultural sector, where production of labor-intensive fresh vegetables, fruits, and nuts has been booming in the last two decades. According to agricultural experts, two factors are primarily responsible: changing consumer tastes (i.e., a preference for more fresh vegetables to maintain a healthier lifestyle) and a virtually inexhaustible reservoir of Mexican hand labor. Thus, employer demand and the Mexican immigrant labor supply have grown in tandem. Unquestionably, California's labor-intensive agricultural industry expanded more rapidly in the 1980s and 1990s than would have been possible in the absence of a plentiful supply—indeed, oversupply—of low-cost immigrant workers (see Martin 1996).

Consistent with the predictions of labor market segmentation theory, the vast majority of Mexican immigrants being added to the labor force in California in the 1970s, 1980s, and 1990s appear to have been complements to—not substitutes for—native-born workers, including members of ethnic and racial minorities (see Marcelli 1997). The growth of the U.S. economy in the past quarter-century has created a large number of low-skilled, so-called bad jobs that do not pay enough to sustain a middle-class standard of living. And because most of these jobs involve arduous manual labor, or at least menial and highly repetitive tasks, they are shunned by most young native-born workers entering the labor force. Most of those jobs have not disappeared, despite all the technological innovation, corporate downsizing, and relocation of production to East Asia, Mexico, and the Caribbean that have occurred in the last ten years or so. And there is no obvious reason why we should expect them to disappear in the foreseeable future.

Whatever happens in the mainstream economy, the demand for immigrant labor will continue to grow in the firms owned and operated by immigrant entrepreneurs. The self-employment rate among Mexican immigrants (6.8 percent, according to the 1990 census data) is still far below that of most other major immigrant populations (see Fairlie and Meyer 1996), and the Mexican immigrant enclave is still behind the Cuban, Korean, and even the Dominican enclaves in terms of capitalization; nevertheless, it is expanding rapidly. Guarnizo (1996, 39) found "a growing archipelago of Mexican businesses [that] traverses the vast Los Angeles metropolitan region." If immigrant-enclave firms already account for 30 percent or more of the low-skilled jobs being created in major cities like Los Angeles and New York, as some recent estimates suggest, a substantial portion of the future demand for immigrant labor is built into the immigration process itself. Nearly 60 percent of the Mexican-owned enterprises represented in Guarnizo's survey in Los Angeles are retail businesses; only 13 percent are manufacturing plants in apparel and other declining industries (Guarnizo 1996, 11). We found the same pattern in San Diego: Mexican immigrant entrepreneurs are concentrated in the restaurant, food processing, construction, and service sectors. All this suggests that Mexican-enclave firms are likely to become a permanent part of the urban economic and cultural landscape in California, just as Dominican-owned firms have become in New York and Cuban-owned firms in Miami (see Smith and Guarnizo 1998).

In this and other ways, the demand for Mexican immigrant labor has become structurally embedded in the U.S. economy. It is no longer meaningful to talk about the "disposability" of this labor source, as if most employers had some realistic alternative to using it. Indeed, more than two-thirds (67 percent) of the firms in our San Diego sample had already experimented with one or more alternatives to employing foreign workers. Rationalization of production to reduce labor requirements was the most commonly pursued option, followed by mechanization, subcontracting, hiring more part-timers, hiring more native-born elderly workers, and moving some production abroad (see Figure 4.4). How had these experiments worked? Only 11 percent of the firms reported that doing any of these things had actually helped them to reduce the proportion of foreign-born workers in their labor force. The vast majority of these firms anticipate the same or even a higher level of reliance on immigrant labor in the future; only 7 percent expect to reduce the proportion of immigrants in their workforce in the foreseeable future. In short, most of

FIGURE 4.4

Alternatives to Immigrant Labor That Have Been Tried by Employer

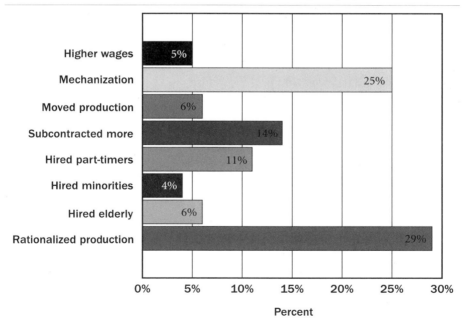

Question asked: "For your company, are there any alternatives to employing foreign workers in order to meet your labor requirements and stay in business?" If so, "What has been tried?" All responses collated.

Source: Sample survey of 112 San Diego County employers, conducted by the Center for U.S.-Mexican Studies, University of California-San Diego, 1996.

these companies see themselves as being locked solidly into the transnational labor market.

In California and other states and regions where Mexicans arriving since 1970 have clustered, employers will be able to draw upon an increasingly stable immigrant labor pool. Since the 1970s the secular trend in Mexican migration to the United States has been toward longer stays and a higher incidence of permanent settlement in the United States (Cornelius 1992). A number of factors on both sides of the border underlie this trend: recurrent economic crises in Mexico (1976–1977, 1982–1989, 1994–present) that have ravaged the country's employment base and widened the real-wage gap between Mexico and the United States, changes in U.S. immigration law (especially the 1986 Immigration Reform and Control Act) that have increased migration for family reunification, and structural changes in the U.S. economy that have increased the demand for nonseasonal, year-round immigrant labor.

When the Bracero program of agricultural contract labor importation ended in 1964, and for up to a decade thereafter, Mexican migration to the United States consisted mainly of a circular flow of mostly young-adult males, who left their immediate relatives behind in Mexico (typically in a small town or rural community), worked in seasonal jobs in the United States (usually for six months or less in a given year), and returned to their place of origin. During the Bracero program such migrants went to the United States legally; after it ended, they continued migrating, illegally. There was a good fit between this kind of Mexican migrant labor and the needs of the U.S. economy, at least as they were understood in the 1960s and early 1970s; that is, the United States mostly needed readily disposable, short-term workers who could be rotated in and out of low-skilled jobs in agriculture and a few other industries, like construction, in which the demand for the product or service fluctuated seasonally or with the business cycle.

Since the early 1970s, we have witnessed a gradual but accelerating shift toward a more socially heterogeneous, year-round, de facto permanent Mexican immigrant population in the United States. To be sure, circular migration by young, lone-male Mexicans did not stop. A recent analysis of data from six states of western Mexico collected between 1982 and 1993 (Reyes 1997) found that about half of the people who migrated from small communities in those states returned to Mexico within two years, and almost 70 percent returned within ten years. But more than one out of four of the people leaving those communities for the United States never went back to Mexico.

Large cities in Mexico are becoming an even more important reservoir of potential migrants and permanent settlers in the United States than rural Mexico. By 1995, according to estimates by INEGI, the Mexican government's statistical agency, 46 percent of the total population of Mexico was living in cities with over 100,000 inhabitants. One-fourth of all Mexicans now live in one of the country's three largest cities: Mexico City, Guadalajara, and Monterrey. Not surprisingly, having been battered so severely by the economic crises of the 1980s and 1990s, the Federal District (Mexico City) has become one of the top four or five sending states for migration to the United States (Cornelius 1992, 157–165). This means that an increasingly large fraction of the migration flow from Mexico to the United States consists of people who have been born and raised in urban areas, who have higher levels of education, and who have worked in nonagricultural occupations if they were in the labor force prior to migration—exactly the type of workers sought by U.S. employers to fill year-round jobs in manufacturing, construction, and service industries.

By enabling some 2 million Mexican undocumented migrants to legalize their status, the amnesty provisions of the 1986 U.S. immigration law were a powerful stimulus to family reunification in the United States. Family heads who had secured amnesty for themselves quickly summoned their wives and children. Psychologically, gaining legal status also raised expectations of financial security and permanence. Our studies in San Diego as well as many other surveys show that the vast majority of Mexicans now migrating to the United States from both urban and rural areas of Mexico are joining close relatives who have preceded them in migration and are now more or less permanently based in the United States. If migrants have that kind of social support network, it is much more likely that they will bring their dependents to live with them in the United States, thereby eliminating the primary incentive for shuttle migration.

Higher rates of permanent settlement in the United States are also very much related to structural transformations of the U.S. economy that have increased the demand for year-round, low-skilled labor. Even in agriculture, recent changes in crop mix and technology have made it possible for many growers to engage in year-round production and have increased the labor intensity of agricultural production. All of the nonagricultural industries in which Mexican immigrants are now heavily represented also offer year-round employment, at least in Sunbelt states.

Urban origins, nonagricultural employment experience, constantly expanding networks of family and friends who can prearrange jobs in the United States, legalization and family reunification on the U.S. side of the border, structural changes in the U.S. economy that increase the demand for nonseasonal, low-skilled labor—all of these factors make the most recent wave of Mexican migrants prime candidates for incorporation into the U.S. economy on a long-term or permanent basis.

The consequences of these mutually reinforcing transformations are readily apparent in the migration and settlement behavior of our sample of immigrant workers in San Diego. More than one-third (35 percent) had arrived in San Diego on their most recent trip to the United States intending to remain there permanently, and another 18 percent planned to stay as long as possible. Thus, well over half of our sample considered themselves to be long stayers, if not permanent settlers, at the moment they arrived in the United States. Another 8 percent saw their stay in the United States as being limited by job tenure: They planned to remain until their current, seasonal job ended. The remaining one-fifth (21 percent) of our interviewees could be classified as "target-earner" migrants—persons who, on arrival, intended to work in the United States only long enough to save a certain amount of money.

By the time we interviewed them, half of the entire sample of immigrant workers had already stayed in the United States longer than they had expected on arrival. When we asked them about their current intentions (as compared with intentions on arrival), nearly 64 percent told us that they see the United States as their future, permanent home. The proportion of respondents viewing themselves as permanent settlers in the United States is up by more than 13 percentage points since 1983, when we conducted our initial survey of immigrant workers in San Diego County (see Table 4.2). The only clearly itinerant subgroup within our 1996 sample was the irregularly employed street-corner workers, but even among them, a clear majority (55 percent) planned to make their permanent home in the United States eventually.

Settlement plans are significantly related to immigration status: Fifty-two percent of the legal immigrants in our sample planned to stay permanently. Even among the illegals, however, a surprisingly high 36 percent told us that they had come to San Diego intending to settle permanently. Moreover, when

TABLE 4.2

Current Settlement Intentions among Mexicans Working in San Diego County

	1983 Survey	**1996 Survey**
Country of Expected Permanent Home:		
United States	50.6 %	63.9 %
Mexico	49.4 %	36.1 %
(number of cases)	(573)	(526)

Note: "Don't know" and nonresponse cases are excluded from the tabulation.

Source: Sample surveys conducted by the Center for U.S.-Mexican Studies, University of California-San Diego, throughout San Diego County.

asked about their current intentions (as compared with intentions on arrival), the undocumented were almost as likely to see the United States as their future, year-round home as legal-resident immigrants (60 and 69 percent, respectively). Overwhelming majorities of both groups expressed an intention to become U.S. citizens eventually (83 percent of the legal immigrants and 75 percent of the currently undocumented, who have a very long way to go before they could qualify for U.S. citizenship, if ever).

In short, all indications are that the current wave of Mexican migrants to the United States is focused mainly on locking in their access to the U.S. labor market rather than leading a transnational existence involving annual, extended physical stays in both Mexico and the United States. After the massive job losses, inflationary spirals, and currency devaluations of the 1980s and 1990s, many Mexicans have simply given up trying to maintain an economic foothold in their place of origin. Mexican immigrants who have lived continuously in the United States for five or more years are now investing in U.S. real estate—buying houses, rather than renting—and starting small businesses in cities like Los Angeles, San Diego, Chicago, and Houston. They are not putting their savings into home construction and small businesses in their communities of origin—certainly not to the extent that they did 10 or 15 years ago. When they do go back, it is typically to visit whatever relatives they still have in their home communities and to spend their vacation time there. Among those with long residence in the United States, their home towns have become places for rest and recreation, not for employment.

As Susan González Baker and her colleagues predict in their contribution to this volume, rapidly rising naturalization rates among Mexican permanent legal immigrants (responding to punitive federal and state-level legislation denying social services to noncitizens, as well as changes in Mexican law that allow naturalized Mexican immigrants to maintain dual nationality) will induce more permanent settlement in the United States. And if the response of San Diego's Mexican migrants to Operation Gatekeeper is any guide, continuing federal government investments in border enforcement will induce more would-be sojourners to extend their stays in the United States, which inevitably increases their likelihood of becoming permanent settlers.

To the extent that Mexican workers stabilize their household arrangements in the United States and limit their stays in Mexico to short, recreational visits, they become a more stable and therefore more attractive labor source for U.S. employers seeking to fill year-round, permanent jobs. Thus, the objective—if not the generally recognized—complementarities between the Mexican immigrant labor supply and U.S. demand will continue to deepen.

CONCLUSION: THE LIMITED EFFICACY OF
IMMIGRATION CONTROLS IN AN IMMIGRANT-DEPENDENT ECONOMY

Our findings are consistent with a body of theory that views international labor migration as the inevitable consequence of powerful market and demographic forces in both labor-importing and labor-exporting countries, reinforced and channeled by social networks that link relatives and friends in the sending and receiving countries (see, for example, Cornelius, Martin, and Hollifield 1994; Massey et al. 1987; Portes and Rumbaut 1996). Such networks give U.S. employers access to virtually inexhaustible reservoirs of foreign-born labor, originating in specific sending regions, local communities, and extended families. From this perspective, contemporary immigration from Third World countries—especially from Mexico, with its more than 100-year tradition of continuous labor migration to the United States—is a highly institutionalized process in which the state may try to intervene, but with policy instruments that are woefully inadequate to affect the millions of individual, family, and corporate decisions that together drive the growth of the immigrant labor force in the United States.

Vigorous debate undoubtedly will continue over the long-term consequences of an immigration flow that is so structurally embedded: the costs and benefits for Mexican and other Latino immigrants themselves, their offspring, African American and other native-born minority workers, and taxpayers at large. But clearly, the traditional labor economics paradigm in which the presence of low-skilled immigrants in the U.S. economy is simply a function of employer greed and convenience, coupled with inadequate governmental regulation of labor markets, has been exhausted. The available evidence suggests that the big-city labor markets in which most Mexican immigrants now participate are considerably more complex—and certainly less subject to manipulation by the state—than most policymakers, average citizens, and some academic researchers would like to believe.

The structural embeddedness of the U.S. demand for Mexican labor has several important implications for public policy. While the general public in California and other key immigrant-receiving states may continue to favor a more restrictive federal immigration policy and various anti-immigrant measures at the state level, small and medium-sized businesses in these same states are likely to resist or evade any serious effort to reduce their access to immigrant labor.

The federal government's most significant attempt to do so thus far has taken the form of the employer sanctions contained in the 1986 immigration law. Employer compliance with these provisions has risen continuously over the past ten years. Among San Diego immigrants whom we interviewed in 1996, 91 percent of those who obtained their current job during 1995 had been required to show documents when they were hired, as compared with 85 percent of those who were hired between November 1986 and December 1994, and only 59 percent among those hired before November 1986, when employer sanctions became federal law. (A State of California employer sanctions state law had been on the books since 1971; see Calavita 1982.)

The impact of employer sanctions on the use of undocumented immigrant labor has been negligible due to the proliferation of fraudulent documents, which employers are not legally obligated to verify. By their own report, 83 percent of the "undocumented" immigrant workers whom we interviewed in San Diego in 1996 had shown documents (apparently borrowed or purchased) when they were hired for their current job. Given the difficulty of proving that an employer has knowingly hired an illegal alien, it is perhaps not surprising that enforcement of the 1986 employer sanctions has been a low priority of the U.S. Immigration and Naturalization Service. The number of INS cases involving potential violations of the sanctions law by employers declined steadily during the 1990s, from 14,311 cases in the 1990 fiscal year to just 5,211 cases in 1996 (Center for Immigration Studies 1997, 20–21).

However, even a much more vigorous and sustained worksite enforcement effort—coupled with some type of nationwide, mandatory-use system for verifying employment eligibility—is unlikely to alter the fundamental dynamics of the labor markets in which Mexican migrants to the United States now participate. Employer preferences for immigrant workers are too well defined, alternatives to this labor source are quite limited (in employers' perceptions if not reality), and the terms of employment in immigrant-dependent businesses are unlikely to improve sufficiently in the foreseeable future to induce the reentry of native-born workers into firms and job categories now dominated by immigrants.

Many immigrant-using businesses pay their entry-level workers just above the legal minimum, but they are not paying illegally low wages or denying fringe benefits that are required by law. Nor are most of the jobs taken by newly arriving Mexican immigrants likely to be upgraded significantly in wages and benefits, given the low level of unionization in small, immigrant-using businesses and the downward pressure being exerted by globalization, that is, the persistent threat that companies (at least the larger ones) will simply move production abroad to take advantage of much lower-cost labor.

Our findings from San Diego and those of Roger Waldinger in Los Angeles (Waldinger 1997c) suggest that the emergence of transnational labor recruitment networks linking employers, their current immigrant employees, and prospective migrants who are relatives or friends of these workers is perhaps the single most potent obstacle to government intervention. After three or four generations, the sociocultural infrastructure of self-sustaining migration from Mexico to San Diego and other U.S. cities with large Mexico-origin populations is firmly in place. Thus, the flow of new migrants persists and the stock of immigrant workers continues to expand, even when macroeconomic conditions in the receiving area would not seem to favor such an influx of labor (as was true during the 1981–1982 and 1990–1993 recessions in California), and even when the U.S. government tries to create formidable new deterrents to illegal immigration.

ACKNOWLEDGMENTS

The research assistance of Marc Rosenblum, Eric Magar, and Rafael Vergara is gratefully acknowledged. Principal financial support for the data collection in San Diego County was provided by the James Irvine Foundation. Additional funding for research assistance was provided by the Center for U.S.-Mexican Studies, University of California-San Diego, and the David Rockefeller Center for Latin American Studies, Harvard University.

NOTES

1. All differences cited are statistically significant, by Pearson chi-square test, at the $p < .05$ level or higher.
2. Owned by a U.S.-born Mexican American, who preferentially hires Mexican-national employees.
3. Evidence from other sources suggests that stepped-up border enforcement is having the same unintended consequence (lengthening the stays of undocumented migrants) elsewhere. For example, the agent in charge of the Cincinnati, Ohio, office of the Immigration and Naturalization Service reported that "With the increased enforcement at the border, we're finding that people can't travel back and forth between the U.S. and Mexico as freely as before. . . . We are seeing people who traditionally worked in the agricultural areas now moving into the cities, and they are remaining in the country longer" (quoted in O'Hanlon 1997). Jorge Durand (see his chapter in this volume) has also found that the tightening of border controls since 1994 has discouraged the traditional pattern of annual returns to Mexico by unaccompanied male migrants working illegally in the United States, while encouraging multiyear stays and intermarriage with permanent U.S. residents.

REFERENCES

Borjas, George J. 1994. "The Economics of Immigration." *Journal of Economic Literature* 32 (December): 1667–1717.

Borjas, George J. 1996. "The New Economics of Immigration." *Atlantic Monthly* 278 (November): 73–80.

Briggs, Vernon M. 1996. *Mass Immigration and the National Interest,* 2nd ed. Armonk, N.Y.: M.E. Sharpe.

Calavita, Kitty. 1982. *California's "Employer Sanctions": The Case of the Disappearing Law.* Research Report Series, no. 39. La Jolla, Calif.: University of California-San Diego, Center for U.S.-Mexican Studies.

Center for Immigration Studies. 1997. *Immigration-Related Statistics—1997.* Backgrounder Series no. 3–97, July. Washington, D.C.

Cornelius, Wayne A. 1989. The U.S. demand for Mexican labor. In *Mexican Migration to the United States: Origins, Consequences, and Policy Options,* ed. W. A. Cornelius and J. A. Bustamante, 25–47. La Jolla, Calif.: University of California-San Diego, Center for U.S.-Mexican Studies.

Cornelius, Wayne A. 1990. Impacts of the 1986 U.S. immigration law on emigration from rural Mexican sending communities. In *Undocumented Migration to the United States: IRCA and the Experience of the 1980s,* ed. F. D. Bean, B. Edmonston, and J. S. Passel. Washington, D.C.: Urban Institute Press.

Cornelius, Wayne A. 1992. From sojourners to settlers: The changing profile of Mexican immigration to the United States. In *U.S.-Mexico Relations: Labor Market Interdependence,* ed. J. A. Bustamante, C. W. Reynolds, and R. A. Hinojosa Ojeda, 155–193. Stanford: Stanford University Press.

Cornelius, Wayne A. 1997. Appearances and realities: Controlling illegal immigration in the United States. In *Temporary Workers or Future Citizens: Japanese and U.S. Migration Policies,* ed. M. Weiner and T. Hanami, 384–427. New York: New York University Press.

Cornelius, Wayne A., Philip L. Martin, and James F. Hollifield, eds. 1994. *Controlling Immigration: A Global Perspective.* Stanford: Stanford University Press.

Fairlie, Robert W., and Bruce D. Meyer. 1996. "Ethnic and Racial Self-Employment Differences and Possible Explanations." *Journal of Human Relations* 31(4).

Gross, Gregory. 1997. Immigrant flow shifts eastward, slows here. *San Diego Union-Tribune,* 24 August, A1, A18.

Guarnizo, Luis. 1996. *The Mexican Ethnic Economy in Los Angeles: Capitalist Accumulation, Class Restructuring, and the Transnationalization of Migration.* Davis, Calif.: California Communities Program, Department of Human and Community Development, University of California, Davis, Working Papers Series.

Marcelli, Enrico A. 1997. The political and economic effects of illegal Mexican immigration to Los Angeles County. Unpublished Ph.D. dissertation, University of Southern California.

Martin, Philip L. 1996. *Promises to Keep: Collective Bargaining in California Agriculture.* Ames, Iowa: Iowa State University Press.

Massey, Douglas S., Rafael Alarcón, Humberto González, and Jorge Durand. 1987. *Return to Aztlán: The Social Process of International Migration from Western Mexico.* Berkeley and Los Angeles: University of California Press.

O'Hanlon, Kevin. 1997. 117 undocumented workers arrested in Ohio. The Associated Press, 7 August.

Portes, Alejandro, and Rubén G. Rumbaut. 1996. *Immigrant America: A Portrait,* 2nd ed. Berkeley: University of California Press.

Repak, Terry A. 1995. *Waiting on Washington: Central American Workers in the Nation's Capital.* Philadelphia: Temple University Press.

Reyes, Belinda I. 1997. *Dynamics of Immigration: Return Migration to Western Mexico.* San Francisco: Public Policy Institute of California.

Smith, Michael P., and Luis Eduardo Guarnizo, eds. 1998. *Transnationalism from Below: Comparative Urban and Community Research,* vol. 6. New Brunswick, N.J.: Transaction.

Waldinger, Roger. 1996. *Still the Promised City? African-Americans and New Immigrants in Post-industrial New York.* Cambridge, Mass.: Harvard University Press.

Waldinger, Roger. 1997a. Ethnicity and opportunity in the plural city. In *Ethnic Los Angeles,* ed. R. Waldinger and M. Bozorgmehr, 445–470. New York: Russell Sage Foundation.

Waldinger, Roger. 1997b. *Beyond the Sidestream: The Language of Work in an Immigrant Metropolis.* Los Angeles: Lewis Center for Regional Policy Studies, University of California, Los Angeles, Working Paper Series, 25.

Waldinger, Roger. 1997c. *Social Capital or Social Closure?—Immigrant Networks in the Labor Market.* Los Angeles: Lewis Center for Regional Policy Studies, University of California, Los Angeles, Working Paper Series, 26.

Commentary

Robert Smith, Barnard College

Wayne Cornelius joins both a public policy and a theoretical debate in his discussion of the structural embeddedness of the demand for Mexican labor in southern California. In my comments, I first summarize his argument and the larger debate he engages, then reflect on the theoretical grounds of each of these arguments and offer comparative evidence from New York and the Northeast, and conclude with some reflections on the implications of these arguments and evidence.

Wayne Cornelius argues that the demand for Mexican labor has become embedded in institutionalized relations between sending communities in Mexico and their members and the second generation in the United States, and between U.S. employers and their Mexican (and other immigrant) employees. Moreover, he argues that because of this institutionalization, public policies such as employer sanctions have not deterred undocumented immigration. He also shows that this demand for labor is steady through business cycles and broadly used throughout the local economy, indicating for him that the use of undocumented workers is not just a stop-gap measure for declining economic sectors. The implication is that the demand for immigrant labor is a structural part of the economy, and that we as a society should not have overly high expectations of our ability to deter immigration by public policy.

His argument answers one part of a position on immigration that also reflects a growing popular opinion and policy consensus: Too many immigrants are coming in and they are too uneducated and hence are costing the United States too much money and endangering our society's future (see, for example, Borjas 1994, 1996; Briggs 1996). Often this school argues that immigration benefits only a small class of people, namely, employers who get cheaper workers and high-income people who can avail themselves of cheaper service providers, and enables them to get rid of their excess workers during downward trends in the business cycle. On the other hand, it is seen to hurt low-income natives who are presumed to compete with immigrants.

Moreover, these low-skilled and uneducated immigrants are coming into an economy that is producing fewer entry-level jobs that promise upward mobility than did low-skilled non-English speakers in the last great wave of migration (which ended with the slamming of the proverbial door with the 1924 immigration reforms). As a result, these immigrants and their native-born children are more likely to consume more in public services—especially schools and health care—than they will contribute. In this view, immigration is mainly the result of employers' greed and the purposeful segregation of the labor market. A common prescription or implication of this school is to stop or greatly decrease immigration, on the assumption that this will better the prospects for low-income natives.

Cornelius' chapter addresses mainly the economic analysis of the demand for Mexican labor, and policy prescriptions concerning that labor, leaving aside issues relating to the second generation that are part of this "limit the numbers" argument. I agree with his analysis about the nature of the demand for immigrant labor and its resistance to public policy, but I also think that questions regarding newcomers and the second generation merit consideration; I return to these issues later. First, I would like to comment on the theoretical significance of Cornelius' chapter and its empirical comparability.

EMBEDDEDNESS, THE MODERN ECONOMY, AND THE INADEQUACY OF CHANGING INCENTIVES FOR CONTROLLING IMMIGRATION

Cornelius is correct in criticizing the limit-the-numbers school for its presumption that changing public policy will effect the desired changes in immigrant behavior. One need only recall the debate over and promises about employer sanctions for the decade or so preceding the passage of the Immigration Reform and Control Act of 1986 to see how difficult it is for public policy to change social behavior. The lack of employer sanctions was (accurately, I think) identified as a main condition facilitating the increasing dependence on undocumented immigration in certain places and industries. It was assumed that repealing the Texas Proviso—which made it illegal for immigrants to work without authorization but exempted employment and its incident practices from penalty—and implementing sanctions would stop or decrease undocumented immigration by eliminating the "jobs magnet." However, the decade since sanctions went into effect presents little evidence that they have deterred the entry or employment of undocumented immigrants, and much evidence that the jobs magnet still pulls migrants north.[1] Moreover, evidence from France's longer experiment with employer sanctions also fails to show that sanctions deter undocumented immigration (for a different view, see Miller 1994). One conclusion is that migration is not transitive: Simply removing the causes that facilitated migration does not necessarily reverse the process because it is cumulatively causal, acquiring a logic of its own over time (see, for example, Massey and Espinoza 1997; Portes and Rumbaut 1994; Zolberg and Smith 1996).

Today, the policy focus is on preventing entry at the border, yet since its initiation in 1994 Operation Gatekeeper does not so far show a decrease in the numbers coming in or staying, though it has moved their arena of operation out of more populated areas in San Diego County. This change could be considered an important policy success in its own right, because it decreases the visibility of undocumented immigrants and makes them less of a political issue. The point that Cornelius makes, which I reinforce here, is that the demand for and delivery of immigrant labor, including undocumented immigrant labor, has been too well institutionalized between the United States and Mexico for the policy changes currently proposed to have the dramatic effects predicted.

There are theoretical and practical reasons for this to be so. Theoretically, the answer has much to do with the concept of embeddedness Cornelius uses to frame his analysis. Contemporary usage of this term owes much to Mark Granovetter's insightful work (1985), but it hails from at least as far back as Polanyi's 1957 analysis of instituted processes, wherein he focused on how economic activity can be conducted without markets, structured through nonmarket relations. The essence of embeddedness can be understood by juxtaposing it with the atomized assumptions of a market-based analysis. In the latter, in order to change observed behavior, one needs merely to change the incentives for them by changing the rules under or institutions within which people act. (Examples of this kind of analysis are the "new institutional economics" or rational choice analysis in political science, or the older form of utilitarian analysis dating from Adam Smith or Jeremy Bentham.) On this view, implementing employer sanctions or increasing the vigilance at the border should significantly decrease or even stop undocumented immigration.

It is precisely the inattention to the embeddedness of immigration and labor markets that leads this incentive-oriented analysis astray. Implementing sanctions has not stopped undocumented immigration and caused a switch toward native labor among employers in southern California, and I doubt that increasing vigilance at the border will have deterrent effects either, though it may have other effects, including increasing the length of stay in the United States. The problem is that labor markets in reality are not just atomized markets where each person competes with every other person as workers. Rather, they are segmented and niched, and competition is collective, group-centered, and ethnic as well as individual (see, for example, Waldinger 1996). Hence, decades of immigration, and the links between particular places and people in Mexico and in the United States that it engenders, as well as larger structural changes in the U.S. and world economies, have led to a situation wherein simply changing incentives by changing laws will not significantly affect migration (see, for example, Massey et al. 1987; Portes and Rumbaut 1994; Zolberg and Smith 1996).

Cornelius addresses another assumption underlying the analysis of the limit-the-numbers school, that is, that our modern economy has fewer and fewer low-wage, unskilled jobs, and is creating mainly better jobs that require increased skill and education levels. If this is true, immigrants can be seen as a subsidy to declining sectors of the economy. This is a classic assumption of modernization theory, postulating new monopoly sectors emerging while old competitive sectors hang on. While there has been a decline in manufacturing in many parts of the United States, this sector remains a significant employer in southern California (Waldinger and Bozorgmehr 1996), and low-wage jobs in service industries are among the fastest-growing job categories in the country (Sassen 1988, 1992). Moreover, the economy is now understood to be more dynamic and multifaceted than previous theories supposed, producing jobs both for the highly skilled and low-skilled workers (see, for example, Sassen 1991, 1988; Mollenkopf and Castells 1991). Hence, it is likely that there will continue to be a demand for people doing the kind of work that low-skilled, poorly educated immigrants do. Moreover, given the course of U.S. demographics, the country is likely to face labor shortages in many of these low-skilled areas in the next 10 to 20 years, while Mexico faces a surplus of low-skilled workers (Reynolds 1983). Another point here is that no matter how highly skilled an economy becomes, there will always be "bad" jobs that higher-status members of that community will not want to do. This is because occupational hierarchies are not just about skill levels but about social locations as well. This enduring social fact will continue to contribute to the demand for immigrant workers.

There is at least one rejoinder on employer sanctions that the public policy school can advance (which has been addressed elsewhere: see Zolberg and Smith 1996). Freeman (1994), for example, argues sensibly that employer sanctions cannot be said to have failed because they have not really been tried yet as they have not been vigilantly enforced. Indeed, the U.S. economy has about 6.5 million employers, while the U.S. Department of Labor can carry out only between 30,000 to 40,000 I-9 (the document one must fill out with information about an applicant's authorization to work) checks per year (Zolberg and Smith 1996). Even in targeted industries (e.g., garments) with a history of high usage of undocumented workers, only about 5 percent of employers are inspected. Thus, even in the worst case, employers have a 95 percent chance that they will not be inspected. Deterrence seems unlikely under these conditions.

However, I do not want to advance an overly socialized conception (e.g., Wrong 1961; Granovetter 1985) of this problem, that is, to argue that changes in public policy or other measures could never reduce immigration. Indeed, it is probable that we could virtually stop illegal border crossing and significantly reduce undocumented immigration—at least for a time—if we were to spend without limit and disregard consequences. This would require a militarization of the border—as occurred in 1951 in Operation Wetback—abandonment of the principle of family reunification in immigration law, elimination of birthright citizenship, stiff penalties for hiring undocumented workers, a national ID card for citizens as well as aliens, and a well-funded, vigilant national agency monitoring ID use and employment: in short, a massive expansion of state intervention.

These moves would be costly in terms of liberty and money. Most Americans do not want a state that intrudes so far into private life, and they are especially loathe to pay for an intrusive state. Removing the principle of family reunification would violate commonly held American, humanitarian standards. Moreover, powerful business interests would object to these measures, arguing that they obstructed free operation of the market. They would also severely disrupt our increasingly important bilateral relationship with Mexico. Finally, they would probably have unanticipated effects. For example, research has shown that when the costs of border crossing go up, one result is that undocumented immigrants stay longer in the United States, thus helping to convert short-term stays into medium- or long-term stays.[2] This seems like a high price to pay to keep 200,000 to 300,000 undocumented people per year—many of whom come to be reunited with their families and legalize their status later—from entering a country of more than 250 million (Warren 1995).

COMPARATIVE PERSPECTIVES ON THE STRUCTURAL EMBEDDEDNESS OF THE DEMAND FOR IMMIGRANT LABOR

Another way to view Cornelius' chapter is comparatively. Does his argument hold for other parts of the United States, or is San Diego an exceptional case? Evidence from the Northeast, especially New York City, suggests that the demand for immigrants is structurally embedded there as well, although there are some differences.

Roger Waldinger (1996) has done an extensive analysis of immigrants and blacks in New York City's economy, examining these issues with penetrating insight. He accounts for the diverging fates of blacks and immigrants using a single, internally consistent theory and pragmatic combinations of data and methodologies. His argument centers around the processes of niche creation and evolution, and ethnic compositional change. Niches are created when ethnic boundaries are established and maintained in certain jobs or industries. Social networks play an important role in this process. Once a niche is established, it provides the ethnic group with the ability to become upwardly mobile within the niche, provided the niche grows. If the niche shrinks while the numbers entering it grow, conflict and downward mobility will result.

Waldinger argued that native blacks and immigrants in New York did not really compete in many industries, such as the garment industry. In the previous wave of immigration earlier in this century, blacks were kept out of most of its jobs by discrimination, while during the second wave since the mid-1960s, blacks were beginning to move in large numbers into public service employment, which offered much better pay, benefits, and working conditions. Immigrants were able to move up in this period in the garment industry, from the mid-1960s to the mid-1980s, because of the ethnic compositional changes that New York's economy was experiencing. The white Jewish and Italian and other merchants and factory owners who were retiring and moving out of the city were not being replaced by their children, who were seeking white collar and professional jobs. Hence, blacks did not go into the garment industry at the time one would have expected because they had better offers. Taken as a whole, Waldinger's analysis offers a picture of the labor market dynamics that create a different kind of embedded demand for immigrant labor.

Another aspect of the embeddedness of demand for immigrant labor that Cornelius addresses stems from the demand for co-ethnic goods, services, and labor (see, for example, Portes and Rumbaut 1994; Bailey and Waldinger 1991). This is also the case in New York City, where the demand created by large immigrant populations sustains a great deal of co-ethnic and immigrant employment. In New York, and increasingly in other cities, we must also differentiate between an "ethnic economy"—involving business only among an ethnic group—and an "immigrant economy"—involving business among non-co-ethnics who are all immigrants. Of particular importance is the demand by immigrant employers not only for the labor of their own ethnic group, but for non-co-ethnic immigrant labor as well.

My own research on Mexicans in New York (Smith 1995, 1996, 1997) offers an example of this kind of structural embeddedness. Much of the surge in demand for Mexican and Central American workers in the late 1980s and early 1990s came from non-Mexican immigrant employers, such as Koreans, Greeks, and Italians, who had very high rates of self-employment.

These high rates of self-employment created dynamics that led to a demand for non-co-ethnic, immigrant labor. First, hiring a co-ethnic employee entails a whole series of reciprocal obligations that hiring a non-co-ethnic does not. For example, in interviews done in the mid-1990s, I learned that Koreans typically had to pay Korean co-ethnics $500 per week, whereas they paid Mexicans only between $180 and $200 per week. Moreover, co-ethnics tried to involve themselves in the business as if they were a member of the owner's family, while Mexicans understood that their relationship was strictly one of employer-employee. Finally, co-ethnic Korean employees often opened their own shop once they had learned the business, thus competing with their former bosses. All these factors contributed to the surge in demand for Mexican and Central American workers by non-co-ethnic immigrant employers. Moreover, because Koreans and other immigrant employers have tight employer networks and Mexicans have tight employee networks, Mexicans soon became known as a preferred labor source among these groups. This provides another example whereby the dynamics of the labor market create a demand for immigrant (here, non-co-ethnic) labor.

This demand did seem to be influenced by fluctuations in the business cycle, a difference from Cornelius' findings that is probably attributable to the differences in the firm sizes and characteristics. The businesses we interviewed were mainly small service or manufacturing firms that spent a relatively large percentage of revenue on labor, and for whom small changes in the economy affected consumer demand significantly. The effect on immigrant hiring, however, was mainly to spur the move away from more expensive co-ethnic hiring and toward less-expensive non-co-ethnic hiring. In either case, there was a demand for immigrant labor stemming from the dynamics of segmented labor markets.

QUEUES, THE SECOND GENERATION, AND THE DEMAND FOR IMMIGRANT LABOR

Waldinger's analysis, and my own, situate the demand for immigrant labor in the dynamics of the labor market. Cornelius' analysis describes the steadiness of this demand for labor from the employer's point of view. These analyses underline that attempts to "just stop" undocumented immigration by turning off the job magnet, raising the costs of immigration, or other simple measures, will not work the way advocates predict. Rather, it is probable that we will continue to have high levels of immigration and that the demand for immigrant labor will continue, but that prospects for low-skilled newcomers, established immigrants, and the second generation will not improve as they did for their predecessors. Of particular importance are the second-generation and 1.5-generation immigrants (those born abroad but raised in the United States), whose futures seem to be most at risk.

Take Waldinger's analysis. His analysis of New York City showed that immigrants moved up through a process of niche creation, by which groups were then able to help themselves advance. What happens when more immigrants come into these niches before the others ahead of them have left, as happened in manufacturing in New York? This is not a problem if the niche grows, but if it shrinks, prospects will be dimmer. Waldinger's current research shows that Mexicans are among the least niched of all groups in Los Angeles, especially in the native-born second generation, putting them at a disadvantage in terms of group mobility.

This concern is increased when one considers Dowell Myers' insightful contribution in this volume. Using innovative methodologies that enable him to follow cohorts through time and hence avoid several measurement errors he sees Borjas (1994) committing, Myers concludes that second-generation Latinos in Los Angeles are in fact adapting well, particularly in terms of high school completion rates. The problem is that the returns to this level of education are less than they were for earlier arrivals. Framed in Borjas' language, it is not the decreasing quality of the immigrants, but of the economy, that accounts for the dimmer prospects of today's Latinos. But returns to education are not strictly linear: There are higher returns to education for years after high school than there are for years before. Indeed, Myers' sample measured education only in terms of high school completion because the census data he used contained too few Latinos who had graduated from college.

What should we do? The limit-the-numbers school would argue that decreasing the numbers of legal immigrants admitted would help the second and 1.5 generation. This might or might not be helpful, but focusing on this to the exclusion of other approaches is a disservice. If fewer legal immigrants from "low-human-capital" countries were admitted, the problem would remain that Mexicans and their children are still concentrated in low-paying occupations and are still not as niched as other groups. The significantly higher rates of high school completion and the lower returns to this education that Myers focuses on point in a more productive direction, especially for the second generation, which is in any case less likely to want to work in the low-paying jobs their parents had. The best investments are policies that increase the college attendance and completion rates, as well as noncollege postsecondary training, for 1.5- and second-generation Mexicans, Mexican Americans, and other immigrants. This would include making public education, especially, more affordable and accessible. This policy would increase the incomes of Mexican immigrants and their children, and hence increase the taxes they pay over their lifetimes and increase their prospects for mobility in an economy that increasingly offers bifurcated opportunities.

NOTES

1. There is, however, some evidence to suggest that at least for a time they did cause people who looked or sounded foreign to be discriminated against in hiring (see Perotti 1994, 37).

2. We can also understand why such measures will probably not be implemented and why sanctions have not been enforced as the result of what has elsewhere been called the Inter-American Migration System (Zolberg and Smith 1996), which highlights the role of three factors in fostering ongoing migration: demographic and economic changes; the actions of states, including the United States, and particularly the influence of business interests; and the manner in which migration becomes a self-feeding process over time, less and less amenable to normal government manipulation. In this view, the drastic reforms suggested above that might affect behavior will not all be adopted because the elements of the system are aligned against their adoption.

REFERENCES

Bailey, Thomas, and Roger Waldinger. 1991. "Primary, Secondary and Enclave Labor Markets: A Training System Approach." *American Sociological Review* 56: 432–445.

Borjas, George. 1994. "The Economics of Immigration." *Journal of Economic Literature* 32 (December): 1667–1717.

Borjas, George. 1996. "The New Economics of Immigration." *Atlantic Monthly* 278 (November): 73–80.

Briggs, Vernon. 1996. *Mass Immigration and the National Interest*, 2nd edition. Armonk, N.Y.: M.E. Sharpe.

Freeman, Gary. 1994. "Can Liberal States Control Unwanted Immigration?" *Annals of the American Academy of Political and Social Science* 534 (July): 17–30.

Granovetter, Mark. 1985. "The Problem of Embeddedness." *American Journal of Sociology* 91 (November): 481–510.

Massey, Douglas, and Kristin Espinoza. 1997. "What's Driving Mexico-U.S. Migration? A Theoretical, Empirical and Policy Analysis." *American Journal of Sociology* 102 (January): 939–999.

Massey, Douglas, Rafael Alarcón, Jorge Durand, and Humberto González. 1987. *Return to Aztlan: The Social Process of Transnational Migration from Western Mexico.* Berkeley: University of California Press.

Miller, Mark J. 1994. "Towards Understanding State Capacity to Prevent Unwanted Migration: Employer Sanctions Enforcement in France, 1975–1990." *West European Politics* 17(2).

Mollenkopf, John, and Manuel Castells. 1991. *Dual City: Restructuring New York.* New York: Russell Sage Foundation.

Polanyi, Karl. 1957. The economy as an instituted process. In *Trade and Markets in the Early Empires,* ed. K. Polanyi, C. Arensberg, and W. H. Pearson. New York: The Free Press.

Portes, Alejandro, and Ruben Rumbaut. 1994. *Immigrant America.* Berkeley: University of California Press.

Perotti, R. 1994. Employer sanctions and the limits of negotiation. In *The Annals of the Academy of Political and Social Science,* ed. M. Miller. Philadelphia: Sage.

Reynolds, Clark W., and Carlos Tello, eds. 1983. *U.S.-Mexico Relations: Economic and Social Aspects.* Stanford, CA: Stanford University Press.

Sassen, Saskia. 1988. *The Mobility of Capital and Labor.* New York and London: Oxford University Press.

Sassen, Saskia. 1991. *The Global City: New York, London, Tokyo.* Princeton: Princeton University Press.

Smith, Robert C. 1995. "Los ausentes siempre presentes": The imagining, making and politics of a transnational migrant community. Ph.D. dissertation, Columbia University.

Smith, Robert C. 1996. Mexicans in New York: Membership and incorporation of a new immigrant group. In *Latinos in New York,* ed. S. Baver and G. Haslip Viera. Notre Dame, Ind.: University of Notre Dame Press.

Smith, Robert C. 1997. Public wages, ethnic niches and racial references: Mexican immigrants and racial minorities in New York City. Draft paper presented at the Eastern Sociological Association Meetings, Baltimore, Maryland.

Waldinger, Roger. 1996. *Still the Promised City? Blacks and Immigrants in Post-Industrial New York.* Cambridge: Harvard University Press.

Waldinger, Roger, and Mehdi Bozorgmehr, eds. 1996. *Ethnic Los Angeles.* New York: Russell Sage Foundation.

Warren, Robert. 1995. Estimates of the undocumented immigrant population residing in the United States by county of origin and state of residence, October, 1992. Paper presented to the Annual Meeting of the Population Association of America, San Francisco, April.

Wrong, Dennis. 1961. "The Oversocialized Conception of Man in Modern Sociology." *American Sociological Review* 26(2): 183–93.

Zolberg, Aristide, and Robert Smith. 1996. *Migration Systems in Comparative Perspective: An Analysis of the Inter-American Migration System with Comparative Reference to the Mediterranean-European System.* Report to the U.S. Department of State, Bureau of Population, Refugees and Migration, through the International Center for Migration, Ethnicity and Citizenship at the New School for Social Research.

Photo by Anna LeVine

Dowell Myers Dowell Myers has lived his life throughout the United States, migrating between the great immigrant destination areas of the nation. Born and raised in Miami, he has spent significant time in New York, Boston, Austin, Texas, and now Los Angeles. An undergraduate education in anthropology at Columbia University kindled his interest in the diverse adaptations of ethnic populations in the city. That was followed by graduate education in urban planning at the University of California-Berkeley and at MIT. Along the way he studied demography and survey research at Harvard University, using these quantitative tools for "people research" to help increase the attention of urban planners to their human constituents.

His current interest in immigration stems from explorations that maximize the information content extracted from census data. Author of *Analysis with Local Census Data: Portraits of Change* (New York: Academic Press, 1992), Myers is a member of the professional advisory committee of the Bureau of the Census. His particular focus is on analysis of changes over time, nesting the life course trajectories of individuals within their evolving housing and urban context. This type of analysis led to a new method that traced birth cohorts within immigrant arrival cohorts, modeling these levels and changes in a statistical framework and linking these trajectories to a graphical display framework, termed the "double cohort method." It is currently being applied to a number of different outcome measures of immigrant adaptation and achievement.

Associate Professor, School of Urban Planning and Development, University of Southern California. Publications also include "Immigration Cohorts and Residential Overcrowding," *Demography,* 1996.

5

Dimensions of Economic Adaptation by Mexican-Origin Men

Dowell Myers
University of Southern California

Mexican immigrants have been the focal point of recent debates over U.S. immigration policy. In some quarters, these are the most unwanted of all the recent immigrants, disparaged for both their often-illegal entry and their very low educational and skill levels. A central point of controversy has been the question of future adaptation: Are these new arrivals doomed to a lifetime of poverty and societal dependency, or are they destined to adapt themselves for economic success? A question not often raised is the degree to which the economic reward system will compensate immigrants for their adaptations.

Economic adaptation of immigrants occurs through a sequence of status attainments leading from educational attainment to occupational mobility and ultimately to earnings achievement. This adaptation occurs over the life cycle and also across generations, making it difficult for analysts to observe from their single vantage point in time. Labor economists have been sorely challenged when applying standard models to changes occurring on multiple temporal dimensions that are collinear or intersecting with one another. Although it is always necessary to simplify reality when constructing quantitative models, some simplifications are more misleading than others. The present study develops a more adequate analysis of economic mobility by native-born workers as an important foundation for judging the relative success of immigrants. Comparisons of changes over time for both immigrants and native-born workers provide a better perspective on the forces that affect their economic success in common.

This chapter evaluates the economic adaptation of Mexican-origin immigrants in southern California, a principal region for immigrant settlement. Three outcome measures are investigated: weekly earnings, occupational status, and educational attainment. First, the educational achievements of different cohorts are analyzed as the foundational step in economic adaptation. The occupational mobility returns to education are then evaluated separately by immigration cohort and birth cohort. Finally, the conversion of occupational attainment into earnings achievement is also of interest, signifying how well occupational mobility is rewarded for different cohorts.

Major attention is given to the multiple temporal dimensions of adaptation, including duration and aging effects, changes across successive arrival cohorts, and changes across successive birth cohorts within arrival cohorts. The latter is often referred to as an age-at-arrival effect. The method developed here adds considerably to our knowledge of adaptation by the 1.5 generation. These insights are gained through application of a recently developed "double cohort" analytical strategy that traces birth cohorts fully nested within immigration cohorts or within the native-born status (Myers and Lee 1996). Primary emphasis in this chapter is given to the visualization of cohorts' progress over time.

Three themes are emphasized: (1) that adaptation occurs not only within adults' careers but also between the careers of parents and children, (2) that the role of growing educational attainment is paramount in the economic adaptation of Mexican immigrants, and (3) that arrivals in the labor market in recent decades—whether immigrant or native born—are not rewarded as fully as more established workers with the same education or the same occupational level. One conclusion is that claims of "declining quality" among immigrants are unwarranted if analysts do not take account also of the falling earnings rewards given to U.S.-born residents. However, a second conclusion may be of greater substantive importance, namely, that the declining reward system reduces the incentives for adaptation to productive economic roles. Despite the rapid transformation of Latino youth (Suárez-Orozco and Suárez-Orozco 1995), lack of economic reward has the risk of fueling the formation of an oppositional culture or second-generation revolt (Perlmann and Waldinger forthcoming).

INTERPRETATIONS OF ECONOMIC ADAPTATION

The size of the migration flow from Mexico, by far the largest contributor to U.S. immigration, together with the low economic status of those migrants, has drawn the attention of critics. Many have pointed out the poverty of this population, adding the speculation that the Mexican immigrants are doomed to remain in poverty without hope of economic assimilation. Indeed, recent data do suggest that Hispanics are the poorest segment of American society, recently falling below the status of blacks in that regard (Goldberg 1997). However, many of the poor are recent newcomers who have not yet had time to advance.

Economic Progress for Mexican Americans?

Changes over time are the main focus of debate. Some allege that Mexican American or Latino economic progress is disguised by the growing numbers of newcomers (Chavez 1991; Myers 1995). So numerous are the poor arrivals that Hispanic poverty seems to grow even though many of the earlier arrivals are upwardly mobile. In fact, a recent report has proclaimed that the movement into the middle class is so strong that a majority of the middle class in the Los Angeles area will soon be composed of Latinos (Rodriguez 1997).

Chapa (1990) has termed this the myth of Hispanic progress. Analyzing 1979 data from the Current Population Survey (CPS), Chapa notes that the status of the third-generation Mexican Americans may not be a true indication of the future status of today's first generation. (He points out that third-generation Asians actually have lower status than first, but no one would expect this cross-sectional pattern to indicate future de-assimilation.) In any event, Chapa also analyzes census data from 1940 to 1980 to show that Mexican Americans, while increasing in education and earnings, are not converging on the status of Anglos, who are advancing even more.

Using more recent CPS data, Bean et al. (1994) show the remarkable educational progress of second-generation over first-generation immigrants, but find a slight downward shift in the third generation. Trejo (1995) also finds that economic progress continues into the third generation of Mexican American settlement in the United States. However, Ortiz (1996) finds very slow progress within the careers of Latino workers in Los Angeles, concluding that they are doomed never to enter the middle class.

Poor Economic Quality?

George Borjas (1985) introduced cohort analysis into immigration research, exploiting new data from the 1980 census, together with those from the 1970 census, to show that the experience of immigration cohorts diverged from that implied by duration differences in the single 1970 cross-section. Chiswick's (1978) early work only had the single cross-section for analysis, leading him to infer that immigrants would surpass the earnings of native-born workers. The results of Borjas' model indicated, instead, that immigrants were faring less well than the native-born population. Borjas attributed the divergent findings to the declining quality of recent immigrants: Once human capital was controlled, the most recent immigrants sustained persistently lower earnings than native-born workers.

The "declining quality" thesis has been criticized on several grounds. The economic concept of quality has an unfortunate implication when expressed in common English. Some have feared the racist implication that the quality of immigrants is declining because the composition of the immigrant flow has shifted from European to Asian and Latin American origins. However, Borjas intended declining quality to signify the declining returns to human capital. Unfortunately, those declining returns are also compounded by *relative* declines in the amounts of human capital. Recent immigrants actually have higher education and other human capital than their predecessors; their human capital is declining only in the relative sense that it is rising more slowly than that of native-born whites (but see Bean et al. 1994). Indeed, recent research has suggested that Mexican-origin immigrants suffer primarily from poor human capital, not low returns to capital (Trejo 1995).

Historical differences also cloud the assessment of immigrant quality. The inference that differences in earnings achievements between cohorts indicate declining quality presumes a constant historical economy. If, on the other hand, labor market conditions shift over time, such that new arrivals in the recent decade receive fewer rewards than earlier arrivals, those intercohort differences would reflect differences in historical economy, not differences in immigrant quality. LaLonde and Topel (1992) and Lindstrom and Massey (1994), among others, draw this conclusion because wage rates fell most sharply since 1970 in the low-skilled categories where Mexican immigrants concentrate. Indeed, the rising volume of new arrivals could create job competition that depresses wages even further, leading to a further appearance of declining quality.

Even the non-Hispanic, white native-born population is suffering from relative slowing of economic progress. Levy and Michel (1991) emphasize the declining income and wealth prospects that began when the baby boom generation came of age. Similarly, Hauser et al. (1996) show that the intergenerational progress of advancing occupational status came to a halt for birth cohorts born after 1950. Both new immigrants and the young native born face the same uncertain economy, but leading immigration research implicitly compares new immigrants with the older native born who are more advantaged, as discussed below.

In sum, the declining quality thesis confuses many different issues of immigration: volume of immigrants, skill mixes, historical changes in labor market conditions, and returns to skills. Mexican-origin immigrants may in fact have rising human capital but suffer declining status relative to the native born, or they may be compared inappropriately with the wrong set of the native born. Adding to the confusion, different layers of relative comparisons often yield divergent results.

Outcome Measures of Economic Adaptation

The most common outcome measure of economic assimilation or adaptation is the wage rate. This prevalence reflects the leadership in the immigration field of labor economists whose concern is for labor market performance adjusted for human capital. An alternative measure might emphasize the gross earnings of immigrants, factoring in not only the wage rate but also hours worked, a measure of effort that is also part of adaptation. Still another alternative would emphasize mechanisms to increase the total income of immigrants and their households.

Income is also important as the best indicator of potential consumption. If immigrants are viewed as consumers rather than workers, then household income is the better measure of economic performance and potential for social incorporation (Lee and Edmonston 1994). Of course, total household income should be adjusted for number of consumers in the household, either on a straight per capita basis, or on a sliding scale such as used in the poverty calculation. Alternatively, Easterlin et al. (1993) argue for adjustment to adult equivalents, not simply number of persons. They show that the population is adapting to changing economic conditions by altering both the number of earners and dependents in households.

The predominant focus on earnings and income has diverted attention from occupational mobility as a precursor to earnings achievement. While earnings may be the end result, the adaptation process occurs first through occupational training and selection. Relatively few studies have addressed occupational mobility directly, in part because this is much less easily summarized than earnings. Kossoudji (1989) analyzed immigrants' occupational status in several broad classifications. Myers (1995) and Myers and Cranford (1998) analyzed immigrants' net progress into and out of selected specific occupations. Alternatively, occupational prestige scores have been used to analyze average occupational status and mobility across generations (Neidert and Farley 1985, Waldinger and Gilbertson 1994). A recent paper by Hauser and Warren (1996) reviews this tradition and proposes a new set of scores for equating occupations identified in the 1980 and 1990 censuses.

Prior to both occupation and earnings achievement lies educational attainment, the key component of human capital used to signify skill level. Most studies of economic adaptation take education simply as a determinant; however, educational attainment is a fundamental aspect of economic adaptation in its own right. Within the lifetime of adult workers, this variable is relatively fixed, but in the context of intergenerational change, educational development is a critical dimension of economic adaptation. Vernez and Abrahamse (1996) show that high school completion depends on duration in the United States as well as the educational attainment of parents and other factors. They note that most Latino immigrants who failed to complete high school are not dropouts because, even if they arrived in the United States by age 15, they never entered the U.S. school system in the first place.

ADAPTATION IN TEMPORAL PERSPECTIVE

As shown, Hispanics' success at economic adaptation has different interpretations. These depend not only on the outcome measures used to infer adaptation, but also on whether status is adjusted for human capital and whether status is judged relative to an external reference group. Underlying all these variations is the essential question of how adaptation proceeds over time. To date, the immigration literature has failed to develop an adequate temporal perspective to comprehensively address this issue.

At least three broadly different temporal dimensions have been used to conceptualize economic adaptation. These include a lifetime or "within career" dimension, an intergenerational or "between careers" dimension, and a successive arrival cohort dimension. In practice, these temporal dimensions are intertwined with the alternative outcome dimensions for measuring adaptation, as well as with the measurement within groups or with respect to an external reference group, and with the decision to measure gross advancement or adjust for human capital.

Temporal Dimensions of Adaptation

Lifetime Career Progress   The most common view of economic adaptation is likely that of lifetime career progress. This is difficult to infer in the short term. Many studies, beginning with Chiswick (1978), have used a single observation year to draw inferences about long-term career outlooks. The assumption is that immigrants' life course progress will follow a time path suggested by age and duration of U.S. residence differences at one point in time. However, Borjas (1985) emphasized the need to use at least two cross-sections in order to distinguish between relatively permanent differences in cohorts and their longitudinal progress.

A second nettlesome problem is that with passing time, cohorts advance not only in duration but also in age; hence, appropriate controls for age (and birth cohort) are indispensable for unbiased estimates of duration effects within careers. A solution to this problem has been proposed by a "double cohort" method that nests birth cohorts within arrival cohorts (Myers and Lee 1996). Unfortunately, Borjas' statistical analysis (1995) has neglected to distinguish birth cohorts from aging effects. Thus, some of the age effects are really inter-birth-cohort differences. Given that the younger generation of native-born workers is falling behind the career progress of their more fortunate parents, failure to adjust for birth cohort leads to upwardly biased age effects. (Ironically, this commits the same cross-sectional fallacy for which Borjas criticized Chiswick.) Compounding this problem, the Borjas method uses the upwardly biased native-born lifetime career as a reference for judging the relative adaptation of immigrants. The implication is that immigrants should advance at the same rate as the false standard linking younger and older men in the cross-section. By this method, both new immigrants and young native-born workers might be judged to have declining quality.

Intergenerational Progress One of the most time-honored themes in research on immigrant assimilation is the advancement of the second over the first generation. Contemporary statistical analyses have carried forward this tradition with analysis of Current Population Survey data (Neidert and Farley 1985; Bean et al. 1994; Trejo 1995). This literature assumes that the immigrant population adapts through its children, and the evidence suggests that full adaptation may take three generations or longer.

Unfortunately, the intergenerational thesis has been divorced from the mainstream of research on adaptation using census data. The decennial census dropped questions on generational affiliation after 1970. Moreover, the new immigrants of the large waves arriving since 1965 are too recent to have raised a second generation to adulthood. Accordingly, immigration scholars have devised a special survey to study the young immigrant children who comprise the 1.5 generation and the emergent second generation (Portes 1995; Rumbaut 1997).

Closely related to the notion of the 1.5 generation is the concept of age-at-arrival effects. That concept is measurable in the census through the intersection of year of arrival and current age of the immigrant. However, to date, the age at arrival has not been integrated in the more general statistical analysis because of statistical identification problems attending the multiple temporal dimensions. The present chapter attempts such an integration through the nesting of birth cohorts inside arrival cohorts. We note that there is no hard boundary definition for the 1.5 generation, although some have suggested that arrival before the age of ten is the cutoff. Instead, we may envision a gradient of adaptation that extends from the oldest adult immigrants to the youngest child immigrants. In a following section we test for such a gradient.

Differences in Status across Arrival Cohorts   A different temporal dimension of adaptation is change across successive arrival cohorts. While this may not represent individuals' adaptation, it is a valid measure of the collective adaptation of the immigrant population. In fact, the claim that immigrants are of declining quality depends on just such an analysis of changes between arrival cohorts. The restructuring thesis cited above also emphasizes the economic role played by successive waves of immigrants drawn into the U.S. labor force. Indeed, in this view, the declining quality judgment may reflect the appropriate adaptation of the immigrant population to a changing economic structure.

Examples of this research design include Morales and Ong (1993), who contrasted the new arrivals of less than ten years' duration in 1980 with subsequent new arrivals in 1990, and Sorensen and Enchautegui (1994), who contrasted a series of duration classes in 1979 with the same duration classes (from subsequent cohorts) in 1989. The latter bears close resemblance to Chiswick's (1978) design, but pools the cross-sectional sample from two different observation years. From this design nothing can be inferred about life course progress over time, only about changes experienced between successive cohorts.

The Timing of Arrival

Adaptation in Time   Our sequence for adaptation posits three successive outcomes leading from educational attainment to occupational mobility and then to earnings achievement. This sequence occurs entirely within the lifetime or career of individual workers. However, adaptation also can be observed between the careers of successive arrival cohorts or between the careers of parents and children in the same arrival cohort. The younger that immigrants arrive, the more likely they are to take advantage of the educational opportunities offered in the United States, acquire better English proficiency, or adapt to the U.S. culture in other economically advantageous ways.

At the same time, all of these changes within careers or between careers are couched within the context of changing historical conditions. In general, earlier waves of immigrant arrivals found lower house prices, better job opportunities, and higher wages than have more recent arrivals. Thus, any comparisons between different arrival cohorts, or younger and older generations within the same arrival cohort, require that we be sensitive to concurrent changes in historical context. As argued above in the critique of the declining quality thesis, the deterioration of economic rewards for workers post-1973 has impeded workers' economic success more than their deficient human capital. The effects of economic restructuring are best captured by measuring the effects on the young native-born population as well as immigrants.

Temporal Stratification of Life Chances   The posited temporal model is focused most fruitfully on the success of the young children who immigrate, the so-called 1.5 generation, comparing their success with that of the young native-born population. Arriving at a very young age, we would expect these immigrant children to develop educational attainment that approaches that of the young native born. At the very least, their high school completion rate should greatly exceed that of older relatives who immigrated at the same time and it may even exceed that of the older native born.

These young children are advantaged by arrival in the U.S. educational system *early in life,* yet they are disadvantaged by arrival in the U.S. labor market *late in history.* A simple model of this divergent temporal stratification is presented in Figure 5.1. The horizontal axis of the model depicts the assumed strong connection between educational attainment, occupational achievement, and ultimate earnings. The outcome of this sequence depends, however, on the temporal position of the worker.

Panel A presents the assumed situation of an immigrant who came to the United States early in life and early in history (before 1970). Arriving at an early age greatly facilitates both educational attainment and development of English proficiency. Arriving early in history means that the young worker entered the labor market and established a career before the wage declines of the late 1970s and competition from large waves of immigrants took their toll. This model would also describe the situation of native-born workers who reached age 20 by 1970 or so.

Panel B describes the situation of an older immigrant who arrived as an adult and missed out on the opportunity for educational attainment. Yet this worker was nevertheless able to enter the labor market while conditions were still favorable. Today these men are in their 50s and are among the best paid in their occupations.

Finally, Panel C depicts the plight of the young immigrant who is advantaged by arriving as a young child but who is disadvantaged by entering the labor market too late. Even though these workers are more skilled than the older generation, they suffer the penalty of arriving too late. This penalty can

FIGURE 5.1

Temporal Stratification of Adaptation Success

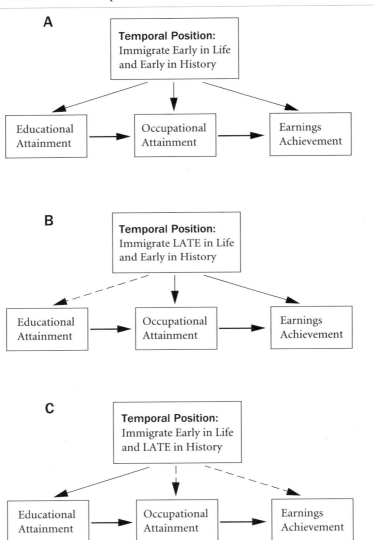

be measured by the earnings premia for a high school degree or for holding a given occupation, comparing the returns for young and old workers while also controlling for their length of experience. The earnings penalty suffered by these workers would not be judged as a measure of their failure to adapt, or of their declining quality; rather, the earnings gap would be more likely a measure of the market's failure to reward workers for their adaptation. If we find that the same penalty applies to young workers who are native born, this suggests a systematic decline in the reward system, one that is likely rooted in the restructuring economy of the late twentieth century.

DOUBLE COHORT ESTIMATION OF ADAPTATION

Our aim is to estimate the process of economic adaptation on multiple temporal dimensions, estimating both the gross changes and those adjusted for skill level, and judging both the progress of immigrants alone and progress relative to the native born. Native-born Mexican Americans are selected for this reference group. They are the most likely role models toward whom the Mexican immigrants might assimilate. Moreover, the relative gap between immigrants and native-borns is much greater among Latinos than among Asians or non-Hispanic whites (Myers 1995).

Cohorts versus Generations

Traditional research related to immigrant progress emphasized generations. One problem emphasized by Chapa (1991) is that the sequence of successive generations cannot be used to define the longitudinal path of progress from the present first generation. A second limitation is that a generation can be 30 years in width, preventing more refined temporal analysis. In contrast, the cohorts used in this analysis are each 10 years wide, providing much smaller chunks of time for comparing immigrant progress. A third, and related, concern is that the post-1965 immigrants have not yet had time to raise a second generation to maturity, thus precluding their analysis unless we resort to smaller-defined cohorts.

Our cohorts are defined by decade of arrival and by decades of birth (converted to ten-year age ranges). Although it is possible to define smaller time widths for cohorts, the ten-year range has substantial advantages.[1] When the two forms of cohorts are jointly identified, it becomes possible to approximate age-at-arrival effects that enable description of the 1.5 generation.

The preferred data for tracing immigrants' changes over time would be panel data, but those are inadequate for longitudinal analysis of immigrants, either because of their limited sample frames, their small sample sizes, or their limited historical coverage (Edmonston 1996). Instead, cohort analysis with census data provides the best opportunity to gain longitudinal insight on immigrant adaptation. While individuals are not traced over time, repeated surveys that sample from cohort populations provide a vehicle for estimating mean characteristics of cohorts over time.

Double Cohort Research Design

The Borjas (1985, 1995) model provided a clear advance over the Chiswick (1978) model, correcting the cross-sectional fallacy of inferring duration effects from simple differences between arrival cohorts. However, the Borjas model retained a different cross-sectional fallacy, inferring aging effects from simple age differences. Immigrants were estimated longitudinally as cohorts, but then they were compared with native-born workers who were estimated cross-sectionally on the age variable. Given that the older native-born workers were much more advantaged than the younger ones (and more advantaged than the young would ever become), this created an upwardly biased comparison standard for immigrants (Myers and Cranford 1998).

The double cohort research design proposed by Myers and Lee (1996) for analysis of changes over time for immigrants corrects this bias by tracking birth cohorts as well as immigrant arrival cohorts. The essence of the double cohort procedure is to nest birth cohorts within immigration cohorts (or within native-born status). Given observations at two separate points in time that include identification of duration (or year of immigration) and age (or birth year), such as with data from two census years, the method permits cohort estimation on both the immigration duration and aging dimensions. As shown by Myers and Lee (1996), immigrants are characterized by dual cohort markers, one related to membership in birth cohorts and another related to membership in immigration cohorts. The parallel to age-period-birth cohort identification is duration-period-immigration cohort. Myers and Lee provide a formal discussion of this dual identification problem and how it can be resolved in immigration research.

Structure of the Model   The data set is first structured in cohorts, assigning individual cases their appropriate cohort markers and deleting observations whose cohorts appear only in a single year (such as the entering cohort in 1990 or the oldest cohort in 1980). Advancement over time for each continuing cohort is then measured by the interaction of census year with cohort, comparing the end-of-interval status attainment with that at the beginning. The relative advancement or assimilation of immigrants is then estimated through higher-level interaction effects that contrast immigrant advancement against native-born advancement in the same birth cohort (see Myers 1996 for more details).

Following is the saturated temporal model that exactly describes the raw data; more limited models can be tested for adequacy of fit. To the temporal variables are added a number of covariate terms (X_i), here represented by education (in the model of occupational attainment and earnings) and occupational attainment (model of earnings only). The model is expressed most simply as follows:

$$A = X + \text{Year} + \text{BC} + \text{MC} + (\text{Year} * \text{BC}) + (\text{Year} * \text{MC})$$
$$+ (\text{BC} * \text{MC}) + (\text{Year} * \text{BC} * \text{MC}) \qquad (1)$$

where

A	= the criterion variable for measuring adaptation: log odds of high school completion, occupational status, or weekly earnings,
Year	= census year (1980 = 0 and 1990 = 1),
BC	= age, or birth cohort, coded in 1980 as 15–24, 25–34, 35–44, or 45–54, and with each cohort ten years older in 1990 (reference group = 45–54 in 1980, 55–64 in 1990),
MC	= immigration duration or year of arrival, coded as 1970s' arrivals, 1960s' arrivals, pre-1960 arrivals (reference group = native born),
X	= educational attainment and/or occupational attainment as covariates,

and the terms enclosed in parentheses are interactions. Additional interactions not shown are formed between the covariates and specific temporal factors, testing whether the covariate effects vary across cohorts or over time. The definition and mean value for each variable is given in Table 5.1.

Finding the Best Model   Unlike previous research that has simply assumed a particular temporal structure for analysis, the alternative temporal structures for describing immigrant advancement can be statistically tested for goodness of fit (Myers 1996). A series of more limited models are tested that are subsets of Equation (1). The best-known test in the case of the logistic regression of high school completion is the significance of the difference in log likelihood ratio chi-square statistics. *F*-tests may be used in the case of ordinary least squares regression. A more general and efficient strategy has been formulated by Raftery (1995), described as the Bayesian Information Criterion (BIC) test. The Raftery method quickly finds the best overall model from a series of alternatives by adjusting the log likelihood ratio chi-square or the *R*-square for degrees of freedom in the fitted parameters and the size of the sample. The BIC test was employed on a series of alternative models estimated for each criterion

TABLE 5.1

Definition and Mean Values of Variable

Variable	Measurement	Mean[a] (Std. Dev.) Occup/Educ. Sample	Earnings[b] Sample
Education	1=High school and college 0=0–11th grade	0.45 (0.50)	0.48 (0.50)
Occupation (Hauser-Warren TSEI Score)		28.79 (10.99)	29.56 (11.08)
Weekly earnings (standardized 40-hour week among full-time year-round workers)		—	459.82 (272.52)
Year	1=1990 0=1980	0.51 (0.50)	0.54 (0.50)
Immigration cohort (reference category: native-born)			
MC2	1=1970s' immigrants 0=Otherwise	0.37 (0.48)	0.35 (0.48)
MC3	1=1960s' immigrants 0=Otherwise	0.14 (0.35)	0.14 (0.35)
MC4	1=pre-1960s' immigrants 0=Otherwise	0.05 (0.22)	0.05 (0.23)
Birth cohort [reference category: 45–54 (in 1980) and 55–64 (in 1990)]			
BC1	1=15–24 (in 1980) and 35–44 (in 1990) 0=Otherwise	0.36 (0.48)	0.32 (0.47)
BC2	1=25–34 (in 1980) and 35–44 (in 1990) 0=Otherwise	0.35 (0.48)	0.36 (0.48)
BC3	1=35–44 (in 1980) and 45–54 (in 1990) 0=Otherwise	0.18 (0.39)	0.19 (0.40)

[a] Means and standard deviations are calculated from the combined 1980 and 1990 samples.
[b] The sample for analysis of earnings is restricted to full-time, year-round workers with positive earnings.

variable. In each case, the lowest (most negative) BIC statistic denoted the best-fitting model.

Once the best-fitting model was selected, the magnitude of variable effects could be evaluated by the coefficients of the estimating equation. The estimates from models will be compared with and without adjustment for educational attainment. Given the complexity of some of the interactions, it is useful to produce "double cohort plots" of the expected values. The ten-year segments of cohort trajectories shown in these plots can be spliced together to simulate lifetime career trajectories following a method described in a later section.

Data

Census data are the most commonly used for studies of immigrant adaptation. This is due to several factors, including the large sample sizes obtainable, the standardized questions across decades, and the superior population coverage of this data source. Data from the Immigration and Naturalization Service pertain only to legal immigrants and lack the detailed economic variables of the census. Current Population Survey data are useful for intercensal years, but are hampered by relatively small sample sizes.

Southern California The great majority of immigration research has focused on the nation as a whole, but the census database permits equally detailed analysis for states, counties, and cities of at least 100,000 population, the threshold for geographic identification in the Public Use Microdata Samples (PUMS). Increasingly, researchers have begun to exploit these opportunities for subnational research (Myers 1992; Espenshade 1997). Many of the dynamics of immigration are more visible at the local level than in the nation as a whole.

The present study draws from the Southern California Immigration Project, which has focused on the broad economic region consisting of the southern seven counties of California ranging from Ventura to San Diego and the Mexican border. This region was home to 17.1 million residents in 1990, 25.1 percent of whom were foreign born (Myers 1995). A total of 4.2 million residents were of Mexican heritage, 46.6 percent of whom were foreign born.

The sample for analysis consists of all Mexican-origin men in the region, including both foreign and native born. Mexican origin is identified through the Hispanic origin question asked in the census.

1980 and 1990 The sample for analysis was drawn from PUMS data collected in both 1980 and 1990. These two cross-sections of microdata are necessary and sufficient to estimate all of the desired temporal effects on adaptation. Without the second cross-section we risk confusing duration or age effects with differences between cohorts that may be relatively permanent. The simple comparison of two cross-sections provides, in essence, "stereoscopic" temporal vision that permits measurement of different changes over time. A third cross-section might be added from the 1970 census (Borjas 1995), but this adds less in the way of insight than it detracts through loss of clarity.

Several advantages attend the pairing of 1980 and 1990 data instead of other possible combinations. Key variables to be used, such as occupational status and Hispanic origin, are coded more consistently in 1980 and 1990 than in 1970. In addition, a smaller sampling fraction was used in 1970 than in the later years, compounding the fact that immigrants prior to 1970 were far less numerous than those in 1980 or 1990. Moreover, the earlier arrivals are still included in the 1980 and 1990 samples, albeit after they have acquired longer duration of U.S. residence (and excluding those that may have emigrated).

Outcome Measures of Adaptation   *Earnings.* The most common measure of economic adaptation has been the earnings or wage rate, reflecting the leadership of labor economists in the study of immigration. A number of variations reflect constraints imposed by different data sets, but analyses of census data usually address annual or weekly earnings of full-time, year-round workers. For this analysis, our sample consists of male workers who worked at least 35 hours per week for at least 48 weeks of the year preceding the census. Earnings of those workers were then standardized to a 40-hour, 52-week basis. Our outcome variable was then defined as the average weekly earnings for the year.

Occupation. Occupational status is an important determinant of earnings and comprises an alternative measure of economic mobility, one that has been analyzed much less often, largely by sociologists. Through the use of changes in mean occupational prestige scores, Neidert and Farley (1985) and Waldinger and Gilbertson (1994) have analyzed the intergenerational mobility of immigrants with Current Population Survey data. Alternatively, Kossoudji (1989) uses a cross-sectional survey to analyze the assignment of immigrants to different occupational classes and estimates earnings within occupations. Still another approach has focused on the odds of entering specific occupations, such as self-employment or factory work (Myers 1995; Myers and Cranford 1998).

The present analysis makes use of occupational status scores newly constructed by Hauser and Warren (1996). Occupations were coded for comparability between the 1980 and 1990 censuses and status scores assigned by evaluation of job holders' characteristics. The total index scores range from a low of 7.13 for shoe machine operators to 80.53 for physicians. The mean score for the Mexican-origin sample is 28.8, corresponding roughly to such occupations as janitor or carpenter.

Educational Attainment. Virtually all studies of economic adaptation include educational attainment as an important measure of human capital that determines earnings and occupation. This variable has been less often carefully considered. Hauser et al. (1996) show that the occupational returns from schooling are highly nonlinear, with weak returns for additional years of schooling before 12th grade and much sharper returns thereafter. They suggest that the low returns estimated for blacks (and Latinos, it may be presumed) are biased by the fact that minorities' education is often truncated to the low-return portion of the response function. Indeed, treating occupational status as a simple linear function of years of education, Neidert and Farley (1985) and Waldinger and Gilbertson (1994) both find very low occupational returns to education for Mexicans and higher than average returns for Asians (who often have very high education). Hauser et al. (1996) propose a nonlinear specification that better captures the effects of education.

Unfortunately, a second problem has emerged from the reconstruction of the education questions in the 1990 census. Whereas previous censuses asked about years of education, the 1990 census switched to asking about certificates and degrees. Analysts using the 1990 data have sought to recode these data back to years of education for use in their standard models, but Mare (1995) demonstrates the incompatibility of these two codings. Exploratory analysis by the present writer shows that the bias lies primarily in the range of those who have completed high school but do not have a college degree. Between 1980 and 1990, there was a sharp upward shift within native-born white cohorts in the percentage that are non-BA, post–high school educated workers, an effect found even among those passing from age 45 to 55, when education should be fairly stable. This shift may arise from respondents volunteering new information on vocational training (e.g., truck driving or beautician school) that was previously omitted from years of education. As a result of this incompatibility, many studies that have compared 1980 and 1990 samples on education reveal a spurious upward shift in the proportion that has completed "some college."

A simple solution resolves the two problems of incompatible coding and nonlinear returns to education, albeit at the loss of some information. Education can be usefully collapsed into three statuses: non–high school completion, high school completion and/or some college, and college graduates. In the present sample, so few proceed to college graduation that educational attainment is defined simply as high school completion or not. While this simple dichotomy may seem to omit useful detail, it avoids both the nonlinearity bias and the coding problems that may otherwise distort analysis of trends and differentials in the effects of education.

FINDINGS

Educational Attainment

Although education is the most commonly used measure of human capital, less often is it considered an important adaptation outcome in its own right. Surely the development of human capital is a critical dimension of economic adaptation. Here we estimate the likelihood that males have completed high school, the first major threshold of educational attainment. The great majority of Mexican immigrants have failed to attain this status (72.7 percent); at the other extreme, very few go on to complete college (3.8 percent).

Completion of high school can be modeled as a function of immigration cohort or native-born status, birth cohort, year of observation, and the joint classifications. Determination of the statistically significant factors to be included was made through comparison of a dozen models. According to the BIC criterion of Raftery (1995), the best-fitting model necessary and sufficient to describe the pattern of educational attainment excludes only the last, highest-level interaction shown in Equation (1). The coefficients estimated from the logistic regression that includes that set of factors are reported in Appendix Table A.1.

For present purposes, the results are best displayed in a double cohort plot, as shown in Figure 5.2. Each tier of the display presents for a different outcome variable the expected values computed from the best-fitting model of statistically significant effects. Each arrow traces a birth cohort from 1980 (white dot) to 1990 (black dot) when it is ten years older. The 1970s' arrivals were only recently settled in 1980 and ten years longer settled in 1990. Separate panels are shown for groups of birth cohorts from progressively earlier arrival waves (or the native born).

The top tier of Figure 5.2 presents cohorts' trajectories of educational attainment. Among the 1970s' arrivals, recently arrived when first observed in 1980, the birth cohorts have uniformly low educational attainment, with the modest exception of the very youngest. Among the 1960s' arrivals, similarly low educational attainment is seen for men who arrived at age 25 or older, but there is a pronounced upward shift into high school completion for the youngest cohort (those aged 15–24 in 1980 who were aged 5–14 shortly after

FIGURE 5.2

Trajectories of Cohort Attainments

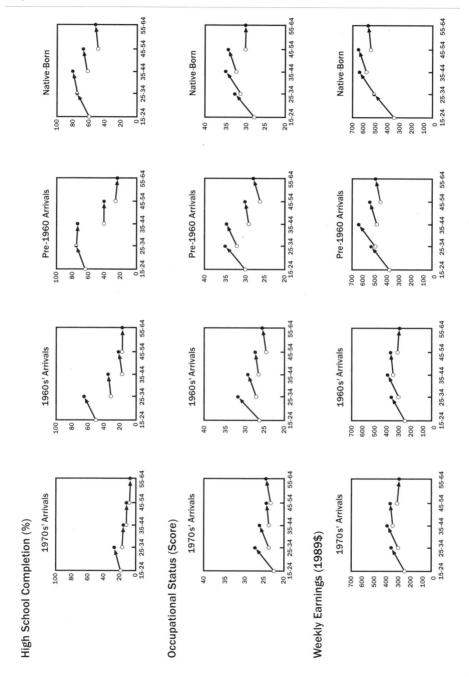

their arrival). In fact, among the pre-1960 arrivals, the two youngest cohorts both rise to higher completion, approximating that for the native born. Overall, this pattern indicates a dramatic rise in educational attainment among what is often called the 1.5 generation. While adult immigrants may not improve their education within their lifetime, the youngest immigrants adapt very quickly.

In principle, the cohort arrows should be flat after age 25, signifying that cohorts retain their educational level through life. However, the slight upward tilt among the native born reflects a general tendency toward "degree inflation" over their lifetime, with the effects of differential mortality by the less educated observable at very old ages.[2] Less understandable is that some immigrant cohorts experienced a decline in high school completion. Research on return migration to Mexico suggests that the opposite should have occurred, because those with a high school degree are less likely to leave California for Mexico (Reyes 1997). This suggests either that the better educated were more likely to migrate out of the region to other parts of the United States (Nogle 1996), or that data error has intruded.[3] Despite these small wrinkles, the overall pattern of educational attainment by cohorts appears remarkably clear-cut.

Occupational Status

Educational attainment provides the essential underpinnings of occupational status, which in turn leads to earnings achievement. We now focus on immigrants' adaptation in terms of occupational attainment, measured by the Hauser-Warren prestige scores. Here we consider both their gross pattern of achievement and that after adjustment for educational level.

The best measure for describing occupational mobility was found to include the same factors as for educational attainment, omitting only the last interaction term in Equation (1). The coefficients from the ordinary least squares regression are presented in Appendix Table A.2. Discussion begins with the gross model before turning to the model that adjusts for education.

The Gross Pattern of Occupational Mobility   As before, the overall pattern of results is best visualized graphically. The second row of Figure 5.2 displays occupational trajectories in a double cohort plot. Within careers, occupational status rises most sharply for cohorts in the youngest age range, but small gains continue throughout the career. Even greater differences are found, however, between cohorts of different arrival decades and ages. Similar to the pattern found for educational attainment, the 1970s' arrivals sustain continued low occupational status in all birth cohorts, while the younger cohorts among the earlier arrivals achieve a substantially elevated status. Indeed, the most dramatic difference is found among the pre-1960 arrivals, where the two youngest cohorts achieve occupational status similar to that of native-born workers, while the two oldest cohorts carry forward a lower status.

The Contribution of Educational Attainment   Much of the difference in occupational attainment between different cohorts may be due to differences in education. Comparison of the education and occupation plots in Figure 5.2 makes this evident. Accordingly, a series of additional models were estimated to directly test the contribution of educational status to explaining occupational attainment. These models ranged from the simple additive effect of education to a combination of interactions linking education and immigration cohort, birth cohort, and year. The aim was to test whether the effect of education was different for different groups or at different times. Following the BIC criterion, the best-fitting model was judged to include the direct effect of the Education variable and the interaction of Education with survey year, immigration arrival cohort, and birth cohort.

Results show that completion of high school has a very large effect on occupational status (8.88 status points). In addition, that effect increased by 1.49 between 1980 and 1990. However, we also find that a high school education yielded lower occupational benefits for recent immigrants than for the native born. High school completion also yielded less occupational mobility for more recent birth cohorts than for the late middle-aged reference cohort. This pattern of differential occupational rewards is displayed in Figure 5.3.

Lifetime Simulations   The ten-year career segments displayed in the middle tier of Figure 5.2 can be envisioned as pieces of longer-term trajectories. The shape of those trajectories is suggested by a sequence of career segments drawn from successive cohorts. Following the double cohort rationale, we can link a birth cohort in the 1970s' arrivals with the next older cohort in the next earlier arrival group. For example, the future path of the 1970s' arrival cohort aged 25–34 in 1980 is suggested by the cohort aged 35–44 in the 1960s' arrival cohort in 1980. The latter is both ten years older and has ten years' longer duration in the United States. In this manner a sequence of segments can be visually traced across the subplots in Figure 5.2.

A compilation of successive career segments is illustrated in Figure 5.4. These seem to line up remarkably well, although not perfectly, and other segment series may be more disjointed. Once the sequence of successive age-duration cohorts are selected, the splicing algorithm joins them smoothly by

FIGURE 5.3

Increased Occupational Status Points Due to High School Completion

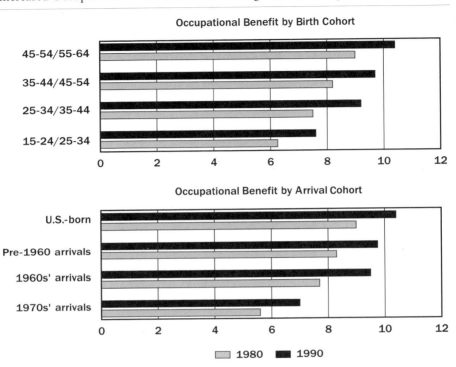

appending the increment of successive segments to the end point of the pre-ceding segment.[4] This procedure is carried out either by summing the relevant series of model coefficients or by manipulating the expected values shown in Figure 5.2. The result is not a statistical estimate or forecast of the future life-time trajectory but a simulation that computes expected lifetime trajectories that would occur if the conditions of the recent past continued in the future. As such, this mode of analysis bears close correspondence to the lifetime sim-ulations presented in Borjas (1995).

Figure 5.5 displays the simulation of lifetime occupational trajectories derived for the 1970s' arrival cohort. A separate trajectory is identified for each birth cohort defined by age in 1980. The plot clearly details the intergenera-tional differences that exist within the 1970s' arrivals, comparing this with the differences within the native-born population, both with and without controls for education. The unadjusted native-born trajectories rise more steeply and reach a higher ultimate level by age 55–64, but the immigrants achieve greater intergenerational progress. Indeed, there is little difference among the native

FIGURE 5.4

Compiling Career Segments of Occupational Trajectories for Successive Arrival-Birth Cohorts Observed 1980 to 1990 (Occupational Status Score)

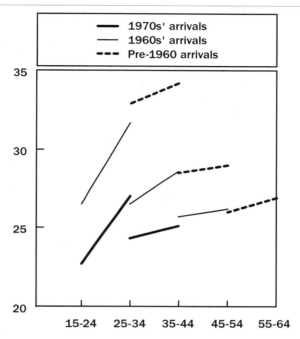

born who were ages 5–14, 15–24, or 25–34 in 1980. In contrast to that compression of successive birth cohorts, among the 1970s' arrivals those three youngest cohorts achieve marked intergenerational gains. This reflects the age-at-arrival benefits accruing to the youngest cohorts, as discussed above.

When educational attainment is controlled, among the native-born population we observe almost no intergenerational progress once the education effects are removed, and the lifetime trajectories are very flat. This reveals the underlying contribution of educational advancement to economic adaptation across native-born cohorts. However, among immigrants, there is still a marked intergenerational upward shift even with education controlled. Thus, immigrants' economic adaptation is strongly aided by completion of high school, but is not solely reliant on that factor. This reflects the benefits of other forms of adaptation, including improved English skills and general acculturation.

Earnings

The outcome most widely used to measure economic adaptation is earnings. Rising earnings signify both increasing labor market value and economic

FIGURE 5.5

Career Occupational Trajectories Simulated for Successive Birth Cohorts of Mexican-Origin Males (Occupational Status Score)

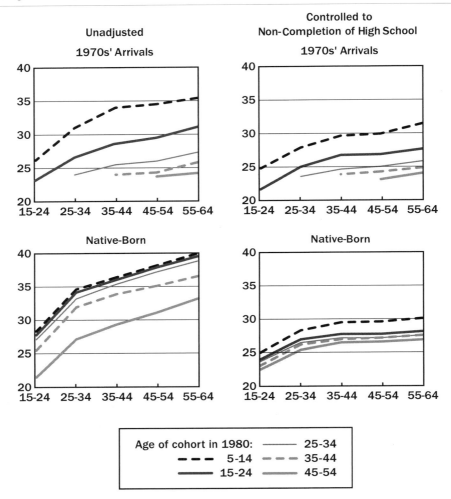

mobility, an outcome dependent also on skill development and occupational attainment. We analyze earnings in a fashion parallel to that of occupation, considering both the gross and education-adjusted patterns of achievement. The returns to occupational attainment are also of substantial interest.

A Model of Earnings Achievement   As before, the model without the highest-level interaction was again found to be the best-fitting model for explaining earnings. Ordinary least squares coefficients from that model are presented in Appendix Table A.3. The overall pattern of earnings mobility is shown in the lower tier of Figure 5.2. Similar to the pattern found for occupational attainment, the 1970s' arrivals sustain low earnings in all birth cohorts, while the younger cohorts among the earlier arrivals achieve substantially higher earnings. However, unlike occupational attainment or the analysis of educational progress, the youngest cohort among earlier arrivals—the 1.5 generation—does not appear to gain as great an advantage over its parents' cohort with regard to earnings. This finding of lower intergenerational progress is even more marked perhaps among the native born.

The Contribution of Educational Attainment   Additional models were estimated to test the contribution of educational status to explaining earnings achievement. Following procedures identical to those for occupational attainment, the aim was to test whether the effect of education varied for different groups or at different times. Under the BIC criterion, the best-fitting model was judged to include the direct effect of the Education variable and the interaction of Education with survey year, immigration arrival cohort, and birth cohort.

Regression coefficients from the best model with education are shown in the middle columns of Appendix Table A.3. Completion of high school has the expected large effect on earnings, adding $149.87 to weekly wages. Moreover, that effect increased by another $56.09 between 1980 and 1990. Unfortunately, we also find that a high school education yielded lower earnings gains for the most recent immigrants than for the native-born, perhaps reflecting the lower value of a foreign education. However, high school completion also yielded progressively lower benefits for successively younger birth cohorts. The pattern of differential rewards for a high school education is shown in Figure 5.6. As that declining benefit pertains to both native-born workers and immigrants, we suspect that it reflects the declining value of a high school degree in the labor market at the time of labor force entry. Whereas a high school degree might have been a distinguishing credential for the older generation, among recent labor market entrants college education may be the credential that sets workers apart. Unfortunately, few Mexican-origin men have college degrees—only 3.8 percent of the foreign born and 12.2 percent of the native born.

The Contribution of Occupational Attainment   A final model of earnings introduces occupational attainment as an additional determinant of earnings along with education (Appendix Table A.3). Interaction terms were selected for this model by comparing additional models that test whether the effect of occupation on earnings was different for different groups or at different times.

FIGURE **5.6**

Weekly Earnings Benefit of High School Completion

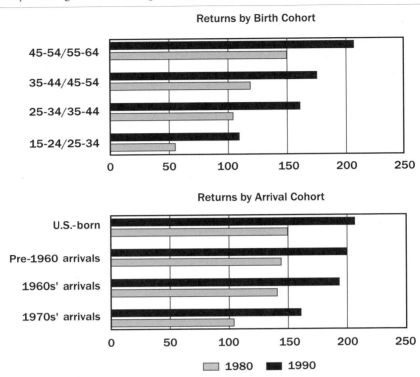

Under the BIC criterion, the best-fitting model including occupation without education was judged to include the direct effect of the Occupational Status variable and the interaction of Occupational Status with survey year and birth cohort. Combining the best occupation set with the best education set dropped out some terms as insignificant. The overall best-fitting model of earnings adds to the occupation set only the direct effect of Education and the interaction of Education with survey year.

The insignificance of an interaction between Occupational Status and immigration arrival cohort is of interest. This signifies that occupational status translates into earnings equally well for native-born workers and immigrants. Moreover, once occupation was added to this model, the interactions of Education with immigration arrival cohort and with birth cohort no longer proved significant. Thus we find a direct and growing effect of education that pertains equally to all workers, but a differential effect of occupation on earnings that differs by birth cohort.

Regression coefficients from the best model including both education and occupation are shown in the two right columns of Appendix Table A.3. Compared with the model without occupation, completion of high school has a smaller direct effect on weekly earnings ($61.44), and that effect increased by only $17.19 between 1980 and 1990. Instead, occupational status contributes a sizable impact on earnings, adding $7.90 for each occupational status point in 1980 and an additional $3.18 in 1990. Thus, occupation received increasing returns over time for the reference cohort aged 45–54 in 1980. However, only workers above a certain occupational level reaped a net gain in earnings. The Year variable carries a large negative coefficient (–$102.98), signifying a decline in earnings for the reference cohort from 1980 to 1990 unless this is offset by the rising returns to occupation implied by the coefficient for the interaction of Year and Occupational Status ($3.18). The break-even point appears to be an occupational score of 32.38 (somewhat above the mean for our sample), above which the added occupation returns over time exceed the negative Year effect and below which workers suffer declining earnings. Younger workers experience somewhat greater career advancement (Year * BC), and so their earnings may continue to rise even at lower occupational levels. Nevertheless, the results underscore a divergence of earnings attainment between higher- and lower-level occupations.

Unfortunately, the estimation also indicates strong stratification of birth cohorts, an effect that is the same in both 1980 and 1990 (see Figure 5.6). Younger cohorts receive lower earnings returns for their occupation than does the middle-aged reference cohort. Whereas the reference cohort received $7.90 per status point in weekly wages, the next younger cohorts received less: –$2.10, –$3.17, and –$6.13, respectively. Although the sharp penalty for the youngest cohort could reflect an apprentice status in their given occupations, this is less likely to be true of the more mature cohorts. Moreover, our model tests indicated that this penalty did not diminish as cohorts grew older and gained more experience.

Lifetime Simulations   The ten-year career segments displayed in the bottom tier of Figure 5.2 can be summarized through compilation into lifetime trajectories, following the method of spliced segments described under occupational attainment. Figure 5.7 displays the results derived for the 1970s' arrival cohort, simulating the lifetime trajectories of birth cohorts defined by their age in 1980. The unadjusted plot clearly details the intergenerational differences that exist within the 1970s' arrivals, comparing this with the differences within the native-born population. The native-born trajectories rise more steeply and reach a higher ultimate level by age 55–64, but the immigrants achieve much greater

FIGURE 5.7

Career Earnings Trajectories Simulated for Successive Birth Cohort of Mexican-Origin Males (Weekly Earnings in 1989 Dollars)

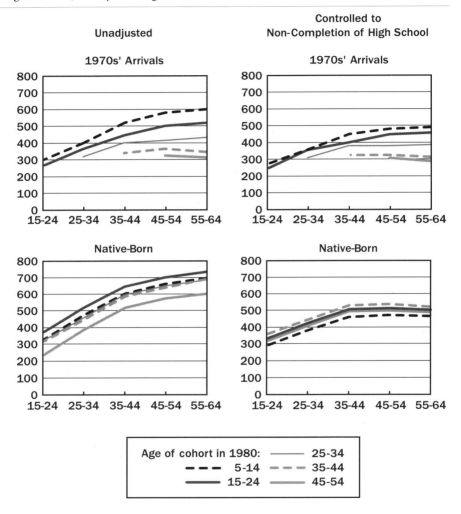

intergenerational progress. Indeed, the native born aged 5–14 in 1980 are falling below the trajectory established by the preceding two cohorts. (Both those aged 15–24 and 25–34 in 1980 are following virtually the same trajectory.)

In contrast to this compression of successive native-born birth cohorts, among the 1970s' arrivals those three youngest cohorts achieve substantial intergenerational gains. This reflects the age-at-arrival benefits accruing to the youngest cohorts, as discussed above.

The adjusted plots use the model estimates controlled for educational attainment. Similar to the case of occupational attainment, among the native born we observe almost no intergenerational progress if the benefits of completing high school are removed, but earnings do rise substantially to age 35–44 before flattening. However, among immigrants, even with education controlled, there is still a marked intergenerational upward shift. Among the immigrants, the younger cohorts are still able to achieve economic mobility in the absence of the educational benefit. While immigrants' earnings achievements may be aided by completion of high school, they are not substantially enhanced. This reflects the lower returns for education that were found when interpreting the model coefficients. Evidently, younger cohorts' investment in human capital development is not fully translating into higher earnings.

CONCLUSION

This paper has approached economic adaptation as having three sequential outcomes. In the first stage, children acquire the educational training needed to develop their human capital for successful labor market performance. By age 20 or 25 their educational attainment is largely set for life. Based on this education, young workers advance into their first jobs and enter occupational trajectories. Those in turn set in motion the earnings trajectories for their careers.

In this manner, the Mexican-origin population adapts economically through the life course progress of its members. However, equally important is the intergenerational progress made by successive cohorts that pass through the educational attainment, occupational formation, and earnings processes. In fact, our evidence seems to show that the process of cohort succession may be most important, because even greater changes occur between immigrant parents and immigrant children than in the lifetimes of adult immigrants.

One outstanding finding of this study is that the young children who immigrate, often termed the 1.5 generation, develop educational attainment that matches that of young native-born workers. Their high school completion rate even exceeds that of older native-born workers. Whereas much is made of the low educational levels of the Latino population, those figures are heavily weighted by both older native-born workers and recent immigrants. The 1.5 generation is a bright exception, and they would seem to be poised for economic success. Indeed, their higher occupational attainment reflects their higher education.

However, an equally outstanding, and disappointing, finding is that the earnings of the best-educated young immigrants are not much higher than those of older men who arrived later in life, but earlier in history, and who even lack a high school education. In fact, the young native born appear to share this same generational failure to advance to higher earnings. This penalty of being born late is reflected both in their lower earnings returns to education and their lower earnings returns to occupation.

What is a young Latino to do? Staying in school and graduating from high school is not enough. Advancing to a decent occupation is not enough. These young men are still disadvantaged relative to their parents' generation. The earnings penalty suffered by these men is not a measure of their failure to adapt. Rather, the earnings gap is a measure of the market's failure to reward them for their adaptation.

Perhaps it could be said that these young workers have not adapted far enough. Certainly they would be better off with a college degree or even a law degree. That would allow them to assume an even higher-prestige occupation. Yet the fact remains that young workers are being penalized today—relative to older men—with lower earnings for the same education and the same job.

This growing generational inequity afflicts the native born at least as much as the immigrants, and it seriously clouds the measurement of immigrants' progress. Studies of immigrants' economic assimilation must be very careful as to their interpretation of the failure of young immigrants. At a time when all Americans under age 45 suffer declining returns, we might all be judged as of declining quality. Instead, the evidence suggests a mounting generational penalty that is rooted in the restructuring economy of the late twentieth century.

The social implications of these falling returns to education and occupation are regrettable, because the declining reward system may discourage others from even trying to adapt. Indeed, as argued by Perlmann and Waldinger (forthcoming) and others, this failure to reward adaptation contributes to the risk of a growing oppositional culture and second-generation revolt. The elders of American society should feel less self-satisfied with their generation's own achievements and more concerned about the declining opportunity structure that is open to their successors, including both immigrants and native-born workers.

ACKNOWLEDGMENTS

Research reported herein is drawn from the Southern California Immigration Project conducted at the University of Southern California with primary support from the Haynes Foundation. The author acknowledges the skillful assistance and comments of Cynthia Cranford, as well as the helpful comments of Nathan Glazer, David Heer, and George Masnick.

APPENDIX TABLE 5.1

High School Completion Estimated by Logistic Regression

Variable	Coefficient	Standard Error
Intercept	−0.038	0.040
Year $(1=1990, 0=1980)^b$	0.143^a	0.060
Immigration Cohort in 1980 (MC, reference = native born)		
1970s' immigrants	−1.895	0.124
1960s' immigrants	−1.473	0.099
Pre-1960 immigrants	−0.886	0.086
Duration Effect with Time (Y * MC, reference = year)		
1970s' immigrants	−0.456	0.048
1960s' immigrants	−0.193	0.059
Pre-1960 immigrants	−0.324	0.089
Birth Cohort in 1980 (BC, reference = 45–54)^c		
15–24	0.502	0.049
25–34	1.290	0.052
35–44	0.643	0.055
Aging Effect with Time (Y * BC, reference = year)		
15–24 to 25–34	0.654	0.068
25–34 to 35–44	0.135	0.070
35–44 to 45–54	0.154	0.075

APPENDIX TABLE 5.1 (CONTINUED)

High School Completion Estimated by Logistic Regression

Variable	Coefficient	Standard Error
Age-at-Arrival Effects (MC * BC, reference = BC)		
For 1970s' immigrants		
15–24	0.078	0.128
25–34	−0.761	0.130
35–44	−0.397	0.139
For 1960s' immigrants		
15–24	0.924	0.110
25–34	−0.475	0.107
35–44	−0.554	0.113
For pre-1960 immigrants		
15–24	1.049	0.179
25–34	0.791	0.119
35–44	−0.078	0.108
Number of Cases	55,310	
Degrees of Freedom	22	
-2 Log Likelihood Model Chi-Square	15,111	

[a] Coefficients in bold are statistically significant at $p < .05$ (more than twice their standard errors).

[b] Year denotes the time trend for the reference cohort: native-born workers aged 45-54 in 1980 and 55-64 in 1990.

[c] BC is estimated for native-born, with differential effects of immigrants captured by MC * BC.

APPENDIX TABLE 5.2

Occupational Attainment Status Scores Estimated by Ordinary Least Squares Regression

Variable	Gross		Adjusted for Education	
	Coefficient	Standard Error	Coefficient	Standard Error
Intercept	30.69[a]	0.20	26.54	0.23
Year (1=1990, 0=1980)[b]	1.88	0.28	0.64	0.29
Immigration Cohort in 1980 (MC, reference = native born)				
1970s' immigrants	−7.17	0.43	−3.81	0.42
1960s' immigrants	−6.07	0.40	−3.27	0.40
Pre-1960 immigrants	−3.75	0.40	−1.82	0.41
Duration Effect with Time (Y * MC, reference = year)				
1970s' immigrants	−1.28	0.20	0.20	0.22
1960s' immigrants	−0.51	0.27	0.39	0.27
Pre-1960 immigrants	−0.60	0.41	0.30	0.40
Birth Cohort in 1980 (BC, reference = 45–54)[c]				
15–24	−2.86	0.23	−2.56	0.27
25–34	1.81	0.24	0.07	0.30
35–44	2.58	0.27	1.45	0.32
Aging Effect with Time (Y * BC, reference = year)				
15–24 to 25–34	3.61	0.31	2.73	0.30
25–34 to 35–44	0.88	0.31	0.53	0.30
35–44 to 45–54	−0.29	0.34	−0.56	0.32
Age-at-Arrival Effects (MC * BC, reference = BC)				
For 1970s' immigrants				
15–24	1.53	0.44	1.49	0.44
25–34	−1.28	0.45	0.40	0.46
35–44	−1.95	0.49	−0.81	0.49
For 1960s' immigrants				
15–24	4.60	0.47	2.94	0.47
25–34	0.52	0.45	1.46	0.45
35–44	−1.15	0.47	0.04	0.46
For pre-1960 immigrants				
15–24	5.98	0.84	4.13	0.82
25–34	4.03	0.53	2.53	0.55
35–44	−0.39	0.52	−0.09	0.50

APPENDIX TABLE 5.2 (CONTINUED)

Occupational Attainment Status Scores Estimated by Ordinary Least Squares Regression

Variable	Gross		Adjusted for Education	
	Coefficient	Standard Error	Coefficient	Standard Error
High School Education (1=completion, 0=noncompletion)	—	—	**8.88**	0.29
Education Effect with Time (Y * HS Education)	—	—	**1.49**	0.19
Differential Education Effect for Immigrants (MC * HS education)				
1970s' immigrants	—	—	**−3.32**	0.23
1960s' immigrants	—	—	**−1.06**	0.29
Pre-1960 immigrants	—	—	−0.63	0.43
Differential Education Effect for Birth Cohorts (BC * HS education)				
15–24	—	—	**−2.70**	0.32
25–34	—	—	**−1.28**	0.33
35–44	—	—	**−0.76**	0.35
Number of Cases	55,309		55,309	
Degrees of Freedom	22		30	
F-Ratio	406.01		505.47	
R-Square	0.1391		0.2153	

[a]Coefficients in bold are statistically significant at $p < .05$ (more than twice their standard errors).

[b]Year denotes the time trend for the reference cohort: native-born workers aged 45–54 in 1980 and 55–64 in 1990.

[c] BC is estimated for the native born, with differential effects of immigrants captured by MC * BC.

APPENDIX TABLE 5.3

Weekly Earnings[a] Estimated by Ordinary Least Squares Regression

Variable	Gross		Adjusted for Education		Adjusted for Occupation & Education	
	Coeff.	Std. Error	Coeff.	Std. Error	Coeff.	Std. Error
Intercept	566.23[b]	5.69	496.05	6.91	301.13	10.95
Year (1=1990, 0=1980)[c]	32.63	8.20	−7.29	8.70	−102.98	11.14
Immigration Cohort in 1980 (MC, reference = native born)						
1970s' immigrants	−248.51	12.59	−192.95	12.82	−169.61	12.20
1960s' immigrants	−169.40	11.93	−125.05	12.12	−107.52	11.44
Pre-1960s immigrants	−86.62	11.60	−53.84	12.14	−46.11	10.99
Duration Effect with Time (Y * MC, reference = year)						
1970s' immigrants	−45.96	6.01	−6.51	6.79	−2.88	6.62
1960s' immigrants	−40.78	7.99	−14.54	8.19	−13.12	7.90
Pre-1960s' immigrants	−3.78	11.88	17.28	11.67	11.76	11.25
Birth Cohort in 1980 (BC, reference = 45–54)[d]						
15–24	−202.54	7.31	−172.72	8.79	−36.52	11.27
25–34	−52.68	6.86	−70.65	9.01	4.55	12.65
35–44	29.61	7.58	16.82	9.46	55.26	14.21
Aging Effect with Time (Y * BC, reference = year)						
15–24 to 25–34	117.79	9.33	103.69	9.29	115.52	9.13
25–34 to 35–44	93.54	9.02	83.36	8.95	89.90	8.68
35–44 to 45–54	26.34	9.73	18.13	9.57	29.64	9.26
Age-at-Arrival Effects (MC * BC, reference = BC)						
For 1970s' immigrants						
15–24	143.42	13.21	123.80	13.55	109.10	12.56
25–34	50.72	13.23	71.52	13.84	55.59	12.79
35–44	−7.64	14.42	7.99	14.89	5.47	13.99
For 1960s' immigrants						
15–24	152.55	14.38	113.90	14.62	98.17	13.61
25–34	72.68	13.09	82.98	13.44	68.22	12.49
35–44	5.35	13.65	25.37	13.96	22.83	13.12

APPENDIX TABLE 5.3 (CONTINUED)

Weekly Earnings[a] Estimated by Ordinary Least Squares Regression

Variable	Gross		Adjusted for Education		Adjusted for Occupation & Education	
	Coeff.	Std. Error	Coeff.	Std. Error	Coeff.	Std. Error
For pre-1960 immigrants						
15–24	**109.97**	24.67	**74.78**	24.74	**67.20**	23.28
25–34	**81.36**	15.18	**48.13**	16.15	**38.16**	14.34
35–44	−4.86	14.94	−4.99	14.96	−2.03	14.16
High School Education (1=completion, 0=noncompletion)						
	—	—	149.87	8.70	**61.44**	4.28
Education Effect with Time (Y * HS education)						
	—	—	56.09	5.98	**17.19**	5.91
Differential Education Effect for Immigrants (MC * HS education)						
1970s' immigrants	—	—	**−41.45**	7.13	—	—
1960s' immigrants	—	—	−11.34	8.71	—	—
Pre-1960 immigrants	—	—	−4.85	12.80	—	—
Differential Education Effect for Birth Cohorts (BC * HS education)						
15–24	—	—	**−91.44**	9.76	—	—
25–34	—	—	**−41.37**	9.86	—	—
35–44	—	—	**−27.53**	10.42	—	—
Occupational Status (Hauser-Warren TSEI Score)						
	—	—	—	—	7.90	0.32
Occupation Effect with Time (Y * occupation)						
	—	—	—	—	3.18	0.26

[a]Standardized 40-hour week in 1989 dollars for full-time, year-round workers.
[b]Coefficients in bold are statistically significant at $p < .05$ (more than twice their standard errors).
[c]Year denotes the time trend for the reference cohort: native-born workers aged 45–54 in 1980 and 55–64 in 1990.
[d]BC is estimated for the native born, with differential effects of immigrants captured by MC * BC.

APPENDIX TABLE 5.3 (CONTINUED)

Weekly Earnings[a] Estimated by Ordinary Least Squares Regression

Variable	Gross		Adjusted for Education		Adjusted for Occupation & Education	
	Coeff.	Std. Error	Coeff.	Std. Error	Coeff.	Std. Error
Differential Occupation Effect for Birth Cohorts (BC * occupation)						
15–24	—	—	—	—	**−6.13**	0.33
25–34	—	—	—	—	**−3.17**	0.35
35–44	—	—	—	—	**−2.10**	0.39
Number of Cases	37,466		37,466		37,466	
Degrees of Freedom	22		30		29	
F-ratio	362.87		335.18		471.96	
R-square	0.1757		0.2117		0.2677	

[a]Standardized 40-hour week in 1989 dollars for full-time, year-round workers.
[b]Coefficients in bold are statistically significant at $p < .05$ (more than twice their standard errors).
[c]Year denotes the time trend for the reference cohort: native-born workers aged 45–54 in 1980 and 55–64 in 1990.
[d]BC is estimated for the native born, with differential effects of immigrants captured by MC * BC.

NOTES

1. Arrivals in the five years prior to the census may be subject to misreporting, with some portion more likely arriving in the preceding five years (Ellis and Wright forthcoming). Use of ten-year cohorts combines the two groups and avoids this data error. Moreover, five-year cohorts on arrival year and age would effectively cut the sample size to one-fourth that of ten-year cohorts. Finally, ten-year cohorts are much more clearly presented than are others.

2. This gradual inflation of high school completion in a middle-aged cohort most likely does not represent additional schooling. Similar upward creep in educational attainment for aging cohorts is observable each decade in national data covering the 1960 to 1990 period (Spain and Bianchi 1996, Table 3.1). This likely represents respondent error in the form of résumé padding.

3. An alternative explanation is respondent error or change in census coverage. Some recent immigrants (likely to have lower educational levels) may have misidentified themselves as arriving in an earlier period, thus dragging down the average educational attainment of that cohort. In addition, lower-educated men may have been undercounted more in 1980 than in 1990 because undercount rates are greater for younger men who are less settled. Better coverage of the cohort in 1990, when it was then older, could cause the educational mix to shift downward.

4. This splicing method extends an algorithm proposed in Pitkin and Myers (1994).

As indicated there, the method avoids the age cohort fallacy of cross-sectional models because each cohort is allowed to have its own level. What is being linked across cohorts is the rate of change in successive ten-year cohort segments, not levels.

REFERENCES

Bean, Frank D., Jorge Chapa, Ruth R. Berg, and Kathryn A. Sowards. 1994. Educational and sociodemographic incorporation among Hispanic immigrants to the United States. In *Immigration and Ethnicity: The Integration of America's Newest Arrivals*, ed. B. Edmonston and J. S. Passel, 73–100. Washington, D.C.: The Urban Institute Press.

Borjas, George J. 1985. "Assimilation, Changes in Cohort Quality, and the Earnings of Immigrants." *Journal of Labor Economics* 3: 463–489.

Borjas, George J. 1995. "Assimilation and Changes in Cohort Quality Revisited: What Happened to Immigrant Earnings in the 1980s?" *Journal of Labor Economics* 13(2): 201–245.

Chapa, Jorge. 1990. "The Myth of Hispanic Progress: Trends in the Educational and Economic Attainment of Mexican Americans." *Journal of Hispanic Policy* 4: 3–18.

Chavez, Linda. 1991. *Out of the Barrio: Towards a New Politics of Hispanic Assimilation.* New York: Basic Books.

Chiswick, Barry R. 1978. "The Effect of Americanization on the Earnings of Foreign-Born Men." *Journal of Political Economy* 86: 897–921.

Cornelius, Wayne A. 1992. From sojourners to settlers: The changing profile of Mexican immigration to the United States." In *U.S.-Mexico Relations: Labor Market Interdependence,* ed. J. Bustamante, C. W. Reynolds, and R. A. Hinojosa Ojeda, 155–195. Stanford: Stanford University Press.

Easterlin, Richard A., Christine M. Schaeffer, and Diane J. Macunovich. 1993. "Will the Baby Boomers Be Less Well Off Than Their Parents? Income, Wealth, and Family Circumstances Over the Life Cycle In The United States." *Population and Development Review* 19(3): 497–521.

Edmonston, Barry, ed. 1996. *Statistics on U.S. Immigration: An Assessment of Data Needs for Future Research.* Report of the National Research Council. Washington, D.C.: National Academy Press.

Ellis, Mark, and Richard Wright. Forthcoming. "When Immigrants Are Not Migrants: Counting Arrivals of the Foreign Born Using the U.S. Census." *International Migration Review.*

Espenshade, Thomas, ed. 1997. *Keys to Successful Immigration: Learning from New Jersey.* Washington, D.C.: The Urban Institute Press.

Goldberg, Carey. 1997. Hispanic households struggle as poorest of the poor in the U.S. *New York Times*, 30 January.

Hauser, Robert M., and John Robert Warren. 1996. Socioeconomic indexes for occupations: A review, update, and critique. CDE Working Paper no. 96-01. Madison, Wis.: University of Wisconsin-Madison, Center for Demography and Ecology.

Hauser, Robert M., John Robert Warren, Min-Hsiung Huang, and Wendy Y. Carter. 1996. Occupational status, education, and social mobility in the meritocracy. Paper presented at the 1996 Meetings of the American Sociological Association, New York, New York.

Kossoudji, Sherrie A. 1989. "Immigrant Worker Assimilation: Is It a Labor Market Phenomenon?" *Journal of Human Resources* 24 (Summer): 494–527.

LaLonde, Robert J., and Robert H. Topel. 1992. The assimilation of immigrants in the U.S. labor market. In *Immigration and the Work Force,* ed. G. J. Borjas and R. B. Freeman, 67–92. Chicago: University of Chicago Press.

Lee, Sharon, and Barry Edmonston. 1994. The socioeconomic status and integration of Asian immigrants. In *Immigration and Ethnicity: The Integration of America's Newest Arrivals,* ed. B. Edmonston and J. S. Passel, 101–138. Washington, D.C.: The Urban Institute Press.

Levy, Frank, and Richard C. Michel. 1991. *The Economic Future of American Families: Income and Wealth Trends.* Washington, D.C.: The Urban Institute Press.

Lindstrom, David P., and Douglas S. Massey. 1994. "Selective Emigration, Cohort Quality, and Models of Immigrant Assimilation." *Social Science Research* 23: 315–349.

Mare, Robert D. 1995. Changes in educational attainment and school enrollment. In *Economic Trends,* 155–213. Vol. 1 of *State of the Union: America in the 1990s,* ed. R. Farley. New York: Russell Sage Foundation.

Morales, Rebecca, and Paul Ong. 1993. The illusion of progress: Latinos in Los Angeles. In *Latinos in a Changing U.S. Economy: Comparative Perspectives on Growing Inequality,* ed. R. Morales and F. Bonilla, 55–84. Newbury Park, Calif.: Sage Publications.

Myers, Dowell. 1992. *Analysis with Local Census Data: Portraits of Change.* New York: Academic Press.

Myers, Dowell. 1995. *The Changing Immigrants of Southern California.* Research Report no. LCRI-95-04R. Los Angeles: University of Southern California, Lusk Center Research Institute.

Myers, Dowell. 1996. A double cohort method for temporal analysis of immigrant adaptation. Unpublished paper.

Myers, Dowell, and Seong Woo Lee. 1996. "Immigration Cohorts and Residential Overcrowding in Southern California." *Demography* 33(1): 51–65.

Myers, Dowell, and Cynthia Cranford. 1998. "Temporal Differentiation in the

Occupational Mobility of Immigrant and Native-Born Latina Workers." *American Sociological Review* 63 (February).

Myers, Dowell, and Seong Woo Lee. Forthcoming. "Immigrant Trajectories into Homeownership: A Temporal Analysis of Residential Assimilation." *International Migration Review.*

Neidert, Lisa J., and Reynolds Farley. 1985. "Assimilation in the United States: An Analysis of Ethnic and Generation Differences in Status and Achievement." *American Sociological Review* 50 (December): 840–850.

Nogle, June Marie. 1996. "Immigrants on the Move: How Migration Increases the Concentration of the Foreign Born." *Center for Immigration Studies Backgrounder* 1 (February): 1–20.

Ortiz, Vilma. 1996. The Mexican-origin population: Permanent working class or emerging middle class? In *Ethnic Los Angeles*, ed. R. Waldinger and M. Bozorgmehr, 247–277. New York: Russell Sage Foundation.

Perlmann, Joel, and Roger Waldinger. Forthcoming. "Second Generation Decline? The Children of Immigrants Past and Present—A Reconsideration." *The Public Interest.*

Pitkin, John R., and Dowell Myers. 1994. "The Specification of Demographic Effects on Housing Demand: Avoiding the Age-Cohort Fallacy." *Journal of Housing Economics* 3 (September): 240–250.

Portes, Alejandro. 1995. Children of immigrants: Segmented assimilation and its determinants. In *The Economic Sociology of Immigration*, ed. A. Portes, 248–280. New York: Russell Sage Foundation.

Raftery, Adrian E. 1995. Bayesian model selection in social research. In *Sociological Methodology 1995*, ed. P. V. Marsden, 111–163. Cambridge, Mass.: Basil Blackwell.

Reyes, Belinda. 1997. *Dynamics of Immigration: Return Migration to Western Mexico.* San Francisco: Public Policy Institute of California.

Rodriguez, Gregory. 1997. The emerging Latino middle class. Malibu, California: Pepperdine University.

Rumbaut, Ruben G. 1997. *Passages to Adulthood: The Adaptation of Children of Immigrants in Southern California.* Report to the Russell Sage Foundation.

Sorensen, Elaine, and Maria Enchautegui. 1994. Immigrant male earnings in the 1980s: Divergent patterns by race and ethnicity. In *Immigration and Ethnicity: The Integration of America's Newest Arrivals*, ed. B. Edmonston and J. S. Passel, 139–161. Washington, D.C.: The Urban Institute Press.

Spain, Daphne, and Suzanne M. Bianchi. 1996. *Balancing Act: Motherhood, Marriage and Employment among American Women.* New York: Russell Sage Foundation.

Suárez-Orozco, Carola, and Marcelo Suárez-Orozco. 1995. *Transformations: Immigration, Family Life and Achievement Motivation among Latino Adolescents.* Palo Alto, Calif.: Stanford University Press.

Trejo, Stephen J. 1995. Intergenerational progress of Mexican-origin workers in the U.S. labor market. Unpublished manuscript, Economics Department, University of California, Santa Barbara.

Vernez, Georges, and Allan Abrahamse. 1996. *How Immigrants Fare in U.S. Education.* Center for Research on Immigration Policy. Santa Monica: Rand Corporation.

Waldinger, Roger, and Greta Gilbertson. 1994. "Immigrants' Progress: Ethnic and Gender Differences among U.S. Immigrants in the 1980s." *Sociological Perspectives* 37: 431–444.

Commentary

Nathan Glazer, Harvard University

This chapter represents a significant advance in our understanding of immigrant economic adaptation in the United States. It builds on the influential work of Barry Chiswick and George Borjas, but by using new techniques it is able to go deeper into the process of economic adaptation and raise new questions about it.

The paper deals only with Mexican-origin men in southern California. It is concerning Mexicans and similar Latin American national-origin groups among the new immigrants of the last three decades that the most important questions about economic adaptation have been raised. European- and Asian-origin groups are generally of higher education and thus generally raise fewer questions about their economic adjustment. Southern California stands first among the immigrant-receiving regions of the United States, and first in the dominance of Mexican immigrants among its large immigrant population.

One can use different approaches to the analysis of immigrant economic adjustment, each of which may give different results. One can contrast immigrants with the native born, one can examine the experience of successive cohorts of immigrants, or one can contrast immigrant with native-born generations of the same group. Chiswick did the first, using the 1970 census and noting how long it took immigrants to achieve parity in earnings with the native born. His results were optimistic as to immigrant adaptation. But this early study was conducted before the mass immigration of the post-1965 years. Borjas went further, using two census years and examining cohorts of immigrants. His results were pessimistic. Successive cohorts of immigrants were of declining quality, measured by education, leading to poorer economic adjustment.

Myers goes further in his analysis, breaking down each successive cohort of immigrants by age at time of arrival. He is thus able to separate out the effects of time of arrival—and undoubtedly one must take account of the fact that economic conditions and opportunities at time of arrival will affect the economic fate of immigrants—and of age at time of arrival because he is using cohorts. Age at time of arrival is a key determinant of earnings and occupational status, by way of its influence on education and educational opportunity. It matters significantly whether an immigrant, whatever the cohort, arrives at the age of 5 and has the benefit of a full career in the American educational system, or at 15, when he might have no or minimal schooling in the United States. Myers develops an ingenious form of graphical representation of the empirical results, which permits us to see the very strong effect of age at arrival on completion of high school (the only measure of education used), mean occupational attainment, and earnings, the three outcome measures that Myers uses (Figures 5.2, 5.5, and 5.7). We see from these displays that young immigrants in the early cohorts (pre-1960 arrivals, or 1960s' arrivals) have a trajectory similar to that of the native born, in completion of high school, attainment of occupational status, and earnings. This much supports Chiswick's optimism. But the experience of the 1970s' arrivals gives more support to Borjas' pessimism.

It seems time of arrival is very important, and getting here earlier has been better for immigrants of the newest waves than getting here later. As Myers summarizes it, "The earnings of the best-educated young immigrants are not much better than that of older men who arrived late in life, and who even lack a high school education. In fact, the young native-born appear to share this same generational failure to advance to higher earnings. The penalty of being born late is reflected both in their lower earnings returns to education and their lower earnings returns to occupation." Against the hypothesis of declining quality, Myers writes: "At a time when all Americans under age 45 suffer declining returns, we might all be judged as of declining quality. Instead, the evidence suggests a mounting generational penalty that is rooted in the restructuring economy of the late twentieth century."

It will be up to other econometricians to analyze these results and see if they stand up. I would nevertheless raise a few questions. As a sociologist who deals with education, I am intrigued at the use economists can make of minimal information on education, in this case high school completion. The first question: Is it possible these declining returns to education for the more recent immigrants reflect the declining quality of education? How one determines that the quality of education has declined is no easy matter. There are the steady complaints about American education in the 1970s through the 1990s, but these may well be paralleled with similar complaints for earlier decades. But there is one major change that has been occurring in the schools of southern California as a consequence of immigration from Mexico and other Latin American countries over the last three decades: The schoolchildren of southern

California have become predominantly Spanish-speaking. Their teachers remained for the most part English-speaking. This increasing number of the Spanish-speaking may well have affected the quality of education, and this may have been reflected in employer judgments. One can think of various analyses that might get to this factor—for example, analyses in other parts of California with a lesser density of Spanish-speaking immigrants.

This raises another and related question: What is the independent effect of density, aside from its effects on the quality of education? As a sociologist of minority groups, one is impressed by the common finding that the earlier arrivals in an immigrant stream do better than the later ones, and that is what we also see in Myers' analysis. Perhaps the declining prospects of later arrivals are affected by the fact that they come into a much more numerous immigrant community. While the numbers of an immigrant group remain small, prejudice, discrimination, and stereotypes do not affect them much; further, while their communities remain small, certain large cultural effects that may limit economic advancement do not yet operate. In other words, it is not only the economic circumstances of time of arrival that affect immigrants, but also their own numbers and weight. This is, I realize, somewhat vague, but one could spell out various possible consequences of density. Certainly this has been an important line of research in considering the economic circumstances of African Americans, as the work of William Wilson illustrates.

Yet a third question arises. California has recently gone through a severe recession, with a recent late recovery. Recessions and recoveries, alas, do not coincide neatly with intercensal periods, but I wonder whether further analysis might not show that the California recession, combined with no particular letup in immigration, has had a serious effect on economic opportunities. This brings us back to one of the big economic questions about immigrants: Do their increasing numbers, leading to increasing competition, not have an important effect on their economic opportunities?

PART IV

Social Themes

CHAPTER SIX

Photo by Anna LeVine

Jorge Durand   My interest in issues of migration began in 1980 when Douglas Massey invited me to participate in his research project on Mexican immigration to the United States. This was the beginning of a long and productive professional and personal relationship that brought us to work in four communities in eastern Mexico, administering surveys and carrying out anthropological interviews. The results of this research were published in the book *Return to Aztlán: The Social Process of International Migration from Western Mexico* (1987). In 1987, we decided to undertake a new project, the Mexican Migration Project, which in its methodological proposal takes off from our previous experience. From the beginning we set as a goal to carry out our work as a team, in an interdisciplinary form, so as to combine methods from anthropology and sociology. Over time, fifty communities have been added to the original four. Each year we continue to add communities and new regions to our database. In this process a large number of researchers in Mexico and the United States work with us in the collection of data in the field and use the information included in the database. As of a number of years, the database became public; it can be accessed via the Internet and allows us to have common access to information of interest to us all.

In addition to quantitative analysis, we have engaged in issues of a more anthropological nature, such as that of ex-votos with migratory themes, which resulted in the book *Miracles on the Border*. Along the same lines is the work that I present here on mixed marriages between Mexicans and North Americans, a phenomenon that, in addition to being novel, is crucial for understanding the new dynamic of migration between Mexico and the United States.

Professor of Geography and Anthropology, University of Guadalajara. Educated at Universidad Iberoamericana, El Colegio de Michoacán and Université de Toulouse Le Mirail. Publications include *Migrations mexicaines aux Etats-Unis* (1996), *Miracles on the Border* (coauthor) (1995), and *Más allá de la línea* (1994).

6

Migration and Integration: Intermarriages among Mexicans and Non-Mexicans in the United States

Jorge Durand
Desmos/University of Guadalajara

At the beginning of this century, two very different migrant processes coincided in the United States. In the north, the doors to European immigration were opened wide at Ellis Island. Although the settlement of these immigrants was often mediated by organizations of conationals, there is little doubt that a process of integration into American society followed their entry (Chermayeff 1991). In contrast, to the south, in El Paso, Texas, thousands of Mexicans were contracted as temporary workers. They did not settle, but came and went from the United States in accordance with the rhythms of fields and factories, following paths opened by the railroads and the advancement of highways.

This temporary and itinerant labor migration did not favor incorporation and integration into American society. On the contrary, the migration patterns that resulted from successive U.S. policies throughout the period reinforced spatial mobility and occupational instability among Mexican workers, a situation that encouraged, when all was said and done, their return to Mexico. The end of the 1920s and beginning of the 1930s witnessed massive deportation campaigns that repatriated nearly a half million migrants to Mexico (Guzmán 1979). Later, the Bracero program of 1942 to 1964 was created by the U.S. Congress to satisfy demand for agricultural labor in the southwestern states and deliberately structured to keep Mexican migration exclusively male, temporary, and rural with respect to both origins and destinations.

During the Bracero period, about 5 million young men from rural areas of the west-central Mexican states were imported into the United States for

seasonal work (Morales 1982). During the subsequent period of undocumented migration (1964–1986), a legal but temporary status gave way to one
that denied Mexican migrants a legal means to remain and be integrated into
U.S. society. Although undocumented workers could easily cross the border
surreptitiously and acquire work in the United States, the threat of a possible
deportation always hung over them. There were exceptions, of course, and
with the passage of time and the succession of generations, some of the
campesinos, and especially their children, were converted into Chicanos.
Among the immigrants themselves, however, the prevailing preference was to
return to Mexico. Indeed, according to data from the Mexican Migration
Project (MMP), about half of all migrants identified in a survey of Mexico's
western region made just one trip to the United States (MMP 1996).

The legal vacuum that had reinforced the temporary and undocumented
character of labor migration from Mexico changed in late 1986. That year the
Immigration Reform and Control Act (IRCA) established a massive legalization program that ultimately allowed more than 2 million Mexican workers to
legitimize their status north of the border. In this way, IRCA launched a new
and entirely different phase of migration linked to legal permanent residence,
yielding an increase in the migration of women and children and a wider participation of families. IRCA also increased participation by migrants of urban
origin and undercut traditional expectations of return migration.

This new context has strongly affected the process of integration into
United States. The ultimate mark of integration, according to demographers,
is intermarriage, indicated by the share of unions formed between Mexicans
and other, previously distant, nationalities. Various authors agree that the rupture of national, ethnic, racial, and religious barriers through intermarriage
signals a crack in the cultural cohesion of a minority and leads the way to
broader integration within a receiving society (Nostrand 1976; Murguía 1982;
Schoen, Nelson, and Collins 1978).

Through a study of one Mexican community with a long tradition of
migration to the United States, this chapter confirms a notable increase in
mixed marriages over the past decade. This finding, however, does not indicate
a unilinear process of integration into American society. Rather, mixed marriages imply the extension of social networks and cultural identities in wider
and more complex ways. The change in migration patterns caused by IRCA
appears to have been a crucial trigger for these new matrimonial dynamics.

This study was carried out in the small city of Ameca, Jalisco, using the tech-
nique of the ethnosurvey, which combines representative survey sampling
with ethnographic fieldwork and archival analysis. In the present instance, I

not only make use of data from a special survey conducted during 1992 but also draw on marriage statistics compiled by civil and church authorities, which recorded 140 cases of marriages to outsiders between 1965 and 1996. This study forms part of the Mexican Migration Project, and draws on field-work undertaken by sociologist Enrique Martínez Curiel of the University of Guadalajara, one of the project research assistants.

A NEW MIGRATION PATTERN

Migration between Mexico and the United States was drastically transformed in 1986 when the United States abruptly decided to change its immigration policy. After IRCA's passage, the legal situation of Mexican migrants in the United States changed dramatically. A recent report of *Migration News* estimates that of 7 million Mexicans in the United States, roughly 1 million are naturalized (14 percent), 4 million are legal resident aliens (57 percent), and 2 million (29 percent) are undocumented (McDonnell 1997). According to fig- ures provided by the Immigration and Naturalization Service (INS), which by tradition tends to inflate estimates of illegal migration, the number of undoc-umented migrants is 2.7 million, which means that they would constitute 38 percent of the total Mexican population.

Migrants legalized under IRCA and those who later achieved legal status through the family reunification provision faced a novel situation, with new opportunities that would have been unimaginable in their previous undocu-mented status: the possibility of lengthening their stay in open-ended fashion, the ability to enter and leave the country at will, the option of naturalizing, the right to access social services for which they had always paid but had hereto-fore been denied, the ability to look for better employment opportunities, and ultimately the freedom to move without fear throughout the United States. Whether they wanted it or not, legality allowed migrants to define new sce-narios for life and work north of the border: Now they could choose their place of residence and employment, the destinations for their savings and investments, their length of stay, and the date of their ultimate return to Mexico.

The change in legal status allowed them to feel, for the first time, a proclivity toward naturalization in United States. Historically, Mexicans were the immi-grant group with the lowest naturalization index: only 3 percent in comparison with 8 percent among Central Americans, 14 percent among Caribbeans, and 16 percent among South Americans in 1993 to 1994 (Department of Labor 1996). In the last two years, however, petitions for naturalization increased dramati-cally among Mexicans. Indeed, 1.1 million Mexicans were naturalized in 1996, and an additional 1.7 million were expected in 1997 (McDonnell 1997). This increase in the number of aspirants for naturalization is attributed to two factors: recent legislation that limits the access of legal residents to key social entitlements (namely Medicare and Medicaid) and the racist attacks on migrants suffered in the wake of California's Proposition 187. Mexicans, feeling vulnerable in the new discriminatory climate, have opted for naturalization in growing numbers as a means of countering the attacks of politicians who have discovered anti-immigrant campaigns to be a powerful vehicle for political mobilization in states such as California and Florida.

In the new, hostile political environment, a change of nationality also reflects a change in attitude on the part of migrants with respect to potential integration north of the border. The upsurge in discrimination obliged them, as never before, to engage in political participation through electoral struggle. As a result, with each passing day the Latino vote becomes more and more of a crucial factor deciding elections in four key states: Arizona, California, Florida, and Texas. The recent victory of Loretta Sánchez in Santa Ana, California, was due largely to the Mexican vote, and especially to the support of just-naturalized voters quickly organized by the Hermandad Mexicana Nacional (McDonnell 1997).

In practical terms, legalization not only opened the possibility of gaining better employment and higher wages but also put Mexicans in a better position to interact with other groups in American society. It afforded them more opportunities for social mobility through changes of employment and residence, and allowed them to gain an improved understanding of the culture and language of the United States. In addition, for many Mexican migrants (and above all the young) it opened new vistas with respect to the possibility of intermarriage.

Those undocumented migrants who, for one reason or another, did not qualify for legalization face a very different situation. Recent increases in the costs and risks of border crossing have obliged them to lengthen their stay north of the border, discouraging the pattern of annual returns to which they had heretofore been accustomed. Undocumented single men who elect to remain in the United States were left with only one road to obtain legal residence papers—marriage. At the same time, meeting and establishing relations with potential mates has become easier. Patterns of living and residence have changed even for the undocumented. The male-only barracks located in agricultural areas have largely been abandoned. Now migrants rent houses and apartments in nearby towns and cities, thus reducing their vulnerability to raids and arrest by the INS.

The new ease of meeting potential mates also follows from transformations of the labor market that generally permit both documented and undocumented migrants relatively free contact with persons of the opposite sex from diverse countries. Indeed, the sexual division of labor has changed in radical ways. Previously, only men could be found in certain activities, or at a minimum there was a strict spatial separation between the work of men and women that limited regular contact. The current trend, however, is to combine tasks in ways that mix men and women within the workplace. Thus, the odds of establishing a romantic relationship have notably increased on the job as well as in residential areas. These new conditions have begun to change marriage patterns among Mexican migrants, as can be seen from the case of Ameca.

THE STUDY OF MIXED MARRIAGES

For a variety of reasons, patterns of intermarriage among migrants to the United States have received little attention in the Mexican literature. First, mixed marriages are relatively new. Until recently, migrants strongly preferred marriage with people from their own places of origin, or at least from other parts of Mexico. Second, censuses and surveys undertaken in Mexico generally offer little quantitative information on intermarriage, and qualitative research is an arduous way of obtaining data on the subject, even locally. Finally, although intermarriage is a phenomenon that affects Mexicans, it transpires in the United States, which hinders studies based on data gathered south of the border.

More attention has been paid to the subject of intermarriage on the U.S. side of the border, with several sources of statistics and analysis. But U.S. studies are at best only approximations to the subject, since most studies focus on Hispanics, Mexican Americans, or Chicanos rather than Mexican immigrants. This blurring of natives and immigrants creates serious problems of theory and definition and presents methodological obstacles to distinguishing separate nationalities, origins, and ethnic ascriptions. Indeed, the trend in U.S. resrach to broaden research to embrace "Latinos" as the relevant group for study impedes understanding of the internal dynamics of the different nationalities that make up that population. One need only recall that between the decades of the 1950s and 1970s there were categorical differences between Chicanos and Mexicans with respect to the demands of the job market (Santamaría 1988). For the former, labor unions provided the principal mechanism for improving conditions of work, especially in agriculture, whereas for the latter, the need to acquire dollars in order to return to Mexico made participation in U.S. labor struggles less urgent. This difference created political tensions that for years widened the social distance between the groups, a gulf that was reflected in matrimonial patterns.

Most research to date has focused on intermarriage between Latinos and Anglos. Based on an analysis of surnames in California, Schoen, Nelson, and Collins (1978) found that during the 1970s there was an increase in the relative frequency of marriages between those with Spanish and Anglo-Saxon last names. They concluded that a narrowing of social distance between the two groups had occurred. According to these authors, the situation of Hispanics differed radically compared with African Americans, who displayed a low rate of intermarriage with Anglos. The Latino pattern generally resembled the intermarriage pattern typical of southern and eastern European immigrants one or two generations earlier. Nevertheless, the authors only asserted that this pattern characterized Hispanics in general, not Mexican immigrants in particular, who still displayed low rates of intermarriage with Anglos (Schoen, Nelson, and Collins 1978).

Murguía's (1982) computations using 1970 data found an exogamy rate of 16 percent for Chicano men and 17 percent for Chicana women. Some years before, in 1953, the rate had been around 14 percent (Nostrand 1976). Thus, according to Murguía, the historical rate of intermarriage between Chicanos and Anglos had just begun to increase in the 1970s. Exogamy tended to be concentrated in urban areas and was more frequent among second- and third-generation Mexicans than among the first. A detailed analysis revealed regional differences as well: Mixed marriages were more frequent in California and New Mexico than in Texas (Murguía 1982). Finally, the analysis reaffirmed Schoen and colleagues' finding that marital barriers between Chicanos and Anglos were not as strong as those between African Americans and whites.

Murguía concluded that what was operating in the case of Chicanos was a combination of ethnic and class barriers. For him, this interaction of ethnic and class barriers explained the relative slowness of Chicano marital assimilation. Intermarriage between Anglos and Chicanos can be expected to increase to the extent that the former's attitudes and behavior toward the latter improve, and to the extent that a process of social mobility occurs in the Chicano community (Murguía 1982). In contrast, for Nostrand (1976) the fact that Chicanos "are assimilated with slowness" follows from three other factors: the persistence of Spanish as a mother tongue, the lack of interest in naturalization among Mexican immigrants, and the low proportion of exogamous marriages. He argued that any change in the assimilation process would have to occur through a modification of one of these indicators.

A recent study by Anderson and Sáenz (1994) analyzed intermarriage from the viewpoint of residential patterns. For them, opportunities for contact are constrained by where one lives, a fact that directly affects the rate of intermarriage between Mexican Americans and Anglos. To the extent that Mexicans are able to move into and integrate within other neighborhoods and share neighboring activities with other groups, their probability of establishing marital relations with non-Latino groups will increase commensurately. Nevertheless, marital change seems to have evolved in a less linear manner than foreseen by prior theory.

AMECA: THE GLOBAL VILLAGE

The city of Ameca, situated in the valley of the same name, is located 77 kilometers to the west of Guadalajara, capital of the state of Jalisco. According to recent census data, the 1995 municipal population was 56,343. Since 1970, rates of population growth in the region have been slow: only 1.24 percent per year during the 1970s, 1.26 percent during the 1980s, and just 0.57 percent from 1990 to 1995. Labor force activities for Amequenses appear to be distributed evenly between two sectors: agriculture and manufacturing. In Ameca these two are interrelated, however, through the old and important San Francisco Refinery, which processes raw cane into sugar. Ameca also plays a commercial role for the broader agrarian region where it is located (Martínez 1995). Nonetheless, shops and work stalls located in commercial and service areas of the city appear to be occupied mainly by women, and indeed at the local level the occupational structure of women is more diversified than that of males.

In this context, it is not strange that migration to the United States became an important and relatively permanent labor option for Amequenses. Over time they learned to combine migration seasonally with the rhythms of a refinery that only offered work during certain months of the year. A representative sample conducted in 1992 revealed that more than half (55 percent) of all households contained someone who had worked in the United States (MMP 1996). Most of these migrants were young men who began emigrating between the ages of 18 and 35 (MMP 1996; Martínez 1995). Historically, most of this movement was temporary, with much shuttling back and forth to cities and towns in California, Illinois, and Nevada (Martínez 1995).

A basic principle of matrimony throughout western Mexico, including Ameca, is that a man should return to his community of origin to seek a wife— if not from there, at least from a neighboring village (González 1973). In the case of Ameca, of course, another extralocal option for matrimony is Guadalajara (Martínez 1995). Thus, despite widespread internal and international migration,

Amequenses turned their gaze toward home when the time came to seek a spouse. In this regard, the community's *fiesta patronal* (feast day of the patron saint) became the key moment for migrants to initiate contacts, formalize engagements, and set marriage dates. Migrant networks anchored in the countryside facilitated the persistence of endogamous ties and reinforced a sense of belonging to the community. The absent son who had begun to go astray north of the border was quickly reintegrated into the community and its obligations through marriage with a nice girl from a local family. The Catholic church, for its part, learned how to protect and watch over its people in places of both origin and destination. In this way, the disruptive by-products of emigration could be controlled with relative success over the years.

Nevertheless, a few cases showed an incipient trend among U.S. migrants to marry among themselves, even if they were from different communities. In this first phase of out-marriage, couples returning to Mexico invariably integrated socially within the community of the husband (Arias 1996). This trend toward exogamy nonetheless became progressively amplified and diversified as internal migration declined in favor of international migration during the 1980s.

The first person to definitively break the norm against exogamy in Ameca was Guadalupe Nava, who in 1965 married Warren Blacker, an American she met in Mexico City. He was a war veteran who, like so many others, decided to retire to Mexico; unlike most others, however, he also sought to marry, have a family, and settle down. Thus, he was something of an unusual case. Over time, however, mixed marriages became more frequent, above all those between migrants who had met in the United States. But it was during the period from 1985 to 1995 that the pace of intermarriage quickened rapidly enough to constitute a meaningful change in the local marriage pattern (see Figure 6.1).

In most cases, we are dealing with migrants who married in the United States when they were illegal (74 percent). Although one of the objectives of these unions was to obtain legal papers, most remained quite stable: The index of divorce and separation is only 16 percent, just four points above the divorce rate estimated for Ameca itself. At present, most intermarried couples reside in the United States (82 percent), with Ameca coming in a distant second (just 7 percent of couples); only a small proportion try to maintain residences in both countries (4 percent). Thus, the intermarried are a population who have largely settled north of the border and whose process of integration must therefore be studied primarily in the United States.

In general, people from Ameca have married persons living in places where they arrive to work (see Figure 6.2). Nonetheless, one sees a greater proclivity toward mixed marriage in urban locations, which confirms the positive relation-

FIGURE 6.1

Mixed Marriages in Ameca, Jalisco, by Year of Marriage

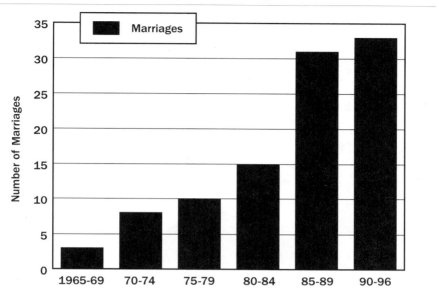

Source: Field work.

ship between urbanism and exogamy noted by Murguía (1982). The spouses of intermarried Amequenses fall into one of four broad categories: Chicanos or other Latinos (44 percent), non-Hispanic white Americans (42 percent), African Americans (3 percent), and other nationalities (11 percent). Beneath this broad grouping, the variety of nationalities represented among the spouses is rather remarkable (see Figure 6.3). Among Latin Americans, in addition to Chicanos, Amequenses have married spouses from five countries in Central America (Costa Rica, El Salvador, Guatemala, Honduras, and Nicaragua), four countries in South America (Brazil, Chile, Peru, and Venezuela), and one from the Caribbean (Puerto Rico). With the exception of one Sioux Indian, all of the North American spouses were of European origin. Europe, the Far East, and the convulsed Middle East also have made marital contact with Amequenses, including spouses from Germany, Korea, Spain, England, Israel, Italy, and Poland. Finally, to complete the panorama we encounter a few marriages with Canadians and Australians. Up to now, the Amequenses involved in mixed marriages have been predominantly male (63 percent), which reflects a migration process that is still predominantly male. Nevertheless, the rate of female out-marriage is notable and indicates the growing departure of women for the north.

FIGURE 6.2

Place Where Amequenses and Foreigners Met

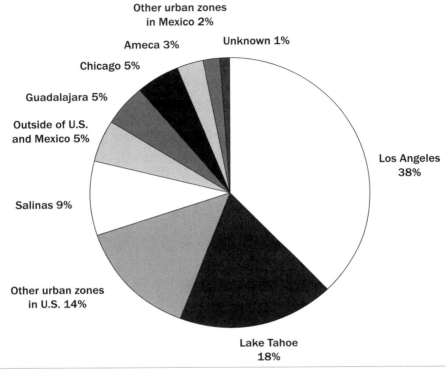

Source: Field work.

FIGURE 6.3

Intermarriages by Sex and Ethnic Origin

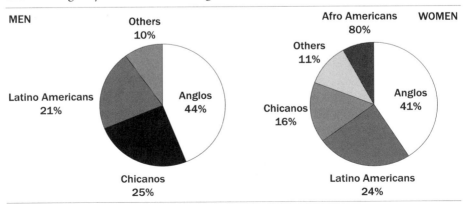

Source: Field work.

In this process of globalization, in fact, it is women who have broadened the marital horizon most significantly, an aspect already noted in studies of exogamy among Chicanas (see Murguía 1982). While men from Ameca clearly divide their preferences between Latinas (46 percent) and Anglo Americans (44 percent), women have opted for a more diverse range of partners. Although Anglos constitute the largest source for husbands (37 percent), second place (31 percent) is held by a diverse range of nationalities, leaving other Latinos relegated to third place in their affections (at 24 percent); only three women (8 percent) married African Americans.

One indication of the change in perceptions regarding intermarriage is the fact that relationships that until a few years ago would have caused irritation and social tension in the community have now come to be seen as a feather in one's cap. A much-discussed marriage between an Amequense and a Korean, for example, conferred great prestige to the family of origin. The reputation of Koreans for achieving economic success in the United States appears to have reached even Ameca.

The new tolerance for mixed marriages is also evident in rituals: Concessions have to be made for in-laws and relatives who arrive from foreign lands with very different music, food, and social customs. In a recent marriage ceremony, the fact that the wedding dinner was illuminated only by candles attracted considerable attention in the community: The bright lights of Mexico had to give way to a more tenuous and romantic light from the north.

CONCLUSIONS

The case of Ameca yields a new and fresh perspective on the long history of migration between Mexico and the United States. The emergence of a new social dynamic involving mixed marriages provides a telling indicator of a new process of settlement, but what stands out most of all is the social acceptance of intermarriages in Ameca, or at least the absence of criticism and outright resistance to the phenomenon. Traditionally communities in Mexico have been jealous and suspicious whenever someone established a romantic relationship outside the locality, or worse yet, from the northern border or the United States (it didn't matter much whether the outsider was Chicano or an Anglo). News of the liaison was enough to unleash a series of stern measures of social control that were quite effective in bringing the transgressor back to the fold. Often, intense social pressure to marry someone from the community was applied.

The new attitude of tolerance may be connected to a fatalistic acceptance of the fact that, like it or not, intermarried couples will probably remain outside the community and construct their lives in the United States. Migrant communities such as Ameca seem to have realized that they have entered a novel era when they must accept a new and distinctive migratory regime with all its consequences, including the rupture of traditional marriage patterns. Amequenses must face and analyze a series of difficult questions about how mixed marriages will be incorporated into the United States, not just Mexico.

At this point we do not know—and it is very difficult to find out from Mexico—what are or will be the nature of the various dilemmas faced by couples with respect to residence, work, education, and politics in the United States, particularly in light of the diversity of nationalities with which they have intermarried. To judge from marriage preferences, above all those of men, the social distance between Chicanos and Mexicans seems to be narrowing, perhaps because they can now unite in the shared goal of constructing a better life in the United States.

What is clear is that this new situation will expand the range of labor and social demands for Latinos more broadly than before. The diverse nature of the marital options chosen by the women from Ameca is especially noteworthy. In a way, one would expect from them more traditional behavior in the selection of a spouse, but this does not seem to be the case. To date, female Amequenses have shown remarkable audacity and originality in their choice of partners. This attitude suggests that the women of today have already begun to break the bonds of traditional society, the repository of the mores and values of rural Mexico. Their new openness toward intermarriage and a diversity of marriage options will inevitably open windows on cultural worlds very different from those of Mexico, suggesting that if something is to be preserved from communities of origin, it must be the task of all, not simply of women.

Intermarriage ultimately implies a fissure in the cultural cohesion of migrant communities within Mexico. At the same time, however, it reinforces a wider Latino identity through pan-Latin intermarriage. The predominance of mixed marriages between Mexicans and Chicanos and between Mexicans and other Latin Americans suggests that the Latino identity that is currently being nourished in the United States with the blood of many veins will ultimately produce a cultural identity richer and more complex than anything we can now imagine.

References

Anderson, Robert, and Rogelio Sáenz. 1994. "Structural Determinants of Mexican American Intermarriage, 1975–1980." *Social Science Quarterly* 75: 515–30.

Arias, Patricia. 1996. Mujeres en los negocios y mujeres de negocios. Unpublished manuscript, University of Guadalajara.

Barbara, Agustín. 1993. "Unions sans Frontieres." *Hommes & Migrations* no. 1167: 10–14.

Chermayeff, Ivan, et al. 1991. *Ellis Island: An Illustrated History of the Immigrant Experience.* New York: Maxwell Macmillan International.

González, Luis. 1973. *Pueblo en Vilo,* 2nd ed. México, D.F.: El Colegio de México.

Guzmán, Ralph. 1979. La repatriación forzosa como solución política concluyente al problema de la emigración ilegal: Una perspectiva histórica. In *Indocumentados. Mitos y Realidades.* México, D.F.: El Colegio de México.

Martínez Curiel, Enrique. 1995. En el norte y el pueblo hay zafra para el obrero: La emigración laboral a Estados Unidos: Un estudio de caso en Ameca Jalisco. Tesis de Licenciatura, Sociología, Universidad de Guadalajara.

McDonnell, Patrick. 1997. "Immigration, Naturalization and Dual Citizenship." *Migration News* 4:2.

Mexican Migration Project (MMP). 1996. Migfile (MRDF). Population Studies Center, University of Pennsylvania.

Morales, Patricia. 1982. *Indocumentados Mexicanos.* México, D.F.: Editorial Grijalbo.

Murguía, Edward. 1982. *Chicano Intermarriage: A Theoretical and Empirical Study.* San Antonio, Texas: Trinity University Press.

Nostrand, L. Richard. 1976. *Los Chicanos: Geografía Histórica Regional.* México, D.F.: SepSetentas.

Santamaría, Arturo. 1988. *La Izquierda Mexicana y los Trabajadores Indocumentados.* México, D.F.: Ediciones de Cultura Popular.

Schoen, Robert, Verne E. Nelson, and Marion Collins. 1978. "Intermarriage Among Spanish Surnamed Californians, 1962–1974." *International Migration Review* 12: 359–369.

U.S. Department of Labor. 1996. *Characteristics and Labor Market Behavior of the Legalized Population Five Years Following Legalization.* Washington, D.C.: Government Printing Office.

Commentary

Merilee Grindle, Harvard University

Jorge Durand's study of migration and marriage as experienced and understood by migrants and those who remain behind in the village of Ameca provides rich insight into the meaning of demographic trends. He explores the relationship between changes in the rules that regulate immigration and citizenship and changes in social behaviors such as the choice of marriage partner and the locality of residence. Moreover, he argues, changes in marriage patterns and residence affect the social and cultural norms of the sending community as well as the political behavior and attitudes of migrants in the receiving country. Ultimately, Durand suggests, we might expect important changes in economic development trends in both the sending and receiving communities. He cites the potential for increasing identification of migrants with labor issues and organizations in the receiving community and decreasing flows of remittance income to the community of origin.

Durand reminds us of the importance of ethnographic studies in the field of migration research. How else can we explore the relationship between the choice of marriage partners and the emergence of cultural tolerance in Mexican villages, or the link between local rituals and globalization of labor markets, or the political consequences of intermarriage between Chicanos and Mexicans? This study of Ameca and its marriages can help us see ways in which conventional wisdom about Mexican migration to "the other side" may have to be revised to accommodate subtle changes in individual and household behavior. His microlevel study, writ large, could carry significant implications for the process of assimilation to the dominant culture of the United States, settlement patterns of mature households, social norms on both sides of the border, and political alliances among Latino citizens.

Yet this study also demonstrates a problem that continues to characterize migration studies: the paucity of middle-range research that could help bridge the gap between macrostudies based on large data sources such as national censuses and microstudies that generate data from local ethnographies. Macrostudies are essential for understanding the dynamics of population changes over time, but always suffer from the inability to get behind the data to consider what is really going on in terms of the lives of real people. Microstudies, in contrast, respond to our need to put flesh and bones on the numbers and to explore hypotheses about causality and consequence, but necessarily suffer from the possibility that they capture idiosyncrasies rather than regularities.

In part, the division of the field into those who focus on macro trends and those who search for fine-grained micro understanding could be the result of disciplinary training, with economists and demographers naturally tending to migrate toward the use of large data sets, while anthropologists gravitate toward the richness of village- or regional-level studies. Professor Durand's work suggests the need for middle-range studies that draw on both macro- and microlevel work to generate hypotheses and find acceptable ways of testing them. In the case of his own work in Ameca, comparative community studies drawing on a sample of migrant sending villages, for example, could bolster the significance of his work. In the case of statistical analyses of large data sets, focused household-level surveys and community-level studies to explore the meaning of the numbers for real human beings and their localities is essential. Both kinds of studies are possible; the paucity of such research may be a result of professional myopia on the part of researchers or the lack of funding for middle-range research. Whatever the causes, the field of migration studies is diminished by the failure to focus more energy on bringing macro- and microlevel research together more fruitfully.

Research at the middle range might also illuminate a question that is raised by Durand's study of Ameca. In the conclusion, he suggests that the cultural changes following from intermarriage between undocumented immigrants from Mexico and members of other Latino groups in the United States as well as those with other sociocultural backgrounds is part of a process of defining new ways of being Latino in the United States. Through the gradual melding of different sociocultural groups, he finds cultural vibrancy and creativity in how communities define themselves as individuals and as groups. In an era in which McDonald's spans the world and Mickey Mouse watches appear in the remotest regions, however, it is worth questioning whether in fact the trends that Durand points to are really new ways of being Latino or evidence of cultural homogenization brought about by globalization. Is the trend toward richer and more complex identities or the slow sapping of distinctiveness through the pervasive impact of globalized sameness? I would like to believe that Durand is right; my fear is that he is not.

Photo by Anna LeVine

E. Richard Brown   My work on immigrants' access to health care, which is a relatively recent interest, came directly from three streams. One stream was my life's work, another was generated by American politics, and the third came from my family roots. The first stream emanated from my own professional and social values. I have spent my professional life studying the factors that affect access to health services and working to improve access for disadvantaged populations in the United States. Immigrants were implicitly, but not explicitly, included in my work until anti-immigrant themes became prominent in political and public policy debates. This second stream, a xenophobic fever that periodically infects the body politic, began to change public policy in ways that would dramatically reduce immigrants' access and pushed me to make their needs an explicit focus of my work. The final stream was my family's own immigrant roots. My parents both came to the United States, my mother from Poland and my father from Russia, when they were young children. Their struggles as poor immigrants shaped their lives and made it difficult for me to ignore the viciousness of efforts to make immigrants scapegoats for real and imagined policy problems.

Director of the University of California, Los Angeles Center for Health Policy Research. Professor, University of California, Los Angeles School of Public Health. Immediate past President, American Public Health Association. Educated at the University of California, Berkeley. Richard Brown has written extensively about issues that affect the accessibility of health care to low-income people.

7

Access to Health Insurance and Health Care for Mexican American Children in Immigrant Families

E. Richard Brown
Roberta Wyn
Hongjian Yu
Abel Valenzuela
Liane Dong
UCLA Center for Health Policy Research

Access to health insurance and to health care are important indicators of socioeconomic opportunity, an ongoing concern in immigration research because social and economic opportunities are important determinants of immigrants' assimilation into U.S. society (Bean et al. 1994; Lee and Edmonston 1994). Access to health services is particularly important for children to ensure that acute and chronic conditions are diagnosed and treated in a timely manner, that health and development are adequately monitored, and that preventive services are provided as recommended (American Academy of Pediatrics 1995). These issues are particularly salient for Mexican immigrants in the United States, who have poorer socioeconomic status than many other immigrant groups.

Health insurance is important because it provides an important degree of financial access to health services. Numerous studies have demonstrated that children who are uninsured—without private health insurance, Medicaid, or any other public coverage—receive fewer physician visits overall, fewer visits for care of chronic conditions, and fewer preventive health services than do insured children (Newacheck, Hughes, and Stoddard 1996; Stoddard, St. Peter, and Newacheck 1994; Wood et al. 1990; Brown 1989).

Although health insurance coverage is important, other factors also influence access. Having a regular provider of care facilitates a connection to the health system; it has been found consistently to increase use of health services (Berk, Schur, and Cantor 1995; Andersen and Davidson 1996). Geographic availability affects use of ambulatory care services and rates of avoidable hospitalizations (Andersen and Davidson 1996; Valdez and Dallek 1991). And cultural factors, including both language barriers and customs, affect access for immigrant and other ethnic and racial minority populations (Aday et al. 1993; Board on Children and Families 1995).

Despite the demonstrable benefits of good access to health care, noncitizens' entitlement to publicly funded health services, as well as to welfare programs and educational services, has become a highly charged policy and political issue (Fix and Passel 1994; General Accounting Office 1995; Clark et al. 1994). In 1996, Congress dramatically reduced the entitlement of both legal and undocumented immigrants to a broad range of federal public assistance programs, including Medicaid. Much of the debate and policy analysis has centered on undocumented and legal immigrant adults, with very little attention to the potential impact of sweeping reforms on children despite the fact that many of the changes taking place disproportionately affect children, particularly immigrant children, and may reduce their access to health care services.

These public policy changes were enacted in the absence of any extensive body of research findings about immigrants' access to health care. The research and theoretical literature on access to health care has focused considerable attention on racial and ethnic disparities, but few studies have examined immigrants' access to health insurance coverage and health care services (Thamer et al. 1997; Edmonston 1996). Latinos have the highest uninsured rates (Mendoza 1994; Valdez et al. 1993; Wyn et al. 1993) and have fewer physician visits for general medical care, acute and chronic conditions, and preventive services than do non-Latino whites (Aday et al. 1993; Wyn et al. 1993; Mendoza 1994; Lieu, Newacheck, and McManus 1993; Vega and Amaro 1994). Studies that specifically focus on Mexicans have found that the percentage of uninsured is higher and health insurance coverage is lower for this group (Trevino et al. 1996; Trevino et al. 1991). However, few studies have examined how immigration and citizenship affect health insurance coverage and access to health care.

This paper examines differences in health insurance coverage and access to health services among Mexican American children living in the United States, comparing noncitizen or immigrant children (first-generation immigrants),

U.S.-citizen or nonimmigrant children in immigrant families, and U.S.-citizen children with U.S.-born parents. The study examines the effects of immigration and citizenship status on uninsurance and access to physician visits among Mexican American children in the United States.

METHODS

The researchers analyzed two large population-based surveys, the March 1996 Current Population Survey and the 1994 National Health Interview Survey, to assess the effects of immigration and citizenship status and other factors on health insurance coverage and on access to health services. The Current Population Survey (CPS) is a national cross-sectional survey conducted by the U.S. Bureau of the Census via phone and in-person to obtain information on employment, unemployment, and demographic status of the noninstitutionalized U.S. civilian population. The March 1996 CPS contains extensive information on household relationships, sources of income, ethnicity, citizenship, immigration status, nativity, and health insurance coverage of each household member. The CPS includes information, usually reported by an adult family member, on approximately 4,600 Mexican American children aged 0 to 17 years in the survey sample.

The National Health Interview Survey (NHIS), administered by the National Center for Health Statistics, is a national in-person survey of the noninstitutionalized population that includes demographic, health status, and utilization information in the core survey. Special supplements were administered in 1994 to provide additional information on health insurance coverage, reported reasons for lack of coverage, and access to health care services. The 1994 NHIS includes information, also reported by an adult family member, on approximately 2,800 Mexican American children aged 0 to 17 in the sample. The NHIS does not contain information on citizenship status, and it contains only limited information on national origin, although it does provide information on whether the child was born in Mexico.

Uninsurance, Immigration, and Citizenship

This study examines Mexican-origin children living in the United States and answers the following questions: Are noncitizen Mexican-origin children at higher risk of being uninsured than U.S.-citizen children in immigrant families? Are U.S.-citizen Mexican-origin children in immigrant families at higher risk of being uninsured than those whose parents were born in the United States? How does the health insurance coverage of Mexican-origin children compare with non-Latino white children?

To answer these questions, we compared the health insurance status of Mexican-origin children who are (1) immigrant noncitizens, (2) U.S. citizens in families with one or more immigrant parents, and (3) U.S. citizens with U.S.-born parents. We used data on children and their families from the March 1996 Current Population Survey to examine health insurance coverage.

Variables Used in the Analysis of Health Insurance Coverage

Our analytic approach is based on the premise that family characteristics strongly influence children's health insurance coverage. We therefore structured the variables, when feasible, to reflect this focus on the family by including information that characterizes the family as well as the child.

Health Insurance Status   The child's health insurance coverage was the outcome variable in this portion of the study. The March CPS asks respondents about health insurance coverage for each family member during the previous calendar year. Children insured by any source at any time during 1995 were counted as insured. Because a person may have multiple sources of coverage reported for 1995, a single hierarchical variable was created to reflect rank ordering of reported health insurance coverage. We counted persons who reported having coverage through their own or a family member's employment at any time during 1995 as covered by employment-based health insurance. Children who did not have any private coverage, but who had Medicaid coverage at any time during the year were counted as having coverage through that federal-state program. Persons who had other public coverage or privately purchased health insurance (i.e., not obtained through employment) were counted as other coverage. Those with no reported coverage of any kind during the year were categorized as uninsured.

Ethnicity   We classified the ethnicity of the child based on parent-reported race and information about origin or descent. Children were categorized as Mexican American if their origin or descent was identified as Mexican American, Mexican, or Chicano, regardless of reported race. For simplicity, in this paper we refer to all children of Mexican ethnicity or national origin as Mexican American. Non-Latino white children were categorized according to parent-identified race.

Immigration and Citizenship Status   We classified children into three immigration and citizenship categories: (1) noncitizen immigrant child, that is, a child who was not born in the United States and is not a U.S. citizen; (2) U.S.-

citizen child (U.S. born or naturalized) in an immigrant family (i.e., one or more parents foreign born, regardless of whether they are U.S. citizens); and (3) U.S.-citizen child with both parents born in the United States (or, in a single-parent family, the one parent U.S. born).

We examined potential differences in access to public or private health insurance coverage among noncitizen children, citizen children in immigrant families, and children in nonimmigrant families. First, we hypothesized that a child's citizenship status would affect whether they received private health insurance or Medicaid coverage. Although legal immigrants, regardless of citizenship status, were entitled to Medicaid in 1995, we anticipated that noncitizen children may have had less access to these benefits. The CPS does not distinguish between legal and undocumented immigrants or refugees and asylees; noncitizens as defined in this paper include all immigrants who are not citizens.

Second, we hypothesized that, even among citizen children, parents' immigration status would affect the child's access to coverage. We expected that citizen children with U.S.-born parents were likely to have the best access to health insurance through employment or private purchase and, in the absence of private coverage, through Medicaid and other public programs. We compared immigrant children's uninsurance rates with those of U.S.-born children, a relative standard.

Family Income Related to Poverty   Children were classified into one of four family-income groups measured in relation to the poverty level, a standard set annually by the federal government and based on total family income from all sources and the number of persons in the family. The groupings used to classify children were below poverty (i.e., less than 100 percent of the federal poverty level), 100 to 199 percent of poverty, and 200 percent plus of poverty. In 1995, the year reflected in the CPS questions on health insurance coverage, the poverty level was set at $15,569 for a family of four.

Family Structure   We categorized a child as living in a two-parent or single-parent family. We expected that single-parent families would, on average, provide fewer opportunities for children to receive health insurance coverage through the employment of a parent. On the other hand, children in low-income single-parent families would be more likely to qualify for Medicaid.

Family Work Status   To examine the effects of labor force participation and employment characteristics on children's health insurance coverage, we classified the family's work status on the basis of the adult (parent) whose labor force participation provided the best opportunity for family members to receive health insurance coverage (we sometimes call this person the primary worker or primary breadwinner). A family was classified as a full-time, full-year employee family if at least one of the parents reported working for an employer at least 35 hours per week for 50 to 52 weeks in 1995; a full-time, part-year employee family if a parent worked for an employer full time for less than 50 weeks; a part-time employee family if no parent worked as a full-time employee but one worked for an employer less than 35 hours a week; self-employed if a parent was self-employed; or nonworking if no parent worked during 1995.

Parent's Educational Status We examined the effect on health insurance coverage of the family's educational status. The educational attainment of the parent whose employment characterizes the family's work status (the primary worker) was used to categorize the family's educational status.

Parent's Duration of Residence in the United States We also examined the effects on health insurance coverage of duration of residence in the United States, measured by the year in which the parent who is the primary worker immigrated to the United States.

UNINSURANCE, ETHNICITY, IMMIGRATION, AND CITIZENSHIP

Noncitizen Mexican American children are much more likely to lack coverage compared with U.S.-born Mexican American children. Over one-half (55 percent) of Mexican noncitizen immigrant children lack coverage—nearly twice the rate for citizen children in immigrant families (29 percent) and three times the rate for citizen children whose parents were born in the United States (18 percent; see Table 7.1).[1] Much of this disparity in uninsured rates is due to differences in access to employment-based coverage through a parent's job. Only 20 percent of noncitizen immigrant Mexican American children have this coverage, in contrast to 34 percent of citizen children in immigrant families and 49 percent of citizen children with U.S.-born parents. However, even this latter group, which has the best employment-based coverage rates among Mexican American children, fares much worse than comparable non-Latino white citizen children with U.S.-born parents, 74 percent of whom have job-based coverage and only 10 percent of whom are uninsured. In fact, noncitizen, non-Latino white children and citizen Mexican American children with U.S.-born parents have comparable employment-based health insurance rates (53 and 49 percent, respectively).

The low rates of employment-based insurance among Mexican American children are partially offset by Medicaid, which covers from one-quarter to one-third

TABLE 7.1

Health Insurance Coverage of Mexican Americans and Non-Latino Whites by Immigration and Citizenship Status, Ages 0–17, United States, 1995

	Uninsured %	Employment Based Insurance %	Medicaid %	Other %	Total %
Mexican American Children					
Citizen child with U.S.-born parents	18 (15, 21)	49 (46, 52)	30 (27, 33)	3 (2, 4)	100 (N=2,470,000)
Citizen child in immigrant family	29 (26, 32)	34 (31, 37)	35 (32, 38)	2 (1, 3)	100 (N=3,549,000)
Noncitizen child	55 (49, 61)	20 (15, 25)	23 (18, 28)	2 (0, 4)	100 (N=842,000)
Non-Latino White Children					
Citizen child with U.S.-born parents	10 (10, 10)	74 (73, 75)	10 (10, 10)	7 (7, 7)	100 (N=43,210,000)
Citizen child in immigrant family	13 (11, 15)	68 (65, 71)	12 (10, 14)	7 (5, 9)	100 (N=2,465,000)
Noncitizen child	14 (8, 20)	53 (45, 61)	23 (16, 30)	10 (5, 15)	100 (N=400,000)

Note: Parentheses provide 95% confidence interval for estimate.

Source: March 1996 Current Population Survey.

of children within each immigrant group. Without Medicaid, these children would have even higher uninsured rates. It is noteworthy that equal proportions of noncitizen, non-Latino white children and noncitizen Mexican American children are covered by Medicaid, but non-Latino white children are more than twice as likely to have employment-based health insurance, which results in a much lower uninsured rate than their Mexican American counterparts.

Uninsured rates vary by social and economic factors, particularly for citizen children (Table 7.2). Noncitizen children whose primary working parent has less than a high school education are particularly disadvantaged: Over one-half (57 percent) of these children are uninsured. Only among Mexican American and non-Latino white citizen children with U.S.-born parents does the primary working parent having at least some college education make a statistically significant difference in reducing the risk of uninsurance.

Among noncitizen children, those with incomes below poverty are more likely to be uninsured. Yet, among these children, uninsured rates are much higher for noncitizen Mexican American children (60 percent of whom are uninsured) than for non-Latino white noncitizen children. A different pattern

TABLE 7.2

Percentage of Children Uninsured by Sociodemographic Characteristics for Mexican Americans and Non-Latino Whites, by Immigration and Citizenship Status, Ages 0-17, United States, 1995

	Mexican American Children			Non-Latino White Children		
	Noncitizen Child	Citizen Child in Immigrant Family	Citizen Child in U.S.-Born Family	Noncitizen Child	Citizen Child in Immigrant Family	Citizen Child in U.S.-Born Family
All Children in Group	55	29	18	14	13	10
Age						
0–5	53	27	15	4	14	10
	(37, 69)	(23, 31)	(11, 19)	(0, 12)	(10, 18)	(9, 11)
6–11	53	30	18	15	14	10
	(44, 62)	(25, 35)	(13, 23)	(5, 26)	(10, 18)	(9, 11)
12–17	57	33	23	18	12	10
	(48, 66)	(27, 39)	(18, 29)	(8, 28)	(8, 16)	(9, 11)
Family Structure						
Married couple with children	57	31	19	13	11	9
	(50, 63)	(28, 34)	(15, 22)	(7, 19)	(9, 13)	(8, 9)
Single adult with children	47	24	18	21	27	16
	(33, 60)	(18, 29)	(14, 22)	(3, 38)	(19, 35)	(14, 17)
Educational Status of Parent						
Less than high school graduation	57	32	22	24	22	23
	(50, 63)	(28, 35)	(17, 27)	(8, 40)	(15, 29)	(21, 25)
High school graduate	37	23	21	13	15	13
	(20, 55)	(17, 29)	(16, 25)	(0, 27)	(10, 20)	(12, 14)
At least some college	a	26	11	11	10	6
		(19, 33)	(7, 15)	(4, 18)	(8, 13)	(6, 7)

Note: Parentheses provide 95% confidence interval for estimate.
a Sample size too small to make a reliable estimate.

Source: March 1996 Current Population Survey.

is seen for citizen children. For citizen children in immigrant families, those with family incomes between 100 and 199 percent of poverty are more likely to lack coverage. For citizen children with U.S.-born parents, uninsured rates are similar for those with incomes below poverty and those at 100 to 199 percent of poverty. These higher or equal rates at 100 to 199 percent of poverty reflect the greater protection that Medicaid offers to poor children compared with those above the poverty level. The patterns for non-Latino white children are even more dramatic.

TABLE 7.2 (CONTINUED)

Percentage of Children Uninsured by Sociodemographic Characteristics for Mexican Americans and Non-Latino Whites, by Immigration and Citizenship Status, Ages 0-17, United States, 1995

	Mexican American Children			Non-Latino White Children		
	Noncitizen Child	Citizen Child in Immigrant Family	Citizen Child in U.S.-Born Family	Noncitizen Child	Citizen Child in Immigrant Family	Citizen Child in U.S.-Born Family
Family Income						
Below poverty	60 (52, 68)	27 (23, 31)	22 (17, 27)	25 (11, 38)	18 (11, 24)	23 (21, 25)
100–199% of poverty	46 (36, 55)	36 (31, 40)	24 (19, 30)	14 (2, 26)	31 (24, 39)	19 (17, 20)
200%+ of poverty	a	20 (15, 26)	11 (7, 14)	7 (1, 14)	7 (5, 9)	6 (5, 6)
Family Work Status						
Full-time, full-year employee	58 (51, 66)	31 (27, 34)	16 (13, 20)	12 (5, 18)	11 (9, 14)	7 (7, 8)
Full-time part-year employee	45 (32, 58)	29 (23, 35)	25 (16, 34)	18 (0, 37)	11 (4, 18)	16 (14, 18)
Part-time employee	a	22 (12, 33)	21 (11, 31)	7 (0, 35)	14 (3, 25)	19 (16, 21)
Duration of Parent's Residence						
Pre-1979	46 (32, 61)	29 (25, 33)	na	10 (0, 38)	12 (9, 15)	na
1980–1983	48 (30, 66)	26 (20, 32)	na	21 (0, 44)	22 (13, 31)	na
1984–1989	56 (46, 65)	33 (27, 39)	na	33 (16, 50)	20 (12, 28)	na
1990–1996	60 (50, 69)	33 (23, 43)	na	7 (2, 13)	16 (5, 27)	na

Medicaid also provides important protection to Mexican American citizen children in immigrant single-parent families; their uninsured rate is lower than for similar children in married-couple families (Table 7.2). This pattern is reversed for non-Latino white citizen children, with lower uninsured rates among those in two-parent families.

The number of hours worked and the duration of work does not show a consistent relationship to insurance coverage across Mexican American immigrant

FIGURE 7.1

Probability of Being Uninsured by Immigration and Citizenship Status, Mexican
American and Non-Latino White Children, Ages 3–5, United States, 1995

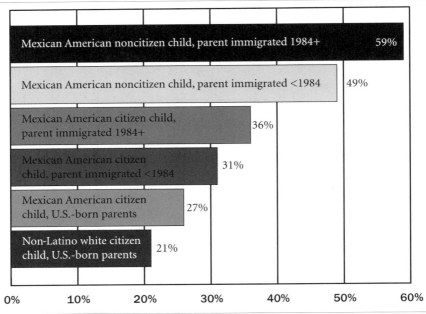

Note: Predicted probabilities are for a child who is female; aged 3 to 5 years; in excellent to good health; living in a two-
parent family, having at least one parent who is employed full-time for the full year, a family income of 100 to 199
percent of the federal poverty level; and whose parent is the primary worker has not graduated high school.

Source: March 1996 Current Population Survey.

groups. However, among Mexican American children in full-time, full-year
working families, citizen Mexican American children with immigrant parents
are twice as likely to lack coverage as are citizen children with U.S.-born parents,
and noncitizen children are over three times as likely (Table 7.2).

Coverage opportunities also differ dramatically between Mexican
Americans and non-Latino whites. Across all Mexican American immigrant
groups, labor force participation does not provide the same degree of health
insurance coverage as seen for comparable non-Latino whites. Particularly
striking are comparisons between noncitizen Mexican American and non-
Latino white children in full-time, full-year employee families. Whereas 58
percent of noncitizen Mexican American children lack coverage, only 12 percent of similar non-Latino whites are uninsured (Table 7.2).

The wide differences in uninsured rates between Mexican American children in immigrant and nonimmigrant families may be due, in part, to differ-

ences between these groups in educational attainment, family work status, family income, and other factors that are highly correlated with uninsurance. To better understand these relationships, we used multivariate analysis to examine the independent effects of immigration and citizenship status on the probability of being uninsured. Figure 7.1, based on our multivariate analysis, illustrates the effects of immigration and citizenship status on the probability of being uninsured among Mexican American children and compared with non-Latino white children with U.S.-born parents. The figure shows how each combination of immigration and citizenship status affects the probability that a child with specific characteristics would be uninsured, holding constant factors other than ethnicity, immigration, and citizenship. We illustrate the effects with a child who is female, aged 3 to 5 years, in excellent to good health, living in a two-parent family in which at least one parent is employed full-time for the full year, where the family income is 100 to 199 percent of the federal poverty level, and where the parent who is the primary worker has not graduated from high school. (The probabilities shown in Figure 7.1 and discussed below are specific to this defined set of characteristics, but another set of characteristics would be likely to demonstrate similar relationships of immigration and citizenship status to the probability of uninsurance.)

Immigration and citizenship status dramatically affect the probability of being uninsured. Mexican American children with the defined characteristics who are noncitizens and whose parents immigrated to the United States in 1984 or later have a probability (or risk) of uninsurance of 59 percent compared with a probability of 49 percent if they are noncitizens whose parents immigrated before 1984, 36 percent if they are citizens whose parents are immigrants who came to the United States in 1984 or later, and 31 percent if they are citizens whose parents are immigrants who immigrated before 1984 (Figure 7.1). It is noteworthy that Mexican American children whose parents were born in the United States have a risk of uninsurance of 27 percent, a lower risk than for other children of Mexican ancestry but a higher risk than for similar non-Latino white children.

THE EFFECTS OF IMMIGRATION STATUS ON ACCESS TO CARE

Does immigration status affect the access of Mexican American children to health services? Do factors that are susceptible to public policy intervention ameliorate any disadvantage that immigrant status may bestow?

To answer these questions, we compared the health care access and use of physician services of children who are immigrants, nonimmigrant children in families with one or more immigrant parents, and nonimmigrant children with U.S.-born parents. We used data on children and their families from the 1994 National Health Interview Survey.

Variables Used in the Analysis of Reasons
for Uninsurance, Health Care Access, and Use of Health Services

The NHIS includes measures of health status, reasons for uninsurance, usual source of care, and use of health services, information that is not available in the CPS. In addition, some variables in the CPS are not available in the NHIS. Variables in the NHIS that are similar to those available in the CPS require no further definition, but we describe those that differ from the CPS variables discussed earlier. As with the analyses of health insurance coverage, we structured several independent variables to characterize the family as well as the child.

Physician Visits   Information on physician visits was obtained using the NHIS question "During the past 12 months about how many times did (child's name) see or talk to a medical doctor or assistant?" We examined the probability of at least one physician visit per year for all children, newborn through age 17. The American Academy of Pediatrics recommends annual preventive care visits for children and adolescents aged 24 months through 17 years (except for ages 7 and 9), and more frequent visits for children under 24 months of age (American Academy of Pediatrics 1995). Thus, our criteria of at least one physician visit per year is a reasonable measure of recommended physician visits.

Usual Person or Source of Care   Information on whether or not the child has a usual person or place for medical care was based on the NHIS question "Is there a particular person or place that (child's name) usually goes to when sick or needs advice about health?" Having a usual source of care has been demonstrated to be a robust measure of access to health services.

Immigrant Status   We classified children into three immigrant groups based on the immigrant status of the child, and for U.S.-born children, the immigrant status of the parents: (1) immigrant child, that is, a child not born in the United States; (2) U.S.-born child who has at least one immigrant parent; and (3) nonimmigrant child, that is, a U.S.-born child with U.S.-born parents (or in a single-parent family, the parent is U.S. born). A child not born in the United States, but who has U.S.-born parents, is also counted as nonimmigrant. The NHIS does not include any questions about citizenship status.

Reason for Lack of Coverage   This information was based on two questions in the NHIS. The first asks respondents which of a series of statements describes why the child is not covered by any health insurance coverage. The second question asks what is the main reason for lack of coverage.

MAIN REASONS FOR LACK
OF COVERAGE AMONG UNINSURED CHILDREN

Regardless of immigrant status, the main reason reported (by adult respondents) for children's lack of coverage is that health insurance is unaffordable (Table 7.3). The expense of health insurance coverage far overshadows any other reason and is reported for 72 percent of immigrant children, 72 percent of U.S.-born children of immigrants, and 76 percent of U.S.-born children with U.S.-born parents. A distant second reason for lack of coverage, and related to affordability, is the unavailability of employment-based health insurance. The dominant role that financial access plays in limiting coverage highlights the need for improving the affordability of coverage, through contributions from employers and/or public programs.

TABLE 7.3

Main Reasons for Lack of Coverage among Uninsured Mexican American Children by Immigration Status, Ages 0-17, United States, 1994

Main Reason for Lack of Health Insurance Coverage	Immigrant Child (%)	U.S.-Born Child of Immigrant Parents (%)	Child and Parents U.S.-Born (%)
Too expensive	72 (63, 81)	72 (65, 79)	76 (68, 84)
Employer does not offer or worker not eligible	9 (3, 15)	11 (6, 16)	10 (4, 16)
Beliefs about coverage	4 (0, 8)	5 (2, 8)	1 (0, 3)
Other options	6 (1, 11)	3 (0, 6)	<1 (0, 3)
Job layoff or unemployed	1 (0, 3)	4 (1, 7)	3 (0, 6)
Other reasons	6 (1, 11)	6 (2, 10)	9 (3, 15)

Note: Parentheses provide 95% confidence interval for estimate.

Source: 1994 National Health Interview Survey.

Belief that coverage is not needed, dissatisfaction with coverage, and lack of belief in health insurance play a minor role in why Mexican Americans do not have coverage, as does the availability of free services or other options to obtain care. Thus, the perceived lack of need for coverage either because of beliefs or other options is not an important reason for lack of coverage for any of the immigrant groups.

USUAL PERSON/PLACE OF CARE

One-third of immigrant Mexican American children (35 percent) lack a usual person or place for health care, compared with 12 percent for Mexican American U.S.-born children with immigrant parents and 8 percent for Mexican American nonimmigrant children (Table 7.4). Within each immigrant status, non-Latino white children are more likely to have a regular connection to the health care system than are comparable Mexican Americans.

For children, having access to a health care provider is critical for reasons beyond treatment for acute care needs. Children need a regular connection for

TABLE 7.4

Percentage of Mexican American and Non-Latino White Children with No Usual Person or Place for Medical Care and Percentage with No Physician Visit during Past Year by Immigration Status, Ages 0–17, United States, 1994

	Mexican American			Non-Latino White		
	Immigrant Child %	U.S.-Born Child of Immigrant Parents %	Child and Parents U.S.-Born %	U.S.-Born Child of Immigrant Child %	Immigrant Parents %	Child and Parents U.S.-Born %
No Usual Source of Care	35 (28, 42)	12 (10, 14)	8 (6, 10)	23 (17, 29)	5 (4, 6)	5 (5, 5)
Did Not Have Physician Visit During Past Year						
All ages: 0–17	42 (35, 49)	23 (20, 26)	21 (17, 24)	27 (21, 31)	16 (13, 18)	17 (16, 18)
Ages 0–2 years	a	8 (4, 12)	3 (0, 6)	a	4 (1, 8)	4 (3, 5)
Ages 3–5 years	22 (5, 39)	13 (8, 18)	11 (5, 16)	19 (4, 34)	9 (5, 13)	10 (9, 12)
Ages 6–17 years	46 (38, 54)	34 (29, 39)	30 (25, 34)	29 (22, 36)	22 (19, 26)	22 (21, 23)

Note: Parentheses provide 95% confidence interval for estimate.
a Sample size too small to make a reliable estimate.

Source: 1994 National Health Interview Survey.

well baby and child checkups, preventive care, and developmental assessment visits.

Among children with a usual source of care, the physician office or private clinic is the most frequently reported site of care across immigrant groups, although it is less common for immigrant children to have this source (Table 7.5). Immigrant children (38 percent) and to a lesser extent children with immigrant parents (20 percent) use public and community clinics at a higher rate than do nonimmigrant children (11 percent), suggesting the critical importance of these safety net providers to Mexican American children in immigrant families.

USE OF HEALTH SERVICES

Among Mexican American children, those who are immigrants are less likely than either those with immigrant parents or those who are nonimmigrants to have had a physician visit during the past year (Table 7.4). Forty-two percent of immigrant children did not have a recent physician visit, compared with 23 percent of children of immigrants and 21 percent of nonimmigrant children. Among children aged 6 to 17 years, immigrant children remain the least likely to have had a physician visit. Mexican American immigrant children and nonimmigrant children in immigrant families are also more likely not to have had a physician visit than similar non-Latino white children.

TABLE 7.5

Type of Usual Source of Care by Immigration Status among Mexican American Children with a Usual Source of Care, Ages 0–17, United States, 1994

	Immigrant Child %	Child of Immigrant Parents %	Nonimmigrant Child %
MD office/private clinic	52 (43, 61)	63 (59, 67)	70 (66, 74)
County/public clinic	18 (11, 25)	13 (10, 16)	7 (5, 9)
Community/migrant clinic	20 (13, 27)	7 (5, 9)	4 (2, 6)
HMO/prepaid group	5 (1, 9)	10 (8, 12)	13 (10, 16)
Emergency room	1 (0, 3)	<1 (0, 2)	<1 (0, 2)
Other	3 (0, 6)	7 (5, 9)	6 (4, 8)

Note: Parentheses provide 95% confidence interval for estimate.

Source: 1994 National Health Interview Survey.

HEALTH INSURANCE COVERAGE,
USUAL SOURCE OF CARE, AND USE OF HEALTH SERVICES

Lower physician use rates may be due, at least in part, to uninsurance or no access to a usual source of care, or both. To understand the factors that influence physician use patterns, we conducted multivariate regression analyses. The models were tested for interactions among key analysis variables by examining the independent effects of these variables on the probability of children receiving at least one physician visit. When an interaction was suspected, based on observed changes in the direction of the coefficient, the presence of an interaction was tested. The models for physician visits account for the interactions found between poverty and immigration status, and education and immigration status.

Figure 7.2, based on multivariate analysis, shows the effects of health insurance coverage and having a usual source of care on the probability of obtaining a doctor visit among U.S.-born Mexican American children in each immigration status. The figure presents predicted probabilities for a child who is female, aged 3 to 5 years, in excellent to good health with no activity limitations, living in a family of four, where the family income is 100 to 199 percent of the federal poverty level, and where the mother has not graduated from high school. In this model, only health insurance coverage, having a usual source of care, and immigration status vary.

Among all three groups of Mexican American children, being uninsured and not having a usual source of care substantially reduce the probability of having at least one physician visit in the past year, while having both Medicaid coverage and a usual source of care provides the best assurance that this minimum will be met. Among immigrant children, those who are uninsured and have no usual source of care have only a 40 percent probability of having a physician visit in a year—a 60 percent risk of not having even one physician visit for preventive or sickness care. It is apparent that having either Medicaid coverage or a usual source of care dramatically improves the probability of a physician visit to 62 and 68 percent, respectively. Having both Medicaid coverage and a usual source of care further improves the probability of a physician visit to 84 percent, thus reducing the risk of not meeting this minimum criterion of access to 16 percent.

U.S.-born children, regardless of whether their parents are U.S. born or immigrants, share similar probabilities of obtaining at least one physician visit when their insurance status and connection to the health system are similar. Those who are uninsured and without a usual source of care have a 61 percent probability of having a physician visit in a year—a 39 percent risk of not visiting a doctor—compared with an 83 percent probability if they are uninsured but have a usual

FIGURE 7.2

Probability of a Physician Visit in Past Year by Immigrant Status, Mexican American Children, Ages 3–5, United States, 1994

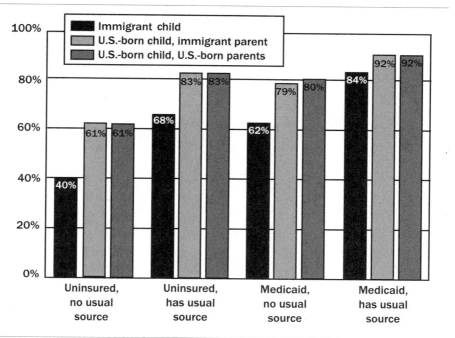

Note: Predicted probabilities are for a U.S.-born child who has at least one immigrant parent; is female; 3 to 5 years of age; in excellent to good health, with no activity limitations; living in a family of four with a family income between 100 and 199 percent of poverty; and whose mother did not graduate from high school.

Source: 1994 National Health Interview Survey.

source of care and a probability of 79 to 80 percent if they have Medicaid but no usual source. Under the most favorable conditions—having both a usual source of care and Medicaid coverage—their probability of a physician visit increases to 92 percent; their risk of not having one thus falls to 8 percent.

DISCUSSION AND POLICY IMPLICATIONS

Being a noncitizen or having immigrant parents puts a Mexican American child living in the United States at greater risk of being uninsured than is experienced by citizen children in native-born families. And being uninsured and without a connection to the health system exposes children, regardless of immigration status, to substantial risks of not being able to access health services to meet their health needs.

These findings underscore the importance of policies that extend health insurance coverage and improve the availability and accessibility of health services to immigrant and nonimmigrant populations, that is, policies that reduce the structural obstacles to immigrant children obtaining health care. A variety of public policies have been established to reduce the structural barriers to health insurance coverage and to health services that we found in this study. Legal immigrants were entitled to Medicaid when these surveys were conducted. In addition, federal, state, and local governments have helped to support community health centers to meet the needs of low-income communities, including those with large concentrations of immigrants. These efforts to improve access were adopted because of widespread beliefs that good access to health care promotes educational achievement and economic opportunity for children and their families. Our study demonstrates the importance of all these programs—Medicaid coverage and community and migrant health centers—for assuring health insurance coverage and access to health services for Mexican American children and especially for those who are immigrants or living in immigrant families.

Recent policy changes, however, are likely to greatly weaken these efforts to ameliorate structural barriers to access in the health system. The Personal Responsibility and Work Opportunity Reconciliation Act of 1996 (H.R. 3734), for example, terminated Medicaid eligibility for most new legal immigrants and, at state option, for legal immigrants who resided in the United States when the legislation was enacted on August 22, 1996. U.S.-citizen children in immigrant families will continue to be eligible for Medicaid, and children who were noncitizen legal immigrants already residing in this country when the legislation was enacted will not lose their Medicaid entitlement if their state opts to continue to cover them (as virtually all states have chosen to do). But children who immigrate legally to the United States after August 22, 1996 will not be eligible for Medicaid unless their families are refugees or asylees, a provision that applies to few Mexican American immigrants.

These policy changes thus may increase uninsurance among immigrant children, while threatened cuts in funding for community health centers and programs that finance care for uninsured low-income persons would curtail their access to health services. These changes are likely to have an adverse effect on the health of both immigrant children and U.S.-citizen children in immigrant families.

ACKNOWLEDGMENTS

The research on which this paper is based is supported by a grant from The Robert Wood Johnson Foundation.

NOTES

1. All references in the text to differences in proportions between groups are statistically significant ($p < .05$) unless otherwise stated.

REFERENCES

Aday, L. A., C. E. Begley, D. R. Lairson, and C. H. Slater. 1993. *Evaluating the Health Care System: Effectiveness, Efficiency and Equity.* Ann Arbor, Mich.: Health Administration Press.

American Academy of Pediatrics. 1995. "Recommendations for Preventive Pediatric Health Care." *Pediatrics* 96(2): 712.

Andersen, R. M., and P. L. Davidson. 1996. Measuring access and trends. In *Changing the U.S. Health Care System: Key Issues in Health Services, Policy, and Management,* ed. R. M. Anderson, T. H. Rice, and G. F. Kominski, 13–40. San Francisco: Jossey-Bass Inc.

Bean, F. D., J. Chapa, R. R. Berg, and K. A. Sowards. 1994. Educational and sociodemographic incorporation among Hispanic immigrants to the United States. In *Immigration and Ethnicity: The Integration of America's Newest Arrivals,* ed. B. Edmonston and J. Passel, 73–100. Washington, D.C.: The Urban Institute Press.

Berk, M. L., C. L. Schur, and J. C. Cantor. 1995. "Ability to Obtain Health Care: Recent Estimates from the Robert Wood Johnson Foundation National Access to Care Survey." *Health Affairs* 14(3):139–46.

Board on Children and Families. 1995. Immigrant children and their families: Issues for research and policy. *The Future of Children: Critical Issues for Children and Youth* 5(2): 72–89.

Brown, E. R. 1989. Access to health insurance in the United States. *Medical Care Review* 46(4): 349–385.

Clark, R. L., J. S. Passel, W. N. Zimmerman, M. E. Fix. 1994. *Fiscal Impacts of Undocumented Aliens: Selected Estimates for Seven States.* Washington, D.C.: The Urban Institute Press.

Edmonston, B., ed. 1996. *Statistics on U.S. Immigration: An Assessment of Data Needs for Future Research.* Washington, D.C.: National Academy Press.

Fix, M., and J. Passel. 1994. *Immigration and Immigrants: Setting the Record Straight.* Washington, D.C.: The Urban Institute Press.

Lee, S. M., and B. Edmonston. 1994. The socioeconomic status and integration of Asian immigrants. In *Immigration and Ethnicity: The Integration of America's Newest Arrivals,* ed. B. Edmonston and J. Passel, 101–138. Washington, D.C.: The Urban Institute Press.

Lieu, T. A., P. W. Newacheck, and M. A. McManus. 1993. "Race, Ethnicity, and Access to Ambulatory Care among U.S. Adolescents." *American Journal of Public Health* 83(7): 960–965.

Mendoza, F. S. 1994. "The Health of Latino Children in the United States." *The Future of Children: Critical Issues for Children and Youth* 4(3): 43–72.

Newacheck, P. W., D. C. Hughes, and J. J. Stoddard. 1996. "Children's Access to Primary Care: Differences by Race, Income, and Insurance Status." *Pediatrics* 7(1): 26–32.

Stoddard, J., R. St. Peter, and P. Newacheck. 1994. "Health Insurance Status and Ambulatory Care in Children." *New England Journal of Medicine* 330: 1421–1425.

Thamer, M., C. Richard, A. W. Casebeer, and N. F. Ray. 1997. "Health Insurance Coverage Among Foreign-Born U.S. Residents: The Impact of Race, Ethnicity, and Length of Residence." *American Journal of Public Health* 87(1): 96–102.

Trevino, F., M. E. Moyer, R. B. Valdez, and M. A. Stroup-Benham. 1991. "Health Insurance Coverage and Utilization of Health Services by Mexican Americans, Mainland Puerto Ricans, and Cuban Americans." *Journal of American Medical Association* 265: 233–237.

Trevino, R. P., F. Trevino, R. Medina, G. Ramirez, and R. Ramirez. 1996. "Health Care Access Among Mexican Americans with Different Health Insurance Coverage." *Journal of Health Care for the Poor and Underserved* 7: 112–121.

U.S. General Accounting Office. 1995. *Illegal Aliens: National Net Cost Estimates Vary Widely.* Report prepared for Congress (GAO/HEHS-95-133). Washington, D.C.: General Accounting Office.

Valdez, R. B., and G. Dallek. 1991. *Does the Health System Serve Black and Latino Communities in Los Angeles County?* Claremont, Calif.: Tomas Rivera Center.

Valdez, R. B., H. Morgenstern, E. R. Brown, R. Wyn, C. Wang, and W. Cumberland. 1993. "Insuring Latinos Against the Costs of Illness." *Journal of American Medical Association* 269: 889–894.

Vega, W. A., and H. Amaro. 1994. "Latino Outlook: Good Health, Uncertain Prognosis." *Annual Review of Public Health* 15: 39–67.

Wood, D. L., R. A. Hayward, C. R. Corey, H. E. Freeman, and M. F. Shapiro. 1990. "Access to Medical Care for Children and Adolescents in the United States." *Pediatrics* 86(5): 666–673.

Wyn, R., E. R. Brown, R. B. Valdez, H. Yu, W. Cumberland, H. Morgenstern, C. Hafner-Eaton, and C. Wang. 1993. *Health Insurance Coverage of California's Latino Population and Their Use of Health Services.* Berkeley: California Policy Seminar, University of California.

Commentary

Felton Earls, Harvard University

This chapter should evoke a sense of anxiety. The reality that we live in a wealthy society that permits millions of children to grow up without the security and benefits of health coverage constitutes a moral wrong. The chapter presents detailed and authoritative analyses of two national data sets that include information on the health status of Latino, Asian, black, and white children. One body of data provides information on access of children at different ages to health services and the other covers the proportion and characteristics of children who lack insurance. Of the three competing hypotheses examined, the results favor a structuralist interpretation. That is, as might be expected, the barriers to health care do not diminish with increasing duration of residence in the United States (the assimilation hypothesis) or with increasing education. The percentage of the uninsured varies from a low of 16 percent for Latino children of U.S.-born parents to 53 percent for Latino children born outside the United States. These percentages translate into well over 2 million uninsured Latino children. The largest number represents children who were born in the United States and who are thus citizens. It is also worth pointing out that these figures are conservative, since the surveys from which they were derived underestimate coverage in a volatile market. The data were also collected just prior to the implementation of restrictive federal policies that construct even more formidable obstacles for immigrant families and children.

The epidemiological observation that some groups of recent Latino immigrants may have better health than those from the same country of origin who have resided in the United States for longer periods of time should be cautiously weighed in relation to the data presented in this paper. If, in fact, increasing duration of residence is associated with worsening health status, then there is all the more reason to insure these families.

The concept of "citizen children" as used by the authors should be underscored. The United States has signed but not ratified the UN Convention of the Rights of the Child. Perhaps this implies that it is not yet legally and ethically bound to the principles established in that universally endorsed document.

But the fact that the United States does not use its considerable resources to provide for the welfare of children results in much avoidable suffering. How much suffering and disability is attributable to 2 million children going uninsured is not known, but whatever the estimate, it is too much.

So where do we go from here? Brown and his colleagues have written a valuable paper that provides the United States with timely and alarming evidence that our policies represent a serious breach. How do we overcome the increasing number of disincentives to provide care for immigrant and other disadvantaged groups of children? Would extending insurance to poor and near-poor families result in overutilization? Some answers are provided in a recent study by Bogard et al. (1997). These investigators examined the rate and type of utilization of poor patients who were just entering a large HMO in Denver, Colorado. The study design permitted the investigators to compare utilization between these new patients and a comparison group of nonsubsidized patients already enrolled. The results were encouraging and should allay the fears that previously uninsured patients will stretch the limits of the charity extended to them.

Health insurance has been driven more by the supply side of the capitalist equation than by the demand side. Why do we have 42 million uninsured and 40 million underinsured citizens? Immigrants are the leading edge of what must become a more vocal demand for services. By carefully constructing these secondary analyses of collected national data, Brown and colleagues have provided a solid study on which to base a sense of urgency and definitive action.

REFERENCES

Bogard, H., D. Pearson Ritzwoller, N. Calogne, K. Shields, and M. Hanraham. 1997. "Extending Health Maintenance Organization to the Uninsured." *Journal of the American Medical Association* 277: 1067–1072.

CHAPTER EIGHT

Photo by Anna LeVine

Enrique Trueba   As a Jesuit missionary among the Mayas in the jungles of Chiapas, I learned of the power of malaria and the powerlessness of the poor even to prevent their children from dying from a poisoned water supply. Born in Mexico City to a family of immigrants from Spain, the tenth sibling in a family of twelve children, I became a Jesuit and spent 18 years of my life with the Jesuit order. But in Chiapas, I felt hopeless and frustrated about the possibility of improving people's lives through my work with the church. I met many anthropologists there and really got to know the local people through their eyes. In 1962, I went to the United States to finish my theological studies and stayed on, becoming an immigrant in this country.

I earned my doctorate in anthropology from the University of Pittsburgh, and became a U.S. citizen in 1972. I began to work in education when the University of Illinois asked me to start an interdisciplinary program there in the 1970s. My work has always been with the marginalized, especially with children. I have worked in the ghettos in Venice, California; I have followed Hmong immigrants on their trail through south-central China; I've worked extensively in Latin America, in Alaska, and with many Latino communities throughout the United States. My interest is to attempt to understand what happens with long-term migrations and the reasons behind the resilience of these immigrants.

Co-Executive Director, The Institute for Urban Education, University of Houston. Educated at Stanford University and University of Pittsburgh. Publications include *Ethnic Identity and Power: Cultural Contexts of Political Action in School and Society* (forthcoming), *Myth or Reality: Adaptive Strategies of Asian Americans in California* (1993), *Healing Multicultural America: Mexican Immigrants Rise to Power in Rural California* (1993), and *Language and Culture in Learning: Teaching Spanish to Native Speakers of Spanish* (1993).

8

The Education of Mexican Immigrant Children

Enrique T. Trueba
University of Houston

A number of scholars feel that the educational progress of Latinos is a topic of serious concern (Portes 1996; Suárez-Orozco and Suárez-Orozco 1995a, 1995b; Valencia 1991). Yet recent studies of the academic success of Latino students in high school and their continued efforts to succeed in their adult lives invite reflection on the supportive role of the family and home environment (Diaz Salcedo 1996). The narratives of academic achievement, in the midst of the narratives of inequity for many Latino students, represent a unique success where failure was expected.

The struggle of Mexicans in what is U.S. territory today did not start with the tens of thousands who began to do unskilled labor there in the late 1800s. Certainly, many Mexicans were living in the Southwest prior to the annexation of Mexican territory by the Guadalupe Hidalgo Treaty of 1848, but many more have come since. In 1900 the U.S. census estimate of Mexican immigrants was 103,393. By 1910, there were 221,915; by 1920, 486,418, and by December 31, 1926, the official count was 890,746 (Gamio 1930, 2).[1] The exploitation of the so-called inferior people and the accepted practice of depriving them of certain rights was common in the last century and in the first decades of this century. The Civil Practice Act of 1850, which excluded Chinese and Indians from testifying against whites, was extended to Mexicans because they were part Indian. The residential segregation of Mexicans firmly established on the West Coast at the turn of the century became the foundation for the widespread segregation of the 1920s and 1930s; Mexicans were not allowed in public facilities such as schools, restaurants, swimming pools, and theaters (Menchaca and Valencia 1990, 230).

We know that there is a close correlation between family poverty and children's educational levels, and between educational and economic development in a country. Furthermore, we have seen the rapid trends of aging in the white population and its decrease both in the labor force and in schools. In fact, the 1970s' predictions of demographic enrollment were too conservative. In the Southwest, the increased immigration of Latino and Asian populations has shifted in two decades both the total number of children in schools and their racial/ethnic balance vis-à-vis the magnitude of the white non-Hispanic population. California will face radical changes before any other state. In 1970 there were only 30 percent ethnic/racial minority students in K–12 public schools. After 140 years of predominantly white enrollment, in 1990, 50 percent of the California public school students belong to ethnic/racial subgroups. There is no numerical majority of whites. By the year 2030, white students will constitute about 30 percent of the total enrollment and Latino students will represent the largest group (44 percent of the total enrollment) (Valencia 1991, 17). Other school demographic projections suggest that the white school-age population will decrease for the country at large, while the Latino school-age population will continue to increase. Latino children (5 to 17 years of age) numbered 6 million in 1982 (9 percent of the national youth population); by 2020 they will number 19 million (25 percent of the country's youth population). That is, the Latino school-age population will more than triple in eight years (Valencia 1991, 18–19).

THE EDUCATION OF MEXICAN IMMIGRANT CHILDREN

The significance of Mexican immigration in contemporary North America is clear (see González Baker et al. and Orfield, this volume). The political, economic, and educational consequences of this phenomenon require a massive, serious, and long-term interdisciplinary approach. California and Texas are the focus of intensive Latino immigration, a population that is now more than ever segregated and neglected (Orfield et al. 1997). As a consequence, Mexican (and other Latino children) become rapidly marginalized and show persistently high dropout rates. What is the role of schools in the face of such a crisis? What are the structural (economic, political, and educational) barriers leading to school failure of Mexican children? Under what conditions is the academic achievement of Mexican children improving? What are the consequences of the increasing lack of cultural sensitivity and the cancellation of affirmative action efforts? These questions cannot be examined in detail here, but they provide the incentive to look into some of the characteristics of the education of Mexican children in North America. There are, however, two important statistical facts that must be presented in advance: the rapid growth of Latino enrollments in the last 25 years and the increasing segregation of Latino students.

According to the Harvard Project on Desegregation (1997), Latino enrollments have increased significantly in California, Texas, New York, Florida, Illinois, Arizona, New Mexico, and New Jersey between 1970 and 1994 (see Table 8.1 and Figure 8.1). Latino enrollments in California, for example, increased 176.3 percent during that period, from 706,900 pupils in 1970 to 1,953,343 in 1994; in Texas, enrollments increased 130.5 percent. The isolation of Latino students has become more acute. The overall trends of black and Latino student segregation in schools continue, but there is a significant increase in these trends for Latinos. Three measures of state rankings in segregation (percentage of Latino students in majority white schools, percentage in minority schools, and percentage of white students in Latino schools) between 1989 to 1990 and 1994 to 1995 show clear trends of marked isolation of Latinos in schools (see Tables 8.2 and 8.3 and Figure 8.2).

These basic facts must be explained in the context of a continued backlash against immigrants (Suárez-Orozco forthcoming).[2] Indeed, new immigrant children face many difficult problems in their adaptation. According to Carola and Marcelo Suárez-Orozco,

> The obvious difficulties that most migrants face include language inadequacies, a general unfamiliarity with the customs and expectations of the new country, limited economic opportunities, poor housing conditions, discrimination, and what psychologists term the "stresses of acculturation". . . Despite these obstacles, many migrants often consider their lot as having improved from what it was in their country of origin. Because of a perception of relative improvement, many migrants may fail to internalize the negative attitudes of the host country toward them, maintaining their country of origin as a point of reference (Suárez-Orozco and Suárez-Orozco 1995b, 325).

Immigrants may sustain their belief of improvement by visiting their villages of origin and displaying their wealth conspicuously (showing off new trucks, good clothes, and spending money; see Ainslie, this volume). The Suárez-Orozcos suggest that immigrants do not see their new life in terms of the ideals of the majority society but in terms of the "old culture," thus holding to a "dual frame of reference" (Suárez-Orozco and Suárez-Orozco 1995b, 325). The adaptive responses of immigrants vary according to their prearrival experience. For example, the key factors determining the educational success of

TABLE 8.1

Growth of Latino Enrollments, 1970–1994

	1970 Enrollment	1994 Enrollment	Change, 1970–1994 Number	Percentage
California	706,900	1,953,343	1,246,443	176.3
Texas	565,900	1,304,269	738,369	130.5
New York	316,600	440,043	123,443	39.0
Florida	65,700	301,206	235,506	358.5
Illinois	78,100	218,568	140,468	179.9
Arizona	85,500	203,097	117,597	137.5
New Mexico	109,300	148,772	39,472	36.1
New Jersey	59,100	148,345	89,245	151.0

Source: DBS Corporation, 1982; 1987; 1991–1992 NCES Common Core of Data Public Education Agency Universe; 1994–1995 NCES Common Core Data School Universe; Harvard Project on Desegregation.

FIGURE 8.1

Growth of Latino Enrollments, 1970–94 States with more than 100,00 Latino Students

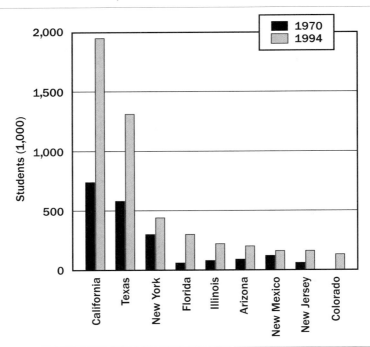

Source: DBS Corp., 1982; 1987; 1991–92 NCES Common Core of Data Public Education Agency Universe; 1994–95 NCES Common Core Data School Universe; Harvard Project on Desegregation.

TABLE 8.2

State Rankings in Segregation of Latino Students by Three Measures, 1989–1990 School Year

Percentage in Majority White Schools		Percentage in 90-100% Minority Schools		Percentage of Whites in Typically Latino Schools	
New York	16.6	New York	54.1	New York	21.5
Texas	21.2	New Jersey	41.4	Texas	26.5
California	22.2	Texas	41.0	California	28.8
New Mexico	23.2	Connecticut	36.8	New Jersey	28.9
New Jersey	24.9	Illinois	35.5	Illinois	31.7
Illinois	25.9	California	33.4	New Mexico	33.3
Florida	32.2	Florida	30.4	Florida	33.8
Connecticut	33.8	Pennsylvania	26.4	Connecticut	33.9
Pennsylvania	40.1	Indiana	21.2	Pennsylvania	41.6
Massachusetts	41.0	New Mexico	17.9	Arizona	42.4

Source: National Center for Education Statistics (NCES), 1989–1990; Harvard Project on Desegregation.

Mexican families are related to the prearrival socioeconomic, cultural, and political experiences that determine their abilities to handle the traumas faced in the United States after their arrival.

A process called marginalization is often associated with conspicuous poverty and isolation in the new country (see Vigil 1988). The lack of com-

TABLE 8.3

State Rankings in Segregation of Latino Students by Three Measures, 1994–1995 School Year

Percentage in Majority White Schools		Percentage in 90-100% Minority Schools		Percentage of Whites in Typically Latino Schools	
New York	13.8	New York	57.3	New York	19.2
California	17.3	New Jersey	43.4	California	24.8
Texas	19.6	Texas	43.0	Texas	25.0
New Mexico	21.6	California	38.7	New Jersey	29.3
Rhode Island	24.8	Illinois	34.9	Illinois	30.9
Illinois	26.5	Connecticut	32.4	New Mexico	31.0
New Jersey	27.3	Florida	27.6	Florida	34.5
Connecticut	31.9	Pennsylvania	25.8	Connecticut	35.0
Florida	33.2	New Mexico	20.0	Rhode Island	38.0
Arizona	34.0	Arizona	18.9	Arizona	38.2

Source: National Center for Education Statistics (NCES), 1994–1995; Harvard Project on Desegregation.

munication with individuals who speak their variety of Spanish and the need to deal with issues dissimilar to those they handled in Mexico create a vacuum of support and a deep sense of anxiety over expectations and norms of appropriate behavior. Poverty is also associated with the nature of immigrants' work, which is often inherently unstable and not well paid; another source of poverty is the urgent needs of the family left behind in Mexico, who expect money to be sent regularly. Furthermore, immigrants often incur debts in order to pay the costs of going north to find employment.

Another factor affecting the adaptive strategies of Mexican immigrants is their degree of literacy (in a broad Freirian sense), that is, their understanding of complex social systems and their ability to handle text related to those systems (contracts, government documents, banks, hospitals, the immigration office, etc.). The marginalization of many Mexican families starts long before they arrive in this country. Their naive notions about the politics of employment, the organization of schools, and the demands of society reflect more a change from rural to urban settings than the change from one country to another. Of course, the added dimension in this country is that in order to acquire the necessary sociopolitical knowledge of appropriate conduct in urban settings, immigrants must first acquire the communicative skills to do so in a second language. To compound the problem, immigrants often take jobs that are exhausting and leave them little time to acquire communicative skills in English. The consequence for the children of immigrants is that soon they are forced to play adult roles in making momentous decisions for their parents because the children know some English and understand the social system a bit better.

A serious problem facing young immigrant families upon their arrival is the neglect and malnutrition of their children. This does not occur only in the case of migrant workers, but also among urban dwellers who are isolated and cannot afford to pay for the cost of child care. Again, to compound these problems, families who have any members without full documentation feel the most vulnerable and therefore do not seek help from social agencies, even if they rightfully qualify to receive assistance. In many instances, workers do not have health insurance or welfare and do not have access to a physician prior to childbirth, or even in the weeks following childbirth (see Brown et al., this volume). Dysfunctional housing conditions increase the chances of health problems and neglect of children. In some cases, even the safety of children is jeopardized in dilapidated housing infested with drug addicts and vandals.

These conditions are also associated with the early recruitment of Mexican children into gangs and with the school dropout phenomenon. If, in the precarious conditions in which families live, the school lacks the resources or

FIGURE 8.2

Latino Segregation by Region, 1994–95 Percent of Latino Students in Region Schools

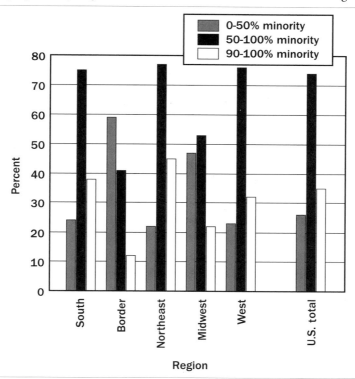

Source: National Center for Education Statistics (NCES), 1994–95; Harvard Project on Desegregation.

interest in providing special attention to immigrant children, then the chances of academic failure increase dramatically. Compounding these problems are the experiences of discrimination, of verbal and physical abuse on the part of mainstream children, and the predominant opinion among teachers that Latino children are low achievers. These experiences create a complex setting in which immigrant children must redefine themselves in the United States, one that can lead them to reject their own family, language, and culture. Such symbolic self-rejection and the formation of a new identity does not necessarily result in embracing school and North American society. A number of scholars have recently dealt with these problems of adaptation in the context of the school environment (Wilson 1991; Gutierrez 1994; Patthey-Chavez 1993; Delgado-Gaitan 1994; Deyhle and Margonis 1995; Gutierrez, Larson, and Kreuter 1995; Bartolomé 1996; Bartolomé and Macedo 1997). Several scholars, using critical pedagogy, offer as a solution "transformative" strategies for teachers and students (based on Freire 1973, 1995; scholars such as Giroux and McLaren 1994; and McLaren 1995, among others).

There is an intimate relationship between the successful adaptation of the entire Mexican family to North America and children's academic success (Suárez-Orozco and Suárez-Orozco 1995a, 1995b; Diaz Salcedo 1996; Trueba 1997). If children manage to retain a strong cultural self-identity and maintain a sense of belonging to their sociocultural community, they seem to achieve well in school. Carola and Marcelo Suárez-Orozco have also shown in their recent studies (1995a, 1995b) that immigrant children's learning ability and social skills deteriorate the longer they are exposed to the alienating environment of American society, which undermines their overall school achievement and adaptation to this society. The traumatic experience of being uprooted, confusion about family values, and a desire for personal survival, coupled with the need for peer support, are bound to lead many youth to become affiliated with gangs (Vigil 1983, 1988, 1989) and to disregard the codes of behavior prescribed by mainstream society.

Frequently, a family takes special precautions to salvage the moral character and overall well-being of a youth by taking him or her back to Mexico for a period of time, to complete his or her education, work under supervision, or marry a local person. There are cases in which the entire family returns to Mexico in order to reeducate teenagers in family values. This is often associated with a serious reassessment of their finances and the risks involved in continuing to work in the United States. The number of repatriated ex–farm workers in Colima, Michoacán, and Jalisco is increasing rapidly (Trueba and González 1997). However, in contrast to the alienation of Mexican immigrant children in major metropolises (such as Los Angeles, Chicago, New York, Houston, etc.), children who live in settings where they can manage to retain their home language and culture, their familiar cultural institutions and networks, seem to survive the trauma of American schooling and to achieve well. This, of course, is the result of a carefully executed plan of education engineered primarily by the mothers, who monitor schooling and defend their language and culture by creating vast networks on both sides of the border, thus supporting their children's strong Mexican identity and their ability to live in a binational and bicultural world (preliminary fieldwork notes by Trueba and González in Comala, Colima, Mexico, 1997)

Some scholars (Martin and Taylor 1996) who intimately know the lives and needs of the seasonal farm worker population in California, as well as the demographic trends in the state, have recently outlined their observations and concerns. Agricultural towns in California are rapidly growing as a result of both immigration and high rates of fertility among immigrants. Between 25 and 50 percent of residents in these towns have incomes below the federal poverty levels, and often live in overgrown labor camps. In these rural communities the correlation between the increase in the immigrant population and the ratios of children in schools is higher than between the population increase and its use of public assistance. Immigration of seasonal farm workers begins with U.S. recruitment during periods of economic downturn in rural Mexico and growth of job opportunities in California. Immigrant families and village networks are instrumental in managing the choice of jobs for persons from particular Mexican communities. Not only are labor market economies in rural communities increasingly layered in a way that passes the costs of farm work onto the most recently arrived immigrants, but this also displaces some migrant workers to areas of urban poverty. To compound the problem, many new immigrants have little education as they enter agricultural life. Rural poverty, thus, has an impact on urban poverty, especially among children. In fact, in California "the transfer of rural poverty to urban poverty highlights the importance of education and training to improve the prospects for California's rural-to-urban migrants in the urban economy" (Martin and Taylor 1996, 2).

The sense that there is no end in sight to the waves of immigrants is pervasive, and demands reflection on the contradiction between immigration and integration policies. Is allowing unregulated immigration from Mexico and Latin America creating rural and urban poverty, and if so, what is likely to happen to the next generation of immigrant children? If the only option left for employers is to import cheap labor from Mexico, then new immigration will bring new poverty and more segregation. The development of new employers from Mexico (see Cornelius, this volume) may indicate that a more profound transformation is occurring among Mexican immigrants and that there is hope for upward mobility. This is also confirmed by some of the work by Dussel Peters, Myers, and González Baker in this volume.

MEXICAN FAMILIES STRUGGLE FOR ECONOMIC SURVIVAL

Primarily for economic reasons, there is a steady stream of immigrants not only from Mexico, but also from Caribbean countries and South America, which now contribute the single largest continental segment (nearly 38 percent) of legal immigrants and over 80 percent of undocumented immigrants to the United States (González Baker et al., this volume).[3] In addition to the role of Mexico in modern migratory movements into the United States, Mexico's economic and political importance was demonstrated by the role of the U.S. government in pursuing the North American Free Trade Agreement (NAFTA) and its diligent response to Mexico's 1994 economic crisis. The flow of Latino immigrants will continue at a rapid pace, and their mainstreaming reflects a more intense globalization of our economies in the American hemisphere.

Foreign-born persons of Mexican origin in 1980 constituted 15 percent of the U.S. population, in 1990 20.7 percent, and in 1994 to 1995, 28.4 percent. The increase of the Mexican-origin population in the United States between 1960 and 1996 is as follows:

1960: 1.7 million (1% of the total U.S. population)
1970: 4.5 million (2.2%)
1980: 8.7 million (3.9%)
1990: 13.3 million (5.4%)
1995: 17 million (6.6%)
1996: 18 million (6.7%) (González Baker, this volume)

It is also significant that the 6.8 million Mexican people born in Mexico and living in the United States represent 38.2 percent of the total Mexican-origin population, and 25.8 percent of all the foreign-born persons in this country. Congruent with the previous indices of growth, the number of naturalized citizens of Mexican origin in 1980 was about half a million; between 1980 and 1996 this figure reached about 1.8 million. It seems that two additional factors have motivated Latinos to become naturalized in the last few months: the impending cuts in social benefits for all immigrants (see Hagan, this volume), and, in the case of Mexicans, the real or symbolic promise of dual nationality, or at least the recognition by the Mexican government, in principle, of their rights to Mexican citizenship.

The popular response to this "browning" of North America is that recent Latino immigrants, now at the bottom of the economic ladder, may remain unassimilated in enduring pockets of poverty. This notion is challenged by scholars who feel that Latino progress is disguised by large and ever-increasing numbers of newcomers. The sheer volume of Latino immigration seems to obscure the upward mobility of earlier arrivals (Myers, this volume). George Borjas (1985, 1995) has defended a model of ongoing deterioration in the human quality of recent immigrants, attributing a lower "human capital" and a "declining quality" to recent Latino arrivals:

> The "declining quality" thesis has been criticized on several grounds. The economic concept of quality has an unfortunate implication when expressed in common English. Some have feared the racist implication

that the quality of immigrants is declining because the composition of the immigrant flow has shifted from European to Asian and Latin American origins. However, Borjas intended declining quality to signify the declining returns to human capital. Unfortunately, those declining returns are compounded by *relative* declines in the amounts of human capital as well. Recent immigrants actually have higher education and other human capital than their predecessors; their human capital is declining only in the relative sense that it is rising more slowly than that of native-born whites (Myers, this volume).

Two factors seem to determine the apparently slow pace of growth of human capital among Latino immigrants: the first is that the rate of the flow of newcomers is greater than the rate of increase in their incomes; the second is the educational point of departure, that is, many newcomers arrive with relatively little formal education. Without the appropriate educational level, upward intergenerational economic mobility is hindered.

Often the main motivation for Latinos who come to work for low wages is to provide their children with a better education. Yet immigrant parents cannot afford to pay for the education of their children. The reality of the exploitation of new immigrants has been clearly stated by Portes:

> The puzzle is whether today's children of immigrants will follow their European predecessors and move steadily into the middle-class mainstream or whether, on the contrary, their ascent will be blocked and they will join children of earlier black and Puerto Rican migrants as part of an expanded multiethnic underclass. As the deteriorating conditions of life in American cities suggest, the question is of more than passing significance for the future of American society (Portes 1996, 3).[4]

According to Myers, there are three broad temporal dimensions that help measure the adaptation of immigrants: lifetime, intergenerational, and successive arrival cohort dimensions. The lifetime dimension follows a path suggested by age and length of residence in the United States. But because individuals move with passing time cohorts not only in length of residence but also in age (along with their birth cohorts) it is important to create double cohorts by putting together birth cohorts with arrival cohorts. Myers explains:

> Given that the younger generation of native-born workers is falling behind the career progress of their more fortunate parents, failure to adjust for

birth cohort leads to upwardly biased age effects. . . . Compounding this problem, the Borjas method uses the upwardly biased native-born lifetime career as a reference for judging the relative adaptation of immigrants. The implication is that immigrants should advance at the same rate as the false standard linking younger and older men in the cross-section. By this method, both new immigrants and young native-born workers might be judged to have declining quality (Myers, this volume).

Intergenerational progress research assumes that immigrants pave the way for their children's adaptation and upward economic mobility. If there is a lack of upward economic mobility from one generation to the next, people assume that there is resistance to assimilation or an incapacity to assimilate. Portes (1995) focused on the so-called 1.5 generation, or young immigrant children, that highlights the age-at-arrival effects. Although there is no clear-cut age to identify the 1.5 generation, one could probably endorse Myers' suggested age of ten years as the cut-off point. Overall, however, change over time is better examined across successive cohorts of newcomers as a measure of collective adaptation of immigrant groups to a new society. According to Myers, the statement about declining quality of immigrants (made by Borjas and others) is based precisely on this type of analysis of change between arrival cohorts.

One of the most important findings of Myers' study is that young immigrant children (or the 1.5 generation) match or exceed the academic achievement of the native-born (they have a higher rate of high school completion). How then do we explain the general statistical data on the low educational achievement of Latinos? Simply by the low achievement of the older native-born population and older recent immigrants. In contrast, the "1.5 generation is a bright exception, and they would seem to be poised for economic success" (Myers, this volume). Another significant finding is that intergenerational educational progress does not necessarily or directly translate into occupational mobility and even less into higher earnings. Myers feels that the explanation for this economic ceiling is that economic restructuring has changed the economic returns to an increase in human capital for the most recent labor force (either immigrants or native-born workers).

SEARCHING FOR HOPE:
THE RESILIENCE OF MEXICAN IMMIGRANTS

As Marcelo Suárez-Orozco has commented (in personal communication and speeches), what is remarkable is not that so many Latino children fail, but that so many succeed in spite of the difficulties they face. I am convinced that the single most important characteristic of Latino immigrants, and particularly of Mexican immigrant families, is their enormous capacity to survive and adapt in the face of arduous life circumstances, poverty, and segregation. The role of Mexican women is at the heart of this resiliency. They are crucial to the maintenance of the home language and culture and a complex binational infrastructure of networks and relationships. Many factors contribute to the retention of the Spanish language: the critical mass of immigrants who speak the language, frequent visits to home towns and cities, and the interdependence between families living on both sides of the border. The organization of functional networks of families and their friends has been most instrumental to the survival of families during difficult economic times, but it has also served as a very strong emotional support system for retaining a strong Mexican identity in the face of the traumas alluded to above by the Suárez-Orozcos (1995a, 1995b, forthcoming). A substantial, although informal, financial cooperative system can also become a powerful political base from which to demand respect for their educational rights, as was the case in Guadalupe, California (Trueba 1997). Traditional organizations of a religious character, in the Mexican tradition, become a strong political enclave and support system in the adaptation of immigrant families to this country (Trueba et al. 1993). In fact, the only way for these families to engage in long-term economic ventures (buying land in Mexico, purchasing homes in the United States, etc.) is through the collective security of the family networks on both sides of the border, collective savings, and commitment to mutual support in times of crisis. The skills to survive emotionally and economically in the worst of situations continue to be a unique characteristic of many immigrant families, who invest every possible resource in the future generation through binational networks of strategically invested scarce resources. This "know-how," which Freire called "knowing the world" in contrast with literacy as "knowing the word," is often the key factor in facilitating the adaptation of the immigrant family (Freire 1973, 1995; Freire and Macedo 1996).

Because Mexican immigrant families have different prearrival experiences and varying degrees of literacy skills and socioeconomic status, their early experiences in the United States and their children's academic success also vary a great deal. The adaptive strategies adopted by new immigrants reflect their previous experiences and determine the pace of adaptation and its ultimate success. One of the least investigated strategies is the binational, bicultural approach to adaptation. Naturally, education is very important to Mexican families. In fact, some children are sent back to Mexico for their elementary education if their experience in American schools becomes unproductive or unbearable. Often, however, children from migrant families in the entire Southwest are well known in school for their absences, which parallel their parents' cycles of unemployment. There are important recent changes associated with the unemployment of immigrants; for example, the replacement of traditional farm workers (those who started to come in the 1960s from central Mexico) by Mixtec or Mayan Indians aggressively recruited by *contratistas* (contractors) in northern Mexico (seeking the cheapest manual labor for agricultural jobs in California). The least sophisticated new workers often tolerate the low pay and abuse because they need work and are unaware of their rights. Although the rural Mexican population in the United States represents only about 20 percent of all Mexicans in the United States (while urban Mexican immigrants are the majority), many of the urban immigrants in the United States come from rural backgrounds and resort to networks and cultural traditions in the United States. The reality of their binational experience is instrumental in their survival, judging from the testimonies of repatriated immigrants in Mexico (see Trueba and González 1997).

From preliminary reports of repatriation studies, it seems that communication between family members on both sides of the border never stops. The economic interdependency of members of the same family residing on either side of the border permits them to engage in a resource exchange and the investment of modest capital to run small businesses. The use of both languages and cultures, as well as the use of capital and labor to support family ventures, continues to provide these families with new economic resources and higher social status. The conspicuous consumption that is discussed by Durand, Parrado, and Massey (1996) has important symbolic functions in marking success and building confidence among those who left Mexico. It is indeed an indirect repayment that compensates the many degrading experiences suffered in the United States. In fact, families and their networks on both sides of the border create an efficient informal social insurance that provides small amounts of cash and emotional support to any person in trouble, with the implied commitment that eventually all will have to reciprocate in kind as crisis or need arises. The penalty for not complying with this reciprocal obligation is abandonment by the family and network on both sides of the border. As they grow up and become fully bilingual, children become an integral part of the network, and are often called to play a role as interpreters and assistants. During important life events all these relationships are played out and ritually sanctioned with religious ceremonies during baptisms, weddings, funerals, and so forth. Also, during certain celebrations (patron saint festivities, Day of the Dead, etc.) relatives get together on either side of the border to renew their commitment to help. An intergenerational agreement is always renewed. More recently, women have come to play a major role in these events because in many instances they have become the financial experts for the family.

CONCLUSION

The following questions continue to intrigue researchers who study Mexican immigration and its consequences for the education of Mexican children:

1. What is the nature of the process of ethnic, racial, and cultural identification of children, and the integration of their inner self, as they face a loss of social status in the United States and increased isolation from both Latino communities and the white communities in this country?
2. What is the cost (emotional, cultural, and psychological) of the apparent socioeconomic advantages of immigration, especially if we consider the heavy financial obligations of immigrants to their families of origin in Mexico?
3. What are the fundamental changes in values and lifestyle, and what are the consequences of such changes for both the survival and prosperity of immigrants in the United States and their temporary presence in Mexico?
4. How do children adjust back in Mexico, and how do they achieve in Mexican schools?
5. For those who return to Mexico for extended periods of time, what is the impact of the socioeconomic, political, and cultural changes they have experienced as they engage in daily life in Mexico?

Binational, bicultural survival is a new fact of life for many Mexican immigrants who do not obtain steady employment in this country and must find creative ways of providing for their family. From preliminary fieldwork in Mexico (see Trueba and González 1997), this is a phenomenon continually increasing both in central Mexico and the U.S. Southwest. It is one of the adaptive strategies for surviving the economic and psychological hardships alluded to by Suárez-Orozco and Suárez-Orozco (1995a, 1995b) as well as by Hondagneu-Sotelo (1994) and by Trueba et al. (1993) that are associated with the experience of working and living in the United States, often in poverty and under oppression.

In the late 1960s, there were more than three times as many blacks as Latinos in the school population, and there was one Latino for every seventeen white students; twenty years later, Latino enrollment is two-thirds of the black student population, and there is one Latino student for every seven whites. The white student population decreased 17 percent, while the Latino student population increased 103 percent in that period (Orfield, cited by Valencia 1991, 18–20). This trend has been accentuated for complex historical reasons in the 1990s (Orfield and Eaton 1996). Paradoxically, the economic and technological future of this country will depend precisely on the educational success of Latinos, blacks, and Asians because by the mid-twenty-first century they will constitute half of the total U.S. population. Latino children are already the majority in many of our schools.

High achievement is only possible for immigrants if we pay attention to what Sonia Diaz Salcedo (1996) considers the most crucial factors of adaptation to schools. Discussing the students in her study, she states:

> They spoke at length about the issues they faced with their parents or guardians, and the impact that their relationships at home have had on their success in school. The themes that surfaced were: resilience and survival, relating to family, the importance of connecting with the culture and ethnicity, developing a sense of responsibility and independence, communication, and spirituality or religious affiliation (Diaz Salcedo 1996, 129).

Diaz Salcedo describes how students spoke lovingly of their parents, who gave them a "loving and caring home life" that provided what they perceived as a supportive environment. In her interviews, Diaz Salcedo suggests that students were grateful to their parents and felt fortunate that their parents provided constant encouragement. In some specific cases, students spoke of the sacrifices made by their mothers in the way they provided a caring, nurturing home for them. This is consistent with the perception of hardships articulated by mothers during the years in which they had to work and take care of their children. Caring for children and providing them with support in their education is at times very difficult and costly for parents, given the exhausting jobs they hold. For example, a young mother, speaking of those years, related to me:

> To me all this has been very hard, especially when my children were younger. I had to prepare lunches and clothing for my oldest son and my daughter the night before and wake them up early to go to school. Then

I had to take my two youngest sons (who were two and four years of age) to my sister's house so she would take care of them while I worked in the fields. I came back home exhausted. I had to see them with *lástima* (pity): "*Mami, Mami*," they said crying. I would reply, "let me make supper" or "let me take a shower." [With tears, she continued] *Bien duro* (real hard). . . (Trueba 1997).

In the Diaz Salcedo study, however, not all of the families of successful students were ideal and exemplary. Those students whose families were less than ideal found other sources of support. Their resourcefulness led them to find the support of surrogate parents, and to find within themselves and their school environment additional support through a strong spiritual life, a strong belief in God, and trust in various church groups. In all cases,

The students also formed their ideas about resilience and survival in the context of their home lives. In turn, they had made the connection to parental support or lack of support in discussing their success at school. For all of them it appeared to be important for someone to say that "they matter." In many cases this "someone" was the mother; in other cases it was someone at school or in their lives outside of school or home (Diaz Salcedo 1996, 131).

In the end, students were aware that they had not chosen their family, but they had many choices open to them; they felt in control of their future. All felt in close emotional connection with their Latino culture, which was "implicit in certain dynamics, and tended to be more explicit in their home contexts" (Diaz Salcedo 1996, 132). These findings are congruent with the work of Carola and Marcelo Suárez-Orozco (1995a, 1995b) and the work I did in central California regarding the unique role that a strong ethnic affiliation plays in the maintenance of the motivation to achieve in school.

In conclusion, there is a conspicuous need for systematic, substantive, and long-term research on the achievement of Mexican children to explore the conditions and circumstances that can make possible a serious change in dropout rates and a marked progress in academic achievement. The research agenda must take into consideration the importance of the family in its binational, bicultural situation. The role of schools in encouraging the use of ethnic cultures to improve achievement continues to be central. School initiatives to prevent the isolation of Mexican families and facilitate their socialization into academic careers are indispensable.

ACKNOWLEDGMENTS

I wish to express my gratitude to Gary Orfield and Marcelo Suárez-Orozco for their reactions to this paper, and their editorial suggestions.

NOTES

1. The U.S. population as of May 1, 1996 was 265,022,000. Of the population 65 years of age and over, whites represent 85 percent, blacks 8 percent, Hispanics 4 percent, and Asian and Pacific Islanders 2 percent. Blacks, Hispanics, Asians and Pacific Islanders, and American Indians account for 34 percent of the U.S. population under 18 years of age. From the over 16 million poor children, one-third (5.6 million) live in working-poor families (that is, having at least one parent working 50 or more weeks a year and making less than $11,821, the poverty standard for 1994). Working-poor families increased 30 percent from 1989 to 1994; most children in these working-poor families are born to women over the age of 25, and half of these children live in two-parent households with one parent working all year. These children (27 percent of whom have no health insurance) are often not immunized, do not do well in school, and are more likely to be poor as adults. From 1985 to 1993, low-birth-weight babies increased 6 percent; violent deaths (suicide, homicide, accidents) among youth aged 15 to 19 increased 10 percent; violent crime arrests of youths aged 10 to 17 rose 66 percent; and single-parent families with children increased 18 percent (*Population Today* 1996, 4–6).

2. As Suárez-Orozco has pointed out insightfully, the United States is currently going through difficult times, when fear of losing one's job, the increase in crime, and the erosion of family values signal social chaos. Anxieties have focused on immigrants and refugees, who are blamed for our problems and our deep and "terrifying sense of homelessness" (Suárez-Orozco 1998, 9–24). Some of this anxiety is related to vast changes in immigration patterns. To understand long-term population trends and the impact of Latinos, we must examine what we know about Latino immigrants from the last three decades. According to Rumbaut (1995, 16–69), in 1990 there were 19.7 million immigrants (defined as people born outside the U.S. territory) in the United States (or 6.8 percent of the U.S. population), of which 8,416,924 were Latinos (including Caribbean), from Cuba, Colombia, Jamaica, Nicaragua, Haiti, the Dominican Republic, Guatemala, El Salvador and Mexico; of that number 4,298,014 were from Mexico. Of all Latino immigrants, 78 percent arrived between 1970 and 1989 (6.5 million, one-third of all immigrants), and 50

percent came in the 1980s; only 27 percent of the Latinos have become U.S. citizens, which is understandable given the recency of their arrival, type of work, rural background, and limited access to assistance. Overall, 60 percent of Mexican immigrants live in California. A person's educational level seems to predict economic level and employment. The highest rates of poverty are found among the populations with the least education: Mexicans, Salvadorans, Guatemalans, Dominicans, and Haitians.

3. While immigration is caused by many complex factors, economists feel that one of the greatest incentives to go north is economic opportunity vis-à-vis the poverty experienced by an ever-increasing unemployed group of able persons. Enrique Dussel Peters (this volume) feels that a major motivation for Mexican immigration to the United States is economic. The chronic lack of stable and well-remunerated jobs in Mexico has created a systematic and permanent flow of immigrants seeking employment in the United States. Part of the problem in Mexico seems to be related to restrictive monetary and credit policies, the import liberalization trends that culminated with the 1994 peso devaluation, and the ever-increasing foreign debt, which together created a surplus of labor in spite of successful economic improvement in the automotive, petrochemical, and electronic industries. In the end, Mexico has not been able to shake off its dependency on imports, and, particularly among the private manufacturing industries, the crises peaked in 1994. The rate of increase among the economically active population far exceeded the pace of economic growth and the demand for domestic labor. One of the most promising, growing industries in Mexico is the maquiladora, with an increase from 5 to 40 percent of total manufacturing employment between 1980 and 1996 (or from 125,000 to 800,000 workers in those years, respectively). But even that represents a very small part of the total economy and will not continue to grow at a fast pace because the market is becoming saturated (Dussel Peters, this volume).

4. Portes goes on to spell out the long-term role of immigration in the structure of the American economy through the sagas of immigrants. Immigrants struggle to find political freedom and economic security. Portes adds:

> The saga reflects accurately many individual experiences, but it is only part of the story. While individual motivations are undoubtedly important, a political economy analysis shows that what drives the process is not the dreams and needs of immigrants but the interests and plans of their prospective employers. Although geopolitical and other considerations have played roles in granting to certain foreign groups access to American territory, the fundamental reason for sustained immigration, at least since the post–Civil War period, has been the labor needs of the economy. . .

Employer associations played a decisive role in recruiting European and Asian labor during the nineteenth century. They organized dependable labor flows from Asia, southeastern Europe, and Mexico at the turn of the century and then succeeded in keeping the immigration door open against nativistic opposition until World War I (Portes 1996, 3–4).

5. Martin and Taylor (1996, 6) suggest that in some rural towns agricultural labor is divided into a three-tiered labor force: The smallest portion of workers, 14 percent, work year round; 20 percent are long-season local workers, and 66 percent are peak season migrants. However, there is a great deal of networking across rural-urban continua within the families of immigrants. In Guadalupe, California, for example, most of the second-generation children who reached high school work in urban areas, in spite of the fact that they were born into Mexican migrant families. I suspect that there is an overall career ladder starting from the lowest-paid jobs in the rural United States to better-paying skilled labor, to professional and business occupations. The mobility from rural to urban within the United States occurs within one generation in most cases (Trueba 1997; and personal interviews in central California). The creative entrepreneurs who repatriate permanently in Mexico, or continue their binational existence, are intimately connected to the flow of "migradollars" sent to Mexico. It is universally recognized that the inflow of migradollars, estimated at some $2 billion a year, directly stimulates higher levels of economic activity, investment, employment, and income growth (Durand, Parrado, and Massey 1996, 423). But there are also many indirect effects, such as the celebration of traditional fiestas:

> In the fiesta, those who have money are expected to spend for the benefit of those who do not. Returning United States migrants with substantial savings feel obligated to spend a share of their funds for the general welfare, covering the lion's share of the costs of the music, fireworks, dances, parades, and religious celebrations—all of which are presented publicly and enjoyed by all, rich or poor (Durand, Parrado, and Massey 1996, 428).

Furthermore, the additional income for Mexicans is estimated at $5.8 billion a year (3 percent of the gross domestic product in 1989), which benefits primarily skilled urban workers and investors, with annual gains of $1.9 million each. Beyond this impact, those 2 billion migradollars could well generate $6.5 billion in manufacturing and services. Thus, unlike other investments, migradollars benefit the people who need money the most, and very little is diverted to those with higher incomes who occupy positions of authority (Durand, Parrado, and Massey 1996, 426–441).

REFERENCES

Bartolomé, L. 1996. Beyond the methods fetish: Toward a humanizing pedagogy. In *Breaking Free: The Transformative Power of Critical Pedagogy*, ed. P. Leistyna, A. Woodrum, and S. Sherblom, 229–252. Reprint Series no. 27. Cambridge, Mass.: Harvard Educational Review.

Bartolomé, L. and D. Macedo. 1997. *Harvard Educational Review* 67(2): 222–242.

Borjas, George J. 1985. "Assimilation, Changes in Cohort Quality, and the Earnings of Immigrants." *Journal of Labor Economics* 3: 463–489.

Borjas, George J. 1995. "Assimilation and Changes in Cohort Quality Revisited: What Happened to Immigrant Earnings in the 1980s?" *Journal of Labor Economics* 13(2): 201–245.

Delgado-Gaitan, C. 1994. "Russian Refugee Families: Accommodating Aspirations Through Education." *Anthropology and Education Quarterly* 25(2): 137–155.

Deyhle, D., and F. Margonis. 1995. "Navajo Mothers and Daughters: Schools, Jobs, and the Family." *Anthropology and Education Quarterly* 16(2): 135–167.

Diaz Salcedo, S. 1996. Successful Latino students at the high school level: A case study of ten students. Ph.D. dissertation, Graduate School of Education, Harvard University.

Durand, J., E. Parrado, and D. S. Massey. 1996. "Migradollars and Development: A Reconsideration of the Mexican Case." *International Migration Review* 30(2): 423–444.

Freire, P. 1973. *Pedagogy of the Oppressed.* New York: Seabury.

Freire, P. 1995. *Pedagogy of Hope: Reliving Pedagogy of the Oppressed.* New York: Continuum.

Freire, P., and D. Macedo. 1996. A dialogue: Culture, language, and race. In *Breaking Free: The Transformative Power of Critical Pedagogy*, ed. P. Leistyna, A. Woodrum, and S. Sherblom, 199–288. Reprint Series no. 27. Cambridge, Mass.: Harvard Education Review.

Freire, P., and D. Macedo. 1987. *Literacy: Reading the Word and Reading the World.* Critical Studies in Education Series. Boston, MA: Bergin and Garvey Publishers.

Hondagneu-Sotelo, P. 1994. *Gendered Transitions: Mexican Experiences of Immigration.* Berkeley: University of California Press.

Gamio, M. [1930] 1971. *Mexican Immigration to the U. S.: A Study of Human Migration and Adjustment.* Reprint. New York: Dover Publications.

Giroux, H., and P. McLaren. 1994. *Between Borders: Pedagogy and the Politics of Cultural Studies.* New York and London: Routledge.

Gutierrez, K. 1994. "How Talk, Context, and Script Shape Contexts for Learning: A Cross-Case Comparison of Journal Sharing." *Linguistics and Education* 5: 335–365.

Gutierrez, K., J. Larson, and B. Kreuter. 1995. "Cultural Tensions in the Scripted Classroom: The Value of the Subjugated Perspective." *Urban Education* 29(4): 410–442.

Martin, P., and E. Taylor. 1996. "Immigration and the Changing Face of Rural California: Summary Report of the Conference Held at Asilomar, June 12–14, 1995." *Rural Migration News.*

McLaren, P. 1995. *Critical Pedagogy and Predatory Culture.* New York and London: Routledge.

Menchaca, M., and R. R. Valencia. 1990. "Anglo-Saxon Ideologies in the 1920s–1930s: Their Impact on the Segregation of Mexican Students in California." *Anthropology and Education Quarterly* 21(3): 222–249.

Orfield G., M. Bachmeier, D. James, and T. Eitle. 1997. Deepening segregation in American public schools. Unpublished manuscript, Harvard Project on School Desegregation, Harvard University.

Orfield, G., and S. E. Eaton, eds. 1996. *Dismantling Desegregation: The Quiet Reversal of Brown v. Board of Education.* New York: The New Press.

Palerm, J. V. 1994. *Immigrant and Migrant Farm Workers in the Santa Maria Valley, California.* Center for Chicano Studies and Department of Anthropology, University of California, Santa Barbara. Sponsored by the Center for Survey Methods Research, Bureau of the Census, Washington, D.C.

Patthey-Chavez, G. 1993. "High School as an Arena for Cultural Conflict and Acculturation for Latino Angelinos." *Anthropology and Education Quarterly* 24(1): 33–60.

Population Today: News, Numbers and Analysis. 1996. 24(8).

Portes, A. 1995. Children of immigrants: Segmented assimilation and its determinants. In *The Economic Sociology of Immigration,* ed. A. Portes, 248–280. New York: Russell Sage Foundation.

Portes, A. 1996. Introduction: Immigration and its aftermath. In *The New Second Generation,* ed. A. Portes, 1–7. New York: Russell Sage Foundation.

Rose, M. 1995. *The Promise of Public Education in America: Possible Lives.* New York and London: Penguin Books.

Suárez-Orozco, C. and M. Suárez-Orozco. 1995a. *Transformations: Immigration, Family Life and Achievement Motivation among Latino Adolescents.* Stanford: Stanford University Press.

Suárez-Orozco, C., and M. Suárez-Orozco. 1995b. Migration: Generational disconti-nuities and the making of Latino identities. In *Ethnic Identity: Creation, Conflict, and Accommodation,* ed. L. Romanucci-Ross and G. De Vos, 321–347. Walnut Creek, CA: AltaMira Press.

Suárez-Orozco, M. 1998. State terrors: Immigrants and refugees in the post-national space. In *Ethnic Identity and Power: Cultural Contexts of Political Action in School and Society,* ed. H. T. Trueba and Y. Zou. New York: SUNY Press.

Trueba, H. T. 1989. *Raising Silent Voices: Educating Linguistic Minorities for the 21st Century.* New York: Harper & Row.

Trueba, H. T., C. Rodriguez, Y. Zou, and H. Cintron. 1993. *Healing Multicultural America: Mexican Immigrants Rise to Power in Rural California.* London, England: Falmer Press.

Trueba, H. T. 1997. A Mexican immigrant community in Central California. Unpublished manuscript, Harvard University.

Trueba, H. T., and J. González. 1997. Repatriation and adaptation: The return of farm workers to Comala, Colima. Unpublished manuscript, University of Colima.

U.S. Bureau of the Census. 1996. *Current Population Reports.* Washington, D.C.: Department of Commerce, Economics and Statistics Administration.

Valencia, R. R. 1991. The plight of Chicano students: An overview of schooling conditions and outcomes. In *Chicano School Failure: An Analysis through Many Windows,* ed. R. R. Valencia, 3–26. London: Falmer Press.

Vigil, D. 1983. "Chicano Gangs: One Response to Mexican Urban Adaptation in the Los Angeles Area." *Urban Anthropology* 12(1): 45–75.

Vigil, D. 1988. "Group Processes and Street Identity: Adolescent Chicano Gang Members." *Ethos* 16(4): 421–444.

Vigil, D. 1989. *Barrio Gangs.* Austin: University of Texas Press.

Wilson, P. 1991. "Trauma of Sioux Indian High School Students." *Anthropology and Education Quarterly* 22(4): 367–383.

Commentary

Gary Orfield, Harvard University

If demography is destiny, the United States is entering a perilous era and seems perversely engaged in implementing policies that will greatly heighten the threat to the American future. Between the mid-twentieth century and the mid-twenty-first century we are being transformed from a nine-tenths white European, English-speaking society with one large minority group, concentrated in the South and a few large northern cities, to a multiracial society with a declining white population and a non-European majority. In that new society, the largest minority group will be Latino, three times as large as the present black population, and many millions will speak Spanish. Political and cultural power will rapidly shift from the East and the Midwest to the West and the South.

Our largest immigrant stream, which is accounting for much of our population growth, includes millions of people with very little education and few skills to prepare them for a bitterly competitive global economy in which the growing rewards are very tightly linked to skills. They tend to enter secondary labor markets with low wages, little mobility, and few exits.

The issues of racial, ethnic, and linguistic differences are likely to become more and more salient as our two largest states become predominantly Latino and many communities try to sort out the cross-pressures of three or four different racial and ethnic groups competing for power and economic opportunity and seeking opportunity through schools. Recent research shows that the major "minority" groups tend to have more intense stereotypes toward each other than whites have of any of them, and there are already bitter political divisions among minorities in some cities.

It should be clear in the post–Cold War era that racial and ethnic cleavages are potentially profoundly destructive if institutions and leaders favoring mutual respect, integration, and pluralism are replaced by demagogues activating stereotypes, fears, and hatred. The Soviet Union collapsed from such forces, not from external conquest. The tragedy of Bosnia follows a long chain of similar events stretching from the Indian subcontinent to Belfast, from Beirut to Indonesia. Our northern neighbor Canada has very recently been through an election in which a major part of the nation came within fractions of a percent of voting to split the nation along lines of language. We could reasonably expect that farsighted leaders would be seeking ways and means to weave together the disparate elements of our changing population with the greatest urgency.

Nowhere should this effort be more intense than in our schools. Unlike most other industrial societies, the United States has a weak system of social welfare provision, one that is becoming more feeble after recent massive cutbacks in welfare, housing, and other programs. Only the schools exist as a major instrument for bringing the society together and giving substance to the central dream—equal opportunity for all. This is particularly true for Latino immigrants, since the Latino population is the youngest major group in the society.

With the best of good will and major resources, the task would still be huge. Schools have much weaker effects than families on children's lives, and population growth is concentrated in overburdened urban school districts that are struggling with many kinds of social and economic problems. A great many low-income families, for example, move every few months because of the lack of affordable housing, giving their children a chaotic educational experience.

Latino immigrants, like earlier black immigrants to big cities, are hard working, ambitious, and deeply concerned about education; they desperately want a better life for their children. Most of their children still have the great benefit of intact families. But the growing populations are often locating in dysfunctional inner cities and decaying suburbs where economic and cultural crises pose a clear and present danger of ghettoization and failure for their children. Too often there is a drastic shift from traditional rural poverty in coherent Mexican villages to chaos and tragedy on vicious streets dominated by heavily armed urban gangs that ridicule the values of parents and the old society.

What our leaders have too often discovered are not the lessons of the dangers of division and inequality but the political benefits of activating stereotypes and playing on fears and social cleavages. As this huge new population arrives asking for incorporation and respect in the society and a fair chance to make it in the mainstream, we are in the process of abandoning many of the limited tools we have to make this work and raising new barriers that block incorporation and mobility.

Since demographic change is already deeply structured into the existing population and we have no policies likely to substantially reduce additional immigration, this means that we are betting that a huge and very rapidly growing community will accept increasing subordination and that the segregated communities and institutions where they are confined will produce acceptance of subordination rather than a countermobilization of beliefs and political leadership built around defiance rather than pluralism.

Latinos are facing intensely isolated and unequal schooling, isolation already more severe even than that of African Americans. They also face a marginalized economic situation. Their family income is now about the same as that of African Americans and has been declining significantly in recent years. The only major policy initiative on their behalf has been bilingual education.

There are now major attacks on bilingual education programs that blame them for the educational problems and lack of incorporation that grow out of poverty, isolation, and discrimination. Latinos are also vulnerable to the conservative attack on the whole array of other civil rights protections that may help them. These attacks target affirmative action college admissions, aid programs, and policies, greatly increasing the cost of college and the courses and test scores required for admission. Programs for minority small businesses, affirmative action hiring, and voting rights enforcement to enhance political representation have also been attacked.

Latino students constituted 13 percent of the enrollment in American public schools by 1994, a proportion higher than the proportion of black students at the height of the civil rights struggle. The West, the region most isolated from the black struggle because of its small black population, is undergoing a vast transformation and now has the smallest share of white students of any region. Predominantly minority areas in terms of school enrollment already include the nation's two most populous states, California and Texas, which are both moving rapidly toward a Latino majority in their school systems. Latino students show the most significant change as a proportion of students in intensely segregated schools, which rose to 34.8 percent of all schools in 1994.

From the 1960s to the mid-1990s, Mexican American areas in the West changed from very substantial desegregation to a level of isolation exceeding that of blacks. Since Latino students are experiencing far higher dropout rates than African Americans, and three-fifths of Latino students live in two states in which education officials have adopted policies ending affirmative action for college admissions, the increasing concentration of students in low-achieving, high-poverty schools where few children prepare competitively for college raises extremely important issues. If the growing community of Latino students is increasingly isolated in inferior schools and standards are raised without the schools having the means to meet them, a vicious cycle of declining opportunity could result.

The relationship between segregation by race and segregation by poverty in public schools across the nation is exceptionally strong. The correlation between the percentage of black and Latino enrollments and the percentage of students receiving free lunches is an extremely high .72. This means that when we talk about racially segregated schools, they are very likely to be segregated by poverty as well.

There is strong and consistent evidence across the United States as well as from other nations that high-poverty schools usually have much lower levels of educational performance by virtually all measures. This is not entirely caused by the school; family background is a more powerful influence. Schools with concentrations of isolated, low-income children have less well-prepared children. Even better-prepared children can be harmed academically if they are placed in a school with few other prepared students and, in some cases, in a social setting where academic achievement is not fostered.

School-level educational achievement scores in many states and in the nation show a very strong relationship between the concentration of poverty and low achievement. This is because high-poverty schools are unequal in many ways that affect educational outcomes. These students' parents are far less educated—a very powerful influence—and these children are much more likely to be living in single-parent homes that are struggling with multiple problems. Children are much more likely to have serious developmental problems and health problems that go untreated. Children move much more often, often moving involuntarily in the course of a school year, meaning that schools often do not have students for sufficient time to make an impact. High-poverty schools have to devote far more time and resources to family and health crises, security, children who come to school not speaking standard English, seriously disturbed children, children with no educational materials in their homes, and many children with very weak educational preparation. These schools tend to draw less-qualified teachers and to hold them for shorter periods of time. They tend to have to invest much more heavily in remediation and much less adequately in advanced and gifted classes and demanding materials. The level of competition and peer group support for educational achievement are much lower in high-poverty schools. Such schools are viewed much more negatively in the community and by institutions of higher education as well as by potential employers. In those states that have implemented high stakes testing that denies graduation or fails students, the high-poverty schools tend to have by far the highest rates of sanctions.

Trueba correctly points out that the educational crisis facing Latinos is compounded in many dimensions. There are massive cultural changes that take place in the process of immigration and entering into new school systems. Newcomer families often have a clearer vision and more hope than those who have been struggling for a generation in a deteriorating urban setting with shrinking economic opportunities and those who have been exposed to the loss of culture between generations. These problems are compounded by prejudice and language differences. Schools can, of course, play important roles in this process and sometimes help replace family influences for those without strong support at home. Sonia Diaz Salcedo and others have described some of the powerful impacts of positive supportive schooling. Typically, however, the schools serving minority concentrated-poverty communities are deteriorating, poorly equipped, staffed with inexperienced teachers who plan to leave as soon as possible, and have few educated or powerful parents.

Latino communities in urban America are deeply threatened by current trends and policies. Most are situated in settings where it is impossible to maintain the old culture through the generations and where the economic threats to both parents and students are often extreme. These communities face the dual pressures of a continuing inflow of economically marginal or illegal workers and the exit of those who have had success in U.S. mainstream institutions. If the economy is raising the stakes on education, and bilingual programs are only a very partial answer and are being cut back, new thinking about educational and residential choices is badly needed. The success or failure of devising and implementing policies directed at these problems will do much to shape large portions of twenty-first-century America.

PART V

Psychocultural Themes

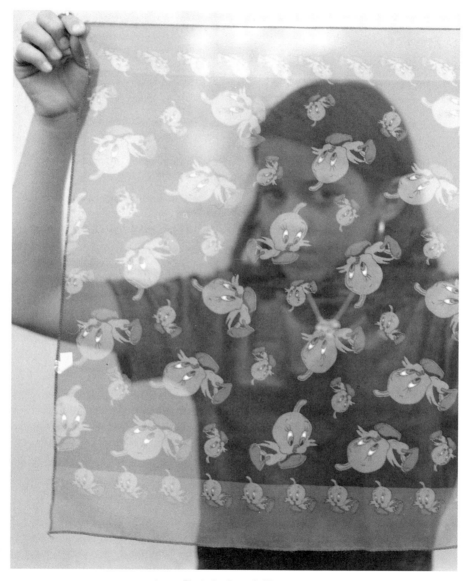

Photo by Anna LeVine

Ricardo Ainslie

The impetus for my work in west Texas was personal. I grew up the son of a Mexican father and an American mother, speaking English in a Mexican world, speaking Spanish in an American world. As a child I had a keen sense for the border; I must have crossed it one hundred times as we flew or drove to visit my mother's family in Texas. The contrast between these two worlds is obvious, but for me there was something almost palpable in the crossing. All of those things we so loosely cluster under the term "culture" impinged directly upon my senses. I always carried two passports, each a kind of magic key to enter its corresponding world. And, always, the feeling I had as I entered one or the other country was of a bit of disingenuousness—hiding one part of my identity from the official examining the documents that certified the other.

—From *No Dancin' In Anson:
An American Story of Race and Social Change*
(Northvale, N.J.: Jason Aronson, Inc., 1995), p. xxi.

This paragraph summarizes an important source of my interest in the experiences, psychological and otherwise, of the immigrant. I am, as reflected in the above excerpt, both an immigrant and not quite an immigrant. I came to the United States to attend college at the age of 17, and for many years held the conviction that I would return home to Mexico. On the other hand, the world I came to was not as foreign, the experienced shifts not as abrupt, as it is in the experience of most immigrants. My background increasingly led me to explore social and psychological experiences where boundaries are crossed and blurred. In *No Dancin'*, the boundaries were historical, social, and psychological boundaries, rather than a discrete geographic boundary, between Anglo and Mexican American worlds that were increasingly shifting within the community of Anson, Texas. Similarly, in my clinical work, I have been particularly interested in patients (immigrants as well as others) whose struggles are linked to psychological crossings that rupture a subjective sense of clear delineation.

Professor and Director of the Counseling Psychology Doctoral Training Program, University of Texas at Austin. Faculty Member, Houston-Galveston Psychoanalytic Institute. Member, Section of Psychologist-Psychoanalyst Practitioners of the American Psychological Association's Division of Psychoanalysis. Educated at University of California, Berkeley and University of Michigan. Publications also include *The Psychology of Twinship* (1997).

9

Cultural Mourning, Immigration, and Engagement: Vignettes from the Mexican Experience

Ricardo C. Ainslie
University of Texas at Austin

In the spring of 1929 Freud wrote to the Swiss psychiatrist Ludwig Binswanger on the occasion of the death of the latter's favorite son:

> Although we know that after such a loss the acute state of mourning will subside, we also know we shall remain inconsolable and will never find a substitute. No matter what may fill the gap, even if it be filled completely, it nevertheless remains something else. And actually this is how it should be. It is the only way of perpetuating that love which we do not want to relinquish (Frankiel 1993, 70).

Loss, Freud is clearly telling us, is inherently paradoxical, setting in motion a psychological effort to resolve that which is inherently unresolvable. It is an experience that creates an emptiness that remains an emptiness despite our efforts to fill it in. Perhaps the most important insight that Freud offers us, however, is that these irresolvable gaps become, again paradoxically, the very means through which we perpetuate our attachment to those whom we have lost. In its own way, mourning negates loss. The lost attachment remains emotionally alive so long as it is mourned.

The immigrant experience represents a special case of mourning in which mourning revolves around the loss of loved people and places occasioned by geographic dislocation.[1] This mourning is not necessarily of such a magnitude as to represent a clinical syndrome. Rather, it represents a psychological context that colors the immigrant's emotional world and that becomes represented at the level of motivation and engagement in ways that are both conscious and unconscious. Notwithstanding the preeminent economic motives that lie behind the decision to leave one's country and the fact that in many instances some measure of economic gain comes from that decision, immigrants are, as Volkan (1993) notes, "perpetual mourners" precisely because they must leave home to achieve those economic goals. In the character of their mourning, in the manner in which immigrants' mourning plays itself out in their individual and collective lives, powerful motivational forces are at work that shape how immigrants alter the worlds into which they have come to live. The immigrant's engagement with the processes of mourning plays an important role in the strategies deployed in managing grief, how the immigrant participates in the new social context, and the nature of his relationship with people and lands that have been left behind.

CULTURE, IDENTITY, AND CULTURAL MOURNING

Individual identity draws heavily from cultural, social, and familial elements that together become the foundation for intrapsychic experience (Erikson 1950). Elsewhere (Ainslie 1995) I have described culture as "both sustentative and suspensory," that is, as a series of sociopsychological enclosures that provide emotional nurturance while psychologically "holding" and organizing us. The subjective experience of culture can be understood, in developmental terms, as having its origins at the beginning of life, in the intimate engagements between parent and child, and increasingly becoming defined or structured by complex social signifiers such as language, ethnicity, and religion, which give culture its hue.

From the beginning of our emotional lives, the social experiences that govern our understanding of the known are seamlessly fused with cultural elements that only later can be reflected upon, becoming discernible to the individual as something "cultural." Neither the toddler in the papoose, nor the young child whose mother sings an "ethnic" lullaby, conceives of himself as immersed in a medium that we term "culture." Children simply experience. Yet from the start that experiencing is densely populated by all of the cultural elements that we come to love and that create for us a sense of the familiar, in both the experiencing and relational aspects of the word. For this reason, identity, in an intimate and psychological sense, is permanently soldered to those characteristics of our experience defined by the peculiarities of our individual parents and families as well as by the cultural elements that have given context to those lives. The link between culture and the deepest features of subjective experience is as ingrained as it is pervasive; this is why cultural dislocation has such profound psychological consequences for the individual.

It is the intimate connection between individual and collective experience that weds individual mourning to cultural mourning. When an immigrant leaves loved ones at home, he or she also leaves the cultural enclosures that have organized and sustained experience. The immigrant simultaneously must come to terms with the loss of family and friends on the one hand, and cultural forms (food, music, art, for example) that have given the immigrant's native world a distinct and highly personal character on the other hand. It is not only people who are mourned, but culture itself, which is inseparable from the loved ones whom it holds. This is the experience that I term cultural mourning. While the motives for migration (voluntary or involuntary) and the conditions left behind (economic, political) vary from person to person, all immigrants lose something essential to their lives in leaving their native homes. While these varied motives may structure the nature of the mourning that must be engaged (for example, the greater the ambivalence about leaving one's country, the more difficult mourning is likely to be), even those whose lives in their country of origin are characterized by conflict and deprivation will experience loss.

LOSS, MOURNING, AND RESTITUTIVE ATTEMPTS: THE PSYCHOLOGICAL "RETURN" AND THE CREATION OF POTENTIAL SPACE

Many have observed the parallel between the formation of the immigrant's new identity after moving to an adopted country and the mourning process that clinicians have come to recognize as characteristic of those who have lost a loved one (Garza-Guerrero 1974; Grinberg and Grinberg 1984; Volkan 1979; Volkan and Zintl 1993). When individuals experience a significant loss, the mourning process proceeds through an internal reworking of the mental representations of that relationship. Hans Loewald (1962), for example, notes that in mourning there is "the relinquishment of external objects and their internalization involves a process of separation, of loss, and restitution" (p. 125). In uncomplicated grief, the mourner loosens ties to the representation of the dead through the work of mourning, gradually forming an identification with that person that promotes growth. Mourning facilitates the processes of internalization that ultimately lead to an experience of separation without psychic loss (Loewald 1962). In normal mourning, then, there is a gradual decathexis of elements of the relationship with the lost one, as well as a claiming of the full range of affect toward the lost one.

A common mechanism in mourning is the use of objects and fantasies that serve to dilute the impact of loss by virtue of maintaining a connection to the deceased. Volkan (1981) terms these activities "linking objects" or "linking phenomena" to indicate the function of such objects or fantasies in the management of grief—they are symbolic bridges to the representation of the dead person. These linking processes "provide a locus for externalized contact between aspects of the mourner's self-representation and aspects of the representation of the deceased. The mourner sees them as containing elements of himself and the one he has lost" (p. 20). These processes are also readily observed in the lives of immigrants who, having left loved ones and loved places behind, must absorb the consequences of that dislocation in order to be able to effectively manage the world into which they have come. In mourning these losses, immigrants keep the people and cultures they have left alive, psychologically, via the use of the linking objects and linking processes described by Volkan.

Donald Winnicott, the eccentric but at times brilliant psychoanalytic theorist, offers us another vantage for understanding the processes of mourning and adaptive efforts to manage them. His theorizing is especially useful in understanding the concept of cultural mourning in that Winnicott weds a child's developing sense of people and the unfolding experience of culture into an indissolvable matrix of experience. Winnicott observed that culture is created out of that realm of experience situated between the infant's desire and the mother's response, in what he termed "the potential space" (Winnicott 1971). The potential space is an intermediate area of experiencing that lies between fantasy and reality, that is, between inner psychic reality and actual or external reality (Ogden 1990). Winnicott's use of the concept was initially intended to capture the psychological experience and struggle of the young child grappling with the need to feel emotionally fused with the mother while simultaneously forced to acknowledge the fact of her separateness. This tension, Winnicott proposed, is resolved via the creation of a domain of psychological experiencing that he termed the potential space. The function of the potential space for the child, and its evolution over the course of development, are not central to the present considerations. However, Winnicott's description of the potential space as pivotal in the management of experiences of separation and dislocation is important. Equally essential is Winnicott's description of the potential space as the area of cultural experience and the area of creative engagement with the world in which we live. These two definitions overlap in cultural mourning.

Winnicott (1951, 1967) theorized that, for the infant, the reality of an internal and an external world, the reality that parent and child are different people with distinct experiences, creates a challenge of momentous proportions. In this sense, children, too, are perpetual mourners. The potential space is the arena within which the child engages and attempts to resolve the tensions created by separateness; it is a domain of experience whose ambiguous status as simultaneously "me" and "not me" allows for the illusion of continuity between self and other while concurrently lending itself to the solution of this spatial and, more important, this experiential distance. Modell (1968) emphasizes that the potential space is actively constructed, rather than passively received, that is, an illusion *created* out of what is interior and what is exterior:

> the transitional inanimate object of the child . . . stands midway between what is created by the inner world and that which exists in the environment . . . It is something other than the self, but the separateness from the self is only partially acknowledged, since the object is given life by the subject. It is a created environment—created in the sense that the properties attributed to the object reflect the inner life of the subject (p. 35).

Whether as children or adults, we manage the ubiquity of dislocation, separation, and loss in our lives through the use of potential space, we construct arenas of experiencing in which we creatively dissolve those tensions, finding within them solutions that bridge the emotional gaps and spaces secondary to separation. For the infant, this might involve an object, say a favorite blanket that has rested between infant and mother in nursing, that becomes a constant comforter to be invoked at those junctures where contact is threatened or vulnerability is experienced. For adults, the manifestations of the potential space are considerably more subtle, insinuated into the worlds we construct, masked by social conventions, but no less amenable to creative engagement and the illusion of restoration of what is lost, as will be illustrated below.

A common feature of the immigrant's mourning is the attempt to deny or dilute the reality of dislocation. There are classic examples: the "new" designations for those communities established by immigrants from places called York, Jersey, or Hampshire; or the Little Italys and the Chinatowns, places within which immigrants have sought to recreate lost worlds. These efforts are transparent in their design: They attempt to mask the reality of loss via the creation of a psychological space, a version of Winnicott's potential space, within which the illusion that they are both "here" and "there," both "now" and "then," is made possible. In this manner, the immigrant mourner is soothed and comforted. Within these enclaves, individual and cultural mourning can be managed and absorbed through the illusion of blurred distances—intrapsychic, territorial, and cultural.

It is important to emphasize that in Winnicott's depiction, the potential space is only partially, and perhaps least interestingly, a retreat from the reality of separation. Most important, in Winnicott's framework the potential space is a form of creative engagement with the problematics of separation and loss, put in the service of constructively, if never perfectly, transcending them. The immigrant, like all mourners, uses the potential space to help resolve the unbearable tensions and contradictions of an existence in which separation brings significant anguish, which may be the case even when separations are chosen and desired. Such resolution facilitates the effective engagement with the new environment.

La Pulga: An Illustrative Potential Space

By midday on any given Sunday, the Austin Country Flea Market, on the eastern margin of the city of Austin, Texas,[2] is bustling. The price of admission is one dollar per carload, and the parking lot is full. Seventy to eighty percent of the 15,000 to 18,000 people who come to the flea market on any given weekend are Hispanic (Gandara 1996), which in Texas means overwhelmingly Mexican or Mexican American. Most of these visitors call the Austin Country Flea Market "La Pulga" ("the flea" in Spanish), reflective of the fact that these immigrants have made the flea market their own. La Pulga has become the quintessential potential space for Mexican immigrants, with or without legal documents, who live and work in and around Austin. La Pulga is very reminiscent of the plazas typical of the towns and villages these immigrants have left. A stage and dance floor are located in the very heart of the square that is formed by the arrangement of vendor's stalls. In front of the stage are metal tables and chairs, and concessions sell food, beer, and soft drinks. Originally, the music ranged from blues and rock and roll to country Western and Mexican Norteño and Tejano music. However, accurately reading the tastes of their predominant clientele, the operators of the flea market now book Norteño and Tejano music almost exclusively. These *conjuntos* play Spanish-language music characteristic of northern Mexico and Texas, but the lyrics closely parallel the motifs typical of American country Western music: lost love, ill fate, and large doses of melancholy. The men sit drinking Mexican beer, eating roasted corn, tacos, gorditas, and other Mexican foods, while watching couples on the dance floor. Many of the women are dressed in their Sunday finest.

La Pulga is concretely the reconstructed world these immigrants have left. Vendor stands sell Mexican videos, classic Mexican movies such as the famous comic Mario Moreno Cantinflas' *El Padrecito* (The Little Priest), Mexico's version of "Funniest Home Videos," and countless Mexican Rodeo movies, an especially popular genre for those from the Mexican provinces. The numerous produce stands are indistinguishable from their Mexican counterparts in terms of their selection of fruit and produce (papayas, mangos, tamarind, sugar cane stalks, and nopales abound, for example) as well as in their atmosphere, with vendors actively beckoning passersby promising the very lowest prices.

However, La Pulga is not only a setting that creates a temporary visual/sensory illusion that one is back home in Mexico, thereby replenishing these immigrants via a reimmersion in the lost familiar, but it is also a space full of the icons of the new culture in which he or she is trying to survive. Many stands reflect this crossroads: Vendors sell T-shirts that declare "Me vale Madre" alongside those with the Texas version: "Don't mess with me." Shirts and caps with the logos of professional American football teams are especially popular. Goods that are identified with the accoutrements of the American middle class, such as dining room sets, Avon skin care products, car care products, and used household appliances—all emblematic of success in the United States—are everywhere to be found. In what we might understand as a bilingual fusion of the somatics of contemporary American life, a sign over a stall selling health care products announces that they are excellent for "Weight loss/Dieta, Stress/Tensión, and Energy/Energía."

The indications are everywhere that La Pulga is a space where one may participate in the cultural forms definitional of American Life: One sees Mexican immigrants dressed in Dallas Cowboy's star Emmett Smith sweat shirts or Guess jeans, eating hot dogs, their children speaking English, carrying bags full of Avon products. A large advertisement for Lite beer seems to capture an important part of the La Pulga spirit. It reads, in English, "Lite Beer: Great Taste, Less Filling," along with the following caption in Spanish: "Que vida Tan Buena, Vivimos en Texas" ("What a good life, We live in Texas").

It is just as evident that La Pulga plays an important function in facilitating the immigrants' adaptation to the new culture with respect to the world of work. One readily finds materials to learn English, for example, on tape or in book and comic book formats. One can also purchase ID cards, an essential item for establishing a life in the United States. Many stalls sell new or used work tools for use in landscaping, construction, carpentry, and automotive repair. New and used clothing that will transform the Mexican immigrant's appearance from rural Mexican to urban, football-jerseyed American are sold at deeply discounted prices. "Connie's Money Den," with a sign indicating that she specializes in "Visa/Mastercard, Notary, Income Tax, Checks, & Immigration"—a kind of fiscal and legal jack-of-all-trades—caters to the needs of the undocumented worker lacking in English skills and sufficiently on the social and economic margins not to have access to these services via more conventional means.

Within La Pulga the Mexican and North American worlds become represented in the ways that cultures always manifest what is distinctly theirs: food, entertainment, and aesthetics, among other social rituals. La Pulga serves as a potential space where Mexican immigrants simultaneously live in the old country and the new, a kind of "as if" world wherein they can momentarily be home again, in the plazas of their villages and towns, while, at the same time, "playing" with the materials of the new culture. Articles catering to the nostalgic are found alongside cultural artifacts that reflect the necessities of work as well as the allure of the new culture. Via the illusion of return, La Pulga provides a restorative function that renews energies, rekindles hopes, and makes it possible to face the next week's hardships of labor, tensions, and discriminations. Simultaneously, La Pulga facilitates the procurement of what is essential for survival in this new environment, be it new cultural identifications (becoming a Dallas Cowboy fan) or purchasing tools needed for work. Winnicott's description of the potential space as a domain of experiencing that is both "me" and "not me," facilitating the transition between known and familiar and unknown psychological terrain, is an apt description of La Pulga—an intermediate zone, culturally, a creative mix of North American and Mexican cultures serving both aesthetic functions as well as comforting, entertaining, and utilitarian functions.

It is in this sense that these immigrant mourners have also altered the American cultural landscape. La Pulga is an illustration of immigrants transforming public space such that Mexicans can now live in the United States as if it were an extension of Mexico (see David Gutiérrez, this volume). However, in emphasizing the *transitional* function, the aspects of La Pulga that serve as *potential space*, I am suggesting more. The particular manner in which immigrants transform this and other public spaces is not merely linked to the recreation within the United States of the culture one has left. In addition, it is a transformation that makes that space *usable* as a resource so that the immigrant may more effectively engage the challenges posed by an unfamiliar culture. These immigrants have seized the flea market and made it their own. In so doing they have simultaneously reconstructed a lost world *and* created a vehicle for effective engagement in the new one. This is precisely what immigrants have always done, thereby shaping the receiving culture, altering its configurations, and all too often provoking deep anxieties among those being changed.[3]

TIME, DISTANCE, AND THE CHARACTER OF CULTURAL MOURNING

Important variables governing the vicissitudes of cultural mourning are the time one has been away from one's native country and the accessibility or ease of return. In the latter respect, Mexican immigrants comprise a unique group in the history of American immigration. The proximity of the two countries and the relative fluidity of their border can alter the character of cultural mourning. One is tempted to add a third variable as well: the emergence of modern communications technologies.[4]

To the extent that the immigrant's ties to the native country are maintained and continuously replenished, mourning is comparatively less necessary. In turn, the maintenance of such links is likely to affect the extent to which the immigrant relinquishes or alters ties to the culture of origin.[5] Accessibility allows immigrants to remain intimately connected to the world they have left, thereby actively sustaining its intrapsychic representations and the fantasy of return. In this context, emotional ties remain rich and potent long after immigrants from other, more distant, countries have been forced (by time, distance, and cultural tensions) to dilute or relinquish them altogether. Mourning does not really take place in the same sense because the link to the native soil remains immediate and is subject to relatively continuous cultural replenishing. One might speculate that such proximity is likely to eventuate in immigrant communities that remain insulated from mainstream American culture for internal reasons rather than those imposed by the host culture. Simply put, they have relatively less to mourn.

The residents of Tehuixtla, Puebla, are one such example.

The Miracle of Tehuixtla

Tehuixtla is a small village high in the mountains of the state of Puebla with a population of approximately 200 inhabitants, its census decimated by rural Mexico's pervasive economic problems.[6] Materially, Tehuixtla simply does not provide enough for its people. As a result, the residents of Tehuixtla have left for the United States in a steady exodus. The character of this migration reflects sociologists' theorizing about the function of immigrant networks in relation to the activation of migration streams (Waldinger 1997). For the residents of Tehuixtla, migration patterns have resulted in three main groupings in this country living in New York, Los Angeles, and Houston. Each of these three clusters is tightly knit, with a great deal of communication within and between groups, as illustrated below. Many of the Tehuixtla expatriots have succeeded in obtaining legal immigrant status by marriage or at the time of the Immigration and Naturalization Service's amnesty program of the late 1980s.

Despite their legal status, the immigrants from Tehuixtla retain a vibrant and intense connection to the town from which they migrated. Most of the year, Tehuixtla is a ghost town. In December, however, the "miracle of Tehuixtla" (*New York Times*, 25 December 1996) takes place as those who have emigrated return and the town's population swells to several thousand during the Posada season (December 16–25) and New Year celebrations. They arrive in caravans of cars, vans, and pickup trucks, bringing their families home in a yearly pilgrimage that reunites them with the dwindling number of town elders, as well as the friends and relatives who have found their destinies in various American cities.

I interviewed two of some fifty Tehuixtla immigrants presently living in the Houston area. One, a 27-year-old man employed as a mechanic, has been in the United States since age 16. The other is a woman of 25 employed as a beautician. Both had obtained their legal papers during the INS amnesty.

The families in Houston, Los Angeles, and New York have a deep and enduring tie to Tehuixtla. In each of these communities, for example, the Tehuixtla immigrants organize annual events (dances, car washes, fund drives) to raise money for the town.[7] These efforts have rebuilt the town's church and the walls of the cemetery, among other community projects. However, the most daunting problem facing the community is the severe shortage of water, potable or otherwise. The town's emigrants have worked hard to find a solution to the water problem. For example, last year they funded efforts to dig a well, but the water from the new well is undrinkable because of its high salt content and the well produces too little. "We can't even shower there like we do here," the mechanic told me. The beautician underscored her concerns with a telling illustration: "We have to bring our own water because the children get sick if they drink the town's water." Increasingly desperate, the Tehuixtla residents living in the United States recently sought the services of a water witch from a nearby village in the hope that his magic will locate water where more conventional means have failed. These efforts also reflect the high level of collaboration among the three expatriate groups, who must agree on goals, raise funds, and coordinate their Tehuixtla projects from their respective communities in the United States.

Tehuixtla's water predicament reflects, both metaphorically and materially, the circumstances that drove its families to seek lives in the United States. The community cannot provide for its members' essential needs—natural resources and economic opportunities that are necessary for their collective survival. But such dire realities have done little to alter the conviction among most of those immigrants that Tehuixtla remains their home, that they are only temporarily living in the United States, and that it is only a matter of time before they return to take up their lives more or less where they left off.[8] Psychologically speaking, for these immigrants Tehuixtla remains part of the psychic present, not a lost past.

For example, both the mechanic and the beautician whom I interviewed spoke of their Houston Tehuixtla compatriots' intent to return. They told of shared plans that included opening a hotel, a shop for automotive repairs, a restaurant, and hardware stores, as well as chicken and hog farms. Many immigrants from the three North American communities have built or are building homes in Tehuixtla, where for most of the year the two-story, cinderblock homes with satellite dishes must seem odd in a town with such a small population, mostly the parents and grandparents of those who have left. In every sense, the immigrants from Tehuixtla are trying to keep their community alive.

The earnestness of these return fantasies, as well as their intensity, is impressive. The proximity of Mexico fuels these hopes. In the lives of these immigrants, Tehuixtla remains a powerful emotional beacon, orienting them toward their homeland. They remain, relative to the experience of many other immigrants, more tightly connected and identified with that community because Tehuixtla is so close and readily accessible. This emotional proximity has implications for the character of their cultural mourning. Their loss is not so complete. Indeed, many believe it to be only transient.

Every Christmas, when the "miracle of Tehuixtla" occurs and the lost children return by the busload and carload from the great urban centers of the United States, that hope is replenished and kept alive. The houses continue to be built, the grandparents renew their acquaintance with grandchildren who show up in Nike shoes and Houston Oilers T-shirts, speaking as much (or more) English as they do Spanish, and everyone hopes that the water witch will resolve the one clear obstacle to their permanent return by finding "sweet water" in sufficient quantities to sustain the thousands who would need it, the thousands who because they retain hope of return, cannot fully mourn the fact that they have had to leave in the first place.

CONCLUSION

While the reasons for leaving their homelands vary immensely, all immigrants are mourners. This spectrum of motivations may mediate, but it cannot alter, the fundamental reality that one has left a world that once was home for another that is not. That irreducible fact has psychological implications for the emotional life of every immigrant.

Epidemiological studies of the immigrant experience indicate that immigration takes a psychological toll. A positive relationship has consistently been found between immigrant status and such mental health indicators as level of depressive symptomatology (e.g., Raymond, Rhoads, and Raymond 1980; Salgado de Snyder and Padilla 1987; Vega et al. 1984). Warheit et al. (1985) report that persons born in Mexico who have immigrated to the United States have more symptoms and psychosocial dysfunction than do Mexican Americans born in the United States, even when such variables as sex, age, marital status, and educational attainment are taken into account. Thus, immigration appears to be a double-edged sword: On the one hand it provides economic opportunities, a potential solution to the poverty that typically motivates immigrants to leave home; on the other hand, the experience of dislocation, coupled with significant acculturative stress attendant to negotiating an unknown culture, results in the noted symptoms.

These issues may be even more complex when one takes gender into account.[9] Salgado de Snyder (1987a, 1987b) reports a strong association between acculturative stress and level of depressive symptomatology among young Mexican immigrant women, who may experience greater levels of acculturative stress when compared with immigrant men. Similarly, immigrant females have been reported to score significantly higher than males on measures of cultural and family conflict (Salgado de Snyder and Padilla 1987), while women with higher ethnic loyalty (maintaining values, maintaining closer links to friends and family back in the country of origin) are reported to have lower levels of self-esteem, social support, and satisfaction, and higher levels of acculturative stress (Salgado de Snyder 1987a). On the other hand, in this same study Salgado de Snyder found that women who were occupied as full-time housewives had significantly higher depressive symptomatology than respondents who were employed outside of the home. It is certainly likely, as some (Baca Zinn 1980; Hondagneu-Sotelo 1992) have argued, that the immigration experience has a profound effect on the structure of roles and values in Mexican immigrant families, shifts that move these families in the direction of more egalitarian gender relations. These shifts suggest that there may be important gender differences in what I have termed cultural mourning.

In normal mourning, the person lost is gradually relinquished via an internalization of that relationship and all that it has meant. With this internalization, the significant features of that relationship become part of the ego. The ego is transformed by the loss, but more so by the reintegration of the lost object through the mourning process, as the mourner revisits the memories and feelings that bound them to the one who has left. In cultural mourning, in addition to mourning lost loved ones, one must mourn the loss of the cultural enclosures that have defined life and given it meaning. The immigrant must resolve both of these losses while simultaneously attempting to construct a new life where essential skills (in terms of language, education, etc.) may be lacking, and where one may or may not be welcomed by the residents of the host country. In doing so, immigrants make use of linking objects and linking processes to help sustain the sense of connection to the lost worlds, a connection that is essential to the maintenance of one's psychological equilibrium. Specifically, immigrants construct transitional areas of experiencing, the potential space, within which they can reduce the feeling of loss and dislocation, if only transiently, while at the same time creatively engage the not-me world of the new culture in which they now live. It is by recreating themselves and simultaneously creating usable, intermediate spaces within their receiving country that immigrants, in their mourning, alter the contours of their new communities.

NOTES

1. The experience of being in a new culture where roles and a variety of organizing assumptions are altered may also represent opportunities that are strongly desired and willingly embraced. The immigrant woman may relish a shift toward egalitarian family relations, for example, or the immigrant man may feel grateful for economic opportunities that allow him to purchase land in his village or to support extended family back home. Mourning is not the *only* experience of the immigrant, and it exists alongside other experiences that structure the immigrant's emotional life.

2. Interestingly, the Austin Country Flea Market is located in neutral territory, ethnically speaking.

3. Candidate Pat Buchanan's Border Stand in the 1996 presidential election is illustrative of these anxieties. Buchanan became a self-appointed spokesperson for the

segment of the American population most threatened by the influx of immigrants from Mexico. Paradoxically, one might argue that a host country's anxieties about being transformed by immigrants taps the same psychological processes at work in the immigrants' mourning: the anxieties mobilized by the loss of the familiar.

4. For example, in one of my visits to La Pulga I interviewed a man selling satellite cable systems from which his clients could receive 16 different Spanish-language stations, 10 of them direct from Mexico. Virtually all of his business is Mexican. Technology has shortened the cultural distance, making it possible to continue inhabiting, psychologically, the world one has left behind. As an immigrant watches a favorite program broadcast from Mexico, his cultural space might be temporarily indistinguishable from that of the relatives he has left in that country.

5. An additional consideration is the degree to which the host culture fosters or inhibits the immigrant's integration—ethnic biases being an obvious example, economic marginalization being another. Jorge Durand (this volume) notes that, historically, Mexican immigrants have very low naturalization rates. One might argue that the proximity between Mexico and the United States has made cultural replenishing easier for Mexican immigrants, thus diluting the motivations for becoming naturalized citizens.

6. See Enrique Dussel Peters' discussion (this volume) of the relationship between recent changes in Mexico's economy and immigration patterns to the United States.

7. Interestingly, these efforts sometimes take place under the dictates of North American cultural norms: The Tehuixtla immigrants often get together on the Fourth of July and Thanksgiving, American holidays that they celebrate and gatherings at which they examine the needs of their community in Mexico.

8. This is in contrast to other Mexican immigrants who report an intention to stay in this country (see Cornelius, this volume).

9. I am indebted to Susan González Baker for her remarks on gender and immigration.

REFERENCES

Ainslie, R. 1995. *No Dancin' in Anson: An American Story of Race and Social Change.* Northvale, N.J.: Jason Aronson Inc.

Baca Zinn, M. 1980. "Employment and Education of Mexican American Women: The Interplay of Modernity and Ethnicity in Eight Families." *Harvard Educational Review* 50: 47–62.

Erikson, E. 1950. *Childhood and Society.* New York: W. W. Norton.

Frankiel, R. V., ed. 1994. *Essential Papers on Object Loss*. New York: New York University Press.

Gandara, Ricardo. 1996. Boots, Vegetables, Phones, Tools and More. *Austin American Statesman*, 15 October.

Garza-Guerrero, A. C. 1974. "Culture Shock: Its Mourning and Vicissitudes of Identity." *Journal of the American Psychoanalytic Association* 22(2): 400–429.

Grinberg, L., and R. Grinberg. 1984. "A Psychoanalytic Study of Migration: Its Normal and Pathological Aspects." *Journal of the American Psychoanalytic Association* 32(1): 13–38.

Hondagneu-Sotelo, Pierrette. 1992. "Overcoming Patriarchal Constraints: The Reconstruction of Gender Relations among Mexican Immigrant Women and Men." *Gender & Society* 6: 393–413.

Loewald, Hans. 1962. Internalization, separation, mourning, and the superego. In *Essential Papers on Object Loss*, ed. R. V. Frankiel, 121–140. New York: New York University Press.

Ogden, T. H. 1990. *The Matrix of the Mind: Object Relations and the Psychoanalytic Dialogue*. Northvale, N.J.: Jason Aronson Inc.

Raymond, J., D. Rhoads, and R. Raymond. 1980. "The Relative Impact of Family and Social Involvement on Chicano Mental Health." *American Journal of Community Psychology* 8: 557–569.

Salgado de Snyder, V. 1987a. Mexican immigrant women: The relationship of ethnic loyalty and social support to acculturative stress and depressive symptomatology. Spanish Speaking Mental Health Research Center, Occasional Paper no. 22: 1–46.

Salgado de Snyder, V. 1987b. "Factors Associated with Acculturative Stress and Depressive Symptomatology among Married Mexican Immigrant Women." *Psychology of Women Quarterly* 11: 475–488.

Salgado de Snyder, V., and A. Padilla. 1987. Social support networks: Their availability and effectiveness. In *Health and Behavior: Research Agenda for Hispanics*, ed. M. Gaviria and J. Arana, 93–107. Chicago: University of Illinois, Simon Bolivar Hispanic-American Psychiatric Research and Training Program.

Vega, W., G. Warheit, J. Auth, and K. Meindhart. 1984. "The Prevalence of Depressive Symptoms among Mexicans and Anglos." *American Journal of Epidemiology* 120: 592–607.

Volkan, V. D. 1979. *Cyprus—War and Adaptation: A Psychoanalytic History of Two Ethnic Groups in Conflict*. Charlottesville, Va.: University Press of Virginia.

Volkan, V. D. 1981. *Linking Objects and Linking Phenomena: A Study of the Forms, Symptoms, Metapsychology, and Therapy of Complicated Mourning*. New York: International Universities Press.

Volkan, V. D. 1993. "Immigrants and Refugees: A Psychodynamic Perspective." *Mind and Human Interaction* 4(2): 63–69.

Volkan, V. D., and E. Zintl. 1993. *Life After Loss: The Lessons of Grief.* New York: Charles Scribner's Sons.

Waldinger, R. 1997. Social capital or social closure? Immigrant networks in the labor market. Paper presented at the Conference on Immigration and the Socio-Cultural Remaking of the North American Space, 11–12 April, at Harvard University, David Rockefeller Center for Latin American Studies, Cambridge, Massachusetts.

Warheit, G. J., W. A. Vega, J. B. Auth, and K. Meinhardt. 1985. "Psychiatric Symptoms and Dysfunctions among Anglos and Mexican Americans: An Epidemiological Study." *Research in Community Mental Health* 5: 3–32.

Winnicott, D. W. 1971. Transitional objects and transitional phenomena. In *Playing and Reality*, 1–25. New York: Basic Books.

Winnicott, D. W. 1971. The location of cultural experience. In *Playing and Reality*, 95–103. New York: Basic Books.

Winnicott, D. W. 1971. Dreaming, fantasying, and living. In *Playing and Reality*, 26–37. New York: Basic Books.

Commentary

Peggy Levitt, Harvard University

In his chapter "Cultural Mourning, Immigration, and Engagement: Vignettes from the Mexican Experience," Ainslie argues that the immigrant experience constitutes a particular type of mourning caused by the loss of people and places brought about by geographic dislocation. Migrants leave behind cultural forms, such as food, music, and art, as well as their families and friends. Just as individuals use linking objects and linking phenomena to manage their grief, so migrants use linking objects and linking processes to "absorb the consequences of their dislocation" and to be able to negotiate the new world to which they have come. And just as children use potential space to manage separation and dislocation, migrants also construct "arenas of experiencing in which we creatively dissolve those tensions, finding within them solutions that bridge the emotional gaps and spaces secondary to separation." For Ainslie, the Little Italys' and Chinatowns throughout the United States are places where migrants seek to create their lost worlds. Within these enclaves, "individual and cultural mourning can be managed and absorbed through the illusion of blurred distances—intrapsychic, territorial and cultural."

Ainslie's concept seems to make good intuitive sense. Most migrants probably experience some feeling of loss and coping. An understanding of the psychological aspects of readjustment and the collective coping strategies that are mounted in response to this process is critical for planners and practitioners working in both sending and receiving communities. To strengthen his notion, I would ask Professor Ainslie to address more directly how varieties of migration experiences alter the process of cultural mourning. I want to make three points.

First, Ainslie acknowledges that the extent to which migrants' ties to their native countries are maintained and reinforced eases mourning. In communities with strong migrant and nonmigrant connections, like Tehuixtla, mourning may be incomplete or temporary. But I do not think Ainslie takes this important point far enough. Increasing numbers of migrants maintain strong, long-term connections to their homelands that alter the cultural mourning process. We would benefit from some exploration of these differences.

In many cases, once migration begins, a dense web of social ties develops, characterized by mutual obligations for assistance, declining risks and costs, and facilitating institutions, which link migrants and nonmigrants and stimulate a self-perpetuating process with an internal momentum of its own (Massey, Goldring, and Durand 1994; Massey et al. 1993). The sustained movement back and forth between the communities of origin and destination, coupled with a recognition of the patterned way in which migration unfolds, prompted some scholars to speak of what are alternatively termed transnational migration circuits (Rouse 1989, 1992), transnational social fields (Basch, Glick-Schiller, and Blanc 1994; Mahler 1996), transnational communities (Levitt 1996; Smith 1995; Goldring 1992; Kearney and Nagengast 1989; Portes 1996; Grasmuck and Pessar 1991) or binational societies (Guarnizo 1994). These ties, both concrete and symbolic, make unique economic activities possible, including long-distance labor markets, collective savings strategies, informal credit associations, and transnational enterprises (Portes and Guarnizo 1990; Sassen 1991; Appadurai 1990). The economic eventually bleeds into the political, cultural, and social realms. As ties strengthen and thicken, a transnational social space or public sphere is created.

What happens within this space is by no means a foregone conclusion. It represents potential that may remain untapped or assume a variety of social forms. It could disintegrate quickly if migrants are incorporated into their host societies and sever their homeland ties. It could be a space where nonmigrants and migrants periodically come together to articulate collective claims (see Gutiérrez, this volume). Or it could develop into a full-fledged transnational community, where both migrants and nonmigrants enact some aspects of their lives simultaneously, though not equally, in multiple settings.

In at least two of these scenarios, cultural mourning would be "incomplete" as Ainslie suggests. This merits further attention because these kinds of sustained transnational ties appear to be increasingly common. Though migrants in the past also sustained contact with their homelands, these ties differ in intensity and duration for contemporary migrants due to (1) ease of travel, communication, and social remittance transmission; (2) the increasingly important role immigrants play in sending-country economies; (3) sending states' attempts to legitimize themselves by providing services to emigrants and their children and to actively create a diasporic nation; (4) the increased importance of the United States in the economic and political futures of sending societies; and (5) constraints to assimilation in the United States, such as diminishing economic opportunities and increased geographic concentration. All of these factors allow migrants to remain connected to their home communities. The idea of cultural mourning would be more useful if Ainslie specified who undergoes it, with respect to what aspects of their lives, and with what consequences. If migrants and nonmigrants stay interlinked, not everyone mourns all aspects of their lives and the place they mourn is also continuously changing.

My second point focuses on Ainslie's notion of identity. Most social scientists have moved away from a notion of identity as fixed and primordial to one in which ethnicity and other ascriptive characteristics can be socially constructed, manipulated, and deployed (Gold 1996). There is still an underlying assumption in much of this work that individuals have one "master" identity, albeit one that can be constructed, manipulated, or strategically deployed. There is also an assumption that identities are fundamentally localized, or that they develop and gain meaning in relation to a single, bounded territory or place. We expect, then, that a migrant feels either Mexican, Mexican American, or Chicano at any particular moment, though we accept that these self-descriptions may change.

In cases where individuals enact their lives transnationally and, I suspect, in other cases as well, the understanding of identity that emerges is a much less cohesive one. In my own work on Dominican migration to Boston, I found that both migrants and nonmigrants managed multiple identities shaped by their particular experience of migration and the organizational opportunities that allowed them to act upon them. The same individual could be island oriented with respect to politics and both Dominican Republic and Boston oriented with respect to the church. These fluid, sometimes conflicting self-perceptions coexisted within the same individual. A further distinction in identity formulation and maintenance must be made by class and gender and between the experiences of those individuals who circulate regularly, those who occasionally visit, and those who remain behind in an increasingly transnationalized environment (Mahler 1996). Though I have a sense that psychologists understand identity differently, a more fluid, less cohesive view would also challenge the notion of cultural mourning. Those who identify with multiple sites or multiple attributes may experience less mourning, or even liberation, when they move.

Finally, my last point concerns what Roger Rouse (1995) calls the logic of identity. He is troubled by our tendency to assume that identity and identity formation are universal aspects of human experience. He argues that we are projecting "key ideas onto the lives of people who think and act quite differently," and that these terms do not unproblematically capture peoples' understandings of "personhood, collectivity, and struggle" (Rouse 1995, 352, 359). I am sure that my own recent experience interviewing Chinese migrants in Boston, who became impatient with and confused by questions of identity but were better able to understand questions about "home," is not unique. This is not to say that some migrants do not mourn the places, people, and self-conceptions they leave behind, but that we need to be aware of the power and politics behind these concepts and the alternative conceptual frameworks that may be at work.

REFERENCES

Appadurai, A. 1990. "Disjuncture and Difference in the Global Cultural Economy." *Theory, Culture, and Society* 7:2–3.

Basch, Linda, Nina Glick-Schiller, and Cristina Szanton Blanc. 1994. *Nations Unbound: Transnational Projects, Postcolonial Predicaments, and Deterritorialized Nation-States.* Switzerland: Gordon and Breach.

Gold, Steven. 1996. *Transnationalism and Vocabularies of Motivation in International Migration: The Case of Israelis in the United States.* Research Paper 96–05. Ann Arbor: Michigan State University, Population Research Group.

Goldring, Luin. 1992. Diversity and community in transnational migration: A comparative study of two Mexico U.S. migrant communities. Ph.D. dissertation, Cornell University.

Goldring, Luin. 1996. "Blurring Borders: Constructing Transnational Community in the Process of U.S.-Mexico Migration." *Research in Community Sociology* 6: 69–104.

Grasmuck, Sherri, and Patricia Pessar. 1991. *Between Two Islands: Dominican International Migration.* Berkeley: University of California Press.

Guarnizo, Luis. 1994. "Los Dominicanyork: The Making of a Binational Society." *Annals of the American Academy of Political and Social Science* 533: 70–86.

Kearney, M., and C. Nagengast. 1989. *Anthropological Perspectives on Transnational Communities in Rural California.* Davis, Calif.: California Institute for Rural Studies, Working Group on Farm Labor and Rural Poverty.

Levitt, P. 1996. Transnationalizing civil and political change: The case of transnational organizational ties between Boston and the Dominican Republic. Ph.D. dissertation, Massachusetts Institute of Technology.

Mahler, S. Forthcoming. "Theoretical and Empirical Contributions Toward a Research Agenda for Transnationalism." *Comparative Urban and Community Research.*

Massey, Douglas, Joaquin Arango, Graeme Hugo, Ali Kouaouci, Adela Pellegrino, and J. Edward Taylor. 1993. "Theories of International Migration: A Review and Appraisal." *Population and Development Review* 19: 431–465.

Massey, Douglas, Luin Goldring, and Jorge Durand. 1994. "Continuities in Transnational Migration: An Analysis of 19 Mexican Communities." *American Journal of Sociology* 99: 1492–1534.

Portes, A. 1996. Transnational communities: Their emergence and significance in the contemporary world-system. In *Latin America and the World Economy*, ed. R. P. Korzeniewicz and W. C. Smith. Westport, Conn.: Greenwood Press.

Portes, A., and Guarnizo, L. 1990. *Tropical Capitalists: U.S. Bound Immigration and Small Enterprise Development in the Dominican Republic*. Working Paper 57. Commission for the Study of International Migration and Cooperative Economic Development.

Rouse, Roger. 1989. Mexican migration to the United States: Family relations in the development of transnational circuits. Ph.D. dissertation, Department of Anthropology, Stanford University.

Rouse, Roger. 1992. Making sense of settlement: Class transformation, cultural struggle, and transnationalism among Mexican migrants in the United States. In *Towards a Transnational Perspective on Migration: Race, Class, Ethnicity, and Nationalism Reconsidered*, ed. N. Glick Schiller, L. Basch, and C. Blanc-Szanton, New York: New York Academy of Sciences.

Rouse, Roger. 1995. "Questions of Identity: Personhood and Collectivity in Transnational Migration to the United States." *Critique of Anthropology* 351–380.

Sassen, S. 1991. *The Global City: New York, London, and Tokyo*. Princeton, N.J.: Princeton University Press.

Smith, R. C. 1995. Los ausentes siempre presentes: The imagining, making and politics of a transnational community between Ticuani, Puebla, Mexico and New York City. Ph.D. dissertation, Columbia University.

CHAPTER TEN

Photo by Anna LeVine

David Gutiérrez   David G. Gutiérrez was born and raised in the Evergreen Heights barrio of East Los Angeles in the home his great-grandmother built there in 1927. Growing up in a neighborhood surrounded by immediate and extended family members, Gutiérrez (who is a fifth-generation Californian on his father's side) attended the same schools that his grandparents and parents had attended in their youth. In many ways, Gutiérrez's interest in immigration is a direct outgrowth of his early life in East Los Angeles, where Mexican Americans, Mexican immigrants, and immigrants and migrants from many other places have lived side by side for generations.

When his family moved to Oceanside, in northern San Diego County, in 1968, Gutiérrez had an opportunity to experience interethnic relations from a very different vantage point. Situated in what was then still a semirural agricultural region, Oceanside was (and remains) an important regional destination for Mexican migrants drawn to employment opportunities in the area's vast truck-crop, citrus, cut-flower, and nursery industries. After finishing high school in Oceanside, Gutiérrez did volunteer work with a local Catholic organization that gathered crop gleanings and other donations for distribution to seasonally unemployed migrants living in the many hidden farm labor camps in the county.

When he began college at the University of California, Santa Barbara, in 1975, Gutiérrez maintained a strong interest in gaining a better understanding of the intersection of regional history, Chicano politics, and the intensifying debate over Mexican immigration. UCSB afforded him the opportunity to combine these interests through formal study and through a series of internships, including a stint with the newly established Congressional Hispanic Caucus in Washington, D.C. After graduating with a degree in U.S. history (with an emphasis in Chicano Studies and immigration history) in 1979, Gutiérrez moved to Washington to accept a position on the legislative staff of Congressman Edward R. Roybal, the veteran Democratic legislator from East Los Angeles.

After a year of working on the Hill (and after seriously considering a career in law), Gutiérrez decided instead to pursue a graduate degree in history. Accepted to the graduate program in history at Stanford University in 1980, he began a course of study that allowed him to combine his lifelong interests in the historical dimensions of Mexican immigration, ethnic-group formation in the United States, and the relationship between Mexican American and Mexican immigrants in American life.

Since leaving Stanford in 1986, Gutiérrez has followed these interests by combining a scholarly career with political activism in immigration and civil rights politics. He has lectured and consulted in both of these broad areas, and has published or edited a number of books and articles, including *Walls and Mirrors: Mexican Americans, Mexican Immigrants, and the Politics of Ethnicity* (1995), and *Between Two Worlds: Mexican Immigrants in the United States* (1996). He is currently working on a book-length study exploring the historical debate over the nature of national citizenship in the United States since World War II. Gutiérrez is Associate Professor in the Department of History and Co-Director of the Southwest History Project at the University of California, San Diego.

10

Ethnic Mexicans and the Transformation of "American" Social Space: Reflections on Recent History

David G. Gutiérrez
University of California, San Diego

Over a recent holiday season, I had a chance to spend a few days in my family's home in the Evergreen Heights neighborhood of East Los Angeles. Built in 1924, my grandmother's home had replaced an even older structure that my great-grandmother, who had emigrated to the United States from Chihuahua at the turn of the century, had built a few years earlier. Between the two buildings, the site had at one time or another been home to four generations of my immediate family and to many more distant friends and relatives who spent various periods of time there over the years. Situated in the heart of what is now one of East L.A.'s largest Mexican barrios, my family's home had stood through the transition of the neighborhood from a semirural suburb to a mixed-race enclave during the thirties, forties, and fifties, and finally to a locale with one of the highest concentrations of Mexican Americans and Mexican immigrants of any place in the United States.

Sitting on a slight rise, the house is usually insulated from noise on the street, but in the late afternoon of the first day of my visit, I was drawn to an unusual sound coming from the street below. Curious, I stepped out to the front porch and saw people on both sides of the street and I could now make out the sounds of them singing, laughing, and just conversing among themselves. Seeing a neighbor whom I knew, I walked over to the fence and asked what was happening. She reminded me that the date was December 12—the feast day of the Virgin of Guadalupe, Mexico's patroness saint—and that the people were celebrating the occasion after having just returned from services at the local Catholic church.

I decided to see some of the celebration for myself, and so I grabbed a jacket and walked down the street toward the church. As I rounded the corner from Folsom Street down the hill onto Fresno Street, I saw that the crowd was much thicker there in front of the old Assumption Church. The scene was also much more festive. The church itself was festooned with wreaths and lights, and the people of the neighborhood had also strung colored lights, streamers, and religious banners from the streetlamps and trees that lined both sides of the crowded street. As was the case up the block, men, women, and children stood around the church or leaned up against walls and fences; some sang, some chatted quietly among themselves, and some sipped *atole* from paper cups.

Although a great many other Mexican Catholics undoubtedly were observing the Virgin's feast day in other parts of Los Angeles that evening, as I strolled back up the hill I was struck by how much the scope of the celebration I observed had changed since my boyhood. As Ricardo Romo (1983), George Sanchez (1993), and other historians have noted (see, for example, Rios-Bustamente and Castillo 1986), the neighborhood has been predominantly Mexican since the 1930s, but I couldn't recall a time in my youth when a religious observance had attracted so many people out onto the streets. To be sure, Mexican Americans and Mexican immigrants in my grandparents' and parents' era and in my own time in the neighborhood had also commemorated important dates on the Catholic religious calendar, but with the exception of weddings and funerals, it was rare to see such celebrations spill out from within the walls of the church itself. But on that cool December evening it seemed that most of the people in a four-block area were participating in the event.

One must take care not to make too much of such impressions, but I would like to suggest here that although the scene I witnessed that evening in the Assumption Church parish in East Los Angeles took place in only one tiny corner of a sprawling metropolitan area of nearly 9 million people, the celebration was symbolic of the many profound—although often unseen—ways in which mass migration from Mexico and other Latin American nations has helped to transform the cultural landscape, social life and practices, and use of public space in southern California and, to a lesser though significant degree, in other areas of the United States. Using this vignette as a point of departure, this chapter is an attempt to place recent migration trends into a broader historical context, to explore some of the social and cultural contradictions these trends expose, and to suggest ways in which the most recent phase of the

Mexican diaspora may well mark a significant departure from previous eras of mass migration from Mexico.

MEXICAN MIGRATION AND THE CLAIMING OF PUBLIC SPACE

Born of the combination of massive economic restructuring, a virtually unbroken three decades of unprecedented northward migration from Mexico, and the demographic revolution that has subsequently resulted, the scene I witnessed that December evening could have taken place in any of literally hundreds of towns and cities in the U.S.-Mexico transborder region. On another level, however, there is nothing particularly novel about ethnic Mexicans appropriating social space in the United States. After all, dating from the first large influx of Mexicans into the United States after 1900, one of the central animating themes of the Mexican diaspora has been the constant augmentation and cultural reinvigoration of existing Mexican American communities in the border states by Mexican immigrants, or the creation of new ethnic enclaves in far-flung pockets of settlement such as Washington's Yakima Valley in the Northwest or the *colonias* established in midwestern industrial cities such as Chicago, Gary, and Detroit.

Poverty and deeply rooted patterns of discrimination against Mexicans in the United States at first compelled Mexican immigrants to occupy marginal spaces of the communities into which they settled, but, like their more recent counterparts, they nevertheless gradually established social networks, economic niches, and an overarching ethnic infrastructure that helped them to adapt to life in the north. The kinds of social networks, businesses, and institutions Mexicans established in the United States were necessarily modest and tenuous, but over time, their investment in homes and various mom-and-pop ventures such as grocery, hardware, and second-hand stores, cafes, barber shops, bars, butcher shops, and bakeries in places like Los Angeles, Tucson, El Paso, and San Antonio helped to transform local social spaces by creating something of a parallel "Mexican" sociocultural world within the political boundaries of the United States. Operating largely within the confines of what the historian Albert Camarillo (1979) described as the relatively "closed social universe" of the barrios and colonias, ethnic Mexicans adapted by creating alternative social spaces within the larger communities in which they lived (see, for example, García 1981; Romo 1983; Gutiérrez 1995a).

Outside the barrios and colonias, Mexicans who had entered the country in the first decades of the century faced very harsh conditions. Barred from many public facilities and forced to work for substandard wages under extreme conditions, ethnic Mexicans occupied a depressed stratum of society that was comparable in socioeconomic terms to that occupied by African Americans and Native Americans. However, while there is no question that Mexican immigrants in the past faced some of the harshest conditions confronted by any group of immigrants coming to the United States, it is also true that after the United States' entry into the Second World War, many immigrants and their second- and third-generation children began to experience significant gains in educational attainment, wages, occupational status, and political rights—and thus gradually began to become acculturated as American citizens. Obviously, even as they progressed as a group, ethnic Mexicans (that is, both citizens and denizens of Mexican descent) continued to lag behind non-Hispanic whites in these areas of social status and welfare, but overall, the clear trend between the 1940s and the late 1960s was for ethnic Mexicans to narrow the gap separating them from the white majority, especially in the areas of wages and occupational status.[1] Similarly, although ethnic Mexicans throughout this period continued to suffer systematic discrimination in education, in employment, in the armed forces, in access to public education and public facilities like movie theaters, swimming pools, and restaurants, and in other social arenas, they also just as clearly made dramatic strides toward empowerment and equal rights by organizing and exerting increasing pressure for reform within the extant American political system (see Gutiérrez 1995a; Gómez-Quiñones 1990; San Miguel 1987; García 1989).

However, in recent years, several trends have helped to disrupt established historical socioeconomic and political patterns and have raised serious questions about the current direction of change. One of the most obvious differences in the current period is the tremendous difference in the scale and scope of transnational migration flows. Whereas the first periods of Mexican migration to the United States were characterized by relatively modest flows stretched out over several decades, the most recent period of migration has brought many more people over a short period of time into a more concentrated area than ever before.

Population growth figures over the past 30 years or so amply demonstrate the point. Spurred by a combination of high birth rates and high levels of legal and unauthorized immigration, the combined citizen and denizen ethnic Mexican population of the United States grew from well less than 5 million in 1970 to more than 8.7 million in 1980, and to more than 14 million by 1990. By early 1997, the combined population of Mexican descent was estimated to be more than 17 million, of whom some 6 to 7 million were born in Mexico.[2] Although ethnic Mexicans are more dispersed than ever before, the major effects of these demographic trends have remained concentrated in just six states. For example, California alone accounts for more than 45 percent of the total ethnic Mexican population of the United States. And along with California, the combined ethnic Mexican population of Texas (29 percent of the total), Arizona (4.6 percent), Illinois (4.6 percent), New Mexico (2.5 percent), and Colorado (2.1 percent) accounts for more than 88 percent of all ethnic Mexicans in the United States (Chávez and Martínez 1996, 26–27; *Hispanic Databook* 1994).

But another crucial characteristic of the recent growth of the ethnic Mexican population is that a great proportion of it has occurred in just a handful of metropolitan areas, with Los Angeles leading the way. As Waldinger, Bozorgmehr, and their colleagues have recently shown in their timely study *Ethnic Los Angeles*, the combined ethnic Mexican population of the Los Angeles region more than doubled from about 1.1 million in 1970 to 2.3 million in 1980, and then grew another 60 percent to more than 3.7 million people in 1990 (Sabagh and Bozorgmehr 1996). The case of Los Angeles may well represent an extreme example of the localized effects of these changes, but shifts in the sociocultural matrix there help illustrate how sustained migration has helped to transform many other American metropolitan areas. Whereas the foreign-born Mexican population of Los Angeles in 1960 was less than 2 percent of the city's total, by 1990 the city's Mexican-origin population had grown to nearly 4 million, of whom 46 percent had been born in Mexico. Another sizable percentage of residents are Spanish-speaking immigrants from Central America (Waldinger and Bozorgmehr 1996). Since Mexican and Latino immigrants tend to be significantly younger and have much higher fertility rates than is true of other Los Angeles residents (and Americans generally), the major impact of recent demographic growth is yet to be seen. Indeed, the demographic structure of the local pan-Latino population (that is, the combined resident population of Latin American descent) is now seen most dramatically in the school-age population. According to a recent analysis published in the *Los Angeles Times*, the population of the huge Los Angeles Unified School District is now nearly 68 percent Latino (of whom 47 percent are of limited English proficiency). In the blue-collar "Hub Cities" directly south of East Los Angeles (Maywood, Bell, Cudahy, Huntington Park, and South Gate) the demographic revolution is even more dramatic. There, the Latino school-age population approaches an astounding 98 percent, of whom 58 percent are of limited English proficiency (Smith 1997).

Although perhaps not as dramatic as the case of Los Angeles, other American cities in the border region have experienced similar demographic shifts. As of 1990, a string of major metropolitan areas in the border region ranging from Yuma, Arizona, in the west to the Brownsville-Harlingen-San Benito metropolitan area in southeast Texas reported Latino population concentrations (which were, of course, overwhelmingly ethnic Mexican) ranging from a low of 38.5 percent (in Yuma) to a high of 93.9 percent (in Laredo, Texas). Within the next 10 to 20 years, it is estimated that ten metropolitan areas in the border states (including Laredo, McAllen-Edinburg-Mission, Brownsville-Harlingen-Benito, Corpus Christi, and San Antonio in Texas; Las Cruces and Santa Fe in New Mexico; and Yuma in Arizona) will have large Latino majorities ranging from a *low* of 66 percent (in San Antonio) to more than 95 percent (in Laredo) ("Top Ten" 1994).

Such trends have been reinforced by similar developments in those cities in northern Mexico that have traditionally served as staging grounds for Mexican migrants and immigrants heading for the United States. Drawn to the prospects of employment in the United States and to burgeoning employment opportunities in maquiladoras in northern Mexico, Mexicans have flocked to these areas by the thousands (see South 1990; Sheridan 1997). As a consequence, since 1940 Mexican cities on or near the international border have been among the fastest-growing places in Mexico. Thus, in Baja California Norte, the cities of Tijuana and Mexicali grew from populations of 16,486 and 18,775 in 1940 to 742,686 and 602,390, respectively, in 1990. In Sonora, the city of Nogales grew from 13,866 in 1940 to more than 107,000 in 1990. In Chihuahua, Ciudad Juárez grew from 48,881 to 797,679; and in Tamaulipas, the border metropolitan areas of Nuevo Laredo, Reynosa, and Matamoros grew from populations of 28,872, 9,412, and 15,699 in 1940 to 217,912, 281,618, and 303,392, respectively, in 1990 (see Arreola and Curtis 1993; Ham-Chande and Weeks 1992).

Demographic shifts of this magnitude have contributed to an expansion of an ethnic Mexican and Latino regional economic, social, and cultural infrastructure that dwarfs that which evolved earlier in the century. For example, in the economic realm, the steady influx of Mexican and Latino immigrants and transmigrants since the early 1970s has contributed to a growth in informal sectors of the regional economy that is perhaps unprecedented in American history. The growth has occurred simultaneously in two directions: the expansion of ethnic entrepreneurship and the growth of the secondary labor market. Although migrants and immigrants have always provided the backbone of the labor force in business enterprises that by their very nature lie largely outside effective government monitoring and regulation (such as the agribusiness, domestic service, and maintenance industries, as well as small, family-run enterprises), in recent years, noncitizen labor drives a huge informal economy that is estimated to represent anywhere from 6 to 12 percent of the United States' annual gross national product (Castells, Portes, and Benton 1989; Simcox 1997).

The impact of this trend has been felt in many different levels of regional society. On a level not easily seen, but crucial nonetheless, Mexican and Latino immigrants have not only continued to supply the low-cost labor that has driven the region's secondary labor market (in occupations in the service, light manufacturing, electronic assembly, construction, furniture, leatherwear, and garment industries) but have also contributed to an unprecedented expansion of the very small firms (defined by the Census Bureau as those employing ten or fewer employees) that often operate beyond the regulation and control of government agencies. In both cases, work in the informal sector is characterized by lax (or nonexistent) enforcement of wage, hour, and safety regulations; extensive home work usually performed for piece rates and no benefits; and a disturbing increase in the use of underage child workers.

On the other hand, however, it is important to note that at least some of these negative trends have been partially offset by a corresponding increase in ethnic entrepreneurship. Although many of the new job opportunities created for immigrants in the region remain in the secondary labor market in entry-level, low-skilled, and semiskilled occupations, the growth of the informal sector has also provided ethnic entrepreneurs with a number of new opportunities. As Mexican and Latino population growth has stimulated growing consumer demand in the ethnic market, native, immigrant, and transmigrant small entrepreneurs have stepped in to provide jobs, goods, and services to this flourishing segment of the regional economy (see, for example, Alvarez 1990; Light and Roach 1996; Portes and Rumbaut 1996).

These ongoing demographic and economic shifts have in turn laid the groundwork for a remarkable cultural transformation of large parts of the United States. Wherever one turns in the region, it is clear that the accelerated process of cultural Latinization that began in the 1970s is gathering steam. Although Latino cultural influences are just beginning to trickle into mainstream American popular cultural forms and practices (in areas such as film, music, literature, and cuisine), much more dramatic changes have already occurred and can be seen in a wide range of Latino cultural production and consumption patterns in the United States.

One of the most compelling examples of such change is the recent proliferation of Spanish-language print and broadcast media networks.[3] Although it is well known that the English-language press has struggled in recent years to maintain readership and advertising revenue, the explosive growth of the pan-Latino population in the United States has allowed the Spanish-language press to move in the opposite direction over the past two decades (see Mott 1991; Chepesiuk 1993; Liebman 1993; Garza 1994). In Los Angeles, for example, circulation of *La Opinión,* the city's major Spanish-language daily, grew 155 percent between 1981 and 1991. Increases in the paper's advertising revenue were even more impressive, growing a full 600 percent in the same period. Other areas in the Southwest have experienced similar rates of growth in Spanish-language print media. The recent growth of Spanish-language broadcast media has been even more spectacular. Aware that the United States now has the fifth-largest concentration of Spanish-speaking people in the world (and that the Latino consumer market itself has grown to more than $280 billion per year), both Latino media entrepreneurs and American advertisers have pumped billions of dollars into radio and television outlets serving this dynamic and volatile market. As a result, radio, television, and cable programming in Spanish-language or bilingual formats has grown steadily since the early 1980s.

Once again, Los Angeles has been in the vanguard of these developments. As recently as 1986, the Los Angeles area had only six Spanish-language radio stations. But by early 1997, 17 of the 82 stations in the huge Los Angeles County/Orange County radio markets were broadcasting exclusively in Spanish. The success of Los Angeles' Spanish-language radio station KLAX-FM provides an even more dramatic example of the breadth and depth of the sociocultural changes that have transformed southern California's radio audience since 1970. KLAX, which specializes in regional Mexican music, shocked the broadcast industry when it became Los Angeles' most popular FM radio station in 1992. The station has ranked either first or second in Los Angeles' market-share ratings ever since. More recently, Los Angeles radio listeners experienced yet another shock when it was announced that the popular alternative rock station KCSA in Glendale (part of the vast media holdings of former cowboy singing star Gene Autrey) had been sold and would immediately switch to a Spanish-language format. Although many English-speaking radio listeners have found these trends mystifying, for a growing number of radio programmers and market researchers, these startling shifts in popular tastes are not at all surprising: Programmers are simply following market growth. As one media executive noted recently, "People ask me what my biggest selling tool is to the Spanish [language] market, and it's the census. Every time fresh demographic information comes in, it recalibrates everything" (Michaelson 1997; see also Baxter 1997).

The rapid expansion of the Spanish-language television networks *Univisión* and *Telemundo* offers further graphic evidence of a growing awareness of the market potential of the Spanish-speaking population of the United States. Although advertising expenditures targeted toward Latinos still remain but a fraction of total television advertising budgets, expenditures by U.S. companies advertising on Spanish-language television alone have shown a steady and significant upward trend, growing at the rate of between 16 and 22 percent each year since 1990. Overall, in 1995 American advertisers spent more than $1.2 billion in Spanish-language television, radio, and print media outlets and expect this trend to continue to accelerate in the near future.[4]

At a more submerged, but no less important level, the growth and development of alternative popular cultural pastimes among Mexican and Latino immigrants—such as listening to the sounds of *banda, conjunto, salsa,* or *rock en español,* or dancing the *merengue* or the *quebradita*—provide another important barometer of the ways immigrants and transmigrants have changed the cultural landscape by transplanting their popular cultural forms and practices across the southwestern United States. Once relegated to the down-in-the-heel beer joints and dance halls of segregated barrios, these musical styles can now be heard on the air 24 hours a day and danced to in hundreds of upscale clubs on both sides of the border (Martínez 1994; González and Rodríguez 1994; Holston 1997).

POLITICS AND SOCIAL SPACE:
THE PARADOX OF ETHNIC MEXICAN POPULATION GROWTH

Given the magnitude of the social, cultural, and economic shifts that have so dramatically changed the social landscape of the southwestern United States, it is truly remarkable how little public discourse has changed to reflect these almost tectonic transformations. Although there is no question that immigration (particularly that which occurs outside of officially sanctioned channels) has recently reemerged as one of the most volatile hot-button issues in the American political arena, it is also clear that much of the rhetoric and analysis utilized in current public debate in the area is virtually identical to the rhetoric and analytical framework used 30, 40, or even 50 years ago.

At the level of official discourse, such thinking has been encouraged and reinforced by American politicians' chronic manipulation of the immigration issue. Numerous examples of this tendency could be cited, but one need only think of the recent presidential campaigns of California Governor Pete Wilson and television commentator and journalist Pat Buchanan to get a sense of the ways politicians have drawn on conventional and increasingly outmoded notions of citizenship, community, and national identity to frame the immigration issue to their best advantage. For example, in his highly publicized presidential campaign, Wilson repeatedly used phrases and images in his speeches and television ads designed to draw stark lines between citizens and "legal" immigrants by emphasizing how "illegal immigrants" were both "breaking the rules" and undercutting the economic position of American citizens "who work hard, pay taxes, and obey the laws" (see, for example, Stall and McDonnell 1993; Weintraub 1994; Wilson 1994; Smith and Tarallo 1995; Shapiro 1997). (Of course, all this occurred while Wilson was busily trying to explain how and why he and his wife had habitually employed undocumented housekeepers earlier in his political career). Buchanan offered a similar gloss on the sanctity of American citizenship and national sovereignty in both op-ed pieces and in his stump speeches during his run for the presidency. For example, in a nationally syndicated op-ed piece that ran in the fall of 1994, Buchanan called for an immediate moratorium on all forms of immigration to the United States to allow the country, as he put it, "to assimilate the tens of millions who have lately arrived." Expressing concern that "the old institutions of assimilation are not doing their work as they once did," Buchanan warned his readers that if they "lack the courage to decide what our country will look like in 2050, others will decide for us, not all of whom share our love of America that seems to be fading away" (Buchanan 1994; see also *Los Angeles Times* 1993; Braun and Fullwood 1996). Another even more caustic example of such thinking was recently sent to the editor of the *San Diego Union-Tribune* (1997) by a disgruntled citizen who asserted:

> Many [people], like me, fail to see how we can have anything in common with a group whose agenda seems to be to create a Spanish-speaking Quebec in much of the United States by demanding totally open borders, unrestricted immigration from Latin America, equality for Spanish, and refusing to learn English or assimilate into the American mainstream. I say this to Hispanics: Until you assimilate and Americanize like the rest of us have, you will never be totally accepted as fellow Americans by the rest of us.

Historically, whether it comes from political leaders or from the citizenry, such rhetoric has proved extremely effective in serving U.S. political and economic interests. As I have argued elsewhere, this kind of discourse has long helped to perform the double task of maintaining an ample and docile "foreign" labor supply while sustaining the illusion that the United States has retained control of its international frontiers. Similarly, by portraying unnaturalized residents as deeply troubling anomalies who are fundamentally out of synch and outside the American political community, individuals employing this kind of analysis have long been able to use the increasingly arbitrary designation of citizenship as a mechanism to obscure the central role both transmigrants and permanent immigrants have played in American economic development (Gutiérrez 1995a, 1995b). Obviously, such rhetoric has also been extremely effective in eliding the extent to which nearly a century of U.S. immigration and labor policies themselves stimulated the kinds of migration flows that are now almost universally derided (Heisler and Heisler 1986; Sassen 1990; Basch, Schiller, and Blanc 1994).

In the contemporary period, such rhetoric continues its disciplinary function by feeding the myth of national unity (or the potential for regained national unity) even when rapid ethnic diversification has deeply undermined that project. As Wilson's and Buchanan's campaigns clearly demonstrate, current appeals to this kind of vision also imply that by adopting an immigration policy designed to reestablish "sovereign control of the nation's borders" and redraw clear distinctions between citizens and aliens, the United States will somehow be returned to a past golden age when societal unity and the political integrity of the American nation-state were unquestioned. And it is important to note that although Wilson, Buchanan, and other politicians who have recently weighed in on the immigration debate differ significantly on specific points of their proposals, virtually all mainstream politicians (including self-described "liberals") continue to draw on the familiar tropes of "assimilation" and the "melting pot" to frame their analysis and appeal to voters.

In the context of an extended period of corporate downsizing and class polarization, increasing racial strife, and the erosion of tax-supported services and institutions, the political appeal of such straightforward, unambiguous notions of citizenship, community, culture, and national identity comes as no surprise. In a period in which so much of the Third World seems to have come to America, and particularly to the Southwest, the comforting idea of the nation as a coherent and unified community spatially located within a clearly demarcated and bounded territory has obvious appeal. But again, one must question the extent to which the political calculus has changed as a result of mass migration and the attendant demographic transformation of the region over the past 30 years. Indeed, a growing number of scholars and social critics have begun to ask whether the ongoing economic, demographic, and cultural shifts that are transforming the region are not signs of a fundamental—and permanent—shift in the meanings of citizenship, national affiliation, and individual and collective identity in the transborder region. The jury may still be out on these questions, but several recent developments are worth considering in this context.

On one fundamental level, it is important to consider how much the scope and scale of international economic activity has changed in the past half-century. There is of course nothing new about the global reach of capitalism, but as the twentieth century comes to a close, dramatic technological advances in communications, transportation, and electronics have allowed multinational firms to utilize resources and mobilize finances more efficiently, expand their markets, and streamline their manufacturing and production processes by outsourcing to regions of the world with the lowest labor costs. These massive shifts, in turn, have helped both to restructure virtually all the national economies in the world and to integrate far-flung regions into the web of economic expansion directed from postindustrial core regions such as the United States, Western Europe, and Japan. As a consequence of this global economic restructuring, millions of people have been set in motion either searching for work in reorganized sectors of their home nation's domestic economy or joining the multiplying millions of those forced to seek work in the international job market (Sassen 1991, 1996a; Kothari 1997).

Over the past three decades, such changes have been felt with particular force in Mexico. Faced with a seemingly endless series of economic and political crises, followed by steep devaluations of the national currency and draconian restructuring of the national debt, Mexico has seen millions of its workers forced first into domestic, and then into transnational, migratory labor streams (see Dussel, this volume). Combined with a virtually insatiable demand for low-wage labor to fuel the secondary labor market in the United States, recent changes in the Mexican economy have sent unprecedented numbers of migrants north seeking work.

In the United States itself, it is also crucial to consider how much the economic "contexts of reception" (to borrow Portes and Rumbaut's apt phrasing) for immigrants and transmigrants have changed since the first influxes of Mexican immigrants entered the United States earlier in the twentieth century (Portes and Rumbaut 1996). As mentioned above, however much previous generations of ethnic Mexicans lagged behind non-Hispanic whites in educational attainment, income levels, occupational mobility, levels of political efficacy, and other socioeconomic indicators, as a group this population did achieve significant measurable progress for several decades following the Second World War. And, although it is true that many ethnic Mexicans (particularly the very poor) did not reap the benefits of the postwar economic boom, it is equally apparent that a great many Mexican Americans did, in fact, benefit and thus were able to achieve a semblance of what might be called the classic trajectory of social and cultural "assimilation" (García 1989; San Miguel 1987).

In recent years, however, there are disturbing signs that the material conditions that in the past acted as necessary precursors to accelerated political, social, and cultural integration have changed for the worse. For example, whereas ethnic Mexicans and their children in most areas in the postwar years had a reasonable chance of moving from entry-level, low-status, unskilled and semiskilled occupations into higher-paying, higher-status, skilled blue-collar occupations, in recent years Mexican immigrants have tended to enter the secondary labor market by taking jobs at the bottom of the economy—and to stay there.[5] More ominously, recent data indicate that native-born American citizens of Mexican descent also appear to be losing ground relative to other Americans. Studies examining income trends in the period between 1959 and 1989 reinforce these findings, indicating that working-class Mexican American citizens in southern California not only had not closed the earnings gap separating them from white workers, but that they appear to have experienced significant economic slippage relative to whites.[6] If one accepts the premise that the "assimilation" of immigrants depends primarily on the existence of a meaningful opportunity for socioeconomic mobility for themselves and their children, recent downward trends in these areas raise serious questions about the continued viability of models of immigrant incorporation that casually predict the inevitable political and cultural integration of many permanent immigrants.

Another critical factor that must be considered when assessing the implications of recent immigration history is the question of how transnational migration circuits linking the United States to Mexico and other Latin American nations have contributed to the gradual erosion of the clear distinctions between "citizens" and "aliens" invoked by politicians like Wilson and Buchanan. Although immigration scholars disagree about how much of the current migratory flow between the United States and Latin America is truly circular, most agree that the migratory circuits first established and elaborated under the auspices of the Bracero program (1942–1964) have helped to create a growing number of "twin" cities or villages that intimately link populations originally from Mexico on both sides of the international frontier (see, for example, Alvarez 1987; Conover 1987; Massey et al. 1987; Massey and Liang 1989; Lidstrom 1996; Cleland 1997a, 1997b). These transnational linkages and communication networks, which continue to shape current migration patterns by deepening historical ties that bind communities in Mexico with those in the United States, have been greatly reinforced during Mexico's current economic crisis by the intensification of remittance flows from ethnic Mexicans in the United States to family, friends, and business associates in Mexico. Estimated to represent anywhere from 4 to 6 billion dollars annually, remittances account for a huge percentage of Mexico's foreign capital inflows, and represent yet another way in which the economy of Mexico is enmeshed with that of the United States (Case 1996). As de la Garza, Orozco, and Baraona (1997) note in a recent study on the phenomenon of remittances in the 1980s and 1990s, "even in major countries like Mexico, with a strong export-oriented market, remittances equal 10% of the total value of its exports and almost as much as the income from tourism."

Considering these trends together, some scholars have gone as far as to argue that the existence of transnational circuits over several generations over the past half-century and more has inevitably transformed the character of international migration by "deterritorializing" communities in sending regions and creating new social spaces in "reterritorialized" locales in the United States for migrants who habitually flow between two or more nation-states.[7] As anthropologist Roger Rouse, one of the leading proponents of this view, has argued, "[transmigrants] are often able to maintain . . . spatially extended relationships [between the United States and Mexico] as actively and effectively as the ties that bind them to their [immediate] neighbors" (Rouse 1996, 254).

It is not neccessary to accept such assertions at face value to recognize that such circular flows have had obvious and lasting effects on ethnic Mexican enclaves north of the international frontier. Of course, the most obvious effect has been to infuse such communities with a more or less constant floating population of migrants and immigrants bringing with them their language, religious practices, customs, and so forth. As so poignantly demonstrated by neighborhood churchgoers in the old Assumption Church parish in East Los Angeles, the influx of immigrants in recent years has expanded the ethnic infrastructure of jobs, communication, entertainment, and local cultural practices in the United States to the extent that, in many ways, Mexicans can now live in the United States as if it were simply a more prosperous extension of Mexico (for a discussion of similar trends in Texas, see Ricardo Ainslie's provocative chapter in this volume).

At a less obvious, but no less important level, the presence in the same neighborhoods (and indeed, often in the same households) of virtually any combination of U.S.-born Mexican Americans, permanent immigrants (both officially sanctioned and undocumented), long-term and short-term sojourners, and the U.S.-born and Mexican-born children of all these groups has greatly complicated the sociocultural matrices in the United States in which individual and collective identities are evolving among ethnic Mexicans in the border region. As sociologist Néstor Rodríguez (1996) notes in a particularly perceptive recent article, habituated over two, three, or more generations to think of themselves as members of transnational communities, individuals engaged in this increasingly common way of life are actively engaged in reconfiguring the social spaces they inhabit in a manner that is largely autonomous and "independent of state authorization and regulation" (see also Hagan 1994). Moreover, as Rodríguez and others have argued, even if legal and unsanctioned migration from Mexico were to slow substantially in the near future (an unlikely event in any case), the demographic momentum established over the past 30 years ensures that the current jumble of cultural, class, and political identities in the border region will continue to splinter and multiply.

I do not mean to suggest here that the entire universe of people's assumptions and expectations about the processes involved in the incorporation of immigrants into American society will suddenly crumble. On the contrary, given the ideological constraints that continue to exert a stranglehold on the immigration issue in American politics, it is likely that discourse will continue to spin around traditional, unilaterally focused modes of thought. Similarly, the current anti-immigrant (and anti-Latino) political climate in the western United States will almost certainly encourage permanent residents to continue to apply for naturalization, to register to vote, and to exercise the franchise, and thus undoubtedly will reinforce the sense among many Americans that the process of immigrant "assimilation" is still working. Clearly, if the regional polity and national political leadership continue to propose punitive measures such as California's Propositions 187 and 209, state- and federally sponsored "English Only" legislation, federal welfare "reform," and other measures perceived to be harmful to the Latino immigrant population, the recent steep increases in rates of naturalization, voter registration, and other forms of formal political mobilization and participation will almost certainly continue to rise.[8]

But at the same time, great care should be taken not to interpret current political events without also taking into account the long-term effects of the structural changes that have already permanently transformed the region. Although it is apparent that the highly charged political climate has played a key role in stimulating an unprecedented surge in applications for U.S. citizenship, more detailed, longitudinal research will need to be conducted to determine the extent to which this trend reflects a new-found sense of (American) patriotism among Mexican and other Latino nationals, or, in a more likely scenario, represents something much more pragmatic, defensive, and instrumental. From my point of view, it makes very little sense to assume that people who heretofore had seen little or no reason to renounce their former national affiliation and/or primary, cultural orientation would now suddenly experience a wholesale change of heart. Along a similar vein, as polit-ical scientists Rodolfo de la Garza (1996), Louis DeSipio (1996a, 1996b), Harry Pachón (Pachón and DeSipio 1994; Pachón 1996), and others have cautioned in research on the political orientation of ethnic Mexicans and Latinos, rising rates of naturalization do not necessarily mean that Latino citizens will auto-matically be able to increase political participation or power—either at the formal or informal levels. Since voting in the United States is strongly corre-lated with age, income, education, and language facility, it is reasonable to expect that ethnic Mexicans and other Latinos will be excluded or will exclude themselves from participation in formal, electoral American politics.[9] Perhaps more important, formal participation in the traditional American politics of citizenship remains an impossibility for the millions of Latino migrants and immigrants who are as yet too young to vote, or who have chosen for a variety of reasons not to become naturalized citizens. It is also important to note that while the recent move in Mexico to explore the possibility of granting dual cit-izenship to the vast expatriate community may eventually encourage more Mexicans to apply for U.S. citizenship, for many the ease of movement between the two countries, strong family and community ties, and a fierce sense of nationalistic pride in Mexico may lead them to continue to live in the uneasy political spaces between the formal national systems of the United States and Mexico.

This does not mean, however, that Mexican and Latino immigrants and transmigrants choosing to opt out of formal electoral politics (in either the United States or Mexico) are apolitical. Indeed, in what is perhaps the supreme irony of the most recent era of migration between the United States and Mexico, the very measures that are now being implemented both to stem the flow of migrants and to cow those already in the country into compliance with increasingly stringent welfare, public health, and public education statutes may well prove the spawning grounds for the emergence of serious dissent in the ethnic Mexican and pan-Latino populations. The framing of the immigra-tion debate within traditional discourses of assimilation and the refusal to impose and seriously enforce legal sanctions against the employers of migrant workers continue to help discipline and control both Mexican migrants and working-class Latino residents by simultaneously demonizing (and criminal-izing) Latinos as foreign, nonintegrated "Others" while continuing to ensure that their labor can be exploited at maximum efficiency. After years of con-doning immigration, and of regulatory practices that ensure open migrant labor flows, American policymakers and employers have also unwittingly helped to create a vast new subnational social space that has virtually guaranteed the emergence of alternative—and potentially deeply subversive—diasporic social identities, cultural frames of reference, and modes of political discourse.

The mainstream media and most political figures have been largely oblivious to this dimension of demographic change, but there are clear signs that ethnic Mexicans and other Latinos are mobilizing and making claims against society in ways that deviate significantly from the historical civil rights trajectory of "minority" populations in the United States, and thus are issuing a serious challenge to what Holston and Appadurai (1996) have termed the "homogenizing" and exclusionary tendencies of traditional national citizenship. These provocative signs have emerged in a number of different contexts. One of the most visible changes has been seen in the recent increase in labor organizing and collective protest activity among both legal and undocumented Latino workers. After years in which American labor organizations shunned their undocumented coworkers, in recent years organizers have made impressive first strides toward organizing both legal and undocumented workers in the janitorial, garment, hotel, restaurant, and construction industries. For example, in California, the recent Justice for Janitors campaign coordinated by the Service Employees International Union (SEIU) and the ongoing efforts of UNITE—the United Needletrades, Industrial and Textile Employees (a union merger of the former Amalgamated Clothing and Textile Workers Union with the International Ladies Garment Workers Union)—are but two of a growing number of examples of the ways in which U.S.-based labor unions are now attempting to organize undocumented workers as well as American citizens. Focusing on bread-and-butter issues of wages, hours, and working conditions and on nontraditional labor issues such as equal access to public education, sexual harassment, child care, and immigration law counseling, these unions have begun to reorient their policy priorities after recognizing that a growing percentage of the American workforce is no longer technically "American." This same recognition has also spurred small unions, union locals, and even American labor giants such as the AFL-CIO and the Teamsters Union to recruit and train Latino organizers and executives to leadership positions. Thus, Latino organizers and executives such as the SEIU's Eliseo Medina, Teamster national vice president John Riojas, and AFL-CIO executive vice president Linda Chavez-Thompson have assumed highly visible—and unprecedentedly influential—leadership positions.[10]

Similarly, the ongoing resurgence of the United Farm Workers Union represents another example of the ways in which U.S.-born Latinos are exploring the possibility of finding common ground with undocumented workers.

Although the UFW historically has fiercely objected to the presence of undocumented workers in the United States, in recent years the union has shown clear signs that it has softened its position. In some areas, union leaders have urged the active recruitment of undocumented workers, arguing that the ties of class and culture that bind workers from both sides of the border are far more important than the divisions created by their different nationalities.[11] In the current climate of intense economic displacement, class polarization, and the transnationalization of labor both in the United States and Latin America, such efforts provide intriguing examples of new experiments in coalition-building outside of the formal structures of regional politics and demonstrate some of the ways in which traditional American civil rights discourses are in some cases being augmented, if not supplanted, by claims for jobs and economic security.

Even more intriguing developments have occurred at the grassroots and transnational levels. For example, one of the most interesting ancillary developments of the recent renaissance of the labor movement has been the grassroots community-organizing efforts of immigrants themselves. Although forced to tread very softly because of their tenuous legal position, immigrants have recently worked outside of existing labor unions and formal political structures to establish worker centers in the United States in an effort, as one observer has put it, to "develop . . . new organizational forms that link economic demands with social justice and political empowerment" (Figueroa 1996b, 24; see also Kidder and McGinn 1995). At an even more provocative level, rank-and-file Latino unionists (and a small but growing number of American union leaders) have begun to forge ties with workers in Mexico and other Latin American nations. For example, one of the most striking offshoots of the recent exposés about the serflike working conditions endured by Central American clothing workers employed by multinational firms such as Nike, the Gap, Guess, Levi-Strauss, and other sportswear and apparel giants has been the growing communication and coordination between American and Latin American labor organizers. Other notable experiments in cooperation and exchange have recently been conducted between the Communication Workers of America (CWA) and STRM, the Mexican telephone workers union, between labor activists associated with the San Diego Labor Council and maquiladora workers in Baja California, and between the Teamsters and independent truckers in Mexico who have had their jobs challenged by some of the provisions of the North American Free Trade Agreement. Again, these efforts have been tentative and sporadic, but are a clear sign that unionists are beginning to take innovative action in response to perceived threats to their livelihoods associated with the globalization of the world economy (see, for example, Figueroa 1996a, 1996b; Haus 1995; Nagengast and Kearney 1990; Smith 1994).

Despite these trends, however, it is also important to keep in mind that this kind of overt organizing and political and quasi-political action remains the exception, rather than the rule, in the everyday lives of most ethnic Mexican immigrants and migrants. Even though the growth of Latino communities has in many ways made it easier for Latino immigrants and migrants to live and move comfortably in a transterritorial "third space" carved out between the political and social worlds of the United States and Latin America, the threat of legal repression from outside the community and conflicts stemming from class and national-origin or cultural differences inside the Mexican and pan-Latino populations will likely contribute to the ongoing fragmentation of these groups into many different shards—and into social behaviors that may strongly militate against their eventual political "assimilation."[12] Indeed, under the circumstances that have evolved over the past 30 or 40 years, it may make more sense to ask why ethnic Mexican and Latino migrants and immigrants would choose to become "assimilated Americans" rather than continuing (as many have for years) to operate in the social and cultural interstices of the nation-states through which they travel, live, and work. As the contradictory forces unleashed by economic globalization continue to tug and pull against the traditional structures that have in the past given citizenship and national affiliation meaning, it may well be that the most logical decision for transmigrants and even permanent immigrants is one that actively (or more probably in most cases, passively) disavows allegiance to a single national entity.

The prognosis, therefore, for ethnic Mexicans and Latinos who have put down permanent roots in or continue to traverse the national territory of the United States is decidedly unsettled. Although the ongoing transformation of cultural geography offers glimpses both of grassroots democratic experimentation and of political repression and violence in the new social spaces of the North American continent, as the state struggles to assert control over its increasingly unruly borders and over the eroding institution of formal citizenship, Latinos will undoubtedly again suffer the brunt of attempts to mediate the growing crisis of the nation in a transnational age.

NOTES

1. For example, median education levels for ethnic Mexicans increased from 5.4 years in 1950 to 7.1 years in 1960, and to 9.2 years in 1970. Income rates showed similar positive incremental changes. Whereas ethnic Mexicans earned only a fraction of what non-Hispanic whites earned during the 1920s and 1930s, after World War II they steadily closed the gap: By 1949, ethnic Mexicans earned about 57 percent of what non-Hispanic whites earned. The percentage inched up to almost 62 percent in 1959 and to 66 percent by 1969. For discussions of the educational attainment of ethnic Mexicans over time, see Grebler, Guzmán, and Moore (1970); Jaffe, Cullen, and Boswell (1980); Bean and Tienda (1987); and Chapa (1990). For income levels and the changing occupational status of ethnic Mexicans over time, see Barrera (1979); Briggs, Fogel, and Schmidt (1977); and Cortes (1980).

2. Recent demographic trends in the Mexican-origin population are explored in Boswell (1979), U.S. Bureau of the Census (1993), and Chávez and Martínez (1996).

3. For an excellent synthetic historical discussion of the expansion of Spanish-language communications media in the United States, see Subervi-Vélez (1994).

4. The recent expansion of Spanish-language broadcast media in the United States is examined in Subervi-Vélez (1994), Zate (1994), Tara (1994), Petrozello (1995, 1996), and Avila (1997).

5. Regional variants exist, but most recent major studies on the economic incorporation of Mexican immigrants have indicated that over the past 30 years Mexican immigrants not only have not closed the gap in earnings relative to non-Hispanic whites but also that this ratio is moving very quickly in the opposite direction. Thus, whereas Mexican immigrant workers in 1970 earned approximately 66 percent of what non-Hispanic white workers earned, by 1989 the average earnings of a Mexican immigrant worker had dropped to 39 percent of that earned by native whites (Chapa 1990; Levin 1996).

6. Whereas Mexican American citizens earned about 81 percent of the median income of non-Hispanic white men in 1959, the figure had dropped to 74 percent in 1982 and to 61 percent by 1989 (Chapa 1990; Levin 1996). Vilma Ortiz's recent work on the Los Angeles metropolitan area, where nearly 4 million people of Mexican descent now live, lends more weight to these findings. In the study, she notes that "[native-born Mexican Americans] and blacks remain substantially behind whites in earnings, and more so . . . than in previous years. The recent changes in the region's labor market appear to have increased the racial bonus enjoyed by whites, reinforcing the preexisting barriers to [Mexican American] progress" (Ortiz 1996).

7. Indeed, some scholars have gone as far as to argue that the process of transnationalization in its various forms has become so pervasive in the late twentieth century that to speak of "immigration" is to employ an outdated and fundamentally flawed framework of analysis. For versions of this position, see Kearney (1991), Sassen (1996b), and Rose (1997).

8. For discussion of these trends in the post–Proposition 187 era, see Gregory Rodríguez (1996), McDonnell and Ramos (1996), Radelat (1997), and Camarillo (1997).

9. These issues are discussed in Brackman and Erie (1993), de la Garza (1996), and DeSipio (1996a, 1996b). For a slightly different line of analysis, see Smith and Tarallo (1995).

10. For the resurgence of ethnic Mexican and Latino labor union activity since the late 1980s, see Haus (1995), Kidder and McGinn (1995), Figueroa (1996b), Aragón (1996), Medina (1996), and Javier Rodríguez (1996).

11. For a brief discussion of the historical evolution of the union's views on undocumented workers, see Gutiérrez (1995a). For the current situation in the UFW, see Haus (1995), Figueroa (1996b), Arax (1996), Silverstein (1996), and Rodríguez and González (1997).

12. For discussion of the contradictory nature of these interstitial social spaces, see, for example, Holston and Appadurai (1996), Appadurai (1996), and Bhabha (1994).

REFERENCES

Alvarez, Robert M., Jr. 1987. *Familia: Migration and Adaptation in Baja and Alta California, 1800–1975*. Berkeley: University of California Press.

Alvarez, Robert M., Jr. 1990. "Mexican Entrepreneurs and Markets in the City of Los Angeles: A Case of an Immigrant Enclave." *Urban Anthropology* 19(1–2): 99–124.

Appadurai, Arjun. 1996. Sovereignty without territoriality: Notes for a postnational geography. In *The Geography of Identity*, ed. P. Yeager, 420–458. Ann Arbor: University of Michigan Press.

Aragón, Raymond G. 1996. It's time to contain the intolerance. *San Diego Union-Tribune*, 12 April.

Arax, Mark. 1996. The UFW gets back its roots. *Los Angeles Times*, 17 February.

Arreola, Daniel D., and James R. Curtis. 1993. *The Mexican Border Cities: Landscape Autonomy and Place Personality*. Tucson: University of Arizona Press.

Avila, Alex. 1997. "Trading Punches: Spanish-Language Television Pounds the Competition in the Fight for Hispanic Advertising Dollars." *Hispanic* (Jan./Feb.): 39–40, 42, 44.

Barrera, Mario. 1979. *Race and Class in the Southwest: A Theory of Racial Inequality.* South Bend, Ind.: University of Notre Dame Press.

Basch, Linda, Nina Glick Schiller, and Christine Szanton Blanc. 1994. *Nations Unbound: Transnational Projects, Postcolonial Predicaments, and Deterritorialized Nation-States.* Basel: Gordon and Breach.

Baxter, Kevin. 1997. L.A.'s Spanish media face new Latino reality. *Los Angeles Times,* 21 August.

Bean, Frank D., and Marta Tienda. 1987. *The Hispanic Population of the United States.* New York: Russell Sage Foundation.

Bhabha, Homi. 1994. *The Location of Culture.* London: Routledge.

Boswell, Thomas D. 1979. "The Growth and Proportional Distribution of the Mexican Stock Population of the United States: 1910–1970." *Mississippi Geographer* 7 (Spring): 57–76.

Brackman, Harold, and Steven P. Erie. 1993. The once and future majority: Latino politics in Los Angeles. In *The California-Mexico Connection,* ed. A. F. Lowenthal and K. Burgess, 196–220. Stanford: Stanford University Press.

Braun, Stephen, and Sam Fullwood, III. 1996. Buchanan gets into shouting match over immigration as Arizona race tightens. *Los Angeles Times,* 24 February.

Briggs, Vernon, Walter Fogel, and Fred H. Schmidt. 1977. *The Chicano Worker.* Austin: University of Texas Press.

Buchanan, Patrick J. 1994. Losing control of America. *San Jose Mercury-News,* 30 October, 7C.

Camarillo, Albert M. 1979. *Chicanos in a Changing Society: From Mexican Pueblos to American Barrios in Santa Barbara and Southern California, 1848–1930.* Cambridge, Mass.: Harvard University Press.

Camarillo, Linda. 1997. "Counting Our Election Returns." *Hispanic* (Jan./Feb.): 108.

Case, Brendan M. 1996. Sending dollars to Mexico is a big, lucrative business. *New York Times,* 14 September.

Castells, Manuel C., Alejandro Portes, and Laura C. Benton, eds. 1989. *The Informal Economy: Studies in Advanced and Less Developed Countries.* Baltimore: Johns Hopkins University Press.

Chapa, Jorge. 1990. "Trends in Educational and Economic Attainment of Mexican-Americans." *Journal of Hispanic Policy* 4: 3–18.

Chávez, Leo R., and Rebecca G. Martínez. 1996. Mexican immigration in the 1980s and beyond: Implications for Chicanas/os. In *Chicanas/Chicanos at the Crossroads: Social, Economic, and Political Change,* ed. D. R. Maciel and I. D. Ortiz, 25–51. Tucson: University of Arizona Press.

Chepesiuk, Ron. 1993. "Hitting Home, Cashing In." *Quill* 81 (Jan./Feb.): 48–49.

Cleland, Nancy. 1997a. Granjenal's life ebbs with exodus. *Los Angeles Times,* 3 August.

Cleland, Nancy. 1997b. In Santa Ana, Mexican villagers re-created community. *Los Angeles Times*, 4 August.

Conover, Ted. 1987. *Coyotes*. New York: Vintage.

Cortes, Carlos E. 1980. Mexicans. In *Harvard Encylopedia of American Ethnic Groups*, ed. Stephan Thernstrom, 697–719. Cambridge: Harvard University Press.

DeSipio, Louis. 1996a. "Making Citizens or Good Citizens? Naturalization as a Predictor of Organizational and Electoral Behavior Among Latino Immigrants." *Hispanic Journal of Behavioral Sciences* 18(2): 194–213.

DeSipio, Louis. 1996b. *Counting on the Latino Vote: Latinos as a New Electorate*. Charlottesville, Va.: University of Virginia Press.

Figueroa, Hector. 1996a. "In the Name of Fashion: Exploitation in the Garment Industry." *NACLA Report on the Americas* 29(4): 24–41.

Figueroa, Hector. 1996b. "The Growing Force of Latino Labor." *NACLA Report on the Americas* 30(3): 19–24.

García, Mario T. 1981. *Desert Immigrants: The Mexicans of El Paso, 1880–1920*. New Haven: Yale University Press.

García, Mario T. 1989. *Mexican Americans: Leadership, Ideology, and Identity, 1930–1960*. New Haven: Yale University Press.

Garza, Melita Marie. 1994. "Growth Market: Mainstream Media Vie for Latino Readers." *Quill* 82 (April): 18–21.

de la Garza, Rodolfo O. 1996. El cuento de los numeros and other Latino political myths. In *Latino Politics in California*, ed. A. Yañez-Chávez, 121–139. La Jolla, Calif.: University of California, San Diego, Center for U.S.-Mexican Studies.

de la Garza, Rodolfo, Manuel Orozco, and Miguel Baraona. 1997. Binational impact of Latino remittances. Unpublished paper, Tomas Rivera Policy Institute.

Gómez-Quiñones, Juan. 1990. *Chicano Politics: Reality and Promise, 1940–1990*. Albuquerque: University of New Mexico Press.

González, Patricia, and Roberto Rodríguez. 1994. "The Tex-Mex Mix." *American Demographics* 16 (June): 40–41.

Grebler, Leo, Ralph C. Guzmán, and Joan W. Moore. 1970. *The Mexican American People: The Nation's Second Largest Majority*. New York: Free Press.

Gutiérrez, David G. 1995a. *Walls and Mirrors: Mexican Americans, Mexican Immigrants and the Politics of Ethnicity*. Berkeley: University of California Press.

Gutiérrez, David G. 1995b. Migration and ethnic politics in a transnational age: Reflections on the California-Mexico border. In *Latino Politics in California*, ed. A. Yañez-Chávez, 121–139. La Jolla, Calif.: University of California, San Diego, Center for U.S.-Mexican Studies.

Hagan, Jacquelin Maria. 1994. *Deciding to Be Legal: A Maya Community in Houston*. Philadelphia: Temple University Press.

Ham-Chande, Roberto, and John R. Weeks. 1992. A demographic perspective on the U.S.-Mexican border. In *Demographic Dynamics of the U.S.-Mexico Border*, ed. J. R. Weeks and R. Ham-Chande, 1–27. El Paso: Texas Western Press.

Haus, Leah. 1995. "Openings in the Wall: Transnational Migrants, Labor Unions, and U.S. Immigration Policy." *International Organization* 49(2): 285–313.

Heisler, Martin O., and Barbara Schmitter Heisler, eds. 1986. *From Foreign Workers to Settlers? Transnational Migration and the Emergence of New Minorities* [Special issue]. *Annals of the American Academy of Political and Social Sciences* (May).

Hispanic Databook of U.S. Cities and Counties. 1994. Milpitas, Calif.: Toucan Valley Publications.

Holston, James, and Arjun Appadurai. 1996. "Cities and Citizenship." *Public Culture* 8(2): 187–204.

Holston, Mark. 1997. "Rock en Español." *Hispanic* (Jan./Feb.): 46, 48, 50, 52.

Jaffe, A. J., Ruth M. Cullen, and Thomas D. Boswell. 1980. *The Changing Demography of Spanish Americans.* New York: Academic Press.

Kearney, Michael. 1991. "Borders and Boundaries of State and Self at the End of Empire." *Journal of Historical Sociology* 4(1): 52–74.

Kidder, Thalia, and Mary McGinn. 1995. "In the Wake of NAFTA: Transnational Workers Networks." *Social Policy* (Summer): 14–21.

Kothari, Rajni. 1997. "Globalization: A World Adrift." *Alternatives* 22(2): 227–267.

Levin, Myron. 1996. A longer journey to the middle class. *Los Angeles Times*, 10 June.

Lidstrom, David P. 1996. "Economic Opportunity in Mexico and Return Migration from the United States." *Demography* 33(3): 357–374.

Liebman, Hanna. 1993. "Newspapers Hablan Español: Major Companies Are Attempting to Reach the Growing Number of Hispanic Readers with Spanish-Language Publications." *Mediaweek*, 16 August, 10.

Light, Ivan, and Elizabeth Roach. 1996. Self-employment: Mobility ladder or economic lifeboat? In *Ethnic Los Angeles*, ed. R. Waldinger and M. Bozorgmehr, 193–214. New York: Russell Sage Foundation.

Los Angeles Times. 1993. GOP is caught napping on immigration. 11 July, M45.

Martínez, Rubén. 1994. "The Shock of the New." *Los Angeles Times Magazine*, 30 January, 10–14, 16, 39.

Massey, Douglas S., Rafael Alarcón, Jorge Durand, and Humberto González. 1987. *Return to Aztlán: The Social Process of International Migration from Western Mexico.* Berkeley: University of California Press.

Massey, Douglas S., and Zai Liang. 1989. "The Long-Term Consequences of a Temporary Worker Program: The U.S. Bracero Experience." *Population Research and Policy Review* 8: 199–226.

McDonnell, Patrick J., and George Ramos. 1996. Latinos make strong showing at polls. *Los Angeles Times*, 8 November, A1, A18.

Medina, Eliseo. 1996. If we don't go back to grassroots politics, we're in trouble. *Los Angeles Times*, 4 May.

Michaelson, Judith. 1997. More radio stations say adios to English. *Los Angeles Times*, 17 March, F1, F7.

Mott, Patrick. 1991. "Finding Gold in the Ethnic Media." *Quill* 79 (May): 34–35.

Nagengast, Carole, and Michael Kearney. 1990. "Mixtec Ethnicity: Social Identity, Political Consciousness, and Political Activism." *Latin American Research Review* 25(2): 61–91.

Ortiz, Vilma. 1996. The Mexican-origin population: Permanent working class or emerging middle class? In *Ethnic Los Angeles*, ed. R. Waldinger and M. Bozorgmehr, 247–278. New York: Russell Sage Foundation.

Pachón, Harry C., and Louis DeSipio. 1994. *New Americans by Choice: Political Perspectives of Latino Immigrants*. Boulder: Westview Press.

Pachón, Harry C. 1996. New citizens are the new target. *Los Angeles Times*, 23 July, B7.

Petrozello, Dona. 1995. "Radio Targets Hispanic Niches." *Broadcasting and Cable*, 13 November, 76.

Petrozello, Dona. 1996. "Audience Shares Swell for Spanish Formats." *Broadcasting and Cable*, 22 January, 122.

Portes, Alejandro, and Ruben Rumbaut. 1996. *Immigrant America: A Portrait*. Berkeley: University of California Press.

Radelat, Ana. 1997. "The Sleeping Giant Wakes." *Hispanic* (Jan./Feb.): 18, 20, 22, 24.

Rios-Bustamente, Antonio, and Pedro Castillo. 1986. *An Illustrated History of Mexican Los Angeles, 1769–1985*. Los Angeles: University of California, Chicano Research Center.

Rodríguez, Gregory. 1996. "The Browning of California." *New Republic*, September 2, 18–19.

Rodríguez, Javier. 1996. A challenge to Latinos. *Los Angeles Times*, 4 April.

Rodríguez, Néstor. 1996. "The Battle of the Border: Notes on Autonomous Migration, Transnational Communities, and the State." *Social Justice* 25(3): 21–39.

Rodríguez, Roberto, and Patrisia González. 1997. César Chávez lives in more than spirit. *Los Angeles Times*, 4 April.

Romo, Ricardo. 1983. *East Los Angeles: History of a Barrio*. Austin: University of Texas Press.

Rose, Frederick. 1997. Mexican immigrants don't stay long in U.S. *Wall Street Journal*, 29 January.

Rouse, Roger. 1996. Mexican migration and the social space of postmodernism. In *Between Two Worlds: Mexican Immigrants in the United States*, ed. D. G. Gutiérrez. Wilmington, Del.: SR Books.

Sabagh, Georges, and Mehdi Bozorgmehr. 1996. Population change: Immigration and ethnic transformation. In *Ethnic Los Angeles*, ed. R. Waldinger and M. Bozorgmehr, 79–107. New York: Russell Sage Foundation.

San Diego Union-Tribune. 1997. Letter to the Editor. 26 September.

San Miguel, Guadalupe, Jr. 1987. *"Let All of Them Take Heed": Mexican Americans and the Campaign for Educational Equality in Texas, 1910–1981.* Austin: University of Texas Press.

Sanchez, George. 1993. *Becoming Mexican American: Ethnicity, Culture, and Identity in Chicano Los Angeles, 1900–1945.* New York: Oxford University Press.

Sassen, Saskia. 1990. "U.S. Immigration Policy toward Mexico in a Global Economy." *Journal of International Affairs* 43(2): 369–383.

Sassen, Saskia. 1991. *The Global City: New York, London, Tokyo.* Princeton: Princeton University Press.

Sassen, Saskia. 1996a. *Losing Control: Sovereignty in an Age of Globalization.* New York: Columbia University Press.

Sassen, Saskia. 1996b. Identity in the global city: Economic and cultural encasements. In *The Geography of Identity*, ed. P. Yeager, 131–151. Ann Arbor: University of Michigan Press.

Shapiro, Michael J. 1997. "Narrating the Nation, Unwelcoming the Stranger: Anti-Immigration Policy in Contemporary 'America.'" *Alternatives* 22: 1–34.

Sheridan, Mary Beth. 1997. Riding the ripples of a border boom. *Los Angeles Times*, 9 June.

Silverstein, Stuart. 1996. The strawberry jam. *Los Angeles Times*, 12 December.

Simcox, David. 1997. "Immigration and Informalization of the Economy: Enrichment or Atomization of Community." *Population and Environment* 18(3): 255–281.

Smith, Doug. 1997. School breakup would tip scales. *Los Angeles Times*, 23 March, A1, A12–A13.

Smith, Michael Peter. 1994. "Can You Imagine? Transnational Migration and the Globalization of Grassroots Politics." *Social Text* 39 (Summer): 15–33.

Smith, Michael Peter, and Bernadette Tarallo. 1995. "Proposition 187: Global Trend or Local Narrative? Explaining Anti-Immigrant Politics in California, Arizona, and Texas." *International Journal of Urban and Regional Research* 19(4): 664–679.

South, Robert B. 1990. "Transnational 'Maquiladora' Location." *Annals of the Association of American Geographers* 80(4): 549–570.

Stall, Bill, and Patrick J. McDonnell. 1993. Wilson urges stiff penalties to deter illegal immigrants. *Los Angeles Times*, 8 August, B1.

Subervi-Vélez, Federico A. 1994. Mass communication and Hispanics. In *Handbook of Hispanic Cultures in the United States: Sociology*, ed. F. Padilla, 304–358. Houston: Arte Publico Press.

Tara, Susen. 1994. "Hispanic Radio Heats Up the Airwaves." *Advertising Age*, 24 January, S8.

"Top Ten Metropolitan Areas in Terms of Percentage Hispanic by 2015." 1994. *American Demographics* 16 (August): 16.

U.S. Bureau of the Census. 1993. *Hispanic Americans Today*. Current Population Reports no. P23-183. Washington, D.C.: Government Printing Office.

Waldinger, Roger, and Mehdi Bozorgmehr. 1996. The making of a multicultural metropolis. In *Ethnic Los Angeles*, ed. R. Waldinger and M. Bozorgmehr. New York: Russell Sage Foundation.

Weintraub, Daniel M. 1994. Wilson ad sparks charge of immigrant bashing. *Los Angeles Times*, 14 May.

Wilson, Pete. 1994. "Securing Our Nation's Borders." *Vital Speeches of the Day*, 15 June, 534–536.

Zate, Mari. 1994. "Radio Reaches New Heights." *Hispanic Business* 16(12): 54.

Commentary

George J. Sanchez, University of Southern California

Reading David Gutiérrez's provocative chapter, I was reminded of the writings of the two Latino public intellectuals who have best captured the ambivalence of the Mexican presence in the American public sphere over the past 50 years: Octavio Paz and Richard Rodriguez. Almost 50 years ago, noted Mexican cultural critic Octavio Paz began his classic on Mexican identity, *The Labyrinth of Solitude*, by writing with scorn about the hyphenated sons of Mexican immigrants—the *pachucos*—that dared to display their emerging culture on the public streets of the city of Angels. He described their immigrant parents living in Los Angeles as acting "like persons who are wearing disguises, who are afraid of a stranger's look because it could strip them and leave them stark naked" (Paz 1961, 13).

While Paz used metaphors of masks and disguises to distinguish Mexican private life from its public appearance, Richard Rodriguez would separate the private from the public by focusing on language 30 years later. In *Hunger of Memory*, published in 1982, Rodriguez wrote approvingly of his moving into the American public sphere by speaking English and abandoning his private family language of Spanish. This book was celebrated by American conservatives for describing the inevitability of cultural loss, a theme connecting it to previous immigrant tales and making the book probably the most assigned book on Mexican Americans in American classrooms for the past 15 years. As George Will explains, Rodriguez "praises what he has lost, but insists that the gain—Americanization: a place in our public—has been worth the pain" (Will 1983).

David Gutiérrez argues in his chapter that Mexican immigrants have arrived in such volume, concentration, and rapidity in the last 20 years that they have thrown off the masks and transformed the public sphere, at least in such cities as Los Angeles. Spanish-speaking neighborhoods, though long segregated, are no longer culturally marginalized, since they dominate the rest of the city. Indeed, reading Gutiérrez, it is the increasingly walled and policed white suburban communities that seem culturally at the margin in Los Angeles, even while they retain economic and political power. For those looking to answer the question of why anti-immigrant feelings have emerged *now*, one should begin by juxtaposing culture and politics in urban areas throughout the Southwest, but particularly in California.

One critical point about this new cultural presence in American public space that Gutiérrez emphasizes is the transformation of the public areas of private industry and voluntary organizations. Commentators like Richard Rodriguez, along with many social scientists, have often concentrated their observations on the impact of government policy and programs in changing the public sphere, from presence in schools and public universities through bilingual education and affirmative action to the opening up of political space for new Hispanic politicians and elected officials. Gutiérrez, while not ignoring these developments, rightly insists on turning our attention toward institutions like the Catholic Church and the media, which have changed the cultural landscape by responding and promoting the presence of the Spanish language in the public sphere in the United States.

I am reminded by Gutiérrez's opening story that one of the largest marches in the history of Los Angeles was held on the *Dia de la Virgen* in December 1934 after the election of Lazaro Cárdenas as President of Mexico (see Sanchez 1993, 167–170). Los Angeles Mexicans, utilizing newfound American political possibilities, mobilized to protest Cárdenas' supposed anti-Catholic attitudes, but were joined by U.S. Catholics from throughout the city—something unlikely in today's ethnically separate politics.

Wayne Cornelius (this volume) and Roger Waldinger (1997) argue that the small business worksite is another area in which the Mexican presence and the public power of Spanish have changed things in a city like Los Angeles, although we know that Spanish never fully abandoned its role in being the language of commerce along the border. Gutiérrez's observations should point social scientists in the direction that Waldinger has already moved: questioning how Mexican immigration has transformed the public space in business, commerce, media, and voluntary organizations like churches and unions. What impact does this transformation have on other Americans? How deep would the anti-immigrant backlash have to go before government and the American public would try to regulate private industry and commerce in cultural interaction? Indeed, I would venture to say that even if our current anti-immigrant backlash rolls back bilingual education and social services, and government efforts at border restriction intensify, we are unlikely to be able to turn back the transformation of the public sphere governed by industry and the media anytime soon.

Despite the moaning and fear-mongering of conservative critics of this trend, like Peter Brimelow in *Alien Nation* (1995), it is important to ask how flexible American public space actually is to these changes. I remember marveling at the ingenuity of the inventor of a simple product being sold at all the car washes on the west side of Los Angeles in the early 1990s that helped the now-handicapped English-only speaker communicate with his or her Spanish-speaking maid or gardener. One would check off a query or comment on a set of fixed English phrases, then peel off the Spanish equivalent on the carbon copy below to hand to the domestic servant. While we might laugh at the extent to which Anglos will go before learning to speak Spanish, it is interesting to look for other signs of accommodation to these changes. Are non-Spanish speakers learning this other public language faster in areas like Los Angeles because of their daily interaction? Have we seen an increase in Spanish language course enrollments in city schools and private industry by non-Spanish speakers?

I am also intrigued, like Gutiérrez, by the development of a "third space" of political and social activity by Mexican immigrants in the United States that goes beyond the disciplinary function of naturalization and citizenship. In my previous work on the cultural world of Mexican immigrants in Los Angeles in the first half of the twentieth century, I noted the "ambivalent Americanism" formed by Mexicans who remained in the United States because of the massive repatriation of the 1930s, which saw one-third of their numbers return to Mexico (Sanchez 1993, 207–226). The response to increasing immigration restriction in this period was to reduce transnational movement by making a choice to either go back or to stay in the United States permanently. Rather than leading toward traditional Americanization, these immigrants turned to the politics of ethnicity and unionization, but not naturalization. More liberalized opportunities for naturalization today, along with co-ethnic agencies designed to help in the process, have helped concretize the citizenship aspects of this ambivalent Americanism. In short, today's pattern of increased permanent settlement, upturn in naturalization, and the potential of growing political mobilization have occurred before in Mexican immigrant communities, but never at the heightened volume we see today.

It is an irony of the political history of Mexicans in the United States that the growth of anti-immigrant sentiment has often led to their political mobilization in America, but with today's numbers and the greater openness to cultural diversity, this mobilization has transformed the public landscape of Los Angeles. The presence of fear and anti-immigrant sentiment *without* widespread deportation—such as occurred in the 1930s—only magnifies the impact of this political mobilization in the United States. In a much-publicized event in the mobilization against Proposition 187, a huge political march just days before the vote was criticized for leading with a Mexican flag on the streets of Los Angeles. Even political commentators opposed to 187 felt that this display of Mexican cultural pride hurt their efforts by demonstrating an anti-American sentiment that offended voters (see McDonnell and Lopez 1994; Berger and Stewart 1994). It will be important for researchers to identify the political symbolism of this third space that can move beyond overtly national symbols, possibly symbols such as the flags of the Virgin of Guadalupe and the black eagle that led most marches of the United Farm Workers. A critical question is whether the ethnic politics of Mexican Americans will provide the mixed symbolism necessary for the immigrant generation to feel empowered in this new public space.

Previous research also indicates that we should not minimize the role of the Mexican national state in changing the public sphere of Mexicans in the United States (see Sanchez 1993, 108–125; Balderrama 1982). While Mexican consular officials in the 1920s and 1930s led efforts at establishing Mexican schools and promoting ethnic celebrations in American barrios, today's Mexican government is considering more fundamental changes in citizenship rights in response to the massive presence of nationals abroad and the threat posed to them by anti-immigrant measures. Whatever finally results from the dual citizenship debate in Mexico, it has already had a tremendous symbolic value to Mexican nationals in the United States by demonstrating to them that they are not considered irreparably lost to the Mexican nation. Possible changes in rules governing the movement of capital and the buying of property by those of Mexican heritage with American nationality are likely to lead to even greater room in which to maneuver in a transnational third space. If discussions continue to move toward increasing the social and economic options in Mexico available to children of Mexican nationals, theoretically possible given the Mexican constitution and an idea already circulating in some circles in Mexico, an even wider set of possibilities lasting over generations will enter this picture.

REFERENCES

Balderrama, Francisco. 1982. *In Defense of La Raza: The Los Angeles Mexican Consulate and the Mexican Community, 1929 to 1936*. Tucson: University of Arizona Press.

Berger, Leslie, and Jocelyn Stewart. 1994. Many angered by Proposition 187 demonstrations. *Los Angeles Times*, 4 November.

Brimelow, Peter. 1995. *Alien Nation: Common Sense about America's Immigration Disaster.* New York: Random House.

McDonnell, Patrick J., and Robert J. Lopez. 1994. L.A. march against Proposition 187 draws 70,000. *Los Angeles Times,* 17 October.

Paz, Octavio. 1961. *The Labyrinth of Solitude.* New York: Grove Press.

Rodriguez, Richard. [1982] 1983. *Hunger of Memory: The Education of Richard Rodriguez.* Reprint. New York: Bantam Books.

Sanchez, George. 1993. *Becoming Mexican American: Ethnicity, Culture, and Identity in Chicano Los Angeles, 1900–1945.* New York: Oxford University Press.

Waldinger, Roger. 1997. Social capital or social closure? Immigrant networks in the labor market. Paper presented at the Conference on Immigration and the Socio-Cultural Remaking of the North American Space, 10–12 April, David Rockefeller Center for Latin American Studies, Harvard University, Cambridge, Massachusetts.

Will, George. 1983. Quoted on inside cover of Richard Rodriguez, *Hunger of Memory: The Education of Richard Rodriguez.* Reprint. New York: Bantam Books.

Photo by Joe Nevins

Peter Andreas's interest in immigration is partly a reflection of his own highly mobile life experience. He spent his childhood years attending 14 schools in three U.S. states and four Latin American countries. His adult life has also been defined by frequent movement rather than the permanence of place. Andreas's research and writing on immigration issues, however, has only developed through a broader interest in the study of policing and the politics of illegal markets. Most of his work to date has focused on U.S. drug control policy, but he has increasingly turned to the study of immigration control due to the striking parallels in the politics and policies that define the two issue-areas. Few other areas of research so fully capture the interaction between politics, economics, and culture, both domestically and internationally. And nowhere is this more transparent than along and across the U.S.-Mexico border, which is the primary focus of Andreas's current research.

Andreas is a Guest Scholar at the Center for U.S.-Mexican Studies (University of California, San Diego) and an SSRC-MacArthur Foundation Fellow on Peace and Security in a Changing World. Beginning in the fall of 1998 he will be an Academy Scholar at Harvard University's Weatherhead Center for International Affairs. Andreas has a B.A. in political science from Swarthmore College and an M.A. in government from Cornell University, where he is currently completing his doctoral dissertation on the politics of U.S. border control in comparative perspective. Recent publications include *Drug War Politics* (coauthor, University of California Press, 1996), "U.S.-Mexico: Open Markets, Closed Border," *Foreign Policy* (summer 1996), "The Rise of the American Crimefare State," *World Policy Journal* (fall 1997), and "The Political Economy of Narco-Corruption in Mexico," *Current History* (April 1998).

11

The U.S. Immigration Control Offensive: Constructing an Image of Order on the Southwest Border

Peter Andreas
Center for U.S.-Mexican Studies
University of California, San Diego

The escalating immigration control campaign along the southwest border provides a striking contrast to the rhetoric and practice of U.S.-Mexican integration in the post-NAFTA era. The trend, it seems, is toward greater policing of cross-border labor flows in the context of a general liberalization of cross-border economic exchange. Thus, while NAFTA and other free market policy initiatives deterritorialize the economy, current border law enforcement initiatives reflect a reassertion of territorial sovereignty. The U.S.-Mexico border, paradoxically, is gaining more political and symbolic significance at the same time as a borderless North American economy is emerging.

I review the Clinton administration's effort to control illegal migration along the southwest border and evaluate some of its most important consequences. I argue that while the border control offensive generates some negative side effects and fails to significantly curb illegal migration and tame the underlying forces that fuel such migration, it very much succeeds in terms of enhancing state claims to territorial authority and creating an image of a more orderly border.[1] The border enforcement campaign also reinforces the myth that the source of the problem (and the solution) is found at the border itself, while obscuring the more awkward realities of an informal transnational labor market.

THE BORDER CONTROL CAMPAIGN:
"PREVENTION THROUGH DETERRENCE"

While the U.S. federal policing presence along the southwest border gradually expanded in the 1980s and early 1990s, this has been overshadowed by the border build-up of the past four years. The Immigration and Naturalization Service (INS), long considered the neglected stepchild of the Department of Justice, is now one of the fastest-growing federal agencies. The INS budget has doubled since 1993, to $3.1 billion in fiscal year 1997, and much of this growth is geared toward southwest border control. This expansion is particularly impressive in an era of fiscal austerity when most other federal agencies are facing budget cuts.[2]

Doris Meissner, the U.S. Commissioner of Immigration, described the INS as "dysfunctional" when she took over, and promised to "reinvent" the agency. A cornerstone of this reinvention process has been southwest border enforcement. Meissner told a Senate committee in October 1996 that "We have done more where border control is concerned in the last two to three years, than I think has been demonstrated over the last two to three decades" (Meissner 1996). And at a January 1997 news conference reviewing the expansion of INS activities, Meissner noted that "Our first priority remains to secure the border" (Associated Press, 14 January 1997).

The Clinton administration had little initial interest in border enforcement matters. Indeed, in early 1993 the administration recommended trimming the number of Border Patrol agents as a cost-saving measure. But Clinton quickly reversed this position in order to ride (rather than be drowned by) the rising restrictionist wave sweeping across the country and in the halls of Congress. Thus, in late July 1993, Clinton announced tough new measures against illegal immigration, including 600 more Border Patrol agents. In announcing the increase, Clinton said, "It's certainly plain to anybody with eyes to see that the Border Patrol is drastically understaffed, breathtakingly understaffed" (Barnes 1993).

Public opinion apparently agrees. As noted in Thomas Espenshade and Maryann Belanger's chapter in this volume, polling data suggest a high level of public enthusiasm for border policing. Thus, perhaps not surprisingly, border control quickly became an arena for the administration to display its law enforcement credentials. In his January 1996 State of the Union address, Clinton highlighted his border enforcement record, noting that "After years and years of neglect, this administration has taken on a strong stand to stiffen protection on our borders." Between 1993 and 1996, the Clinton administration increased the size of the Border Patrol by 45 percent. Attorney General

Janet Reno even appointed a "border czar" to coordinate all southwest border enforcement initiatives. The Illegal Immigration Reform and Immigration Responsibility Act of 1996, which the president signed on September 30, 1996, authorizes nearly a doubling of the Border Patrol by the year 2001, increasing the number of agents from 5,175 to 10,000. The new legislation also calls for additional measures to toughen border enforcement, including a controversial triple fence along 14 miles south of San Diego and increased penalties for alien smuggling.

The new legislation reinforces and builds on a strategy the INS calls "prevention through deterrence." The main goal is to discourage unauthorized entry along the southwest border—through more fencing, surveillance equipment, and law enforcement personnel—rather than having to apprehend entrants once they've crossed into the United States. Such an approach was first operationalized by the Border Patrol in El Paso in September 1993. Operation Blockade (later given the more diplomatic name Hold-the-Line) deployed 450 agents working overtime to cover a 20-mile stretch of the border. Apprehensions plummeted. Silvestre Reyes, the El Paso sector Border Patrol chief who planned the operation, became an overnight hero (and was even elected as a representative to Congress in November of 1996).

What began as a local and experimental law enforcement initiative has become an institutionalized centerpiece of southwest border control. This high-profile display of concentrated force gained the immediate attention of Washington, the media, and leaders in other border states who were eager to repeat the El Paso success story. The powerful appeal of the El Paso campaign was that the results were both immediate and visible. This proved politically irresistible. In 1994, the INS announced a broader adoption of the prevention-through-deterrence strategy to concentrate on the key points of illegal entry along the border. In October 1994, Operation Gatekeeper was launched south of San Diego, and Operation Safeguard was initiated in Nogales, Arizona. Most recently, operation Rio Grande began in east Texas in August 1997. While Gatekeeper originally focused on the 14 westernmost miles of the border, in October 1996 the INS announced an extension of Gatekeeper to include the 66 westernmost miles. The size of the Border Patrol in both San Diego and Nogales has doubled in the last two years. New staffing has been matched by new equipment: In San Diego, for example, the Border Patrol received 800 more vehicles, 28 additional infrared night scopes, and 600 more underground sensors between 1994 and 1996.

The support role of the military and the National Guard in border enforcement is also expanding. Law enforcement is assisted by 350 members of the

Marine and Army units that are part of the military's Joint Task Force 6, which was formed in 1988 to assist in southwest border drug control efforts. In January 1996 the administration announced a strengthening of the cooperation and coordination between law enforcement and the military on the border. In making the announcement, Meissner said, "Think of this as one team, different roles, different uniforms, but with the same game plan—and that is to restore the rule of law to the border" (Meissner and Reno 1996).

Although prohibited from making arrests, military personnel assist the INS by operating night scopes, motion sensors, and communications equipment, as well as building and maintaining roads and fences. For example, along the border south of San Diego, Army reservists have constructed a 10-foot-high steel wall made up of 180,000 metal sheets originally designed to create temporary landing fields. Similarly, in Nogales, Army engineers in 1994 and 1995 constructed a 15-foot-tall steel mat fence that is almost five miles long, stretching from one end of town to the other. New fencing is going up elsewhere along the border as well. For example, in January 1996 construction began on a 1.3-mile-long fence in Sunland Park, New Mexico, the first fence of its kind in the state. Similarly, a 10-foot-high fence is being erected to separate the border towns of Jacume, Mexico, and Jacumba in east San Diego County.

Experimental military technologies are also being adapted for border control purposes: For example, the Border Patrol is evaluating a photo identification system that came out of the CIA and the Department of Defense. Other devices include an electronic current that stops a fleeing car, a camera that can see into vehicles to check for hidden passengers, and a computer that checks commuters by voiceprint. A Border Research and Technology Center was opened in March 1995 to adapt military and intelligence technology to the problems of border control (*San Diego Union-Tribune*, 18 March 1995).

As part of the effort to make the border a more meaningful deterrent, the administration has also significantly toughened the penalties for alien smugglers and document forgers, and has dramatically increased the number of inspectors at the ports of entry to detect those attempting to enter through fraudulent document use. In 1996, for example, INS staffing at ports of entry increased by 50 percent—the largest port of entry staffing increase in history (INS 1996a). At the port of entry south of San Diego, users of false documents may now be prosecuted for repeat violations, and vehicles may also be confiscated (*Migration News*, February 1997).

Although each initiative is designed to meet distinct demographic and geographic challenges, operations Hold-the-Line, Gatekeeper, Safeguard, and Rio Grande share a similar underlying logic: Increase enforcement resources and concentrate them along the busiest entry points for illegal migration, disrupting the human traffic and forcing migrants to attempt entry along more difficult, remote areas and at official ports of entry that are presumably easier for the Border Patrol to regulate. Raising the risk and difficulty of entry, in turn, forces more migrants to turn to smugglers and increases the price of being smuggled. The end result, border control strategists argue, is that many migrants are inhibited from even attempting to cross, and many of those who try fail repeatedly, leading them to give up due to frustration and lack of resources.

INS officials praise the results of the prevention-through-deterrence strategy. As a consequence of their efforts, the INS says, "The border is harder to cross now than at any time in history" (INS 1996b). Southwest border control, Meissner stated in October 1996, is "showing dramatic success" (Meissner 1996). The persistence of the border crossers "isn't working," she said, meaning that "people that are crossing repeatedly and are being apprehended by us ultimately run out of both money to take care of themselves and of the willingness to try" (Meissner 1995). Official assessments on the ground level are equally celebratory: Commenting on Operation Gatekeeper, Johnny Williams, the Border Patrol chief for the San Diego sector, has claimed that "This is probably the single largest accomplishment in the Border Patrol's history" (*New York Times*, 28 August 1996).

However, redirecting the population flow is very different from reducing it. Noticeably missing from INS progress reports is any claim that illegal migration is actually down. Illegal entry is certainly more difficult and dangerous, but little evidence has been provided to suggest that large numbers of migrants are giving up and returning home (see Cornelius 1997).

EVALUATING THE BORDER CONTROL STRATEGY

Policy evaluation in the area of border control is a curious and unsatisfying business. The ambiguity of the measures is simultaneously a source of frustration and cover for those who make and implement policy.[3] In today's heated political climate over immigration issues, measuring policy progress has become a delicate art of political persuasion and packaging. More so than in most policy areas, appearances matter enormously.

Unwrapping the political packaging reveals that border control is both a stunning success and a stunning failure—depending on how one defines the problem and interprets the evidence. Almost every indicator that the administration points to as a sign of policy success can be read as a sign of failure. Similarly, every indicator that critics claim reflects policy failure is either conveniently downplayed or interpreted by administration officials as a sign of success. An examination of the interplay between law enforcement and law evasion along the southwest border suggests both the power and limits of border controls. While intensified border enforcement fails as a serious deterrent, it does significantly influence the location, difficulty, form, and frequency of entry. This has crucial consequences in terms of public and media perception, the political or material rewards for key actors (law enforcement agencies, elected leaders, smugglers), and certainly for the migrants themselves.

Whereas the border was once largely a nuisance for many clandestine crossers, the recent border build-up has clearly made it a much more serious (and more dangerous) challenge.[4] As law enforcement concentrates on the easiest and most heavily used crossing points, the human traffic is disrupted, dispersed, and displaced. Many migrants have turned to more remote entry points away from those urban areas targeted by operations Hold-the-Line, Gatekeeper, and Safeguard. Thus, for example, apprehensions in the El Paso sector remain far below the levels prior to Operation Hold-the-Line, but have jumped dramatically to the west in New Mexico and Arizona.[5] Similarly, apprehension numbers in the Imperial Beach sector south of San Diego (traditionally the single most important gateway for illegal migration along the entire border) have plummeted since Gatekeeper began, but arrests have shot up in the more remote eastern portions of San Diego county.[6]

One of the more predictable consequences of making the border crossing more difficult and risky is to push what was once a relatively simple illegal act (crossing the border without authorization) into a wider web of illegality. Past patterns of illegal migration across the U.S.-Mexico border can be characterized almost as a form of "self-smuggling" (i.e., the traditional role of the smuggler, or coyote, was limited and localized). However, the recent tightening of border controls increases the migrant's dependence on the connections and skills of professional people-smugglers. The cost of being smuggled across the border has consequently risen with the risks. For example, the price for being smuggled to Los Angeles roughly doubled between 1994 and 1996 (*Migration News*, March 1996). Overall, smuggling fees have increased from $250–$300 to $500 or more (*Migration News*, February 1997).

From the perspective of the border enforcers, this is a key indicator of policy success: It is more difficult and more expensive for migrants to cross. However, higher smuggling costs may not be as successful a deterrent as administration officials claim, given that travel costs are often paid for by relatives in the United States rather than by the migrants (Martin 1996). At the same time, higher smuggling costs do succeed in fueling the growth of increasingly sophisticated and well-organized binational people-smuggling organizations. This is fully recognized by administration officials. As Miguel Vallina, the assistant chief of the Border Patrol in San Diego points out, "The more difficult the crossing, the better the business for the smugglers" (*Los Angeles Times*, 5 February 1995). Meissner explains that "[A]s we improve our enforcement, we increase the smuggling of aliens that occurs, because it is harder to cross and so therefore people turn more and more to smugglers" (Meissner and Reno 1996). But while Meissner recognizes the fact that the Border Patrol is creating business for the smugglers, she also says that we are "moving as aggressively as we can . . . so that we can put them [the smugglers] out of business" (U.S. House 1996). Thus, on the one hand, she acknowledges that more enforcement fuels more smuggling, yet on the other hand insists that more enforcement can also bring an end to smuggling.

However, smugglers are, at core, service providers (even if abusive ones), and as long as there is a strong demand for their services, smuggling organizations will thrive. Aggressive enforcement certainly puts some smugglers out of business, but in the process simply creates business for competing smugglers. Thus, what is one smuggler's loss is another's gain. And the high profits of the business (inflated by law enforcement pressure) ensures that there will be smugglers willing to take the risks that come with the job.[7] In short, while arresting more smugglers provides a body count for officials needing to show progress in controlling the border, it does not necessarily reduce smuggling.[8]

Meanwhile, the persistence and expansion of smuggling provides the rationale for even tougher laws and tougher enforcement—reflected, for example, in the most recent immigration law and the fact that migration smuggling is increasingly treated as a form of organized crime. Yet it is the border enforcement offensive itself that has helped turn migration into a growing organized crime problem.[9]

Forcing migrants to attempt crossing at official ports of entry also creates additional strains on law enforcement. This is illustrated at the port of entry at San Ysidro south of San Diego, the busiest land border crossing in the world. As a staff report of the U.S. Commission for Immigration Reform (1995) observed, "Inspectors are frustrated that they must often choose between a thorough inspection which slows traffic or an expedited one that keeps traffic moving" (p. 14). Operation Gatekeeper, it should be emphasized, makes the inspector's task even more difficult and frustrating. For example, the INS claims that Gatekeeper sparked a 40 percent rise in the use of fraudulent documents to cross the border at ports of entry. Officials have an increasingly difficult time reconciling two objectives: On the one hand, to facilitate the growing volume of legitimate border crossings, but on the other hand to control the growing volume of illegitimate crossings that result from stepped-up border enforcement between the ports of entry.

In January 1996, for example, INS officials reported that they were overwhelmed by the sudden influx of migrants attempting to enter through fraudulent document use at the San Ysidro port of entry. In January 1997, the INS beefed up the number of inspectors in anticipation of a similar post-holiday rush (overall, the number of inspectors at the San Ysidro port of entry has doubled in the past year). Such crackdowns, however, are constrained by the sheer volume of legitimate border crossings. Forty thousand people cross the border legally every day to work. About 40 million people and 15 million cars a year now enter the United States through the ports of entry south of San Diego. Overall, 230 million people and 82 million cars enter the United States from Mexico every year (*Migration News*, February 1997). As these numbers continue to grow through the process of economic integration, weeding out the illegal from the legal crossers becomes ever more difficult.

The tightening of border controls also influences the frequency of clandestine border crossings. A majority of Mexican migrants do not stay in the United States permanently but go back and forth across the border, almost as a form of transnational commuting. But as a result of tighter border controls, many of these migrants are prolonging their stay and even settling down permanently in the United States (when the commute becomes too difficult and costly, then the incentive to relocate closer to the workplace increases). As the Urban Institute's Jeffrey Passel points out, "there's a trade-off between deterring illegal immigration and converting temporary migration into permanent migration" (*San Francisco Chronicle*, 3 September 1996). A staff report of the U.S. Commission on Immigration Reform (1995) reaches a similar conclusion, noting that some migrants "are choosing to remain in the United States for longer periods so that they do not face the problem of re-entering when they are ready to return to the U.S." A study of Operation Hold-the-Line by Frank Bean and his colleagues (1994) suggests that many migrants continue to cross illegally, but stay on the U.S. side for longer periods in the El Paso area because the crossing is more difficult than before. Interestingly, in terms of the administration's goal of lowering border apprehension statistics, this is policy success (migrants stay longer and thus cross fewer times), but in terms of reducing the illegal migrant population this is not only an indicator of policy failure but of a counterproductive policy.

Meanwhile, there is no indication of a labor shortage in those sectors of the economy that rely on illegal migrant workers. As the U.S. Commission on

Immigration Reform (1995) noted in its evaluation of Gatekeeper, "By one measure, Operation Gatekeeper appears to have had little effect—the availability of workers in industries that are dependent on illegal alien labor" (p. 7). As the chapters by Wayne Cornelius and Susan González Baker et al. document, employer demand for migrant workers persists at very high levels. Yet it is here that INS enforcement efforts are noticeably least focused. According to the president's 1994 *Report on Immigration*, "Everyone agrees that the primary incentive for illegal immigration is employment. Workplace enforcement of labor standards and employer sanctions are the instruments for reducing that incentive" (*Accepting the Immigration Challenge* 1994). Yet despite such public statements, only about 2 percent of the fiscal year (FY) 1996 INS budget was devoted to employer sanctions enforcement (*Migration News*, November 1996). When asked why only a fraction of INS spending is devoted to targeting the workplace, Meissner simply replied, "We have always argued that the centerpiece of effective enforcement must be the border, and that it must be backed up with employer enforcement" (Federal News Service, 8 February 1996).

Although the administration has begun to push for more workplace enforcement, including the hiring of hundreds of additional inspectors, the trend for most of the decade has actually been toward a relaxation of workplace monitoring. For example, there were about 6,000 INS investigations of employers for immigration violations in FY 1995, a drop from almost 15,000 in FY 1989 (*Migration News*, April 1996). Moreover, the INS generally settles cases for less than half of the amount assessed in fines against employers of illegal migrant workers (*Migration News*, November 1996). The most recent immigration control legislation focuses largely on border control while doing little to remedy the anemic condition of workplace controls. The current enforcement strategy, in other words, is not a major departure from the past practice of primarily targeting illegal migrants rather than the employers who hire them.

At the same time, little is being done to tame the broader economic transformations in Mexico that help fuel continued mass migration. Mexico's sweeping market-based reforms (such as the liberalization of agriculture) are, at least in the short and medium term, reinforcing the incentives for Mexican workers to migrate to the United States (some of these structural changes in Mexico's economy are outlined in the chapter by Enrique Dussel Peters). Moreover, the collapse of the peso and subsequent economic crisis widened the U.S.-Mexico wage gap from 8:1 to 12:1.

Given the limits and consequences of the current U.S. approach to curbing illegal migration, one must ask why it nevertheless sustains such enormous public support and continues to receive such high praise from administration officials. Indeed, even when some of the shortcomings of the strategy are recognized and acknowledged, the solution is assumed to be escalation rather than any fundamental reevaluation. Such policy persistence and escalation points to an underappreciated fact: Failing and flawed policies can nevertheless be successful from a political and psychological perspective. The border *appears* more orderly at those crossing points that are most visible to the public and the media's eye. Migration flows are less visible because they are more dispersed, more remote, and more clandestine. In a relatively brief period of time, a much greater *sense* of order has been created along the most visible and contested sections of the border.

This imposition of orderliness is powerfully illustrated by photographs (displayed at a Border Patrol sector office south of San Diego) taken of the same stretch of the border before and after Operation Gatekeeper. They provide sharply contrasting images of chaos and order. The picture taken of a key area of the border before Gatekeeper shows a mangled and twisted chain-link border fence and crowds of people milling about on both sides, seemingly oblivious of the border line. The Border Patrol is nowhere to be seen. The image is one of a border that is defied, defeated, and undefended.

The picture of the same area after Gatekeeper was initiated, however, shows a sturdy steel-wall fence, backed up by powerful stadium lights and four-wheel drive Border Patrol vehicles stationed every few hundred feet or so alertly monitoring the line. There are no groups of people milling about on either side of the fence. The image is one of a border that deters and defends against unauthorized crossings. In the case of Gatekeeper, "The game is to try and focus as much attention as possible on one small piece of real estate," explains T. J. Bonner, the president of the National Border Patrol Council. "You then hope everyone ignores the fact that we're being totally overrun in the rest of the sector." The truth, Bonner says, is that "it's bursting out all over—Arizona, New Mexico, parts of Texas" (*Los Angeles Times*, 6 July 1996).[10]

From a purely political and bureaucratic perspective, appearances can have high payoffs: For the INS, the border campaign has brought with it an unprecedented injection of resources and heightened prestige and credibility to an agency that has long been neglected and maligned; for elected leaders, it has won votes in key states and provided an inoculation against political attacks that they are soft on illegal immigration. Regardless of one's own views about border control, the political success of the Clinton strategy should be acknowledged and taken seriously. Both liberal and conservative critics often neglect this fact in their efforts to portray the policy as either draconian and inhumane or puny and ineffective.

It is tempting, of course, to cynically dismiss or belittle the heightened appearance of order along the most populated stretches of the border as merely a psychological ploy for short-term political gain (see, for example, Graham 1996). However, for those in charge of border enforcement, how Congress and the broader public *feel* about the integrity of the border is arguably as important as the actual deterrent effect of the border. The deterrence function of borders has always been as much about image as reality, a political fiction providing an appearance of control that helps reproduce and reinforce state legitimacy. Indeed, the very premise of the current push to "regain control of the border" reinforces the myth that the border was actually controlled in the first place. It also perpetuates the myth that the problem and the solution are located at the border rather than having to confront the problems of formally managing a transnational labor market. In other words, statecraft in this case is not merely about curbing illegal migration but about propping up state claims to territorial authority. In short, the symbolic and perceptual effects of border enforcement are arguably more politically important than the actual deterrent effects.

CONCLUSION

Immigration control initiatives such as Gatekeeper and Hold-the-Line are ultimately about re-crafting the image of the U.S.-Mexico border. How these law enforcement moves shape the perceptions of the spectators (Congress, the media, local residents in border areas, the broader public) is as critical as the countermoves of the clandestine border crossers. Border policing, in other words, is very much a spectator sport, but in this particular case the objective is to pacify rather than inflame the passions of the spectators.[11] In this effort, the administration's border control offensive is not only a strategic move in an endless game of cat-and-mouse but also reflects a fundamental change in the rules of the game itself: The most visible forms of entry—groups of illegal migrants openly crossing near urban areas—are no longer tolerated. Thus, for the border crossers, evading the border enforcers is now a longer and more complex game requiring greater patience and stealth. With persistence, they eventually make it across the line, but in a much less visible (and thus less politically embarrassing) manner than before. So far, it seems, the game for the border enforcers has been less about winning (achieving deterrence) and more about projecting a winning image.

In the absence of large-scale job creation in Mexico (to reduce the migration push on the supply side) and much tighter workplace regulations (to

reduce the employment pull on the demand side), domestic political impera-
tives dictate that border policing will continue to escalate. While the United
States and Mexico have signed agreements to respect the human rights of
migrants, do more to combat smuggling organizations, and increase bilateral
cooperation, left politely unmentioned is that socioeconomic trends in both
countries are likely to propel continued high levels of migration, at least in the
short and medium term. Unable or unwilling to make more fundamental policy changes, the delicate political task facing U.S. policymakers will be to regulate and channel the unauthorized influx of migrant labor in a manner that
minimizes cross-border tensions while maximizing the appearance of an
orderly and secure border.

ACKNOWLEDGMENTS

Research for this chapter was made possible by an SSRC-MacArthur
Foundation Fellowship on Peace and Security in a Changing World. I also
thank the Center for U.S.-Mexican Studies at the University of California, San
Diego.

NOTES

1. For an earlier analysis that points to the significance of maintaining the image of
   border control, see Portes (1983).
2. As one press report noted, "While other federal agencies face severe cutbacks or
   even dismantling, the INS can barely keep up with the money being funneled its
   way. For example, a year ago when the agency sought 700 new border-control
   agents, Congress approved 800" (Knight-Ridder News Service, 20 March 1996).
   This year the agency plans on hiring 1,000 new Border Patrol agents. In the scram-
   ble to meet its hiring targets, the INS has even established an around-the-clock
   hotline to find new Border Patrol applicants (United Press International, 14
   January 1997).
3. For example, border arrest statistics are notoriously limited as indicators in that
   they do not indicate how many people actually cross the border undetected and do
   not indicate how many people are repeat offenders.
4. In an effort to bypass Gatekeeper, for example, 14 border crossers died from exposure to the cold and one was killed in a traffic accident during a two-week period
   in January 1997. In the summer of 1996, heat exhaustion claimed the lives of more
   than a dozen crossers (*San Diego Union-Tribune*, January 25, 1997).

5. The greatest deterrent effect of the El Paso operation has been on local commuters from Ciudad Juarez rather than on long-distance migrants; see Bean et al. (1994).

6. In the first nine months of Gatekeeper, apprehensions in the Imperial Beach sector dropped sharply, but in the eastern sectors of San Diego county, apprehensions skyrocketed from 1,785 in the first nine months of fiscal year 1994 to 21,000 in 1995, and reached 60,000 in 1996 (*Migration News*, October 1996).

7. As the risks and penalties for smuggling rise, so does the smugglers' willingness to take more extreme measures to evade law enforcement. This partly explains the rise in high-speed chases and accidents that result when smugglers try to avoid INS highway checkpoints.

8. For example, in San Diego there was a 65 percent increase in the prosecution of alien smugglers between fiscal year 1995 and fiscal year 1996 (INS 1996b).

9. Despite the increasing importance of smuggling organizations in facilitating migration, there is remarkably little work in the immigration literature on this topic.

10. Some San Diego Border Patrol agents reportedly complained that supervisors urged them to underreport arrests along the westernmost points of the border and to overreport apprehensions to the east. In some cases, apprehended migrants were reportedly transported east before being processed (*Migration News*, August 1996).

11. For an analysis of politics as a spectator sport, see Edelman (1964).

REFERENCES

Accepting the Immigration Challenge: The President's Report on Immigration. 1994. Washington, D.C.: Government Printing Office.

Alvord, Valerie. 1997. Reno firm on halting border crossers. *San Diego Union-Tribune*, 25 January.

Barnes, Fred. 1993. "No Entry: The Republicans' Immigration War." *New Republic*, 8 November.

Bean, Frank, R. Chanove, R. G. Cushing, R. de la Garza, G. Freeman, C. W. Haynes, and D. Spencer. 1994. "Illegal Mexican Migration and the United States-Mexican Border: The Effects of Operation Hold-the-Line on El Paso/Juarez." Population Research Center, University of Texas at Austin.

Cornelius, Wayne. 1997. Appearances and realities: Controlling illegal immigration in the United States. In *Temporary Workers or Future Citizens: Japanese and U.S. Migration Policies*, ed. M. Weiner and T. Hanami. London: Macmillan.

Edelman, Murray. 1964. *The Symbolic Uses of Politics*. Urbana, Ill.: University of Illinois Press.

Graham, Wade. 1996. "Masters of the Game: How the U.S. Protects the Traffic in Cheap Mexican Labor." *Harpers* (July).

Martin, Philip. 1996. The Mexican crisis and Mexico-U.S. migration. Unpublished manuscript.

Meissner, Doris. 1995. Foreign Press Center briefing, Washington, D.C., 23 October.

Meissner, Doris. 1996. Testimony before the Senate Judiciary Committee Subcommittee on Immigration, 2 October.

Meissner, Doris, and Janet Reno. 1996. News conference. Washington D.C., 12 January.

Portes, Alejandro. 1983. Of borders and states: A skeptical note on the legislative control of immigration. In *America's New Immigration Law: Origins, Rationales, and Potential Consequences*, ed. W. Cornelius and R. A. Montoya. La Jolla, Calif.: University of California-San Diego, Center for U.S.-Mexican Studies.

Sandia National Laboratories. 1993. *Systematic Analysis of the Southwest Border*, Vol. 1. Report prepared for the U.S. Immigration and Naturalization Service.

U.S. Commission on Immigration Reform. 1995. *Staff Report on Border Law Enforcement and Removal Initiatives in San Diego, California*. Washington, D.C.: Government Printing Office.

U.S. House. 1996. Hearings of the Commerce, Justice, State, and Judiciary Subcommittee of the House Appropriations Committee, 8 May.

U.S. Immigration and Naturalization Service. 1996a. *Building a Comprehensive Southwest Border Enforcement Strategy*. Washington, D.C.: Government Printing Office.

U.S. Immigration and Naturalization Service. 1996b. *Operation Gatekeeper: Two Years of Progress*. Washington, D.C.: Government Printing Office.

Commentary

Jacqueline Hagan, University of Houston

The principal argument put forth by Andreas is both intriguing and convincing. The U.S. policing campaign along the southwest border has failed as a policy because it is not achieving its central goal of "deterrence through prevention." It nonetheless enjoys considerable public and administrative support because intensified and concentrated activities at key and visible points of entry have affected the location, difficulty, and mode of unauthorized entry. Andreas convincingly suggests that by disrupting and redirecting the flows, U.S. enforcement policy efforts succeed in creating an image of a more orderly border and a strong nation-state in command of its territory.

Both policy analysts and migrant communities have had reason to be skeptical of this most recent border campaign. They observed early on the limits of enforcement strategies with the implementation of the Immigration Reform and Control Act of 1986. Ten years later they listened to the rhetorical arguments of Clinton's border campaign that hastily ushered in further border enforcement efforts with the passage of the Illegal Immigration Reform and Responsibility Act of 1996 (IRAIRA). This skepticism seems warranted. Despite the rapid expansion of U.S. federal policing efforts along the 2,000-mile southwest border during the past decade, it remains uncertain whether and to what extent these increased enforcement activities have decreased the overall volume of unauthorized entry along that border (Martin 1993; Bean et al. 1994; Espenshade 1994; Singer and Massey 1997).

More important, perhaps, than the question of the effectiveness of the new border control campaign—which will not be fully determined until current trends of increased enforcement operations run their course—are the implications of enhanced enforcement provisions of IRAIRA for civil and human rights. Dubbed the "Mexican Exclusion Act" by many of its critics since the law's teeth are largely directed toward the south, the "reforms" (as they are diplomatically referred to by IRAIRA's architects) embedded in IRAIRA have potentially devastating consequences for the human rights of undocumented migrants, the civil rights of asylum seekers, legal residents, and U.S. citizens, as well as the future survival of transnational border communities and regional and binational integration efforts.

The cornerstone of IRAIRA—improvements to border and interior enforcement—appears to be based on a contradictory and rhetorical connection between immigration, organized drug and people smuggling, and terrorism. Border patrol agents claim that often they are unable to distinguish migrants from drug traffickers. In essence, the words "alien" and "drug smugglers" have become married in official pronouncements. There is, however, a contradiction underlying official statements and actions. For example, as Andreas notes, U.S. administration officials argue that increased border enforcement can put a stop to human smuggling, but at the same time they recognize that policing is good for the smuggling business. However, what appears at first to be contradictory may indeed be a purposeful strategy on the part of the border campaign. By forcing migrants to rely on coyotes, the flows may become more organized and therefore more controllable.

Despite official claims of the link between undocumented migration and organized smuggling, the empirical evidence supporting this connection is scanty at best. For example, a recent study by Singer and Massey (1997) found that while the odds of apprehension were dramatically lower for initial crossers traveling with either a coyote, guide, relative or friend, the form of crossing for the more seasoned migrant has no influence on the likelihood of apprehension.

The cost of criminalizing undocumented migration is the apparent demoralization of people who are, after all, doing what millions of Americans have done before, namely, coming to America to seek a better life—a sad departure for a nation that has long boasted of the welcome it extends to immigrants. There are even more tragic human costs for some would-be crossers. By channeling would-be migrants into areas more remote from major, and hence more visible, U.S. population centers, along more circuitous routes and across more dangerous mountain, ranch, and desert terrains, the costs in terms of personal safety mount. Indeed, in the period from 1993 through 1996, at least 1,185 migrants died trying to cross the southwest border into the United States (Eschbach et al. 1997). Moreover, media reports indicate that a growing number of these fatalities occur away from the border in the desolate ranch lands of south Texas and the barren deserts of Mexico and Arizona. Tragically, many of the dead are never identified and are hastily buried in unmarked graves in pauper cemeteries along the border. These human costs, although staggering and mounting, remain outside the concerns of official policy.

The policing of the border also has implications for the civil rights of persons living in border communities, including legal residents and U.S. citizens. A number of projects and organizations developed to document and curtail the violation of human rights in immigration law enforcement found that a substantial number of victims who report psychological and physical abuse from U.S. enforcement officials are U.S. citizens and legal residents. Not surprisingly, the large majority are Latino (AFSC 1992; Koulish et al. 1994).

Continuing to draw on a rather shaky, but publicly appealing, relationship between immigration, drug trafficking, and terrorism, the security provisions of IRAIRA authorize wiretapping for the investigation of alien and/or drug smuggling, promote INS agreements with local and state law enforcement arms, allow for preinspection at foreign airports, and even go so far as to initiate the training of airline personnel to detect fraudulent documents and suspect would-be immigrants. The national security provisions of IRAIRA also usher in IDENT, a national fingerprint database system created to track undocumented migrants and keep them from entering and working in the United States. This system has potentially chilling implications for the power of government to monitor and control both immigrants and citizens. Are these policies moving the United States toward the creation of a national population register that must be consulted to verify the eligibility of U.S. citizens to earn a livelihood?

Similarly draconian are IRAIRA's revisions in the conditions and grounds for exclusion and removal of inadmissible (another new diplomatic term) and deportable aliens, including asylum seekers. Under these most recent revisions, the definition of deportable crimes for both undocumented persons and legal residents is expanded. Moreover, the denial of asylum is made easier by turning over the initial decision to INS inspectors and investigators at the port of entry and restricting the time frame during which an asylum seeker can appeal the initial decision. It is clear that one of the major intentions of IRAIRA was the exclusion of asylum seekers. Yet, as the history of immigration policy and trends has demonstrated, policies that shut out one admissible category of immigrants usually usher in another. Thus, we shouldn't be surprised in the coming years to see an increase in numbers in another entry category—irregular entries.

Equally chilling are those IRAIRA provisions that change the deeming process by which legal residents and U.S. citizens can bring relatives to the United States and those that restrict a host of social service benefits for large segments of the legal resident population. Under Subtitle C of the new law, sponsors must now show that they have an income of at least 125 percent of the federal poverty line. These exclusionary provisions not only create new categories of persons (e.g., qualified/unqualified legal resident) and thus potentially further fragment groups by immigration status, but also challenge the foundation of U.S. immigration policy and core democratic values by undermining family reunification principles and skewing sponsorship opportunities away from the poor.

Hardest hit by these measures, of course, will be impoverished immigrant communities, many of which are located along the U.S.-Mexico border. For example, in Hidalgo, Texas, one border site of my current research on the effects of immigration and welfare reform, the poverty rate is one of the highest in the country and unemployment stands at 18 percent. One in every twelve residents is a legal immigrant receiving some form of public assistance, and many of these poor households are composed of persons of mixed immigration and eligibility statuses with low levels of education and English literacy. In these communities, which experience the twin blows and harsh realities of border policing and welfare repeal, fear and uncertainty prevail.

At some point in these immigration debates we must ask ourselves the following questions: How far are we willing to go in the name of immigration control? How many deaths are acceptable to the United States in its quest to enforce its borders? Is the United States showing the same respect and concern for the value of life for all groups in its territory? Are we prepared for the consequences of what Jonas (1996, 76) refers to as "the spill over effect"? That is, will an expansion of policies first designed to exclude undocumented migrants spread to include the denial of services and rights to some legal resident groups? Will we be deceived into accepting these spillovers as the collateral damage needed to accomplish our primary goal of exclusion? If unchecked, this dynamic could eventually spread to affect the civil rights and liberties of naturalized and native-born U.S. citizens alike.

In some ways, I see an analogy between the current battle to control immigration and the war waged in this country against drugs. Just as we expanded police authority in the name of the drug war, we are now seeking to expand enforcement in the name of immigration control. Civil libertarians have done a good job of documenting the human and civil rights costs of the drug war. Perhaps the time has come for us to broaden our research agenda to include the documentation of the civil and human costs of immigration control.

References

American Friends Service Committee (AFSC). 1992. *Sealing Our Borders: The Human Toll*. Third Report of the Immigration Law Enforcement Monitoring Project (ILEMP). A Project of the Mexico-U.S. Border Program. Philadelphia. February.

Bean, Frank, Roland Chanove, Robert Cushing, Rodolfo de la Garza, Gary Freeman, Charles Haynes and David Spencer. 1994. *Illegal Mexican Migration and the United States/Mexico Border: The Effects of Operation Hold-the-Line on El Paso/Juárez*. Washington D.C.: U.S. Commission on Immigration Reform.

Eschbach, Karl, Jacqueline Hagan, Nestor Rodriguez, Ruben Hernandez Léon, and Stanley Bailey. 1997. *Death at the Border*. Working Paper Series 97-2. Houston: Center for Immigration Research.

Espenshade, Thomas. 1994. "Does the Threat of Border Apprehension Deter Undocumented U.S. Immigration?" *Population and Development Review* 20(4): 871–892.

Jonas, Susanne. 1996. "Rethinking Immigration Policy and Citizenship in the Americas." *Social Justice: A Journal of Crime, Conflict and World Order* 23(3): 68–85.

Koulish, Robert E., Manuel Escobedo, Raquel Rubio-Goldsmith, and John Rober Warren. 1994. *U.S. Immigration Authorities and Victims of Human and Civil Rights Abuses: The Border Interaction Project Study of South Tucson, Arizona and South Texas*. Working Paper Series 20. Mexican American Studies and Research Center.

Martin, John L. 1993. "Operation Blockade: A Bullying Tactic or a Border Control Model?" *Backgrounder*. Washington D.C.: Center for Immigration Studies.

Singer, Audrey, and Douglas Massey. 1997. The social process of undocumented border cossing. Paper presented at the meetings of the Latin American Studies Association, 19 April, Guadalajara.

CHAPTER TWELVE

Photo by Anna LeVine

Thomas J. Espenshade   My immigrant ancestors on my father's side included three brothers from the area around Espenschied in Germany who came to the United States in 1787 and settled near Lancaster and Harrisburg, Pennsylvania. My siblings and I are in the sixth generation of Espenshades in the United States. Interestingly, my brother and I are the first in our branch of the family to settle outside the relatively small Pennsylvania Dutch section of the state and marry persons from different ethnic backgrounds. I became interested in immigration research in the early 1980s when I was working at The Urban Institute in Washington, D.C. It was a puzzle in mathematical demography that first attracted my attention. Subsequently, I was part of a team that was studying the social and economic impacts of Mexican immigration into southern California. It was that study that sparked my later substantive interests that have led me down many fascinating avenues of inquiry.

Professor of Sociology and Faculty Associate at the Office of Population Research, Princeton University. Educated at The College of Wooster, Yale University, and Princeton University. Research interests focus on public opinion toward immigrants, the fiscal impacts of immigration, and models of undocumented migration to the United States. Publications include *Keys to Successful Immigration: Implications of the New Jersey Experience* (1997), *A Stone's Throw from Ellis Island: Economic Implications of Immigration to New Jersey* (1994), and *The Fourth Wave: California's Newest Immigrants* (coauthor) (1985).

12

Immigration and Public Opinion

Thomas J. Espenshade and Maryann Belanger
Office of Population Research, Princeton University

Immigration to the United States is accelerating, and foreign-born individuals account for a rising share of the total U.S. population. Data from the Current Population Survey show that the proportion of foreign-born U.S. residents reached 9.3 percent in March 1996, up from 7.9 percent in 1990, and nearly double the 1970 figure of 4.8 percent (Hansen and Faber 1997; Bureau of the Census 1995). Persons born outside the United States now constitute the largest fraction of the U.S. population since the Second World War. Of the nearly 25 million foreign-born U.S. residents, more than one-quarter arrived in this country since 1990, and another 34 percent entered during the 1980s. California is home to the largest number of immigrants (8 million), and New York ranks second with 3.2 million. Other states with at least a million foreign-born residents include Florida, Texas, New Jersey, and Illinois (Hansen and Faber 1997).

According to the 1990 U.S. census, 21.7 percent (or 4.3 million individuals) of the total U.S. foreign-born population of 19.8 million persons were born in Mexico (Bureau of the Census 1993). By March 1996 this proportion had increased to 27.2 percent, and the estimated size of the foreign-born population originating in Mexico had grown to 6.7 million (Hansen and Faber 1997). The Philippines is the second-largest country of origin, accounting for 1.2 million individuals, or just 4.7 percent of the foreign-born total.

Legal immigration to the United States has risen in every decade beginning with the 1940s and reached a total of 7.3 million aliens admitted for lawful permanent residence between 1981 and 1990. For the 1991 to 1995 fiscal years combined, legal immigration totaled 5.2 million (INS 1997), suggesting that the 1990s may set an historic record.[1] Mexico sends more legal migrants to the

United States than any other country. So far in the 1990s, 1.5 million permanent resident visas (or 28 percent of the total) have been granted to Mexican nationals. This figure is twice the total for all of Europe (728,000). In fiscal years 1991 to 1992 the Mexican totals were substantially lifted above their secular trends by the legalization program surrounding the 1986 Immigration Reform and Control Act (IRCA). But even in 1995, when IRCA visas numbered just 4,300, Mexico still led the list of sending countries with 89,900 visas out of a total of 720,500. The former Soviet Union was second with 54,500 permanent resident visas, followed by the Philippines with 51,000. All of Africa comprised 42,500 visas, less than half the number allotted to Mexican nationals (INS 1997).

In addition to its substantial contribution to legal U.S. immigration, Mexico is also the leading source country for undocumented migration to the United States. Of the estimated 2.06 million undocumented aliens enumerated in the 1980 census, 1.13 million persons, or more than one-half of the total, were born in Mexico (Warren and Passel 1987). Many of these illegal immigrants took advantage of an amnesty program that was a condition of IRCA's passage. For example, in a study of nearly 6,200 newly legalized aliens who had lived in the United States continuously since January 1, 1982, the Immigration and Naturalization Service (INS) found that 70 percent came from Mexico (INS 1992). Despite the fact that more than 2.8 million formerly illegal migrants and their dependents eventually received permanent legal resident status under IRCA (INS 1997), there were still an estimated 5 million undocumented migrants resident in the United States in October 1996 (Department of Justice 1997). An estimated 2.7 million persons born in Mexico accounted for 54 percent of this total. Roughly five out of every six illegal migrants from Mexico entered the United States without inspection, whereas the remaining 16 percent overstayed the terms of their visas. According to the INS, the size of the illegal resident population in the United States is growing by an average of roughly 275,000 persons per year (Department of Justice 1997).

Growing anxiety over the presence of immigrants in the United States has accompanied the rise in immigration. Recent trends in immigration attitudes are graphed in Figure 12.1. The solid dark line plots the fraction of public opinion survey respondents in a series of nationwide polls who feel that the level of immigration to the United States should be decreased. The trend is relatively flat until sometime after 1975, when it rises abruptly. The evidence suggests that the United States has entered a neorestrictionist era in the past two decades.[2] The annual U.S. unemployment rate is also shown in Figure 12.1. The two series are highly correlated, with the exception of a few years near

FIGURE 12.1

Percentage of American Public Who Want Immigration Decreased and Trend in U.S. Unemployment Rate

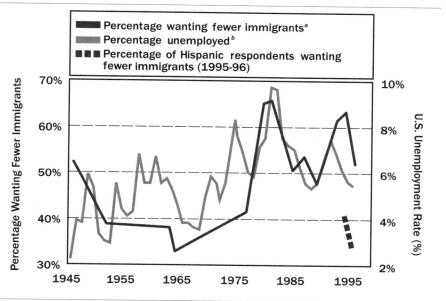

[a] Source: Simon and Alexander (1993); POLL database, Dialog Information Services, Inc.
[b] Source: U.S. Bureau of the Census, *Statistical Abstract of the United States* (various issues); U.S. Bureau of the Census (1975); and Data Stream database.

1960 when public opinion data are missing. Similar patterns have emerged in Canadian data (Tienhara 1974; Palmer 1994). They suggest that Americans' attitudes toward immigrants are partially conditioned by the state of the macroeconomy and that these attitudes harden when employment prospects for native workers dim.[3]

Results from other contemporary polls are consistent with the negative attitudes toward immigrants shown in Figure 12.1. Nearly two-thirds of adults in a January 1995 nationwide survey conducted by the Scripps Howard News Service said they did not think that most Americans still wanted to extend to immigrants the kind of invitation carved on the Statue of Liberty: "Give me your tired, your poor, your huddled masses yearning to breathe free." In a January 1996 poll of national registered voters, two-thirds of respondents believed the U.S. government was doing too little to restrict immigration, and just 7 percent thought it was overregulating immigration flows. Finally, in a

July 1996 national poll conducted by the *Washington Post*, almost one-half of all respondents worried either a great deal or a good amount that immigration is changing this country for the worse; only one-quarter of respondents expressed a similar degree of concern that the United States will shut the door to new immigrants and the dream of a melting-pot nation will be lost.

After reviewing a century's worth of media and public opinion coverage of immigration issues, Rita Simon (1985) concluded, "The most remarkable observation I can make is that so many people were admitted to the United States when there was so little enthusiasm for them for such long periods of time" (p. xv). This contrast is especially poignant in the neorestrictionist era, because an apparent disjuncture has developed between federal initiatives that have continued to liberalize legal immigration policy and American public opinion, which has become more restrictionist toward immigrants (Harwood 1986, 201).[4] An understanding of this paradox rests on three elements: (1) American attitudes toward immigration are often ambivalent; (2) opinions frequently are not strongly held, even if they are negative; and (3) vocal pro-immigrant interest groups have been successful in capturing the attention of federal policymakers (Espenshade and Calhoun 1992).

The purpose of this chapter is to take a fresh look at American attitudes toward U.S. immigration. In doing so, we will illustrate two points made in the previous paragraph: Attitudes are often ambivalent, and they typically are not strongly held. Our research extends the analysis in Espenshade and Belanger (1997) in several ways: New issues are explored; some prior questions are reexamined in the light of new data; and, whenever possible, answers to public opinion questions are shown separately for all respondents and for a subsample of Hispanic respondents. Despite the prominence of Mexican migration to the United States, few opinion polls ask questions specifically about Mexican migrants. As a consequence, our analysis in many cases will emphasize differences in how legal and illegal immigration are perceived and in how attitudes of Hispanic respondents compare with other sample participants.

PRIOR RESEARCH

Nonwhites, and blacks in particular, may hold more restrictionist immigration views for fear of job competition from migrants (Harwood 1985; Cain and Kiewiet 1986; Simon 1985). Briggs (1995), for example, has argued that the urban black labor force has been adversely affected by the resurgence of mass immigration into cities of the North and West. In a 1983 survey conducted for the Federation for American Immigration Reform, 82 percent of African Americans believed that illegal immigrants take jobs away from native workers, compared with 58 percent of Hispanic Americans (Harwood 1986; see also Jackson 1995; Sullivan 1995). And in a 1989 Texas survey, blacks showed more concern about the effects of undocumented migration than Hispanics (Tarrance and Associates 1989). At the same time, however, blacks may feel a sense of solidarity with other people of color, and perhaps this sentiment also extends to current immigrants, many of whom are nonwhite (Tanton 1995).

A feeling of solidarity with immigrants might also shape the attitudes of Hispanics and Asians, because most of the recent legal and undocumented migrants to the United States come from either Latin America or Asia (Fix and Passel 1994). It may not be surprising, therefore, that Hispanics display more pro-immigrant views than non-Hispanics (Cain and Kiewiet 1986; Miller, Polinard, and Wrinkle 1984; Harwood 1983, 1985; Day 1989). This relation is sometimes explained by a cultural affinity hypothesis (Espenshade and Calhoun 1993). Cultural and ethnic ties to recent immigrants promote pro-immigrant attitudes and appeals for more liberal immigration policies (Day 1989, 1990).

In June 1983 the Field Research Corporation conducted a telephone survey of public attitudes toward immigration among 1,031 residents in the six urban counties of southern California. Nearly nine out of ten respondents (87.5 percent) believed that the illegal immigration situation in southern California represented either a "very" or "somewhat" serious problem. Two-thirds of sample participants felt that the influx of illegal or undocumented immigrants into southern California was having an overall unfavorable effect on the state as a whole. Hispanic respondents were somewhat less likely than African Americans to view illegal immigration and undocumented migrants in a negative light (Muller and Espenshade 1985).

Multiple regression analysis showed that the characteristics of survey respondents and their perceptions of migrants' behavior affect the way residents in southern California view both undocumented migrants and the overall impact of illegal immigration (Espenshade and Calhoun 1993). The most salient respondent traits are age, education, and ethnicity. Older survey participants were more likely to see illegal immigration in negative terms, whereas having more education and being Hispanic were each associated with greater optimism about undocumented migrants and illegal migration. In some models, blacks were significantly more likely than non-Hispanic whites (the reference group) to view illegal immigration as a serious problem. At the same time, respondents who cast immigrants as poor and welfare dependent or as making little effort to learn English voiced some of the most unfavorable rankings concerning undocumented immigration and its effects.

In a June 1993 CBS News/*New York Times* national poll, 1,363 adults were asked, "Should immigration into the United States be kept at its present level, increased, or decreased?" An analysis by Espenshade and Hempstead (1996) found that, in comparison with non-Hispanic whites (the omitted category for ethnic contrasts), Hispanic, black, and Asian respondents were more likely to express pro-immigration views. Both gross and net effects were statistically significant for blacks. Neither effect was significant for Hispanics, and Asians fell in between.[5] Findings with respect to Hispanic attitudes conform to results in de la Garza (1985) and de la Garza, Falcon, and Garcia (1993). The CBS News/*New York Times* poll did not ask Hispanic respondents to which national-origin group they belonged, nor were questions asked about citizenship or place of birth. Yet recent research has shown that a monolithic or homogeneous "Hispanic community" does not exist. Many people prefer to identify instead in national-origin terms such as Mexican American, Puerto Rican, or Cuban. In the Latino National Political Survey (LNPS) more respondents preferred to be called "American" than "Latino" (de la Garza et al. 1992).[6]

The fact that blacks were significantly more positive about immigration than whites is also of interest. This finding runs counter to other results (Espenshade and Calhoun 1993) and to the general perception that African Americans are one subgroup of the population that is likely to be apprehensive about higher immigration (Muller and Espenshade 1985). It may be that blacks' positive attitudes reflected a low concern about job competition and perhaps a new affinity based on socioeconomic status. At the same time, blacks may have developed a new cultural affinity for black immigrants while attempting to reclaim their own African heritage.

More than 1,200 New Jersey residents were interviewed in September 1994 concerning their attitudes about immigrants in the state. Among other things, each sampled individual was asked, "Would you like to see the number of immigrants in New Jersey increased, kept at the present level, or decreased?" A regression analysis of respondents' answers to this question against their demographic and socioeconomic characteristics generally supported the cultural affinity/ethnic solidarity hypothesis. Blacks, Asians, and Hispanics were all significantly more likely than non-Hispanic whites in New Jersey to prefer the same or a higher number of immigrants. The Asian effect was especially large and significant (Espenshade 1997).

Finally, Espenshade and Belanger (1997) explored what is known about attitudes and reactions toward Mexican migration to the United States. Two broad conclusions emerge from their analysis of public opinion surveys conducted over more than three decades. One is that Latin American and

Caribbean migrants in general, and Mexican migrants in particular, rank somewhere near the bottom in terms of how Americans view immigrants from different parts of the world. European immigrants are most favored, and Asians fall in the middle. In comparison with Latin American migrants, Asian immigrants are perceived to be less likely to use welfare or to commit crimes, and more likely to work hard, to have strong family values, and to do well in school. Only in terms of being overly competitive are Asians viewed less favorably than Latino migrants. Although the American public feels that the United States is admitting too many migrants from both Latin American and Asian countries, they are more likely to feel this way about Hispanic migrants.

Second, individuals are substantially more concerned about problems surrounding illegal migration than they are about legal immigration. They feel that the federal government can and should be doing more to control the flow of undocumented migrants into the country. By margins of roughly nine to one, Americans believe that stricter control of our borders and coastlines is a good idea. But support begins to waver once specific measures are introduced. Overall, there seems to be a policy tradeoff between measures that are effective and those that will receive broad approval. Many measures that might be expected to cut rather deeply into illegal immigration are seen by the American public as too harsh and are not supported.

NEW FINDINGS

The poll results presented in this chapter are based on data from the Public Opinion Location Library (POLL) database, a comprehensive online retrieval system for polling data provided by Dialog Information Services and compiled from survey data collected by the Roper Center for Public Opinion Research at the University of Connecticut. POLL currently contains the full text and complete responses to more than 230,000 survey questions.[7] In the past, the POLL database contained only the aggregate distribution of responses to survey items. New information is being added, however, that allows users to see the survey results broken down to the level of race, ethnicity, gender, age, education, geographic location in the United States, and political party affiliation. As of September 1996, these detailed breakdowns were available for more than half the public opinion online surveys from January 1995 forward. Given the orientation of other chapters in this volume around new Mexico-U.S. research, we break out the responses of Hispanic individuals whenever possible and compare them with those of all sample members.

Specifying keywords relating to Mexico or Mexican and to immigration, migration, or migrant netted fewer than two dozen questions that had appeared on national public opinion polls between 1979 and 1997. Many of these concerned how respondents thought the North American Free Trade Agreement (NAFTA) would affect Mexican migration to the United States. Because this information was insufficient to support an analysis, we broadened the search to include such other identifiers as Hispanic, Latin American, Latino, illegal, and welfare, and we eliminated any time constraints on survey dates.

Our main results are shown in a set of appendix tables. They are based on national surveys conducted by 20 polling organizations during a 30-year period between the mid-1960s and 1997, with an emphasis on data collected since 1990. The findings are grouped into three broad categories: the perceived economic consequences of immigration, policies toward legal and illegal immigration, and the relative importance of immigration issues. Six different issues are explored in the appendix tables, encompassing 12 separate survey questions. In many instances, the same (or nearly the same) question was asked several times, making it possible to identify trends in the data.

Perceived Economic Consequences of Immigration

Two central concerns surrounding the economic consequences of U.S. immigration are that immigrants have adverse labor market and fiscal impacts on natives (Smith and Edmonston 1997). It is often said that immigrants take jobs away from native workers and/or lower the wages natives can earn. Moreover, on the fiscal side, some claim that immigrants are a burden on native taxpayers because immigrants use more in publicly provided services than they pay for with their taxes. There also is evidence from both local and national opinion polls that Americans have more negative assessments about immigration when they believe that immigrants harm the employment and earnings opportunities of natives and that immigrants are a fiscal drain on natives (Espenshade and Calhoun 1993; Espenshade and Hempstead 1996; Espenshade 1997). These issues are explored on a national scale in questions 1 to 4.

Question 1 concerns whether American adults believe that today's immigrants are competing for jobs with natives. A minority of respondents feels that immigrants take jobs from American citizens, whereas half or more believe that immigrants are filling jobs that natives do not want. Sample individuals who identified themselves as Hispanic are less likely than all respondents to perceive job market competition. Somewhere between one-quarter and one-third of Hispanic individuals feel that immigrants are labor market substitutes for natives. In general, Hispanics have more positive assessments than all respondents about the labor market impact of immigrants. These findings are consistent with a cultural affinity hypothesis.[8]

Question 2 rephrases question 1 in terms of the labor market impact of *illegal* or undocumented migrants. Americans are more likely to believe that illegal immigrants are competing with natives, but the proportions are not overwhelming. Between one-half and 70 percent of all respondents view undocumented migrants as labor market competitors with native workers. Results in the last column appear to be an anomaly, but one needs to consider the qualifiers added to the kinds of jobs—"menial" and "good." It may be that poll participants are reacting to the kinds of jobs that undocumented migrants have, rather than to the question of job competition. The data in question 2 are older than those in question 1, and this fact may also have something to do with the different patterns observed in the responses.

Most empirical research has been unable to detect large labor market effects, either positive or negative, associated with immigration. The literature has been ably summarized by Borjas (1994) and by Friedberg and Hunt (1995). The main conclusion, based largely on cross-sectional data, is that there are only "modest effects of immigrants on natives' labor market outcomes" (Friedberg and Hunt 1995, 35). A potentially important qualifier has been added by Manson, Espenshade, and Muller (1985); Filer (1992); Frey (1995); and White and Hunter (1993). It may be the case that some natives are displaced by foreign workers, but if these native workers move out of high immigrant-impact areas to labor markets where they perceive better opportunities, then cross-sectional studies may fail to detect negative wage or employment effects. Economists have argued that native labor flows across regions dilute the adverse labor market effects of immigration (Borjas, Freeman, and Katz 1996) and that, if these effects were properly accounted for, the large-scale immigration of less-skilled workers may explain perhaps one-third of the recent relative decline in the wages of less-educated native workers (Borjas 1996).

A second topic of economic consequence concerns the fiscal impact of immigrants. How much do immigrants pay in taxes to federal, state, and local governments, how large are the benefits immigrants receive in return, and how do the two amounts compare within various jurisdictions? Some attitudinal evidence on these issues is provided in questions 3 and 4. Respondents are asked in question 3 whether America can still "afford" to keep its doors open to newcomers. Typically, small majorities feel that America should continue to keep the door open to immigrants. Responses are not drastically different whether the question is framed in terms of all immigrants or just legal immigrants. In this instance, responses of Hispanic participants are quite similar to those of all respondents.

Perceptions about immigrants' fiscal effects are also tapped in question 4, although the wording of the primary question combines elements of both job competition and fiscal effects. A slight majority of all respondents tends to view immigrants today as a burden on the United States. The question asked in the March 1996 Princeton Survey Research Associates (PSRNEW) poll elicited a large fraction of "don't knows," but the last part of the question (". . . by using up more than their fair share of tax dollars and government services") requires persons to make a technical judgment that many respondents may have felt incapable of making. The last column in question 4 comes closest to raising a specific fiscal impact issue. There is again a high proportion of respondents who say "don't know."[9] The data seem to indicate that individuals are better able to respond to questions that are generally worded than to narrower matters that may be perceived as too esoteric. In contrast to all respondents, Hispanic sample members typically feel that immigrants strengthen the United States. Here, then, is another instance in which Latinos have more optimistic evaluations.

Numerous fiscal impact studies exist. Using census data, Borjas (1994) found that immigrants were slightly less likely than natives to receive cash welfare benefits in 1970, but that immigrant households were overrepresented among the welfare population by 1990 (the fraction of immigrant households receiving welfare was 1.7 percentage points higher than the fraction of native households—9.1 versus 7.4 percent). Moreover, tracking immigrant cohorts over time revealed that immigrants "assimilate into welfare" the longer they are in the United States. Panel data for 1984 to 1991 from the Survey of Income and Program Participation showed little difference between natives and immigrants in the probability of receiving cash welfare benefits, but a larger native-immigrant differential emerged when other programs were included (Borjas and Hilton 1996). The fraction of immigrant households receiving some kind of public assistance was 50 percent larger than the native fraction (21 versus 14 percent).

Much less work has gone into examining the *net* fiscal costs of migrants (Espenshade 1996). Fix and Passel (1994) assert that "Contrary to the public's perception, when all levels of government are considered together, immigrants generate significantly more in taxes paid than they cost in services received" (p. 57). These effects are not uniformly distributed across all levels of government. Immigrant households appear to be a fiscal asset only for the federal government. Revenues and expenditures are more or less equal for state governments, and it is typically at the local level where immigrants are the greatest fiscal drain (Rothman and Espenshade 1992; Smith and Edmonston 1997). In some states, both immigrant and native households receive more benefits than they pay for with taxes, but the negative effects associated with immigrant households are greater than those for natives, especially at the local govern-ment level (Garvey and Espenshade 1997).

Legal and Illegal Immigration

The distinction between legal and undocumented migration becomes impor-tant when the focus is on Mexico, because an estimated 40 percent of Mexican immigrants in the United States are here without authorization. Moreover, Mexico and illegal immigration are highly intertwined in the public's mind. In a March 1995 survey, for example, one-third of those interviewed said that ille-gal immigration into the United States was their "greatest worry about the future of Mexico" (Espenshade and Belanger 1997).

Questions 5 and 6 ascertain the public's attitudes toward legal and illegal immigration. To begin with, it is interesting to note that immigration is labeled for respondents as a "problem." When respondents are asked their views about legal immigration in question 5, answers are more or less evenly distributed across all four response categories. If "major" and "moderate" categories are grouped and if "minor" and "no problem" are combined, then the distribution of Hispanic responses is quite similar to that for all responses. Within these aggregations, however, Hispanics are less likely than all adults to see legal immigration as a problem.

Respondents are asked in question 6 how problematic they think illegal immigration is. When thinking about legal versus illegal immigration, Americans are more than twice as likely to say that illegal immigration is a major problem. Roughly two-thirds of all respondents see illegal immigration as a major problem.[10] Unauthorized migration as a "moderate" problem is the next most common response. Very few respondents had no opinion. Moreover, as illustrated by the *Los Angeles Times* polls, responses are remark-ably consistent when question wording is constant. In contrast to the response patterns for legal immigration, Hispanic respondents are just as likely as all respondents to view illegal immigration as either a major or moderate prob-lem. This could be because undocumented immigration, much of it from Mexico or otherwise from Latin America, stigmatizes Hispanic members of the U.S. population whether they themselves are legal or not.[11]

Opinion polls taken during 1995 and 1996 on the subject of illegal immi-gration reveal that, when asked about the legal status of today's immigrants, more people believe that the majority of immigrants in the United States are here illegally.[12] They also suggest that most of the American public feels that the country is losing ground against the problem of unauthorized immigra-tion and that the flow of illegal immigrants will increase over the next decade, that nearly 90 percent of registered voters would like to see President Clinton "crack down" on illegal immigration during his second term, and that nearly everyone feels that it is the responsibility of the federal government to control illegal immigration. Other evidence suggests that Americans feel that the United States has a problem with border security, that the federal government should and can be doing more to cope with the problem, and that the public is willing to support doing more. On the other hand, attitudes are often ambivalent. Whereas many Americans support the general principle of controlling illegal immigration, this support sometimes wavers when respondents are confronted with specific tactics (Espenshade and Belanger 1997).

Some of these tactics include patrolling U.S. borders more strictly, adding more Border Patrol agents, erecting fences in high-traffic areas, digging ditches, building a wall along the border, and charging a small toll or user fee to enter the country. Other measures that have been discussed or implemented include employer sanctions, amnesty programs, and the use of national identification cards. In November 1994, voters in California tried to take the control of undocumented immigration into their own hands by passing Proposition 187 by a 3 to 2 margin. This initiative denies public education, health care (except emergency medical services), and social services to undocumented migrants. Moreover, the failed Gallegly amendment to the 1996 immigration reform bill that was approved by Congress in September 1996 would have permitted school districts to deny public schooling to undocumented immigrant schoolchildren. Proposition 187 and the Gallegly amendment assume that many undocumented migrants come to the United States to take advantage of the social welfare system and that illegal immigration could be curbed if undocumented migrants were denied substantial access to these benefits.

Question 7 asks respondents whether it is fair to characterize recent immigrants to the United States as welfare prone. This question does not distinguish between legal and unauthorized immigrants. Nevertheless, in both the 1985 and the 1993 Yankelovich surveys, more than half of all survey participants agreed with this depiction of U.S. migrants. But respondents differentiated sharply between Asian and Latin American immigrants. The latter are thought to be much more likely to end up on welfare.

In question 8 the American public is asked how it feels about measures such as those specified by Proposition 187 that would deny education, health care, and other social services to illegal immigrants. The American public generally supports these measures, and support appears to grow over the period covered (compare answers to the July 1993 and July 1995 Gallup surveys when the identical question was asked). On the other hand, the degree of support depends on how a specific question is phrased; it is strongest when couched in terms of denying welfare and weaker when only schools and hospitals are mentioned. References to denying "public assistance" garner levels of support intermediate between "welfare" and "schools and hospitals."

Furthermore, support for measures denying social services to illegal immigrants weakens whenever the prospect of harming children is raised and strengthens if adults only appear to be affected (compare question wording in table notes *e* and *f*). Some of the lukewarm enthusiasm for these policies that was evident during August and September of 1996 may be related to negative publicity that surrounded debate and passage of the welfare reform bill in August 1996. Although enacted welfare reforms primarily affect legal U.S. immigrants, these issues may be easily confused in the minds of many people. Finally, with the exception of the January 1995 ABC poll, Hispanic respondents are considerably less supportive of denying social services to illegal immigrants than are all respondents. There is also an apparent trend; a gap between all respondents and the subsample of Hispanic survey participants emerges in a second ABC poll in January 1995 and continues to widen through the August 1996 ABC News/ *Washington Post* poll, when the likelihood of Latinos supporting these measures is just one-half of that for all Americans (23 percent versus 49 percent).

Dramatic changes are in store for U.S. immigrants as a result of federal welfare and immigration reform legislation enacted in August and September of 1996. The thrust of these reforms is to deny legal immigrants access to means-tested public benefits to which they had previously been entitled and to reduce eligibility by tightening criteria (Espenshade and Huber forthcoming). Respondents are asked in question 9 how they feel about measures to deny welfare to legal immigrants as part of a set of measures to reform the federal welfare system. Answers appear to depend on question wording, because support for the general proposal fluctuates between 37 and 82 percent. Respondents seem most opposed to blanket prohibitions that make no exceptions (see table notes *h* and *k*), and more supportive when questions are worded to differentiate between deserving and undeserving immigrants. Persons who appear to the general public to be most deserving are immigrants who work hard and pay taxes and those who have become U.S. citizens. Having lived in the United States for at least five years also serves as an important qualifier (compare table note *c*). Overall, the American public is most supportive of welfare cuts to legal immigrants if these cuts are targeted on immigrants who have not become U.S. citizens and who have lived in the United States for fewer than five years.

The highest level of support for cutting benefits to legal immigrants (82 percent) was registered in the August 1996 *Los Angeles Times* survey, but the question wording suggests that not all of the support has to do with immigration provisions.

In comparison with all respondents, Hispanic respondents typically profess either the same or lower levels of agreement with welfare cuts for legal immigrants. There does not appear to be an obvious explanation for why the Latino support is sometimes equal to and sometimes less than the support registered by all Americans. For example, question wording in both table notes *a* and *i* refers to denying welfare to noncitizens. In the former case, Hispanic support is much less than that for the general public, whereas in the latter instance the two groups are more similar.

Relative Importance of Immigration Issues

The evidence presented so far suggests that the American public views immigration, and especially undocumented or illegal immigration, as a serious problem facing the United States, that it believes the federal government has the responsibility to do something about the problem, and that the public wants the government to take stronger action. At the same time, it is important to understand that opinion polls usually elicit such levels of support when the word "immigration" is specifically mentioned in a question, especially if reference is also made to "illegal" immigration or if immigration is characterized as a "problem." It is instructive to know how the American public evaluates the seriousness of immigration issues relative to other problems Americans face. These matters are taken up in this section.

In questions 10 to 12, respondents are faced with a series of open-ended questions designed to assess the relative importance of a variety of potentially important issues. No specific cues are provided for the significance of immigration. The importance of immigration issues is now cast in a dramatically different light. Immigration typically ranks lower than "don't know" when respondents are asked in question 10 about the "most important problem" facing the United States today. Moreover, there is no obvious trend in the percentage of respondents who think immigration is the most important problem. Crime is generally perceived to be the number-one issue, followed by concerns over jobs and the state of the economy, and then by high taxes and government spending. One of these three issues is usually mentioned by roughly half of all respondents as being most important. There is some evidence that concerns over moral decline in America have become more salient to the general public.

Question 11 narrows the focus of question 10 to that part of the country where the respondent lives. The dominance of the crime issue is clearly evident at the beginning of the period. By November 1996 its importance is almost halved, but it continues to be the single most important issue. Jobs and the economy, along with taxes and government spending, appear to have gained in significance. However, when all three issues are combined, their collective importance has decreased only slightly, from 58 percent to 52 percent of respondents citing one of them as the number-one problem. A miscellaneous collection of smaller issues grouped into the "Other" category has gained in prominence. Once again, immigration commands little attention as the number-one problem; roughly five times as many respondents instead said "don't know."

In question 12 the framing of the question is narrowed even more to include the most important problems "that you and your family are most concerned about." But the overall pattern of responses is unchanged. Crime and jobs vie for top billing, and taxes and government spending come in third place. Together, these three issues contend for a relatively stable fraction (between 50 and 60 percent) of all responses. Immigration issues are barely mentioned and exhibit no discernible trend.

DISCUSSION

Our examination of contemporary American attitudes toward U.S. immigration points to three main conclusions. First, attitudes often appear ambivalent. Sharply different responses can be triggered to seemingly similar questions by slight changes in question wording. In particular, some words or phrases appear to have acquired symbolically important meanings to many Americans, and the invocation of these phrases can predispose respondents to react in predictable ways. Our analysis has identified at least four critical axes: (1) children versus adults as targeted populations, (2) legal versus illegal immigrants as potentially affected groups, (3) education and health benefits versus welfare benefits, and (4) citizens versus noncitizens. In each of these paired comparisons, the category or group mentioned first seems to have acquired a quasi-protected status. Proposals to cut back on immigration flows or on benefits to immigrants typically receive less support when they are perceived as primarily affecting children, legal immigrants, education and health benefits, and citizens. Conversely, these measures are likely to receive more positive responses when they are viewed as targeting adults only, welfare benefits, illegal immigrants, and noncitizens.

Second, the comparisons between the responses of all Americans and the subsamples of Hispanic Americans reveal that Latinos usually have either the same or more positive assessments about immigration and its consequences than does the general public. This evidence lends additional support to the cultural affinity/ethnic solidarity hypothesis whereby respondents who have the closest ethnic and/or cultural ties to immigrants are expected to exhibit the strongest pro-immigrant attitudes.

Finally, after examining the relevance of public opinion to U.S. immigration policy, Pascual-Moran (1987) concluded that foreign policy considerations are preeminent over public opinion, especially when the latter is not tightly organized into well-defined and powerful pressure groups; that cumulative public opinion has a greater impact on the policy process than do sporadic manifestations of public concern; and that the state of the economy, particularly as it relates to unemployment, has an effect on policymakers and on the public's opinion on immigration matters. Since the 1970s, U.S. public opinion on immigration has not been well organized or effectively articulated. In fact, as Harwood (1986) observed, "What is significant about the current neorestrictionism is the fact that the public's attitude toward immigration policy is both inconsistent, especially on the issue of illegal immigration, and lacking in intensity" (p. 205). Our analysis supports Harwood's conclusions. Despite professing a strong concern with immigration issues, especially when illegal immigration is cued as a problem for survey respondents, the general public is substantially less worried about immigration than it is about crime, job opportunities, and family economic security. Perhaps the most sobering finding in this study is that immigration ranks below "don't know" among the most important problems facing the United States today.

At the beginning of this chapter, we noted that the volume of both legal and undocumented immigration to the United States is running at or close to historic levels. At the same time, the United States was at a low point during the early 1990s in terms of public support for further immigration and immigrant-related services. It may seem difficult to reconcile the apparent lack of fit between public opinion and public policy in the area of immigration.

There does not appear to be a discrepancy, however, with regard to undocumented immigration. Our earlier poll results showed that the American public believes illegal immigration is a serious problem and wants the federal government to do more to control illegal entry. Although the success of its policies can be debated, the U.S. Congress has made an effort during the past decade to reduce illegal immigration. First in the 1986 Immigration Reform and Control Act and then in the 1996 Illegal Immigration Reform and Immigrant Responsibility Act, Congress authorized expanded resources for the U.S. Border Patrol, for locating and deporting undocumented migrants who had settled in the U.S. interior, and for new employer sanctions programs whereby it became unlawful for the first time for employers knowingly to hire undocumented migrants.

Moreover, the 1996 welfare reform act (also known as the Personal Responsibility and Work Opportunity Reconciliation Act) made major changes in noncitizen eligibility for welfare by reforming the entitlement policy for poor families and imposing new limits on alien access to welfare and other social services. Most of these restrictions apply to new immigrants who come to the United States after August 1996, but some affect current immigrants as well. Under the terms of the welfare reform bill as originally enacted, the total cost savings to the federal government from reduced eligibility for immigrants are estimated at $20 to 25 billion for the six-year period between 1997 and 2002. This is approximately 45 percent of the projected $54 billion savings from the entire welfare reform bill (Espenshade, Baraka, and Huber 1997).[13] State-led initiatives, such as California's Proposition 187, are also consistent with public sentiment to reduce immigrant-related services.

If there is any inconsistency between public opinion and immigration policy, it is with respect to legal immigration. But even here the facts are open to several interpretations. It is not obvious whether the low support for immigration during the early 1990s that is shown in Figure 12.1 pertains to total, legal, or illegal immigration. Survey questions underlying Figure 12.1 are typically framed in terms of immigration in general, without specifying legal or illegal, although we know from other polling results that most Americans mistakenly believe that the majority of U.S. immigrants are here illegally. One interpretation of the trends in Figure 12.1, then, is that the public is currently exhibiting low support primarily for illegal immigration.

If this interpretation is correct, then a liberal legal immigration policy would not be extraordinary. We have already observed that people do not react to legal and illegal immigration in the same way. Appendix questions 1 and 2 show that the public regards illegal immigrants as more likely than legal immigrants to be competing for jobs with native workers. And questions 5 and 6 indicate that survey participants are more likely to view illegal immigration as a serious problem than legal immigration. Under the circumstances, current U.S. immigration policy, which aims to close the back door to illegal immigration while holding open the front door to legal immigration, may be largely consistent with public attitudes.

But even if we were to suppose that Figure 12.1 is reflecting currently low support for both illegal and legal immigration, the resulting incongruity with an expansive legal immigration policy may nevertheless be understandable. We know from Harwood (1986) and Pascual-Moran (1987) that public opinion may not always be relevant when Congress formulates immigration policy because foreign policy considerations frequently dominate over public opinion, public opinion about immigration is often ambivalent and lacking in intensity, and pro-immigration interest groups are able to make their voices heard over those of the general public. The results in this paper substantiate the conclusions that American attitudes concerning immigration are frequently soft and malleable and that they are not always strongly held.

This last observation raises a final question. If people commonly rank immigration low on a list of priorities, then why has immigration policy had such high visibility? There are several possible responses. First, there are numerous well-organized interest groups at both ends of the ideological spectrum whose existence depends on keeping immigration issues alive. Second, Congress may be misreading public opinion on immigration. The salience of immigration issues in opinion polls is usually greatest when respondents are prompted to think about immigration as an issue, especially if immigration is characterized for survey participants as "illegal" or a "problem." But without these specific cues, most Americans will not readily identify immigration issues as those issues about which they care the most. Third, immigration has sometimes been seized on by politicians to symbolize the high cost of government. Recent debates in Congress over welfare reform or, at the state level, over the cost of providing public schooling to illegal immigrant children provide evidence for this practice. At the same time, public opinion is more susceptible to manipulation when the economy is performing poorly. Now that the economy has turned around (and more aliens are applying for citizenship under threat of losing their access to means-tested public benefit programs), governors and mayors are either toning down their anti-immigrant rhetoric or competing to celebrate the immigrant experience. Finally, immigration has sometimes been seized on by the media to symbolize the failure of U.S. immigration policy. Televised images of the bombing of the World Trade Center, the disgorging of hundreds of illegal Chinese immigrants after the *Golden Venture* ran aground, and undocumented migrants climbing walls and crawling through fences along the Mexico-U.S. border evoke threats to U.S. sovereignty that have perhaps higher perceived significance in the aftermath of the Cold War.

APPENDIX

ABBREVIATIONS FOR APPENDIX TABLES

ABC: ABC News
ABCWP: ABC News/*Washington Post*
CBS: CBS News
CBSNYT: Columbia Broadcasting System/*New York Times*
GALLUP: Gallup Organization
KRC: K.R.C. Communications Research
LAT: *Los Angeles Times*
MELL: The Tarrance Group, and Mellman, Lazarus and Lake
NBC: Hart and Teeter Research Companies
NBCWSJ: Hart and Teeter Research Companies
NYT: *New York Times*
ORC: Opinion Research Corporation
PSRA: Princeton Survey Research Associates
PSRNEW: Princeton Survey Research Associates
SCRIPP: Scripps Howard News Service/Ohio University
TARR: Tarrance Group and Lake Research
WASHP: *Washington Post*
YANK: Yankelovich, Skelly and White
YANKCS: Yankelovich Clancy Shulman
YANKP: Yankelovich Partners, Inc.

APPENDIX TABLE 12.1

Job Competition – Question 1

NYT, CBSNYT, PSRNEW: Do you think immigrants coming to this country today mostly take jobs away from American citizens, or do they mostly take jobs Americans don't want?

	NYT 12/95 (%)	CBSNYT 2/96 (%)	PSRNEW 3/96[a] (%)
All Respondents			
Take jobs from American citizens	36	39	21
Take jobs Americans don't want	55	51	65[b]
Both (vol.)	—	7	—
Don't know	10	3	14
N	1,265	1,223	500
Hispanic Respondents			
Take jobs from American citizens	26	33	
Take jobs Americans don't want	72	64	
Both (vol.)	—	0	
Don't know	2	4	
N	69	62	

[a] "Thinking about the immigrants who have moved into your community in recent years, what effect (if any) do you think these recent immigrants are having on job opportunities for you and your family members? Are they making things better, making things worse, or not making much difference either way?"

[b] Includes "better" (5 percent) and "not much difference" (60 percent).

APPENDIX TABLE 12.2
Job Competition – Question 2

LAT, YANKCS: Do you think illegal aliens take jobs that nobody wants, or do you think they take jobs away from Americans who need them?

	LAT 10/80 (%)	LAT 3/81 (%)	YANKCS 7/86[b] (%)[c]	YANKCS 7/86[d] (%)
All Respondents				
Take jobs nobody wants	39	40	26	70
Compete with Americans	52	48	71	16
Some of both (vol.)	—	—	—	10
Not sure	9[a]	12	3	3
N	2,853	1,681	1,017	1,017

[a] Includes 1% who refused to answer.

[b] "Illegal aliens often come to this country to find jobs. To what extent do you feel illegal aliens from Mexico take jobs away from American workers—a lot, sometimes, only a little, or not at all?"

[c] Take jobs nobody wants = only a little (21%) and not at all (5%). Compete with Americans = a lot (38%) and sometimes (33%).

[d] "Do you think that illegal aliens from Mexico mostly take menial jobs that American workers don't want, or do they mostly compete with American workers for good jobs?"

APPENDIX TABLE 12.3
Fiscal Impacts – Question 3

CBSNYT, ABCWP: Which comes closer to your opinion: (1) America should always welcome some immigrants, or (2) America cannot afford to open its doors to any newcomers?

	CBSNYT 10/95 (%)	CBSNYT 10/95 (%)	CBSNYT 2/96 (%)	ABCWP 3/96[a] (%)
All Respondents				
Welcome some	54	55	60	48
Cannot afford any	42	42	35	50
Don't know	4	3	5	2
N	1,077	1,269	1,223	1,512
Hispanic Respondents				
Welcome some	48	45	63	50
Cannot afford any	47	49	34	50
Don't know	6	6	3	0
N	31	33	62	72

[a] "The U.S. should always welcome some legal immigrants, or the U.S. can't afford any new legal immigrants."

APPENDIX TABLE 12.4

Fiscal Impacts – Question 4

PSRNEW, ABC, LAT: Please tell me which one of the following statements comes closer to your own view: Immigrants today strengthen our country because of their hard work and talents, or immigrants today are a burden on our country because they take our jobs, housing, and health care.

	PSRNEW 6/95 (%)	PSRNEW 3/96[a] (%)	ABC 5/96[c] (%)	LAT 8/96[d] (%)
All Respondents				
Strengthen	40	31	42	13
Burden	52	36	53	58
Both (vol.)	—	8	—	6
Don't know	8	25[b]	5	23
N	945	500	1,024	1,572
Hispanic Respondents				
Strengthen	56		53	
Burden	39		46	
Both (vol.)	—		—	
Don't know	6		1	
N	150		50	

[a] "On balance, do you think recent immigrants have done more to help your community with their hard work and talents or have done more to hurt your community by using up more than their fair share of tax dollars and government services?"

[b] Includes 5 percent of respondents who said their community had no recent immigrants.

[c] "Please tell me if you agree or disagree with the following statement: Immigrants take more from this country than they contribute to this country." Those who agree (disagree) were coded as "burden" ("strengthen").

[d] "Generally speaking, do you think that immigrants to the United States take more from the U.S. economy through social services and unemployment than they contribute through taxes and productivity or do they contribute more through taxes and productivity than they take through social services and unemployment, or haven't you heard enough about that yet to say?"

APPENDIX TABLE 12.5

Importance of Legal and Illegal Immigration – Question 5

LAT, YANKP: How big a problem is the amount of legal immigration into the United States? Is it a major problem, a moderate-sized problem, a minor problem or not a problem at all?

	LAT 9/93 (%)	YANKP 9/93[a] (%)	LAT 4/96 (%)	LAT 8/96 (%)
All Respondents				
Major problem	30	15[b]	21	29
Moderate problem	26	49	24	23
Minor problem	21	—	21	18
No problem	19	35	27	25
Not sure	4	1	6	5
N	1,491	1,108	1,374	1,572
Hispanic Respondents				
Major problem			11	
Moderate problem			35	
Minor problem			16	
No problem			33	
Not sure			5	
N			45	

[a] "Does the presence of legal aliens in this country concern you a great deal, somewhat, or not at all?"
[b] Great deal (15%), somewhat (49%), not at all (35%), not sure (1%).

APPENDIX TABLE 12.6

Importance of Legal and Illegal Immigration – Question 6

LAT, YANKP, PSRA: How big a problem is the amount of illegal immigration into the United States? Is it a major problem, a moderate-sized problem, a minor problem or not a problem at all?

	LAT 9/93 (%)	YANKP 9/93[a] (%)	PSRA 1/96[c] (%)	LAT 4/96 (%)	LAT 8/96 (%)
All Respondents					
Major problem	62	48[b]	35[d]	63	70
Moderate problem	22	40	41	21	18
Minor problem	10	—	22	10	7
No problem	4	12	—	3	2
Not sure	2	1	2	3	3
N	1,491	1,108	1,206	1,374	1,572
Hispanic Respondents					
Major problem			35[e]	66	
Moderate problem			38	17	
Minor problem			22	15	
No problem			—	2	
Not sure			6	0	
N			57	45	

[a] "Does the presence of illegal aliens in this country concern you a great deal, somewhat, or not at all?"

[b] Great deal (48%), somewhat (40%), not at all (12%), not sure (1%).

[c] "How important a problem for the country is illegal immigration?"

[d] One of the most important (35%), important, but not most important (41%), not too important (22%), don't know/refused (2%).

[e] One of the most important (35%), important, but not most important (38%), not too important (22%), don't know/refused (6%).

APPENDIX TABLE 12.7

Denying Social Services to Illegal Immigrants – Question 7

YANK, GALLUP, YANKP: I am going to read you some statements that are some-times made about people who have immigrated from other countries in the last ten years. Tell me, in general, whether you think that statement applies to immigrants moving here in the past ten years or does not apply. . . . End up on welfare.

	YANK 4/85 (%)	(Latin America) GALLUP 7/93[a] (%)	(Asia) GALLUP 7/93[b] (%)	YANKP 9/93 (%)
All Respondents				
Applies	59	60	38	54
Does not apply	21	27	53	30
Applies to some/not others	15	—	—	10
Not sure	5	13	9	5
N	1,014	1,002	1,002	1,108

[a] "Please tell me whether each of the following characteristics does or does not apply to immigrants from Latin American countries. . . . Often end up on welfare."
[b] "Please tell me whether each of the following characteristics does or does not apply to immigrants from Asian countries. . . . Often end up on welfare."

APPENDIX TABLE 12.8

Denying Social Services to Illegal Immigrants – Question 8

GALLUP, YANKP, SCRIPP, ABC, PSRA, NBC, NBCWSJ, ABCWP: Please tell me whether you would generally favor or oppose each of the following steps which have been proposed as a way of reducing illegal immigration into the U.S. . . . Not allow-ing illegal immigrants to use American schools and hospitals.

	GALLUP 7/93 (%)	YANKP 9/93[a] (%)	GALLUP 12/94[b] (%)	GALLUP 12/94[c] (%)	SCRIPP 1/95[d] (%)	ABC 1/95[e] (%)	ABC 1/95[f] (%)	GALLUP 6/95[g] (%)
All Respondents								
Favor/Agree	40	47	57	63	44	93	65	67
Oppose/Disagree	57	48	39	34	46	6	31	28
No opinion	3	6	4	4	10	1	4	5
N	1,002	1,108	1,016	1,016	1,022	1,145	1,145	1,311
Hispanic Respondents								
Favor/Agree						91	53	
Oppose/Disagree						9	40	
No opinion						0	7	
N						58	58	

APPENDIX TABLE **12.8** (CONTINUED)

Denying Social Services to Illegal Immigrants – Question 8

GALLUP, YANKP, SCRIPP, ABC, PSRA, NBC, NBCWSJ, ABCWP: Please tell me whether you would generally favor or oppose each of the following steps which have been proposed as a way of reducing illegal immigration into the U.S. . . . Not allowing illegal immigrants to use American schools and hospitals.

	GALLUP 7/95 (%)	PSRA 10/95[h] (%)	YANKP 5/96[a] (%)	NBC 8/96[i] (%)	NBCWSJ 8/96[i] (%)	ABCWP 8/96[j] (%)	LAT 9/96[k] (%)
All Respondents							
Favor/Agree	50	58	53	45	48	49	48
Oppose/Disagree	45	40	41	41	44	48	45
No opinion	4	2	6	14	8	3	7
N	801	2,000	1,011	819	1,203	1,514	1,522
Hispanic Respondents							
Favor/Agree	26		25		30	23	
Oppose/Disagree	68		69		65	77	
No opinion	6		6		5	0	
N	18		29		47	64	

[a] "Stop providing government health benefits and public education to illegal immigrants and their children."

[b] "Would you favor or oppose a proposal to eliminate all forms of public assistance, including education and health benefits, to all illegal immigrants and their children?"

[c] "Voters in California recently approved a proposal to eliminate those benefits (public assistance including education and health benefits) for illegal immigrants. Would you favor or oppose a similar proposal in your state?"

[d] "California has passed a law banning public school enrollment and government-provided medical care for the children of illegal immigrants. Would you like to see such a law passed for the entire nation?"

[e] "The government . . . should not provide welfare, or public assistance payments, to people from other countries who entered this country illegally."

[f] "The government . . . should not provide welfare, or public assistance payments, to illegal immigrants who have children that were born here."

[g] "Are you in favor of or opposed to eliminating free public education, school lunches, and other benefits to children of immigrants who are in the U.S. illegally?"

[h] "Illegal immigrants and their children should not be allowed to receive education, health and welfare benefits."

[i] "Do you think that the children of illegal immigrants . . . should not be permitted to attend U.S. public schools?"

[j] "Do you favor or oppose a law barring illegal immigrants from public schools, public hospitals and other state-run social services?"

[k] "Do you favor or oppose barring children of illegal immigrants from attending public schools?"

APPENDIX TABLE 12.9
Support for Welfare Reform – Question 9

MELL, LAT, GALLUP, KRC, PSRNEW, YANKP, CBSNYT: Do you favor or oppose the following suggestion to reform the welfare system: Deny welfare to legal immigrants?

	MELL 11/93 (%)	MELL 11/93[a] (%)	LAT 4/94[b] (%)	GALLUP 4/94[c] (%)	GALLUP 12/94[d] (%)	KRC 12/94[e] (%)
All Respondents						
Favor/Yes	37	69	54	69	56	64
Oppose/No	55	25	40	28	40	27
Don't know/ Refused	8	6	6	3	4	9
N	1,000	1,000	1,682	1,002	1,014	1,200
Hispanic Respondents						
Favor/Yes	40	36	42	52	39	63
Oppose/No	54	54	54	48	55	28
Don't know/ Refused	7	9	4	0	6	9
N	26	26	102	31	25	68

[a] "Deny welfare to legal immigrants until they become citizens."

[b] "In order to pay the cost of the job training and child care under welfare reform, some have proposed denying welfare benefits, with the exception of emergency medical care, to legal immigrants who are not American citizens, even if this would cause such people hardship. Do you favor or oppose this proposal?"

[c] "In order to pay for changes in the welfare system, would you favor or oppose each of the following: Cut all aid to immigrants who have entered the United States legally until they have lived here at least five years."

[d] "Now here are some possible changes to the welfare system. Please tell me whether you would favor or oppose each one: Cut all aid to immigrants who have entered the United States legally until they have lived here at least five years."

[e] "Several proposals have been made recently to change the welfare system in the United States. As I read each of the following, please tell me if you favor or oppose that proposal: Government should limit or deny welfare aid to noncitizens. This would include most legal immigrants as well as all illegal immigrants."

[f] "Do you favor or oppose . . . ending federal benefits to legal immigrants who are not U.S. citizens, even if they work and pay taxes?"

[g] "Please tell me whether you favor or oppose each of the following proposals . . . Making legal immigrants ineligible for most welfare benefits, such as food stamps and Medicaid."

[h] "Do you think immigrants who live in the United States legally should be ineligible to apply for welfare?"

[i] "Do you favor or oppose denying legal immigrants who are not American citizens the right to receive welfare benefits?"

[j] "As you may know, a welfare reform bill has just passed in Congress and President (Bill) Clinton said he will sign it. The legislation requires that welfare recipients work within two years of applying for benefits, it eliminates eligibility for most federal benefits for most legal immigrants until they become citizens, it requires able-bodied adults with no dependent children to work 20 hours per week in order to be eligible for food stamps, and it imposes a five-year lifetime cap on welfare benefits whether or not a person can find a job. Do you favor or oppose the new welfare reform bill?"

[k] "As you may know, last month a national welfare reform bill was signed into law. One of the provisions of the bill is that legal immigrants would stop getting government benefits, such as Medicaid, food stamps, and aid to the elderly. Do you approve or disapprove of this provision of the welfare reform bill that stops the benefits of legal immigrants?"

APPENDIX TABLE 12.9 (CONTINUED)

Support for Welfare Reform – Question 9

MELL, LAT, GALLUP, KRC, PSRNEW, YANKP, CBSNYT: Do you favor or oppose the following suggestion to reform the welfare system: Deny welfare to legal immigrants?

	PSRNEW 1/95[f] (%)	YANKP 3/95[g] (%)	CBSNYT 12/95[h] (%)	CBSNYT 8/96[i] (%)	LAT 8/96[j] (%)	LAT 9/96[k] (%)
All Respondents						
Favor/Yes	39	55	42	69	82	40
Oppose/No	56	40	54	27	14	54
Don't know/ Refused	5	5	5	4	4	6
N	757	800	1,111	1,166	1,572	1,522
Hispanic Respondents						
Favor/Yes		51	30	61		
Oppose/No		37	62	32		
Don't know/ Refused		11	8	7		
N		25	41	45		

APPENDIX TABLE 12.10

Immigration Issues in a Wider Context – Question 10

LAT, ORC, GALLUP, ABCWP, CBS, CBSNYT, WASHP, YANKP, ABC: What do you think is the most important problem facing this country today?

	LAT 6/93 (%)	LAT 9/93 (%)	ORC 1/94 (%)	GALLUP 1/95 (%)	ABCWP 3/95 (%)
All Respondents					
Immigration/Illegal aliens	*	*	*	1	*
Crime[a]	14	23	28	21	29
Jobs/Economic growth[b]	30	22	16	20	12
Taxes/Govt. spending[c]	14	9	4	15	6
Health care[d]	9	17	13	8	5
Poverty[e]	4	3	7	6	5
Moral decline[f]	7	5	10	8	10
Other[g]	20	18	18	24	28
Don't know	2	3	8	2	2
N	1,474	1,491	2,018	1,002	1,524

	CBS 6/95 (%)	GALLUP 7/95 (%)	CBSNYT 8/95 (%)	CBSNYT 10/95 (%)	WASHP 10/95 (%)
All Respondents					
Immigration/Illegal aliens	1	2	1	1	*
Crime[a]	21	23	18	20	27
Jobs/Economic growth[b]	16	17	21	19	10
Taxes/Govt. spending[c]	12	9	6	10	7
Health care[d]	8	4	9	12	7
Poverty[e]	5	5	5	4	6
Moral decline[f]	7	11	10	6	13
Other[g]	21	25	23	25	26
Don't know	9	4	7	2	4
N	977	801	1,478	1,269	839

* = less than 0.5 percent.

[a] Includes violence, drugs, uncontrolled youth, guns.

[b] Includes economy in general, unemployment, cost of living, inflation, recession.

[c] Includes federal budget deficit, federal debt.

[d] Includes hospitals, Medicare increases, senior citizen benefits.

[e] Includes hunger, homelessness.

[f] Includes ethics and society, government corruption, dissatisfaction with government, politicians.

[g] Includes environment and pollution, AIDS, race relations, abortion, godlessness, lack of leadership, foreign relations, foreign aid, family breakdown, war and peace, education, welfare reform, international trade, overpopulation, judicial system.

APPENDIX TABLE 12.10 (CONTINUED)

Immigration Issues in a Wider Context – Question 10

LAT, ORC, GALLUP, ABCWP, CBS, CBSNYT, WASHP, YANKP, ABC: What do you think is the most important problem facing this country today?

	GALLUP 1/96 (%)	GALLUP 5/96 (%)	CBSNYT 8/96 (%)	YANKP 9/96 (%)	ABC 1/97 (%)	GALLUP 1/97 (%)
All Respondents						
Immigration/ Illegal aliens	1	3	1	1	*	1
Crime[a]	13	19	15	19	29	25
Jobs/Economic growth[b]	14	19	16	11	15	17
Taxes/Govt. spending[c]	22	13	14	12	10	9
Health care[d]	7	5	6	5	3	5
Poverty[e]	5	3	3	3	7	6
Moral decline[f]	13	14	7	19	14	6
Other[g]	22	22	29	21	25	28
Don't know	4	5	9	8	0	6
N	1,039	1,001	1,138	2,080	1,206	1,005

APPENDIX TABLE 12.11

Immigration Issues in a Wider Context – Question 11

MELL, TARR: What do you think is the number one problem facing this part of the country today?

	MELL 8/94 (%)	MELL 10/94 (%)	MELL 4/95 (%)	MELL 1/96 (%)	TARR 11/96 (%)
All Respondents					
Immigration/Illegal aliens	1	1	1	1	2
Crime[a]	41	39	32	26	22
Jobs/Economic growth[b]	12	14	15	16	17
Taxes/Govt. spending[c]	5	6	11	14	13
Health care[d]	8	5	5	3	5
Poverty[e]	1	1	2	2	1
Moral decline[f]	8	8	9	12	9
Other[g]	15	21	19	20	23
Don't know	6	4	6	5	6
N	1,000	1,000	1,000	1,000	1,000

[a] Includes violence, drugs, uncontrolled youth, guns.

[b] Includes economy in general, unemployment, cost of living, inflation, recession.

[c] Includes federal budget deficit, federal debt.

[d] Includes hospitals, Medicare increases, senior citizen benefits.

[e] Includes hunger, homelessness.

[f] Includes ethics and society, government corruption, dissatisfaction with government, politicians.

[g] Includes racism, welfare reform, Bill Clinton, education, environment, growth and overdevelopment, abortion, AIDS, foreign affairs, child care, children's issues, agriculture.

APPENDIX TABLE 12.12

Immigration Issues in a Wider Context – Question 12

MELL, TARR: What do you think is the number-one problem facing this part of the country today—that is, what is the problem that you and your family are most concerned about?

	MELL 4/93 (%)	MELL 6/93 (%)	MELL 5/94 (%)	TARR 9/96 (%)	TARR 10/96 (%)
All Respondents					
Immigration/Illegal aliens	*	1	1	*	2
Crime[a]	12	22	43	20	23
Jobs/Economic growth[b]	33	27	17	21	16
Taxes/Govt. spending[c]	14	12	4	8	13
Health care[d]	11	10	6	5	7
Poverty[e]	1	2	2	1	1
Moral decline[f]	7	7	6	8	5
Other[g]	17	17	11	28	25
Don't know	3	3	8	6	5
N	1,000	1,000	1,000	1,000	1,000

* = less than 0.5 percent.

[a] Includes violence, drugs, uncontrolled youth, guns.

[b] Includes economy in general, unemployment, cost of living, inflation, recession.

[c] Includes federal budget deficit, federal debt.

[d] Includes hospitals, Medicare increases, senior citizen benefits.

[e] Includes hunger, homelessness.

[f] Includes ethics and society, government corruption, dissatisfaction with government, politicians.

[g] Includes racism, welfare reform, Bill Clinton, education, environment, abortion, foreign affairs, children's issues.

ACKNOWLEDGMENTS

Partial support for this research was provided by grants from the Andrew W. Mellon Foundation and the National Institute of Child Health and Human Development. The authors gratefully acknowledge the helpful comments of Michael Jones-Correa, Wayne Cornelius, Marcelo Suárez-Orozco, and other conference participants, as well as the capable technical assistance of Melanie Adams and Deanna Lewis.

NOTES

1. The previous record for a single decade was established between 1901 and 1910 when 8.8 million legal immigrants were admitted to the United States.

2. The dashed line in Figure 12.1 corresponds to the views of Hispanic respondents. Substantially smaller proportions of Hispanic respondents than of all respondents feel that U.S. immigration should be reduced.

3. Further corroboration for this interpretation is provided by recent poll data from New Jersey (Espenshade 1997). New Jersey residents who said they thought the number of immigrants in the state should be reduced were asked open-ended questions about the reasons for their views. The most common response related to fears that there are not enough jobs to go around and that immigrants take jobs away from native workers. Almost 40 percent of adults who preferred fewer immigrants cited this factor. Other important reasons related to concerns that New Jersey is already overcrowded and does not need more people (cited by 17 percent of respondents wanting fewer immigrants) and that immigrants place a welfare, social service, and educational burden on the state, causing taxes to rise (12 percent).

4. A progressive liberalization extends from the Refugee Act of 1980 to the 1986 Immigration Reform and Control Act that granted amnesty to almost 3 million former undocumented migrants and their dependents through to the Immigration Act of 1990 that increased the total number of legal immigrants entering the United States annually during fiscal years 1992 to 1994 to 714,000, excluding refugees (Papademetriou 1990). Efforts to reduce the volume of legal immigration in the last Congress by linking legal immigration reform with a popular bill to strengthen controls over undocumented migration failed when the two bills were uncoupled and legal immigration reform was taken off the legislative agenda.

5. The *gross* effects refer to the regression coefficients on the race and ethnic identifiers when the only other predictors in the model include respondents' demographic and

socioeconomic background characteristics. The *net* effects of race and ethnicity are measured after including additional variables for respondents' attitudes about the state of the macroeconomy, feelings of social and political alienation, indicators of an isolationist mentality on international economic matters and foreign policy, and attitudes about the consequences of immigration.

6. Moreover, immigration attitudes differ by national-origin group, citizenship status, and region of the country. Data from the LNPS show that clear majorities of Puerto Rican and Cuban respondents disagreed with the statement that preference should be given to immigrants from Latin America in U.S. immigration law, whereas Mexican Americans were more evenly split. On the other hand, the likelihood of agreeing with the proposition was significantly higher for noncitizens than for citizens. More than 70 percent of each of the Latino-origin groups, but especially Mexicans and Puerto Ricans, agreed that there are too many immigrants coming to the United States. Noncitizens were more likely to support the statement than citizens (de la Garza et al. 1992; de la Garza, Falcon, Garcia, and Garcia 1993). In a recent study of Latinos in New York, Florida, Texas, and California, there were large differences in Latino national-origin attitudes toward immigration across states. Mexican Americans in Texas are similar to Cubans, but in California, Mexicans and Puerto Ricans are more similar (Rodolfo de la Garza, personal communication, 19 February 1996).

7. Some of these pertain to immigration, but POLL covers the full spectrum of public-interest issues (for example, politics, government, public institutions, international affairs, business, social issues and attitudes, and consumer issues and preferences).

8. The empty space for Hispanic respondents beneath the March 1996 PSRNEW survey indicates that the POLL data do not separately identify Hispanic individuals.

9. The 1994 New Jersey immigration poll asked respondents, "Do you think that immigrants to New Jersey receive more in education, health, and other state benefits than they pay for with their taxes, or do they pay more taxes than they receive in benefits, or are the two amounts about the same?" Three of five respondents believed immigrants were a fiscal burden; only 6 percent refused to answer or said "don't know." When the same question was asked about illegal immigrants in New Jersey, the proportion characterizing immigrants as a burden rose to 67 percent, and 11 percent responded "don't know" (Espenshade 1997).

10. In addition, overwhelming proportions (85 percent) of respondents to a July 1993 Princeton Survey Research Associates poll believed that illegal immigration is a more serious problem for the United States today than in the past.

11. Further evidence that Americans indicate they consider illegal immigration to be a serious problem whenever interviewers provide specific cues for the issue is given by results from an October 1994 NBC News/*Wall Street Journal* survey. When

asked, "Which one or two of these issues will be most important to you in this year's (1994) elections for Congress . . . crime, welfare reform, jobs and economic growth, health care, taxes and government spending, illegal immigration, foreign affairs?" Twenty percent of participants mentioned illegal immigration. Crime, cited most often, was mentioned by 33 percent of respondents.

12. For example, 48 percent of respondents to a January 1995 Scripps Howard News Service poll believed that most immigrants in the United States are here illegally. Just 40 percent believed most immigrants are legal, and 12 percent had no opinion. Somewhat surprisingly, one-third of respondents in the same poll reported having known someone who was in this country illegally. Other polls also suggest that the American public vastly exaggerates the share of the U.S. foreign-born population that is in the country illegally (Espenshade and Hempstead 1996).

13. As a result of the balanced-budget agreement reached between Congress and the White House in 1997, many of the Supplemental Security Income benefits for current immigrants that were threatened by the welfare reform act are being restored.

REFERENCES

Borjas, George J. 1994. "The Economics of Immigration." *Journal of Economic Literature* 32(4): 1667–1717.

Borjas, George J. 1996. "The New Economics of Immigration." *Atlantic Monthly* 278 (November): 72–80.

Borjas, George J., Richard B. Freeman, and Lawrence F. Katz. 1996. "Searching for the Effect of Immigration on the Labor Market." *American Economic Review* 86(2): 246–251.

Borjas, George J., and Lynette Hilton. 1996. "Immigration and the Welfare State: Immigrant Participation in Means-Tested Entitlement Programs." *Quarterly Journal of Economics* 111(2): 575–604.

Briggs, Vernon M., Jr. 1995. "Immigration Policy Sends Blacks Back to the South." *The Social Contract* 5(4): 270–271.

Cain, Bruce, and Roderick Kiewiet. 1986. "California's Coming Minority Majority." *Public Opinion* 9 (February/March): 50–52.

Day, Christine L. 1989. U.S. Hispanics and immigration reform. Paper presented at the Annual Meeting of the Midwest Political Science Association, 13–15 April, Chicago, Illinois.

Day, Christine L. 1990. Ethnocentrism, economic competition, and attitudes toward U.S. immigration policy. Paper presented at the Annual Meeting of the Midwest Political Science Association, 5–7 April, Chicago, Illinois.

de la Garza, Rodolfo O. 1985. Mexican Americans, Mexican immigrants, and immigration reform. In *Clamor at the Gates*, ed. N. Glazer, 93–105. San Francisco: Institute for Contemporary Studies.

de la Garza, Rodolfo O., Louis DeSipio, F. Chris Garcia, John Garcia, and Angelo Falcon. 1992. *Latino Voices: Mexican, Puerto Rican, and Cuban Perspectives on American Politics*. Boulder, Colo.: Westview Press.

de la Garza, Rodolfo O., Angelo Falcon, and F. Chris Garcia. 1993. *Ethnicity and Attitudes Towards Immigration Policy: The Case of Mexicans, Puerto Ricans and Cubans in the United States*. Texas Population Research Center Paper no. 13.11. Austin: University of Texas.

de la Garza, Rodolfo O., Angelo Falcon, F. Chris Garcia, and John A. Garcia. 1993. "Attitudes Toward U.S. Immigration Policy: The Case of Mexicans, Puerto Ricans and Cubans." *Migration World* 21(2/3): 13–17.

Espenshade, Thomas J. 1996. *Fiscal Impacts of Immigrants and the Shrinking Welfare State*. Office of Population Research Working Paper no. 96-1. Princeton, N.J.: Princeton University.

Espenshade, Thomas J. 1997. Taking the pulse of public opinion toward immigrants. In *Keys to Successful Immigration: Implications of the New Jersey Experience*, ed. T. J. Espenshade, 89–116. Washington, D.C.: The Urban Institute Press.

Espenshade, Thomas J., and Maryann Belanger. 1997. U.S. public perceptions and reactions to Mexican migration. In *At the Crossroads: Mexican Migration and U.S. Policy*, ed. F. D. Bean, R. O. de la Garza, B. R. Roberts, and S. Weintraub, 227–261. New York: Rowman and Littlefield Publishers, Inc.

Espenshade, Thomas J., and Charles A. Calhoun. 1992. *Public Opinion Toward Illegal Immigration and Undocumented Migrants in Southern California*. Working Paper no. 92-2. Princeton, N.J.: Princeton University, Office of Population Research. March.

Espenshade, Thomas J., and Charles A. Calhoun. 1993. "An Analysis of Public Opinion Toward Undocumented Immigration." *Population Research and Policy Review* 12(3): 189–224.

Espenshade, Thomas J., and Katherine Hempstead. 1996. "Contemporary American Attitudes Toward U.S. Immigration." *International Migration Review* 30(2): 535–570.

Espenshade, Thomas J., and Gregory A. Huber. Forthcoming. Antecedents and consequences of tightening welfare eligibility for U.S. immigrants. In *Immigration, Citizenship, and the Welfare State: Germany and the United States in Comparison*, ed. H. Kurthen, J. Fijalkowski, and G. Wagner.

Espenshade, Thomas J., Jessica L. Baraka, and Gregory A. Huber. 1997. "Implications of the 1996 Welfare and Immigration Reform Acts for U.S. Immigration." *Population and Development Review* 23(4): 769–801.

Filer, Randall K. 1992. The effect of immigrant arrivals on migratory patterns of native workers. In *Immigration and the Work Force: Economic Consequences for the United States and Source Areas*, ed. G. J. Borjas and R. B. Freeman, 245–269. Chicago: The University of Chicago Press.

Fix, Michael, and Jeffrey S. Passel. 1994. *Immigration and Immigrants: Setting the Record Straight*. Washington, D.C.: The Urban Institute Press.

Frey, William H. 1995. The new geography of population shifts: Trends toward Balkanization. In *Social Trends*, 271–334. Vol. 2 of *State of the Union—America in the 1990s*, ed. R. Farley. New York: Russell Sage Foundation.

Friedberg, Rachel, and Jennifer Hunt. 1995. "The Impact of Immigrants on Host Country Wages, Employment and Growth." *Journal of Economic Perspectives* 9(2): 23–44.

Garvey, Deborah L., and Thomas J. Espenshade. 1997. State and local fiscal impacts of New Jersey's immigrant and native households. In *Keys to Successful Immigration: Implications of the New Jersey Experience*, ed. T. J. Espenshade, 139–172. Washington, D.C.: The Urban Institute Press.

Hansen, Kristin A., and Carol S. Faber. 1997. *The Foreign-Born Population: 1996*. Current Population Reports P20-494. Washington, D.C.: Government Printing Office. March.

Harwood, Edwin. 1983. "Alienation: American Attitudes Toward Immigration." *Public Opinion* 6 (June/July): 49–51.

Harwood, Edwin. 1985. How should we enforce immigration law? In *Clamor at the Gates*, ed. N. Glazer, 73–91. San Francisco: Institute for Contemporary Studies.

Harwood, Edwin. 1986. American public opinion and U.S. immigration policy. In *Immigration and American Public Policy* [Special issue], ed. R. J. Simon. *The Annals of the American Academy of Political and Social Science* 487 (September): 202–212. Beverly Hills: Sage Publications.

Jackson, Jacquelyne Johnson. 1995. "Competition Between Blacks and Immigrants." *The Social Contract* 5(4): 247–254.

Manson, Donald M., Thomas J. Espenshade, and Thomas Muller. 1985. "Mexican Immigration to Southern California: Issues of Job Competition and Worker Mobility." *Review of Regional Studies* 15(2): 21–33.

Miller, Lawrence W., Jerry L. Polinard, and Robert D. Wrinkle. 1984. "Attitudes Toward Undocumented Workers: The Mexican American Perspective." *Social Science Quarterly* 65 (June): 482–494.

Muller, Thomas, and Thomas J. Espenshade. 1985. *The Fourth Wave: California's Newest Immigrants*. Washington, D.C.: The Urban Institute Press.

Palmer, Douglas L. 1994. *Anatomy of an Attitude: Origins of the Attitude Toward the Level of Immigration to Canada*. Ottawa, Canada: Citizenship and Immigration Canada, Strategic Planning and Research. February 3.

Papademetriou, Demetrios G. 1990. *The Immigration Act of 1990*. Report prepared for the Bureau of International Labor Affairs, U.S. Department of Labor. Washington, D.C. December.

Pascual-Moran, Vanessa. 1987. The shadow of public opinion and various interlocking issues on U.S. immigration policy: 1965–1982. Unpublished Ph.D. dissertation, Columbia University.

Rothman, Eric S., and Thomas J. Espenshade. 1992. "Fiscal Impacts of Immigration to the United States." *Population Index* 58(3): 381–415.

Simon, Rita J. 1985. *Public Opinion and the Immigrant: Print Media Coverage, 1880–1980*. Lexington, Mass.: Lexington Books, D.C. Heath and Company.

Simon, Rita J., and Susan H. Alexander. 1993. *The Ambivalent Welcome: Print Media, Public Opinion and Immigration*. Westport, Conn.: Praeger.

Smith, James P., and Barry Edmonston, eds. 1997. *The New Americans: Economic, Demographic, and Fiscal Effects of Immigration*. Washington, D.C.: National Academy Press.

Sullivan, John. 1995. "Immigration and African Americans." *The Social Contract* 5(4): 259–261.

Tanton, John. 1995. "Back to the Back of the Bus?" *The Social Contract* 5(4): 239.

Tarrance and Associates. 1989. *Research Report: California Immigration Survey*. Houston, Texas. April.

Tienhara, N. 1974. *Canadian Views on Immigration and Population: An Analysis of Post-War Gallup Polls*. Ottawa: Information Canada.

U.S. Bureau of the Census. 1975. *Historical Statistics of the United States: Colonial Times to 1970*, Part I. Washington, D.C.: Government Printing Office.

U.S. Bureau of the Census. 1993. *The Foreign-Born Population in the United States: 1990*. Subject Report CP-3-1. Washington, D.C.: Government Printing Office. July.

U.S. Bureau of the Census. 1995. The Foreign-Born Population: 1994. Current Population Reports P20-486. Washington, D.C.: Government Printing Office. August.

U.S. Department of Justice. 1997. "Estimates of the Unauthorized Immigrant Population Residing in the United States: October 1996." *Backgrounder*. Washington, D.C.: Office of Policy and Planning, U.S. Immigration and Naturalization Service. January.

U.S. Immigration and Naturalization Service (INS). 1992. *Immigration Reform and Control Act: Report on the Legalized Alien Population*. M-375. Washington, D.C.: Government Printing Office. March.

U.S. Immigration and Naturalization Service (INS). 1997. *1995 Statistical Yearbook of the Immigration and Naturalization Service*. M-367. Washington, D.C.: Government Printing Office. March.

Warren, Robert, and Jeffrey S. Passel. 1987. "A Count of the Uncountable: Estimates of Undocumented Aliens Counted in the 1980 United States Census." *Demography* 24(3): 375–393.

White, Michael J., and Lori M. Hunter. 1993. *The Migratory Response of Native-Born Workers to the Presence of Immigrants in the Labor Market.* Working Paper Series 93-08. Providence, R.I.: Brown University, Population Studies and Training Center.

Commentary

Michael Jones-Correa, Harvard University

Since 1970, the numbers of new immigrants as a proportion of the U.S. population have doubled, from 4.8 to 9.7 percent in 1990, and to almost 11 percent in 1997. The single largest group of new immigrants is Mexican, accounting for 21.7 percent of the foreign-born population of the United States. The increase in immigration has been accompanied by a corresponding rise in public anxiety about immigration and its consequences. Politicians have played off this anxiety, raising the specter of a fragmenting American culture, a border out of control, and a sea of uncomprehending and incomprehensible immigrants, stubbornly keeping to their own language.

As Espenshade and Belanger point out, there is a puzzle here: They note Rita Simon's observation that the curious thing is that so many people have been admitted to the United States while there was so little enthusiasm for new immigration over such long periods of time (Simon 1985, xv). Since 1965 the United States has seen the liberalization of federal immigration policy at the same time as public opinion has become more restrictionist. Why is this?

The answer that Espenshade and his coauthors give (Espenshade and Calhoun 1993; and Espenshade and Belanger, this volume) is that three elements are key to understanding the puzzle. First, American attitudes toward immigration are often inconsistent or ambivalent. Second, opinions are not strongly held, even if they are negative. And third, pro-immigrant groups have been successful at capturing the attention of federal policymakers. In their chapter in this volume, Espenshade and Belanger focus on the first two elements, particularly on the inconsistency of the public's opinions on the immigration issue.

The authors analyze polling questions from national polls ranging from the 1960s to 1997, focusing in more detail on a collection of national surveys carried out from 1992 to 1996. Pulling together this polling data, they focus on three areas of questioning: queries on respondents' views of the perceived economic consequences of immigration; that is, what they thought the impact would be on earnings and jobs; respondents' views toward legal and illegal immigration; and respondents' relative ranking of the immigration issue compared with their other concerns. In general the findings in the current study are consistent with previous literature. The polls seem to indicate that the American public views immigration as a serious problem and wants stronger action from the federal government. The twist that Espenshade and Belanger add here is that when the public is asked to evaluate immigration as a problem relative to other issues, respondents end up ranking immigration very low on their scale of concerns.

The authors offer three conclusions for the reader to take away. First, they conclude that the symbolic import of words is key: The public responds more favorably to immigrant issues if they are perceived as concerning children, education or health benefits, or citizens. Conversely, respondents are more prepared to respond negatively if these same issues apply to adults, welfare benefits, and undocumented aliens. Second, Latinos tend to be more positive than other groups when evaluating immigration, though not dramatically so. This finding indicates support for the cultural affinity hypothesis. Third, anti-immigrant public opinion is not well organized and tends to be inconsistent. The public has negative views about immigration, but these rank low on their general ranking of concerns. I want to respond to all three of the authors' conclusions, though not necessarily in the order given.

Espenshade and Belanger's strongest conclusion is that anti-immigrant opinion is often ambivalent or inconsistent. However, it seems to me, particularly given Espenshade and Belanger's striking chart showing the match between unemployment rates and anti-immigrant sentiment, that public opinion is actually very consistent. As they note, since the early 1960s the rise in anti-immigrant sentiment has almost perfectly followed the unemployment rate. The two variables are highly correlated, which is presumably evidence for some kind of internal consistency to anti-immigrant opinion. However, while correlated, the one variable doesn't necessarily *predict* the other. Indeed, evidence of this kind of causal connection is weak: Why would unemployment drive anti-immigrant sentiment when the research so far indicates that immigration's effects on unemployment rates are minimal?

The authors also note that public opinion is ambivalent, and here I am much more in agreement. There are other values that come into play when people are asked to evaluate the immigration question. Espenshade and Belanger's first conclusion, on the importance of how the issue is slanted, is illuminating here. It makes a difference if we're talking about children versus adults, citizens versus noncitizens, and so forth, but the ambivalence here seems to be following a set of norms—that is, people are trying to make distinctions between "deserving" and "undeserving" immigrants. Americans, Espenshade and Belanger note, want to make distinctions in immigration policy: They want a more restrictive policy, but they are opposed to blanket provisions without any exceptions.[1]

This deserving/undeserving distinction goes far beyond immigrant politics. It has deep roots in historical debates about the right to protection under the government's umbrella (Skocpol 1992), as well as shading much of the discussion taking place today about social rights and welfare. For instance, in contemporary debates on welfare, Americans remain concerned about the poor but don't want to encourage a "culture of poverty" that encourages people to remain on the dole. The current solution seems to be to move people into workfare, a transitional phase between welfare and moving into full participation in the workforce (see Murray and Jackson 1986; Niskanen 1997).[2] Whatever its effectiveness as policy, workfare can be seen as an example of the American penchant for trying to find the balance between what they see as conflicting ends, as a compromise between compassion and responsibility.

Espenshade and Belanger's finding that people actually rank immigration quite low on their list of concerns is quite significant. When asked what their most important concern is, or to list several of their most important concerns, immigration barely appears on respondents' radar screens. I think this finding does a lot to answer the puzzle of why we have such high levels of immigration if so many people seem unhappy with it. It seems immigration policy is relatively insulated from public opinion to begin with, and that the general public, while unhappy with the policy, doesn't think it is of sufficient importance to get involved.

Immigration, then, is at the opposite end of the spectrum from issues like abortion, which mobilize voters around a particular question, at times to the exception of all others. Feelings in the abortion debate, for example, are often narrow, but deep. These single-issue partisans become engaged, for better or worse, in the body politic (see Verba, Scholzman, and Brady 1995, 392–415; Scott and Schuman 1988). Their volunteering, donations of money, and voting may all be driven by that same single issue. A politician's stand on the issue may swing a sizable number of votes in an election. Immigration, on the other hand, seems to engage the feelings of a broad segment of the public, but only in a very shallow way. The immigration issue is not enough to galvanize voters by itself—a realization that came too late, and at great cost, to both Pat Buchanan's and Governor Pete Wilson's campaign teams in the 1992 presidential race.

The combination of breadth and shallowness of feeling on the immigration issue creates an inherently unstable policy situation in which public opinion can be manipulated at little cost to politicians and policy can be made by relatively few players, since the majority of the public is on the sidelines. On the one hand, immigration policy is an area of technocratic expertise, driven by specialized staffs in Congress, lobbying groups, and the relevant government agencies. Deals can be struck involving a relatively small number of people, many of whom have worked with one another for years as they move through the revolving doors of Washington politics. Examples of this are the liberalizing 1965 Immigration and Nationality Act, the 1990 Immigration Act, and the battles through 1996 and 1997 over whether to exclude legal immigrants from Medicaid and welfare benefits. In the day-to-day business of politics, technocrats usually have the final say in shaping immigration law.

On the other hand, over the last century immigration has played an important symbolic function in American political rhetoric. Both proponents and detractors have used immigration to define a sense of American identity and nationalism. This is no less the case today. Immigration serves as mirror in which everyone sees their own reflection as American citizens. Of course everyone, seeing themselves, sees a different reflection. The symbolic role of immigration politics helps explain why immigration policy has had such high visibility in the media, and why certain politicians have tried to capitalize on the perceived public unhappiness with immigration. It also helps explain why immigration policy is so vulnerable to interpretation and to false impressions.

One of the questions that arises in the course of reading Espenshade and Belanger's chapter is why, given that so much of the public is presumably interested in the issue, are there so many misconceptions about immigrants and immigration? Why are stereotypes about immigrants, particularly Latin American immigrants, so prevalent? For instance, when respondents are asked to rank immigrants arriving to the United States from around the world, why are Mexicans ranked so persistently at the low end of the scale (Espenshade and Belanger, this volume)? Why do people believe Latin American immigrants are more likely than other immigrants to commit crimes and take advantage of welfare, and less likely to work hard, do well in school, and have strong family values? In part these views are likely related to another misperception: Espenshade and Belanger note that the 1995 and 1996 polls show that most people think that the vast majority of immigrants to the United States enter the country illegally. This is patently false. The ratio of illegal immigrants to documented permanent legal residents in the United States is at most one in five. One of the results of this false belief is that there has been a persistent concern over the last two decades, at times approaching hysteria, about "controlling the border" (see, for example, Peter Andreas' chapter in this volume on the symbolic politics of the border). Finally, most people seem to believe that immigrants are an economic drain, and specifically, that they take away American jobs. Actual research on this matter indicates that the net effect of immigration is probably close to neutral. In their reviews of the literature, Borjas (1994) and Friedberg and Hunt (1995) both conclude that job loss, if any, is minimal. The comprehensive National Academy of Sciences report (Smith and Edmonston 1997) on the effects of immigration comes to the same conclusion. Taken together, these misperceptions show a staggering amount of misinformation on the immigration issue.

These stereotypes exist and persist because the public immigration debate is often less about facts than about perceptions. The persistence of stereotypes raises questions about the role of opinion leaders and the media. The role these actors play is suggested by Espenshade and Belanger, who note that

> [public] attitudes often appear inconsistent. Sharply different responses can be triggered to seemingly similar questions by slight changes in question wording. In particular, some words or phrases appear to have acquired symbolically important meanings to many Americans, and the invocation of these phrases can predispose respondents to react in predictable ways.

The public is bombarded by ideologically and symbolically loaded rhetoric designed to sway them for or against immigration.[3]

Even Hispanics are not immune from these stereotypes, inflated arguments, xenophobic reactions, and protectionist sentiments. Though Espenshade and Belanger find that Latinos are generally equally or more favorable toward immigration than non-Hispanic whites, their findings are remarkably tepid. Espenshade and Belanger note that Hispanic support for immigration is "variable."[4] Indeed, other recent findings have suggested there is wide variance among Latinos' views on immigration, by class, by education, and by region (de la Garza 1985; de la Garza, Falcon, and Garcia 1993). That such variations should exist is not surprising. At least some Latinos are potentially competing with immigrants for the same jobs—or more to the point, *believe* they may be competing—so that economic concerns may outweigh ideological concerns and feelings of cultural commonalities. On the other hand, particularly for younger, better-educated Latinos, the feeling is that Hispanic Americans are all being tarred with the same brush: If all Latinos are going to be perceived as illegal immigrants, then for goodness' sake, we'd better defend immigrants, even if they are illegal. After all, if we are seen as them, then they are us.

There are times, then, when the rhetorical and symbolic aspects of the immigration debate overwhelm the backdoor politics of the technocrats. These moments are triggered by periods of economic uncertainty, as indicated by higher unemployment rates. While unemployment in itself is not caused by immigration, the uncertainty and anxiety of high unemployment periods open the door to the manipulation of immigration and other related symbolic issues, like English Only and Proposition 187 (Diamond 1996; Smith and Tarallo 1995; Citrin et al. 1990). That unemployment is not itself the cause of anti-immigrant sentiment is reflected in the absence of much of a relationship, since 1995, between the superficial indicators of economic well-being and public opinion on immigration. While the economy continues to record historically low inflation and unemployment figures, anti-immigrant feeling has not significantly fallen. Uncertainty and anxiety have persisted, in spite of low unemployment. However, anxiety can be driven by other sources of unease: concerns about job stability and the changing role of the worker in a globalizing economy, for instance, as well as unease about cultural issues like language, citizenship, and national identity. Espenshade and Hempstead find, for example, that anti-immigrant sentiment is associated with feelings of political alienation, economic pessimism, and casting a vote for antiestablishment politicians like Ross Perot in the 1988 and 1992 presidential elections (see Espenshade and Hempstead 1996, 550–553).

Some policymakers, like some of those failed candidates in the 1992 presidential race, may misread the public's stance on the immigration issue and believe that polls indicate a more fundamental discontent than is the case. A deeper understanding of the polling data (after reading Espenshade and Belanger, of course) would let them see that public opinion on immigration, while widely negative, is only an inch deep. But others take advantage precisely of the shallowness of the public's concerns, and may feel free to manipulate the symbolic aspects of the immigration debate—arrayed around language, nationalism, citizenship—in order to score points on what appears to them to be a low-cost valence issue. The symbolic politics of immigration might help explain why, even while the economy in the 1990s has been performing better than any time in the last four decades and unemployment is at historic lows, anti-immigrant sentiment remains quite high. Unemployment is linked only indirectly to anti-immigrant sentiment—the key variables are feelings of uncertainty and alienation, which, properly spun by opinion makers, then are used to target immigrants as symbolic scapegoats for deeper anxieties in the American republic.

Espenshade and Belanger's comprehensive examination of polling data across time lays the foundation for a more nuanced discussion of the relationship of public opinion to the immigration debate. Their findings that respondents indicate that they are dissatisfied with current levels of immigration, but that they rank immigration low on their ranking of overall concerns, suggest that public opinion on immigration issues is broad but shallow. I suggest in this essay that the shallowness of public opinion on these questions leaves the field open to technocratic and symbolic approaches to immigration, driven by policymakers and opinion leaders. The outlines of this argument, however, have yet to be filled. The relationship between the technocratic and symbolic aspects of the immigration debate needs to be developed. Further empirical research on what Espenshade elsewhere calls the "alienation hypothesis"—that alienation from the mainstream and uncertainty about the economic future is associated with anti-immigrant sentiment (Espenshade and Hempstead 1996)—is needed. We could do worse here than to return to Joseph Gusfield's *Symbolic Crusade,* which provides the classic account of the dynamics of status anxieties in American politics (Gusfield 1963). In short, the anxieties driving anti-immigrant sentiment, and their connection to the broader American political landscape of the 1980s and 1990s, need to be elaborated.

NOTES

1. There is a disjuncture, too, between how people respond in polls on their views on individual migrants—their neighbors—and immigrants in the abstract. Individuals are almost always seen more favorably, regardless of their national origin or race, than the abstractions. Anti-immigrant sentiment, seen side by side with often gentler sentiments toward individuals, is in keeping with the usual justification for prejudicial views, which always begins, "Well, some of my best friends are. . . ."

2. Just how broad this discourse of deserving and undeserving is was made clear to me in the course of interviews I was undertaking on the aftermath of civil disturbances in four cities. The public, it seems, is much more willing to compensate a homeowner who has built his or her house on a barrier reef that has been destroyed by a periodic hurricane than it is to compensate someone who has lost his or her business in a riot. The first is an act of God; the second has human causation, and therefore surely someone can be found to pay restitution. Of course, it's rarely this simple.

3. In this sense the immigration debate fits into Daniel Rodgers' paradigm of "contested truths"—symbolically charged "keywords" at the core of the American political debate. See Rodgers (1987).

4. Espenshade's own work has been mixed on this point: Espenshade and his co-authors have concluded at times that Latinos are slightly, but not significantly, more pro-immigration than non-Hispanic whites (Espenshade and Hempstead 1996) and at other times that there is, in fact, some support for the cultural affinity hypothesis (Espenshade and Calhoun 1993). Much of the work that has been done in this area, however, has been hobbled by small sample sizes for Hispanics in national surveys.

References

Borjas, George. 1994. "The Economics of Immigration." *Journal of Economic Literature* 32(4): 1667–1717.

Citrin, Jack, Beth Reingold, Evelyn Waters, and Donald P. Green. 1990. "The 'Official English' Movement and Symbolic Politics of Language in the United States." *Western Political Quarterly* 43(3): 535–560.

de la Garza, Rodolfo O. 1985. Mexican Americans, Mexican immigrants, and immigration reform. In *Clamor at the Gates,* ed. N. Glazer, 93–105. San Francisco: Institute for Contemporary Studies.

de la Garza, Rodolfo O., Angelo Falcon, and F. Chris Garcia. 1993. *Ethnicity and Attitudes Toward Immigration Policy: The Case of Mexicans, Puerto Ricans, and Cubans in the United States.* Texas Population Research Center Paper no. 13.11. Austin: University of Texas.

Diamond, Sara. 1996. "Right-Wing Politics and the Anti-Immigration Cause." *Social Justice* 23(3): 154–168.

Espenshade, Thomas, and Charles A. Calhoun. 1993. "An Analysis of Public Opinion Toward Undocumented Immigration." *Population Research and Policy Review* 12: 189–224.

Espenshade, Thomas, and Katherine Hempstead. 1996. "Contemporary American Attitudes Toward U.S. Immigration." *International Migration Review* 30 (Summer): 535–570.

Friedberg, Rachel, and Jennifer Hunt. 1995. "The Impact of Immigrants on Host Country Wages, Employment and Growth." *Journal of Economic Perspectives* 9(2): 23–44.

Gusfield, Joseph. 1963. *Symbolic Crusade: Status Politics and the American Temperance Movement.* Urbana, Ill.: University of Illinois Press.

Murray, Charles, and Jesse Jackson. 1986. "What Does the Government Owe the Poor [Discussion]." *Harper's Magazine* 272 (April): 35–46.

Niskanen, William A. 1997. "Welfare and the Culture of Poverty." *The Cato Journal* 16(1): 1–15.

Rodgers, Daniel T. 1987. *Contested Truths: Keywords in American Politics Since Independence.* New York: Basic Books.

Scott, Jacqueline, and Howard Schuman. 1988. "Attitude Strength and Social Action in the Abortion Dispute." *American Sociological Review* 53: 785–793.

Simon, Rita. 1985. *Public Opinion and the Immigrant: Print Media Coverage, 1880–1980.* Lexington, Mass.: Lexington Books, D.C. Heath and Company.

Skocpol, Theda. 1992. *Protecting Soldiers and Mothers.* Cambridge: Harvard University Press.

Smith, James P., and Barry Edmonston. 1997. *The New Americans: Economic, Demographic and Fiscal Effects of Immigration.* Washington, D.C.: National Academy Press.

Smith, Michael Pete, and Bernadette Tarallo. 1995. "Proposition 187: Global Trend or Local Narrative? Explaining Anti-Immigrant Politics in California, Arizona and Texas." *International Journal of Urban and Regional Research* 19(4): 664–676.

Verba, Sidney, Kay Lehman Scholzman, and Henry E. Brady. 1995. *Voice and Equality: Civic Voluntarism in American Politics.* Cambridge: Harvard University Press.

Epilogue

Marcelo M. Suárez-Orozco
Harvard University

Although immigration has been gathering momentum over the last three decades, only recently has it become a sharply focused policy and research issue. Before the 1990s, immigration as a concern seemed limited mostly to ethnic politicians and powerful business interests, largely in California, who were attentive to the need to maintain a large pool of foreign workers to do the impossible jobs natives didn't want to do. Other than that, the general attitude toward immigration was one of "benign neglect" (Martin 1994, 83). Immigration, as American as apple pie, was simply not a big deal: Immigrants came, immigrants assimilated, and in a couple of generations or so they become proud and loyal Americans.

By the early 1990s all of this began to change. A number of developments contributed to a sudden shift in public attention. The economic recession generated strong anti-immigration sentiment, feeding isolationist and nativist impulses. During the 1991 presidential primaries, Pat Buchanan—challenging then-President George Bush for the Republican nomination—began a nationwide debate when he claimed that the U.S. borders were being overwhelmed by illegal immigrants from Latin America and that "Zulu immigrants" (surely a code name for immigrants of color) did not fit into American culture as well as Anglo-Saxon Europeans.

Another wave of public debate over immigration began when Zoë Baird, President Clinton's first nominee for the office of Attorney General, removed herself from consideration when it was revealed that she had hired two undocumented immigrants from Latin America as domestic workers. A few months later, the participation of illegal immigrants in the terrorist bombing of Manhattan's World Trade Center injected another dose of anxiety into the public debate. By then, immigration began to dominate the headlines that both reflect and foment public discourse.

In the area of basic research, immigration went from being a low-status field of inquiry, mostly generating "low theory" in a handful of disciplines—prominent among them being labor economics, demography, sociology, and cultural anthropology—to a place of high priority in the scientific agenda of many influential national and international agencies. By 1996 the National Research Council had created a blue-ribbon commission of leading scholars of immigration (including Tom Espenshade and Mary Waters, contributors to this volume) to examine the relevant data on the socioeconomic and demographic consequences of immigration. In 1997, the Binational Study on Immigration (including Frank Bean, Agustín Escobar Latapi, and Sidney Weintraub, contributors to this volume)—with funding from the Mexican and U.S. governments as well as the private sector—began working on a binational study of migration between Mexico and the United States. Likewise, the National Science Foundation and the National Institutes of Health, as well as a number of influential private foundations such as the Spencer Foundation, suddenly gave immigration research a high priority.

Why this change? Surely, the numbers involved are impressive: Since 1990 the United States has been accepting, on average, nearly 1 million new legal immigrants each year. The economic downturn of the early 1990s, which, paradoxically, hit traditional immigrant destinations such as California and Texas hard, surely contributed to concern about the economic consequences of immigration. Suddenly, many began asking, Have immigrants become redundant, taking away jobs from native workers, hence contributing to their unemployment? Are immigrants depressing the wages of native workers? And what about the fiscal implications of large-scale immigration? Do immigrants "pay their way" taxwise? Or are they simply a load that must be carried by native taxpayers? All of these questions, and many others, found themselves in various ways into public debate, political positions, and scientific and quasi-scientific research.

In addition to the absolute numbers of new immigrants and the complex economic consequences of immigration, a third fact may help account for the sudden change in attention. Over the last three decades, immigration to the United States has been thoroughly dominated by the non-English-speaking developing world. Many are anxiously asking how these nonwhite, non-Europeans will adapt to American culture and its public institutions. And, perhaps more important, how is the United States going to be changed by them? Because of history, geography, economics, and demography, Mexican immigration has become the dominant locus of concern.

The study of Mexican immigration to the United States reveals a number of analytically delicious paradoxes. It is an issue that at once unites and divides the two neighboring countries. While powerful interests in the United States have achieved significant gains via large-scale immigration, Mexican immigration also generates a great deal of ambivalence in terms of U.S. public opinion and attitudes. While immigration spawns substantial wealth for Mexico—particularly in areas of high emigration to the United States—Mexico also loses important human capital as many of its more ambitious and entrepreneurial citizens choose to pursue their fortunes north of "the line." Policy initiatives making crossing the border more difficult—in theory, to deter the substantial flows of undocumented Mexican immigration to the United States—seem to be slowing down the number of Mexican immigrants *returning* home after trying their fortunes in the United States.

Perhaps the most important paradox is that Mexican immigration to the United States is at once paradigmatic of the new immigration—particularly of low-skilled, non-European, non-English-speaking people from the South moving in large numbers to the North—and a unique case that must be set apart from all other immigration. Mexicans in the United States are at once immigrants and nonimmigrants: The original Mexican-origin population in the United States did not move to the United States; rather, the United States moved to them when Mexico lost an enormous portion of its northern territories to the United States.

Newly arrived Mexican immigrants are, in the apt metaphor used by Massey and his colleagues, "returning to Aztlán." No other immigrant group shares this unique historical feature with Mexicans, although, of course, Native Americans and African Americans share with them the fact that their earliest experiences in the United States were as "involuntary minorities," not as voluntary immigrants (Ogbu 1997). These groups found themselves in a subordinate position of power vis-à-vis a dominant Euro-American majority that not only exploited them economically but disparaged them psychologically and culturally as inferior, violent, and lazy.

A version of this symbolic apparatus colors how many in the United States view Mexican immigrants. In recent years, it has taken the form of a near-hysterical anti-immigrant sentiment largely focused on Mexico. Such forms of what George De Vos (1997) has called "psychological disparagement" generate impossible cultural double binds, especially for many Mexican immigrant children who are being asked to "Americanize" just as they face toxic dosages of emotional and symbolic violence. The anti-immigrant ethos in many parts of the United States is making the psychologically complicated process of Americanization even more difficult for many Mexican immigrant children. Many Mexican-origin youth responded to what they saw as an attack in the form of Proposition 187 by proudly—some said defiantly—displaying Mexican flags in street demonstrations in Los Angeles, San Diego, and San

Francisco. Some observers noted that the Mexican flag incident generated a backlash and insured passage of the controversial proposition.

The huge U.S.-Mexican border connects two vastly unequal countries. The paradoxes are endless: It is both the most porous border in the world and the most heavily guarded. It is a line that at once separates and unites two cultures, two languages, and two economies. Another way in which Mexican immigration to the United States is a unique phenomenon—unlike all other immigration to United States today—is that both proximity and size matter. There is now a critical mass of Mexican immigrants in the United States, generating a demographic and cultural momentum whose effects will be felt for decades to come. They tend to settle, in great numbers, in three states: Today fully 85 percent of all Mexican immigrants live in California, Texas, and Illinois.

The explosive growth of the Spanish-speaking mass media, new communication technologies that instantaneously connect large numbers of Mexican immigrants to their areas of origin, the seasonal movement back and forth between Mexico and the United States among those immigrants who can afford it, the more or less uninterrupted flow of new arrivals from Mexico—along with the cultural double binds Mexican immigrants face—structure the cultural adaptations and identities of Mexican immigrants in unique ways. Some data suggest that Mexican immigrants tend to retain their home language more systematically than other immigrants, such as new immigrants from Asia (Portes 1997). Rather than following a unilinear path of assimilation toward Americanization, large numbers of Mexican immigrants and their children are crafting new hybrid cultural identities and styles of adaptation.

The large number of undocumented Mexican immigrants in the United States also distinguishes the Mexican experience from that of other immigrant groups. Today there are between 2 and 2.5 million undocumented Mexican immigrants in the United States. During the 1980s, 2 million undocumented Mexican immigrants legalized their status under the Immigration Reform and Control Act (IRCA) of 1986. The anemic employer sanctions under IRCA, the continued demand for Mexican labor in various sectors of the U.S. economy, the enduring U.S.-Mexico wage differential, and the powerful transnational social networks linking Mexican towns and cities to the United States generate a strong momentum for ongoing unauthorized immigration—a momentum that has not yet been deterred by the massive border control buildup at the international frontier.

It is also paradoxical that the new border control initiatives are making it more likely that undocumented Mexican immigrants who would ordinarily return to Mexico now seem to stay *longer* in the United States. Large numbers of poor and low-skilled undocumented immigrants are marginalized and forced to live, in the words of Leo Chavez, "shadowed lives," with no prospect for integration into the mainstream (Chavez 1992). Particularly worrisome is the marginalization of large numbers of undocumented immigrant children in light of recent legislation that would exclude them from publicly funded services. The long-term consequences of the marginalization of large numbers of immigrants are likely to be quite negative in economic, social, and human terms.

The pattern of marginalization is not only affecting undocumented immigrants. While Mexican immigrants are an extremely heterogeneous group—today in the United States there are more Mexican immigrant professionals than immigrant professionals from any other group—large numbers of Mexican immigrants are low-skilled workers. These workers are entering an American economy facing profound transformations, including massive losses in the manufacturing sector. The U.S. economy is characterized by growing inequality, where large numbers of low-skilled and unskilled redundant workers have little or no prospect of status mobility. This new economic landscape will shape the long-term adaptations of large numbers of unskilled and low-skilled Mexican workers.

A critical but understudied and undertheorized aspect of Mexican immigration to the United States is the experience of children. Large numbers of Mexican immigrant children are entering American public schools at a time when many large inner-city districts are collapsing. Mexican immigrant children tend to enroll in highly segregated, poor, and violent inner-city schools. These schools are overpopulated and understaffed. Qualified teachers are in short supply. Bilingual education—eternally controversial in the United States—is now facing a head-on challenge in California, the state most heavily affected by Mexican immigration. While many Mexican immigrant children do extraordinarily well in schools, as a group they tend to receive lower grades and lower scores in standardized achievement tests than other immigrant children. They also tend to have higher suspension rates and dropout rates than other immigrant children (Portes 1997). While most immigrant youngsters who give up on school before graduating will join their relatives in the ethnic economy and service sector, others may gravitate toward a gang culture ready to quickly socialize new arrivals into a lucrative alternative economy in which drug taking and dealing are a growing part of the economic and cultural ethos.

The current research on immigration is quite uneven. During the 1960s there was a concentrated research effort to empirically examine issues of race, poverty, and education, mostly focused on African Americans and poor whites. Since the 1980s, at a time when immigration was transforming major American cities, any further progress in basic research on urban issues has been eroded. We know much about some topics (such as demography) and next to nothing about others (such as the political behavior of the Mexican-origin population of the United States in light of the unprecedented legal changes taking place in both countries). Much of the research on immigration today is superficial and contradictory, such as the work on the fiscal consequences of immigration.

Perhaps no other issue is in more urgent need of serious scholarship than the children of immigrants. In the area of children, the research is quite scattered: There is a little on bilingual education, a little on cultural identities, a little on health, a little on students in high school, and a little on the transition to college and the world of work. There is a lack of basic research on a variety of problems. Why do immigrant girls do better than boys in schools? Why do some schools have a better record in educating immigrant children than other schools? Why is it that over time many Mexican immigrant children seem to dampen their optimism and faith in schools as the primary avenue for status mobility?

Immigration will continue to be a powerful vector of change on both sides of the border. We need a better understanding of how immigration is transforming both countries. If the availability of jobs on the U.S. side decreases and Mexican wages improve, the recent historically high flows will decrease but not likely cease—family reunification and transnational networks will continue to play a part in immigration. We need a major research agenda to examine the long-term causes and consequences of Mexican immigration to the United States—from changing fertility rates (both in Mexico and among Mexican immigrants in the United States), to the future of the Spanish language in the United States, to the impact of NAFTA on immigration, to the consequences of the recent immigration legislation. We need better theoretical understandings of the multiple paths taken by Mexican immigrants in their long-term adaptations. We need more interdisciplinary dialogue. This volume is a contribution to that vision.

REFERENCES

Chavez, L. R. 1992. *Shadowed Lives: Undocumented Immigrants in American Society.* Fort Worth, Tex.: Harcourt Brace College Publishers.

De Vos, G. 1997. Themes in the cultural psychology of immigration. Paper presented to the Harvard Immigration Projects, 21 November, Harvard University, Cambridge, Massachusetts.

Martin, P. 1994. The United States: Benign neglect toward immigration. In *Controlling Immigration: A Global Perspective*, ed. W. Cornelius, P. L. Martin, and J. Hollifield, 83–99. Stanford: Stanford University Press.

Ogbu, J. 1997. The study of identity among immigrants and non-immigrant minorities. Paper presented to the Harvard Immigration Projects, 7 November, Harvard University, Cambridge, Massachusetts.

Portes, A. 1997. The new second generation. Paper presented to the Jerome Levy Economics Institute of Bard College, 24 October, Annandale-on-the-Hudson, New York.

Index

San Diego County labor market
study and, 132
Social space
Austin County Flea Market (La Pulga)
illustration of, 26, 290–293
changes in East Los Angeles as example of, 307–309
community-organizing efforts and,
326–327
cultural mourning and creation of
potential, 288–290
demographic changes and, 312–313
ethnic Mexicans and transformation
of, 309–327
political involvement and, 317–327
regional economic, social, and cultural infrastructure changes and,
314–315
Spanish-language mass media and,
315–317
Social themes, 12, 18–23, 205–280
Sociocultural conditions (general)
immigration and globalizing trends
in, 12
impact of emigrants on, in countries
of origin, 10
Sociocultural conditions (Mexico),
migration and changes in, 8
Sociocultural conditions (U.S.)
health insurance coverage of
Mexican American children
related to, 230–236
Mexican immigration and changes
in, 8, 18–23
need to understand impact of
Mexican immigration on, 8
rhetoric on immigration and,
322–323
segregation of Mexican immigrants
and, 19
transformation of social space and.
See Social space
Sorenson, Elaine, 166
South, Robert B., 314
Southern California Immigration
Project, 173

Space. See Social space
Spain, Daphne, 196n2
Spanish language, 33n6
employment of immigrants and, 11
mass media, 10, 28, 315–317
St. Peter, R., 227
Stall, Bill, 318
Steinberg, L., 22, 42n44
Steinhauer, J., 10, 28, 34n10
Stewart, Jocelyn, 339
Stoddard, J. J., 227
STPS, 56
STRM, 326
Suárez-Orozco, Carola, 21, 22, 23, 24,
160, 253, 255, 260, 265, 267
Suárez-Orozco, Marcelo M., 3–44, 21,
22, 23, 24, 34n15, 38n31, 160, 253,
255, 260, 262, 265, 267, 270n2,
413–418
Subervi-Vélez, Federico A., 328n3,
328n4
Sue, S., 21, 22
Sullivan, John, 369
Sunland Park, New Mexico, 346
Suro, R., 27
Szekely, Gabriel, 86

Taniura, Taeko, 72n2
Tanton, John, 369
Tara, Susen, 328n4
Tarallo, Bernadette, 318, 329n9, 400
Tarrance and Associates, 369
Taylor, E., 260, 261, 272n5
Tehuixtla, Mexico, return of immi-
grants from, 25, 293–295
Teitelbaum, Michael, 81
Television, Spanish-language, 315–316
Texas. See also Border region
connections to country of origin of
immigrants in, 25
illegal immigrant settlement in, 100
Mexican immigrants in, 11, 91, 96
predominance of Latino students in
schools in, 23, 252
Thamer, M., 228